TV NORTH

TV NORTH

everything you wanted to
know about canadian television

Peter Kenter

with notes by Martin Levin

whitecap
vancouver/toronto

Acknowledgments

I would like to thank: my editor Kathy Evans for her cheerful diligence in editing this mammoth manuscript; Leone Earls and the staff at the CBC Reference Library for their kind assistance in researching this book; Blaine Allan, professor of Social Sciences and Humanities, Film Studies, at Queens University, for making his research into early television available to me; Trevor Evans; and my dear little wife, Amanda, for her support and patience during the rather lengthy preparation of this book.

The information in this book is true and complete to the best of our knowledge. All recommendations are made without guarantee on the part of the author or Whitecap Books Ltd. The author and publisher disclaim any liability in connection with the use of this information. For additional information, please contact Whitecap Books Ltd., 351 Lynn Avenue, North Vancouver, BC V7J 2C4.

Edited by Kathy Evans
Proofread by Elizabeth Salomons
Cover design by Maxine Lea
Interior design by Peter Kenter
Art direction by Roberta Batchelor
Cover photographs courtesy the Canadian Broadcasting Corporation and (far right) Franz Russell
All photographs and images not otherwise credited are part of the author's collection,
or believed to be in the public domain.
Interior chapter head illustrations by Jason Schneider

Printed and bound in Canada

National Library of Canada Cataloguing in Publication Data
Kenter, Peter.
TV North

Includes index.
ISBN 1-55285-146-X

1. Television programs—Canada—History. 2. Television broadcasting—Canada—History. I. Levin, Martin (Martin W.) II. Title.
PN1992.3.C3K46 2000   791.45'0971   C00-911184-0

The publisher acknowledges the support of the Canada Council for the Arts and the Cultural Services Branch of the Government of British Columbia for our publishing program. We acknowledge the financial support of the Government of Canada through the Book Publishing Development Program for our publishing activities.

Contents

INTRODUCTION

Ask me for a list of my ten favourite TV shows of all time and I won't name a single Canadian program. Growing up in Toronto, I could choose between watching local Canadian stations or a string of stations from just across the border in Buffalo, beaming in programs from ABC, NBC, and CBS. It wasn't much of a contest: *The Munsters* vs. *Don Messer's Jubilee*; *Lost in Space* vs. *Hymn Sing*; *The Avengers* vs. *Wojeck*. The local loser was always pinned decisively to the mat in lightning-quick matches. A generous helping of American programming rebroadcast on Canadian networks didn't help the local cause either. Would I prefer back-to-back broadcasts of the same episode of *Gilligan's Island* or a Canadian nature documentary on the plight of the sea cucumber?

"Gilligan, you've done it again." And again.

The term "Canadian television" conjures up few magical images and suggests all the charm of monotonous educational programming we were forced to sit through at school when a television strapped to a towering metal cart was wheeled into the classroom. "Canadian television" suggests unfunny comedies pushing lame jokes top-loaded with Canadian references, and unfortunate documentaries about abandoned prairie towns and the dietary habits of northern denizens. It's the type of programming you'd swear was conceived by government bureaucrats instead of artists. It's programming so self-righteous beneath its Canadian-content halo that it doesn't care whether you enjoy it—or even watch it.

But while I despise the concept of "Canadian television," I feel a certain fondness for some of the individual programs that slipped through television bureaucracies, government policies, Canadian-content regulations, and tough American competition to emerge as smart, entertaining, or weirdly memorable despite the odds. Programs like *Butternut Square* and *Mr. Dressup*, *Chez Hélène*, *Johnny Jellybean*, and *Uncle Bobby*, that stuck to the wallpaper of comforting pre-adult memories. Family competitions for *Headline Hunters* victory (I always won). Episodes of *Hymn Sing* before summer evening church services. Catching bits and pieces of the bizarre *Hilarious House of Frightenstein* while eating breakfast or waiting for the school bus. Coming home for lunch to the well-established American/Canadian combo: *The Flintstones* (in colour) back-to-back with *The Littlest Hobo* (in black and white). After school spent watching the strangely compelling *The Trouble With Tracy*.

I looked forward to the quarterly Wayne and Shuster specials that were de rigueur viewing for high school cafeteria "did ya see" discussions: "Did ya see the 'Kung Fu' sketch? Did ya see the part where Shuster got nailed by an avalanche of pumpernickel? Or the biblical football playoff between the Philistine Phillies and the Jericho Jets? Or the guest appearance by Eddie Shack?" Of course we saw it. *Everybody* watched the Wayne and Shuster specials (even though our attention might have flagged a little during the songs).

I enjoyed the long-haired humour of Hart Pomerantz and Lorne Michaels in *The Hart and Lorne Terrific Hour* specials, featuring Pomerantz's disconcertingly convincing beaver impersonation, or a mockumentary on Dutch Puck Disease, a biological plague destroying Welland's puck crops and devastating the NHL.

But, whether the shows were good or bad, we have very few records of them. Other than a very few exceptions, there's little to mark Canada's TV heritage. While Americans create meticulous records of their own television minutiae, there are no epitaphs for home-grown Canadian programs, like the game shows *Anything You Can Do, This Is the Law,* and *Definition;* or for dramatic series like *Cannonball, Hawkeye,* or *Seaway.* There are no handy reference guides for *Adventures in Rainbow Country, The Beachcombers,* or *Red Fisher,* or for impossible-to-ignore misfires like *The Starlost* and *The Trouble With Tracy.*

When I began to research this book, I discovered something alarming. Not only was there no authoritative reference material for Canadian television, but TV networks and local stations were disposing of archival television material with willful abandon. Tapes are erased, film deteriorates with age, and reams of photos, press releases, and production material wind up in trash bins. Some programs survive only as single lines in the TV listings section of local newspapers—we don't know who starred or even what the program was about. Recollections fade, and Canadian television pioneers, in their memoirs, present conflicting information about the programs they created. A few books dissect select aspects of home-grown television programming, with all the entertainment value of a quadratic equation.

TV North offers a record of Canada's television programming history before any more details slip from the collective unconscious, and from the archives, across the country.

It's only fair to admit that *TV North* is a subjective work containing a cross-section of Canadian programming, but certainly not all of it. I was more likely to include programs appearing on major networks in prime time (evening hours) and children's programming, with an emphasis on older or more unusual material. Other programs were included simply because I have a soft spot for them. Programs less likely to make the cut include sports shows (which would require a book of their own to do them justice), and less remarkable, short-lived efforts. Always an issue in program selection: the scarcity of reference material and limited access to it. Only one network offered the use of its archives; the others refused access to what little material they had left.

While I've made a valiant effort at accuracy, double-checking some spellings or scheduling information proved near impossible. Even network press releases often disagree with each other on important details, while Canada's numerous time zones, and the fickle broadcasting habits of individual stations, make a hash of accurate scheduling information. But I know there are people out there who will be able to correct a spelling error, provide a programming detail, supply an actor's name, or send in an old publicity photo. I welcome your gentle admonishment and/or contributions. I'm counting on you to make subsequent editions of *TV North* bigger, better—and even more fun.

Peter Kenter
2001

To comment, join the TV North *mailing list, or for news on the upcoming* TV North *website, e-mail* tvnorth@earthlink.net.

Ad and Lib

CBC
Comedy
First Broadcast: Monday, April 12, 1954, 6:30 p.m.
Final Year Broadcast: 1954
Running Time: 15 min.

Cast:
Ad . . . . Joe Austin
Lib . . . . Larry Mann

Weekday visits with Ad and Lib, general-store proprietors who were a dang sight smarter than "city folk." Dialogue was ad libbed.

Adderly

Global
Adventure/Comedy
First Broadcast: Monday, February 16, 1987, 10:00 p.m.
Final Year Broadcast: 1989
Running Time: 60 min.

Cast:
V. H. Adderly . . . . Winston Rekert
Melville Greenspan. . . . . Jonathan Welsh
Mona Ellerby . . . . Dixie Seatle
Major Jonathan B. Clack . . . . Ken Pogue

A former top agent in Covert Operations, Adderly is tortured by enemy spies who smash his hand to smithereens. Shifted to a desk job, in the dreary basement offices of ISI (International Security and Intelligence), his new trademark is a black leather glove disguising his artificial appendage. Under the direction of Miscellaneous Affairs, Adderly keeps his injured finger in the espionage pie and drags staff members into the action: administrative secretary Mona (who has a crush on him), simpering bureaucrat Greenspan, and bureau chief Major Clack.

Fast-paced and reasonably clever, this show was part of a package of Canadian offerings used by CBS television to provide low-cost, first-run programming in midnight time slots. Adderly was a minor character in the book *Pocock and Pitt* by Elliot Baker (the V. H. stands for Virgil Homer, says the author).

Potential buyer CBS hated the novel's European setting, so it was relocated to that *Twilight-Zone*-ish Canada where citizens avoid any reference to their home and native land, leading Americans to believe they're watching a bona fide U.S. production. Though Rekert may turn a statement into an interrogative by tacking on the occasional "eh?," he's also seen flying to Toronto—from Toronto.

The Canadian premiere occurred a mere six months after the program's U.S. debut.

Addison Spotlight Theatre
See: *Sunshine Sketches*

Adventures in Rainbow Country

CBC
Drama
First Broadcast: Sunday, September 20, 1970, 10:00 p.m.
Final Year Broadcast: 1971
Running Time: 30 min.

Cast:
Nancy Williams. . . . . Lois Maxwell
Billy Williams . . . . Stephen Cottier
Hannah Williams . . . . Susan Conway
Pete Gawa . . . . Buckley Petawabano
Dennis Mogubgub. Wally Koster
Roger Lemieux. . . . . Albert Millaire
Dougal MacGregor . . . . Alan Mills

The Forest Rangers in bell bottoms, this Canadian/Australian/British co-production ran for one season before it was relegated to network rerun hell until 1977. Maxwell (James Bond's original Miss Moneypenny)

CBC

Rainbow crew: From left to right, Buckley Petawabano, Stephen Cottier, and Alan Mills patrol Rainbow Country from on high.

with a viewership of more than 4,600,000 — 55th place on a list dominated by U.S. programs. A planned feature film, *Return to Rainbow Country*, never flew, though the script was used as the basis for a novel.

The critics jeer: "[Cottier's] principle dramatic device is to hunch up his shoulders in petulance, thus rendering nearly perfect his...impersonation of Doris Day."—Leslie Millin, *The Globe and Mail*

"...absolutely hilarious...I broke up over the dialogue, which is at a literary level only a shade below Dick and Jane." — Bob Blackburn, *Toronto Telegram*

"...poorly written, awkwardly motivated and ham-handedly historical." — Blaik Kirby, *The Globe and Mail*

played a presumed widow (nobody can find missing Dad!) who moves daughter Hannah and son Billy to Northern Ontario. Where's Rainbow Country? The town of Whitefish Falls, population 25, about 80 km north of Sudbury.

Most of the adventures featured Billy and his friend Pete, an Ojibway neighbour. Opening credits featured moderately stirring theme music and aerial shots of bush pilot Mogubgub's seaplane flying over Rainbow Country itself. Lemieux was a millionaire playboy photographer. Folksinger Mills played a tugboat pilot.

A surprise ratings success, CBC failed to order more episodes before the production company broke up. A 1986 Nielsen survey of the most-watched programs on Canadian television lists an episode of this show as the highest-rated Canadian-produced program,

The Adventures of Chich

CBC
Children's
First Broadcast: Monday, October 6, 1958, 5:15 p.m.
Final Year Broadcast: 1959
Running Time: 15 min.

Hosts: Tom Kneebone, Larry Mann, Helene Winston
Voices of:
Uncle Chichimus/Holly Hock . . . . John Conway

Uncle Chich rose from self-imposed puppet limbo, courtesy of puppeteer Conway, to spoof famous fairy tales. Kneebone, Mann, and Winston shared co-host duties. Conway was also puppeteer. The series continued to 1966 on local Ottawa TV. Also known as *Uncle Chichimus* and *Uncle Chichimus Tells a Story*.

The Adventures of Snelgrove Snail

Syndicated: 1980
Children's
Running Time: 30 min.

Voices of:
Snelgrove Snail/Terry Turtle/Professor Periwinkle
. . . . Donald W. Reid
Herman the Hermit Crab/Sid the Squid/Stanley the Starfish . . . . George Robertson
Constance Cowrie/Carrie Cowrie . . . . Helene Buwalda
Clement Clam/Conrad Crepidula . . . . Marc Reid
Olivia Van Oysterbed/Lulu Limpet . . . . Joyce Clarke
Dr. Lionel Limpet . . . . Barrie McLean

Gastropod music: This record album was produced as a tie-in for the children's series *The Adventures of Snelgrove Snail.*

THE SNAILSVILLE GASTROPOD JAMBOREE!

Songs from the popular television series "The Adventures of Snelgrove Snail"

They don't make 'em like this anymore—but they keep showing 'em to keep Cancon watchdogs happy. Puppet students in the undersea town of Snailsville learn extremely simple lessons in life and love while avoiding the extended reach of Sid the Squid, dedicated to making sushi of the town's inhabitants.

A sort of musical version of the 1970s *Waterville Gang* (Olivia Van Oysterbed bears a striking resemblance to Pearl Van Oyster), the show spawned at least one record album, *The Snailsville Gastropod Jamboree!*, featuring such standards as "Obesity," "Happy Turtle," "Ramses Crepidula," and "A Hot Time in Snailsville."

Alliteration would seemingly limit the available names for the burgeoning population of undersea residents. And what the heck's a crepidula?

Adventures of the Black Stallion

YTV
Children's
First Broadcast: Monday, September 10, 1990, 8:00 p.m.
Final Year Broadcast: 1993
Running Time: 30 min.

Cast:

Henry Dailey . . . . Mickey Rooney
Alec Ramsey . . . . Richard Ian Cox
Belle Ramsey . . . . Michelle Goodger
Pierre Chastel . . . . Jean-Paul Solal
Catherine Rousseau . . . . Virginie Demians
Nicole Berthier . . . . Marianne Filali
Nathaniel MacKay . . . . David Taylor

"The Black" is back, and Canada's got him. Walter Farley's novel begat a 1979 feature film and a 1983 sequel, which begat this TV hoss opera.

The show treated viewers to further adventures of the popular stallion owned and trained by Alec and widowed mom Belle at Hopeful Farms.

In episodes filmed in France, Nicole was a teenage stable hand with a crush on Alec; Pierre and Catherine added another French element as nasty show competitors. Rooney returned from the first film as trainer Dailey; Nathaniel was Dailey's nephew. A Canada/France/New Zealand co-production. Guest stars included Canadians Conrad Bain, Yvonne DeCarlo, and Margot Kidder.

Alliance Atlantis

Black Stallion **brigade:** From left to right, Marianne Filali, Mickey Rooney, The Black, and Richard Cox.

The critics jeer: "Parents will find *Black Stallion* a bore...." — Antonia Zerbisias, *The Toronto Star*

The Adventures of Tugboat Annie

See: *Tugboat Annie*

After Hours

CBC
Musical Variety
First Broadcast: Friday, May 8, 1953, 10:00 p.m.
Final Year Broadcast: 1954
Running Time: 30 min. and 60 min.

Host: Rick Campbell
Regular Performers: John Aylesworth, Jill Foster, Frank Peppiatt

The show featured live comedy and filmed band performances. The TV-screen debut of writers Peppiatt and Aylesworth, who went on to write for *Rowan and Martin's Laugh-In* and create *Hee Haw*.

Afternoon Delight

CBC
Discussion
First Broadcast: Wednesday, July 30, 1979, 3:00 p.m.
Final Year Broadcast: 1983
Running Time: 60 min. and 30 min.

Host: John Donabie
Contributors: Max Haines, Earl McRae

A weekday series looking at male-female relationships. Crime writer Haines presented tales involving crimes of passion, and sports writer McRae interviewed male athletes and their "sports widows." The show ran Tuesdays and Thursdays in its final season.

The Age of Uncertainty

CBC
Documentary
First Broadcast: Monday, March 28, 1972, 10:00 p.m.
Final Year Broadcast: 1972
Running Time: 60 min.

Host: John Kenneth Galbraith

A critically acclaimed look at the history of industrialization, co-produced by CBC, the BBC, OECA, and PBS for a whopping $2 million. The final segment, a round table at Canadian expatriate Galbraith's Vermont farm, featured an impressive guest list, including endocrinologist Dr. Hans Selye, former British PM Edward Heath, U.S. historian Arthur Schlessinger, and then-U.S. Secretary of State Henry Kissinger. The program's opening credits featured arresting imagery in the style of René Magritte.

The critics cheer: "Considered simply as an economic and socio-political view of history of the last two centuries, *The Age of Uncertainty* is without equal in the history of television." — Chris Dunkley, *Financial Times*

The critics jeer: "I defy you to remain awake…as a TV performer [Galbraith] is a total dud." — Chris Dunkley, *Financial Times*

A Go Go '66

CTV
Musical Variety
First Broadcast: Thursday, September 15, 1966, 9:00 p.m.
Final Year Broadcast: 1967
Running Time: 30 min.

Host: Mike Darrow
The A Go Go Dancers: Lynda Chankin, Linda Christopher, Claudette Houchen, Diane Webb
Music: Robbie Lane and His Disciples

A northern take on *Shindig* featuring four hip go-go girls and guest acts including The Charmaines and Little Caesar. Wicked William (Bill Cudmore) of the Disciples occasionally left his piano for frantic harmonica solos. Go-go costumes were supplied by Marilyn Brooks. Succeeded by *It's Happening* after the sudden implosion of the go-go craze.

Air Waves

CBC
Situation Comedy
First Broadcast: Monday, January 27, 1986, 7:30 p.m.
Final Year Broadcast: 1988
Running Time: 30 min.

Cast:
Zoe Lipton	Ingrid Veninger
Jean Lipton	Roberta Maxwell
Bobby	Roland Hewgill
Mark	Kimble Hall
Alex	Alec Willows
Ariel	Taborah Johnson
Matt	Christopher Bolton
Dale Campbell	Patrick Rose
Greg	Gordon Michael Woolvett
Kate	Patricia Hamilton

One of the few programs that tried to capture at least a smidgen of life in the 1980s, this effort proved too taxing for viewers who couldn't handle its deliberate, gentle rhythm. Three generations of Liptons faced the trials of urban life from different perspectives: teenaged post-secondary school drop-out Zoe, talk-show host mom Jean, and 63-year-old university student Grandpa Bobby. Mark was Jean's radio-station (CJEX 790) boss, Alex employed Zoe at the trendy Alibi club, Ariel was Zoe's co-worker/best friend. The second season added Zoe's cousin, Matt, and interviewer Dale.

The critics cheer: "If only for daring to be different, it deserves to be nurtured." — Rick Groen, *The Globe and Mail*

A Is For Aardvark

CBC
Educational
First Broadcast: Wednesday, July 7, 1954, 10:00 p.m.
Final Year Broadcast: 1954
Running Time: 30 min.

Hosts: Lister Sinclair, James Bannerman

A summer series: Sinclair (a.k.a. The Bearded Brain) and Bannerman picked through the alphabet, beginning with Aristotle, until rudely interrupted by cancellation at "N" (Bannerman's letter). Sinclair picked up the ball on CBC radio, 30 years later.

The Alan Hamel Comedy Bag

CBC
Variety
First Broadcast: Saturday, September 23, 1972, 7:00 p.m.
Final Year Broadcast: 1973
Running Time: 30 min.

Host: Alan Hamel

This show featured comedy sketches and U.S. guests (including two appearances by Broderick Crawford). Cheap, unsuccessful foreign-sale bait. And that title!

The critics jeer: "...so bad that Alan Hamel couldn't give it away." — Heather Robertson, *Maclean's*

The Alan Hamel Show

CTV
Variety/Talk Show
First Broadcast: Saturday, September 20, 1976, 2:00 p.m.
Final Year Broadcast: 1980
Running Time: 60 min.

Host: Alan Hamel

Toothy Hamel did a good impression of a U.S. talk-show host in this middle-of-the-road gabfest. One stand-out feature was an instant opinion-poll meter.

The Alan Thicke Show

CTV
Variety/Talk Show
First Broadcast: Monday, September 15, 1980, 1:00 p.m.
Final Year Broadcast: 1983
Running Time: 30 min.

Host: Alan Thicke

After Alan Hamel's departure from *The Alan Hamel Show*, CTV used fill-in hosts Thicke, David Steinberg, Ronnie Prophet, and Helen Shaver, among others, to bridge the gap until Thicke was appointed to the full-time throne. Thicke had already hit it big in the U.S., writing theme songs for such TV-show stalwarts as *The Facts of Life* and *Diff'rent Strokes* and scripting U.S. cult comedy favourite *Fernwood 2Night* and its successor, *America 2Night*. The cunning network culled bits of the daytime show and ran them at night as *Prime Cuts*.

The Albertans

CBC
Drama
First Broadcast: Sunday, January 14, 1979, 9:00 p.m.
Final Year Broadcast: 1979
Running Time: 60 min.

Cast:
Don MacIntosh . . . . Leslie Nielsen
Peter Wallen . . . . Gary Reineke
Carl Hardin . . . . George Waight
Marjanne . . . . Frances Hyland
Clair . . . . Anne Collings
Hans Keller . . . . Daniel Pilon
Isaac . . . . George Clutesi
Johnny . . . . Albert Angus

Leslie does *Dallas* as Nielsen played an oil tycoon in this three-episode series featuring interwoven stories set in Alberta. The drama centred on a multi-million-dollar oil deal, Native land claims, romance, eco-terrorism, and business intrigue.

Albert J. Steed

CHCH-TV
Children's
First Broadcast: Monday, September 28, 1964, 11:30 a.m.
Final Year Broadcast: 1968
Running Time: 90 min.

Host: Bill Lawrence
Puppeteer: Leon Mangoff
Voice of:
Albert J. Steed/Sebastian . . . . Bill Lawrence

Were you brought up in a barn? Thousands of children were, thanks to "Uncle" Bill Lawrence and his puppets: the dull-witted stallion Albert J. Steed and "chatterbox" doggie-pal Sebastian. This six-day-a-week stalwart featured anything that could be used to fill three hours: stories, viewer mail, saying grace, eating the sponsor's breakfast cereal, and watching serialized chunks of the British *Sir Lancelot* program or segments from Lawrence's *Tiny Talent Time* show. Albert boasted a range of about a dozen comments: "Mix it and stir it, stir it and mix it," or "My old one broke; now I have a new one." Sebastian's signature line after tying on the feedbag was: "I'm full up to the tip of my little tail." On the final episode, the puppets went to live with Albert's grandmother. A spinoff starring Lawrence was called *The Very Interesting Room*.

Host Bill Lawrence on Albert J. Steed:

"Albert was such a strained voice that I couldn't do it consistently. We recorded about a dozen comments and used them for the entire series. I would record Sebastian's voice the day before and we would alter the speed on playback. The people in the control booth would fire out random comments, just to see how I'd react. In the middle of a story segment, I'd hear Albert say, 'It really, really works.' Then I'd have to cover up for it. We'd stretch out the story segments to build up Canadian content, so CHCH could show American programming. If I could stretch a reading of *The Three Bears* to 12 minutes, they could show Merv Griffin that afternoon."

Albert's Place

CBC
Children's
First Broadcast: Wednesday, July 1, 1959, 5:00 p.m.
Final Year Broadcast: 1959
Running Time: 15 min.

Cast:
The Handyman. . . . . Robert Clothier
The Storyteller . . . . Nonie Stewart
Songs: John Chappell

In a cluttered attic, Albert the puppet entertained human guests.

CBC

Maritime music in half-hour doses: The cast of CBC's popular musical variety series *All Around the Circle*.

Alfred Hitchcock Presents

Syndicated: 1987
Anthology
Running Time: 30 min.

Host: Alfred Hitchcock

Want to make a quick buck? Re-film old *Alfred Hitchcock Presents* TV scripts, adding some up-to-date references. Not authentic enough? Then colourize old intros and extros of the master himself from the original *Alfred Hitchcock Presents* and bookend the new shows with them. That was NBC's original idea in 1985 when it jumped on the concept during a television writers' strike. When the show failed, the producers transplanted the idea to Canada, using imported U.S. actors and Canadian supporting players for a syndicated series padded with new stories.

In all fairness, Hitchcock directed only a handful of original episodes, but many of these updated episodes look cheap and cheesy, while Hitchcock's decades-old intros sparkle by comparison.

All Around the Circle

CBC
Musical Variety
First Broadcast: Friday, June 30, 1969, 5:30 p.m.
Final Year Broadcast: 1975
Running Time: 30 min.

Host: Doug Laite
Regular Performers: John White, Evan Purchase, Don Randell, Carol Brothers, Ray Walsh and his band

This Newfoundland musical series danced all around the schedule with the vigour of a Highland fling. Song and dance numbers were heavily influenced by English, Scottish, and Irish standards.

Set in a church hall, Laite provided comic relief as Uncle Eli, a hidebound, geriatric fisherman. Produced in St. John's, among other locations. Broadcast locally in Newfoundland between 1964 and 1969, then appearing as a CBC summer series only until 1973.

The critics cheer: "…a simple but fast and joyous half-hour of rousing sea shanties performed with exceptional voices and a good Newfie twang…."—Heather Robertson, *Maclean's*

Al Oeming—Man of the North

CBC
Nature Documentary
First Broadcast: Saturday, March 29, 1980, 7:00 p.m.
Final Year Broadcast: 1980
Running Time: 30 min.

Host: Leslie Nielsen

Albertan wildlife preservationist Oeming travelled across the country to trap endangered animals for his world-famous Alberta Game Farm, located near Edmonton. The series featured Oeming's efforts to preserve wolverines, grizzly bears, and other endangered species. Oeming was credited with single-handedly saving the grey owl from extinction. A syndicated 1960s program, *Alberta Game Farm*, was hosted by Oeming.

Alphabet Soup

CBC
Children's
First Broadcast: Tuesday, October 5, 1971, 5:00 p.m.
Final Year Broadcast: 1973
Running Time: 30 min.

Hosts: Marc Stone (1971–72), Trudy Young (1971–73),
    Lynne Griffin (1972–73), Mavis Kerr (1972–73)
Voice of:
Arbuckle the Alligator . . . . Roy Leslie

Programs centred around a topic beginning with a different letter of the alphabet. Arbuckle the Alligator co-hosted. In an anachronistic rebroadcast by YTV in 1990, viewers were invited to send in audience response cards using a 6-cent stamp.

Notable segments: Doug Henning (A for Abracadabra); Pierre Berton (K for Klondike; Peter Appleyard (X for Xylophone); and Don Harron (T for Tongue (??!).

The Amazing World of Kreskin

CTV
Magic
First Broadcast: Sunday, January 17, 1972, 8:30 p.m.
Final Year Broadcast: 1978
Running Time: 30 min.

Host: Kreskin
Announcer: Bill Luxton

Kreskin

Self-billed as "the world's foremost mentalist," Kreskin showcased his mental prowess, divining audience secrets and performing elaborate experiments with audience volunteers, using playing cards, sealed envelopes, and locked boxes.

A guest star (usually American) would help him perform a more spectacular mental feat. A very typical episode: Barbara Feldon sends mental messages from the CN Tower to small watercraft anchored off the shore of Lake Ontario.

Kreskin scrupulously denied that he derived powers from the occult. Viewers could buy a "You Can Be Kreskin" magic kit or a "Kreskin's ESP" game.

Anne of Green Gables

See: *Road to Avonlea*

Anything You Can Do

CTV
Game Show
First Broadcast: Monday, September 13, 1971, 3:30 p.m.
Final Year Broadcast: 1974
Running Time: 30 min.

Hosts: Gene Wood (1971–72), Don Harron (1972–74)
Announcer: Bill Luxton

"It's a man's world! It's a woman's world! It's the battle of the ages! It's the battle of the sexes! It's Anything You Can Do!"
    —Opening, *Anything You Can Do*

A wretched take on U.S. game show *Beat the Clock*, pitting two teams of three people in a battle of the sexes (contestants were often related or married) with guys picking gals' challenges, and vice versa. Stunts featured common elements: balloons, ladders, basketball nets, shaving cream, beanbags, and wastepaper baskets.

The host assigned a time limit to the stunt, and the program's zany theme music kicked in until contestants were frozen in their tracks by a raucous air-horn blast. The team with the lowest time totals would win copious prizes (sewing machines, deep fat fryers).

Original host Wood was better known as the voice who introduced fighting families on the U.S. game show *The Family Feud*. Shown briefly on ABC in 1971–72.

The series' defining moment: eager contestants diaper a kewpie doll, then roll a massive blob of bread dough across the stage.

Are You Afraid of the Dark?

Syndicated: 1992
Horror/Children's
Running Time: 30 min.

Cast—Are You Afraid of the Dark?:
Frank	Jason Alisharan
Gary	Ross Hull
Betty Ann	Raine Pare-Coull
Kiki	Jodie Resther
Kristen	Rachel Blanchard
David	Nathaniel Moreau
Eric	Jacob Tierney
Tucker	Daniel DeSanto
Sam	Joanna Garcia

Cast—Are You Afraid of the Dark? (1999):
Tucker	Daniel DeSanto
Vange	Vanessa Lengies
Quinn	Kareem Blackwell
Megan	Elisha Cuthbert
Andy	David Deveau

The Midnight Society was a group of tweenagers who shared spooky campfire tales heavy on suspense but light on violence.

Export versions featured minor changes: campfires were a no-no in France, and Americans, who watched on Nickelodeon, wanted to hear more U.S. references. The initial series ran until 1996. A second series, *Are You Afraid of the Dark? (1999)*, debuted in 1998, with only Tucker returning.

Ark on the Move

CBC
Nature
First Broadcast: Monday, January 4, 1982, 4:00 p.m.
Final Year Broadcast: 1982
Running Time: 30 min.

Host: Gerald Durrell

A sequel to *The Stationary Ark* featuring famous naturalist Durrell travelling the world in search of endangered species to study and rescue—geckos, pigeons, and ring-tailed lemurs among them. Durrell was accompanied by wife Lee and assistant John Hartley. Filmed largely in Madagascar and the island of Mauritius, whose inhabitants hunted the dodo bird into extinction centuries earlier.

The Associates

CTV
Drama
First Broadcast: Tuesday, January 16, 2001, 8:00 p.m.
Final Year Broadcast: —
Running Time: 60 min.

Cast:
Benjamin Hardaway	Demore Barnes
Jonah Gleason	Shaun Benson
Robyn Parsons	Tamara Hickey
Mitch Barnsworth	Gabriel Hogan
Amy Kassan	Jennie Raymond
Angus MacGregor	R.H. Thomson

"The law like you've never seen it before." Well, perhaps not in the last couple of days or so. The adventures of a quintet of twenty-something neophyte lawyers in the Toronto offices (a flapping Canadian flag in the opening credits lets you know this really is Canada, not a pretend American city) of the prestigious law firm Young, Barnsworth & King. The new crew includes: tight-ass Barnes; lackadaisical British playboy Hogan (with Beatle-esque coiffe to distinguish him from his Traders character); beautiful but icy Raymond; Southern belle Hickey, fresh from Austin, Texas; and, ex-Montrealer Benson, resident mensch and supporter of lost causes. Senior partner MacGregor supervises the new brood from his 27th floor office. Also the name of a 1979 ABC sit-com featuring Martin Short.

Astroboy

Syndicated: 1986
Animated
Running Time: 30 min.

"Soaring high in the skies, he may be small but only in size..."

North American audiences of 1963 took a shine to Japanese cartoon star Astroboy, known in Japan as The Mighty Atom. Criticized for what was then considered hyper-violence, the program was quietly pulled from NBC's Saturday schedule. Twenty years later, new programs appeared in colour, with the violence toned down a notch and the addition of the Canadian-produced soundtracks in English and French (*le Petit Astro*). Based on comic books published in 1951 by Osamu Tezuka, the stories are set in Futuropolis, a city of the 21st century. Astroboy is a surrogate robot son, built by a scientist whose wife and child had been killed in an accident. Designed with retractable feet, Astroboy uses his legs as rocket tubes to fly into action, fighting crime on Earth and in space. Thoughtful and engaging, the program deals with fairly sophisticated concepts: prejudice against machines, and a UN document known as the *Bill of Robot Rights,* for example.

While many character names differ from the 1963 series, there's one way to spot the Canadian version: Astro's non-super sister is known as Astrogirl in the original series, as Sarah in the Canadian version, and as Uran in international cuts. The Canadian cast is uncredited.

At Home With John Newmark

CBC
Music
First Broadcast: Sunday, September 5, 1954, 10:30 p.m.
Final Year Broadcast: 1954
Running Time: 30 min.

Host: John Newmark

Not pianist Newmark's real home, but a Montreal studio mock-up, where he performed chamber music. Guest performers included musicians Noel Brunet, Walter and Otto Joachim, Lucien Robert, Irene Salemka, and Newmark's cat.

Atlantic Summer

CBC
Variety/Discussion
First Broadcast: Monday, August 7, 1978, 1:00 p.m.
Final Year Broadcast: 1979
Running Time: 60 min.

Host: Denny Doherty
Co-Hosts: Sharon Dunne, Shirley Newhook

Doherty, formerly of the band the Mamas and the Papas, tried his hand as a summer talk-show host. Taped outdoors in Halifax and St. John's, the 1978 series was plagued by rough weather, including prop-twisting, microphone-popping sou'westers.

Aubrey and Gus

CBC
Children's
First Broadcast: Monday, September 26, 1955, 4:45 p.m.
Final Year Broadcast: 1956
Running Time: 15 min.

Narrator: Dick Thomas
Cast:
Gus . . . . Lloyd Jones
Voice of:
Peter the Skunk . . . . Norma Macmillan
Aubrey . . . . Garry Lay
Puppeteer: Elizabeth Merton

Communication gap, raccoon-style. Aubrey the raccoon puppet can't talk to ring-tailed family members so he searches for his other half—a boy who grunts in coon lingo—to arrange an exchange of language skills. Gus, another boy, assists.

Audubon Wildlife Theatre

CBC
Nature
First Broadcast: Saturday, April 13, 1968, 6:00 p.m.
Final Year Broadcast: 1974
Running Time: 30 min.

Host: Bob Davidson
Narrator: Robert C. Hermes

This critically acclaimed nature series was produced in association with the Audubon Societies of the U.S. and Canada. Syndicated repeats ran well into the 1980s.

Backstretch

CBC
Drama
First Broadcast: Thursday, December 1, 1983, 8:00 p.m.
Final Year Broadcast: 1985
Running Time: 60 min.

Cast:

Marge Aylesworth . . . . Florence Patterson
Charlie Aylesworth. . . . . Frank Adamson
Ray Foley . . . . Peter MacNeill
Jack Stoness . . . . Robert King
Tom Hutchinson. . . . . Peter Millard
Ronny . . . . Danny Pawlick
Delbert Purvis. Sneezy Waters
Elva. . . . . Diana Belshaw
Kelly . . . . Martha Burns

After husband Charlie kills himself, Marge Aylesworth takes over the down-and-out Ettrick Raceway (a horse track located somewhere in Southern Ontario.) Jockey Ray supports Marge's efforts, but nasty track secretary Tom and rider Jack conspire to undermine her. Ronny is jockey Delbert's assistant, Elva is Delbert's wife, and Kelly works at the snack bar. Originally a four-part mini-series.

The critics cheer: "There's a goldmine of hometown characters, each with real life quirks." — Tom McDougall, *The Vancouver Sun*

The critics jeer: "The style of *Backstretch* is dishpan dull...comes up with a bad case of the blahs." — Jim Bawden, *The Toronto Star*

The Bananas

CBC
Children's
First Broadcast: Thursday, January 2, 1969, 4:30 p.m.
Final Year Broadcast: 1969
Running Time: 30 min.

The Bananas: Bonnie-Carol Case, John Davies, Melody Greer, François-Regis Klanfer
Cast:
The Great Announcer . . . . Alan Maitland

Set in Bananaland, this series debuted a mere four months after the wildly successful *Banana Splits Adventure Hour* on U.S. television. Four "Bananas"—hip kids playing multiple roles—were selected from auditions in Toronto and Montreal to perform satirical skits, songs, and dances. Non-human characters included: the Big Mouth, an on-screen autocrat who traded information for wheelbarrows full of food; the Blob, an amorphous electronic creature with an identity crisis; and an Official, Certified, Genuine, Grade-A Gorilla. Segments include: "The Reverse," in which children and adults switch roles.

Producer Rod Coneybeare on *The Bananas:*

"I was trying to create a program that was wry, ironic, and sardonic—something to get the audience to question things around them. It represented a sort of civilized iconoclasm that I believe kids should be exposed to. It was quite successful with audiences, but it died for lack of funds—it was expensive for the time. We probably should have changed the title after the U.S. program aired, but the CBC really liked the name, so we stuck with it."

Bantam Roundup
See: *Junior Roundup*

Barney Boomer

CBC
Children's
First Broadcast: Tuesday, September 12, 1967, 4:30 p.m.
Final Year Broadcast: 1968
Running Time: 22 min.

Cast:

Barney Boomer . . . . John Clayton

Florence Kozy . . . . Lynn Gorman

Councillor Edgar Q. Russell. . . . . Franz Russell

Trudy . . . . Trudy Young

Captain Boomer. Rex Sevenoaks

Ma Parkin . . . . Claire Drainie

Mr. Andrews . . . . Claude Rae

Sam Oliver. . . . . Gerard Parkes

Susan . . . . Belinda Montgomery

Franz Russell

After an abortive attempt to explore the Great Lakes, young Barney Boomer moors his houseboat at Sixteen Harbour in Cedarville to write the Great Canadian Novel, despite the opposition of Councillor Edgar Q. Russell, who can't abide a commoner laying anchor near the Cedarville Yacht Club.

Barney's uncle, Captain Boomer, lived in a lighthouse, Florence Kozy owned a convenience store, and actress Trudy Young played herself. Described as *Peyton Place* for kids, the series was seen several times per week. After dumping Barney, the series was revamped as *Upside Town*. *Swingaround*, a kiddie quiz show, padded out the half-hour.

"...he lived on a houseboat and bored everybody to death...." — Roy Shields, *The Toronto Star*

Barris and Company

CBC
Musical Variety
First Broadcast: Saturday, September 21, 1969, 10:30 p.m.
Final Year Broadcast: 1970
Running Time: 30 min.

Host: Alex Barris
Announcer: Janet Baird
Music: Guido Basso

Another program jammed in the iffy time slot following *Hockey Night in Canada*. *Globe and Mail* columnist and television personality Barris hosted this whipping boy for everything wrong with Canadian television. Promoted with the unsubstantiated claim: "TV viewers asked for Barris—and Barris is back," this disaster collected record numbers of scathing reviews.

Even Doug Nixon, CBC's director of television entertainment, candidly told press: "We made a mistake with Barris. From now on we'll have to give priority to talent." Wayne and Shuster jumped to Barris' defence, claiming critics had unfairly sunk the show, but disastrous ratings told a different story.

Barris, who blamed producers, devoted a chapter to this embarrassment in his autobiography, *The Pierce-Arrow Showroom Is Leaking*. Alex Trebek, current host of U.S. game show *Jeopardy*, was originally slated as announcer.

Barney sails into town: John Clayton, us CBC's Barney Boomer, pilots his minuscule houseboat into Cedarville's Sixteen Harbour.

The critics cheer (sort of): "...it's a bland package, but it's all amiable enough...a good mixture of conversation, comedy and music. I wouldn't go out of my way to see it, but it was no strain at all to watch."—Bob Blackburn, *Toronto Telegram*

The critics jeer: "...I caught him plugging a major supermarket, a frankfurter victualer and, excruciatingly, his own son. To me it was pathetically obvious that the major weakness of the program was Poor Alex himself. He had neither the confidence radiated by a professional host, nor the chutzpah that would enable an amateur to get away with it."—Douglas Marshall, *Maclean's*

"...the worst single show I have ever seen on television...patiently aimed at the rubes who'll watch anything that moves.... The fallout is still at a perilous level from the bomb that was Barris' first variety show [*The Barris Beat*] a decade ago...."—Patrick Scott, *The Toronto Star*

"No show in the history of Canadian TV has ever received such unanimously bad press." —Nathan Cohen, *The Toronto Star*

The Barris Beat

CBC
Musical Variety
First Broadcast: Wednesday, July 4, 1956, 9:00 p.m.
Final Year Broadcast: 1957
Running Time: 30 min.

Host: Alex Barris
Announcer: Bruce Marsh
Music: Betty Jean Ferguson, Roy Roberts, The Gino Silvi Octet
Orchestra Leader: Bill Isbister
Regular Performers: Jack Duffy, Larry Mann, Gloria Lambert, Maggie St. Clair, Sammy Sales
Cast:
The Billboard Girl . . . . Sheila Billing/Babs Christie

Barris was a maple-flavoured Steve Allen, an ex-American taking a stab at Canadian late-night variety, in a mixture of music, interviews, and sketch comedy.

Real-life reporter Barris played one in a continuing segment, assisted by copy boy Duffy. In a challenge to modern standards of journalistic integrity, Barris mercilessly promoted the program in his *Toronto Telegram* column. ("Well, what do you know! We've got a real, live movie star on tomorrow night's *Barris Beat.* He's Zippy the chimp [who] played Cheeta in the Tarzan movies.") Singer Ferguson was Miss Canada of 1948.

Directed and produced by Norman Jewison. The show was demoted from weekly to twice-monthly appearances before cancellation.

The critics cheer: "…Barris is a clever ad-libber, a probing interviewer, a suitably obtuse straight man, a ham, and many other things. But above all he's an 'idea' man. This makes the show exciting—and unpredictable." — Charles McGregor, *Toronto Telegram*

CBC

The Beat Goes On: Alex Barris (right) and associates perform newspaper shtick on *The Barris Beat.*

The Beachcombers

CBC
Adventure
First Broadcast: Sunday, October 1, 1972, 7:30 p.m.
Final Year Broadcast: 1991
Running Time: 30 min.

Cast:
Nick Adonidas . . . . Bruno Gerussi
Molly Carmody . . . . Rae Brown
Hughie . . . . Bob Park
Margaret . . . . Nancy Chapple, Juliet Randall
McCloskey . . . . Reg Romero
Ol' Relic . . . . Robert Clothier
Jesse Jim . . . . Pat John
Gus Calhoun . . . . Stefan Winfield
Laurel . . . . Marianne Jones
Constable John Constable . . . . Jackson Davies
Constable Samantha Jones . . . . Diane Stapley
RCMP Colonel Norman Brewster . . . . Don Granberry
Pat O'Gorman . . . . Dione Luther
Sara . . . . Charlene Aleck
Graham . . . . Cam Bancroft
Pat's Grandfather John . . . . Joe Austin
Dana Battle . . . . Janet-Laine Green
Sam Battle . . . . Beau Heaton
Tommy . . . . Cory Douglas
Ceece Neville . . . . Joseph Golland
Harv Haywood . . . . Heath Lamberts

Cigar-chompin' lumber scavenger Nick Adonidas was the unlikely hero of this preposterously long-running series set on the British Columbia coast. Nick rented a room in Molly's Reach, a truck-stop diner, and plucked timber from Howe Sound with his boat, the *Persephone.* Molly's grandchildren Hughie and younger sister Margaret lived with her. Jesse Jim was Nick's partner, and Relic was a hard-cheating competitor. Constable Jones was a minor love interest for Nick. McCloskey was the garbage man. Hughie joined Nick's salvage company in 1981, and Molly left to get married in 1986.

In an earth-shattering departure from tradition, the word "The" was dropped from the series title in its 17th season. In that year, divorcee Dana Battle and her son took over the cafe, Jesse and wife Laurel moved into their own home, Nick moved in with Jack, and Constable John (who also had an eye for Dana) became a corporal.

Guest stars included The Irish Rovers, former pop singer fave René Simard, and David Suzuki as themselves, Chief Dan

George, and Gordon Pinsent in the recurring role of John Kelsey, The Hexman, an evil magician.

In a wild departure from the series' quiet tone, the concluding episode saw Nick quitting the business as a new breed of violent, gun-toting beachcombers move in on his aquatic turf.

The series defied serious criticism by achieving its extremely modest goals—even Gerussi admitted the show wasn't art—but cancellation after 19 years left an unusually shaped hole in the Canadian TV landscape. Filmed in Gibson, British Columbia, the series was seen in more than 40 countries. Real-life beachcomber John Smith served as technical advisor.

The critics cheer: "A high camp mellerdrama with stilted dialogue and wooden gestures…. The production, like the scenery, is splendid; it has a strange and cheerful innocence which is never found in American shows." — Heather Robertson, *Maclean's*

Beat the Clock

CTV
Game Show
First Broadcast: Monday, September 14, 1970
Final Year Broadcast: 1974
Running Time: 30 min.

Hosts: Jack Narz (1970–72), Gene Wood (1972–74)
Announcer: Gene Wood (1970–72)

A revival of the old game show seen on CBS and ABC during the 1950s and early 1960s. Teams of two contestants competed to perform inane stunts within the time limits set by a huge orange clock (superimposed on the screen in white during stunts). Winners of each round got to choose one of the letters in the show's title from a "cash board" to reveal money prizes ranging between $25 and $200. Contestants also joined forces with a celebrity guest (the likes of performers Cab Calloway, Peggy Cass, Bob Denver, William Shatner, Tom Poston, and Betty White) or chose to bet $50 on the clock or the star in a solo celebrity stunt. A 1969–70 season was produced in New York; subsequent seasons were filmed in Montreal. CTV stations ran the show in different time slots to suit local schedules.

A 1979 U.S. revival on CBS featured Canadian Monty Hall as host, with Narz as announcer.

CBC

Beyond Reality

Syndicated: 1991
Science Fiction
Running Time: 30 min.

Cast:
Laura Wingate	Shari Belafonte
J. J. Stillman	Carl Marotte
Celia Powell	Nicole deBoer

Two university parapsychologists investigate the paranormal. Wingate was the true believer, J. J. was the skeptic, and graduate assistant Celia helped. Filmed in Toronto and seen on the USA Network. Two seasons were filmed.

Beachcombin': Bruno Gerussi (left) and Pat John in the impossibly long-running CBC family series, *The Beachcombers.*

Beating the Clock: Host Jack Narz (with microphone) cheers contestants who use an inflatable Mr. Magoo doll to knock stuffed poodles into a cardboard box.

CFCF-TV

Psychic phenomenon: Paul Soles was host of CBC's oddball psychic game show *Beyond Reason*.

Beyond Reason

CBC
Game Show
First Broadcast: Monday, June 27, 1977, 9:00 p.m.
Final Year Broadcast: 1980
Running Time: 30 min.

Host: Paul Soles (1979–80)
Moderator: Bill Guest (1977–78)
Adjudicator: Allen Spraggett (1977–78)
Panelists: Geoff Gray-Cobb (astrologer), Marcel Broekman (palmist), Irene Hughes (clairvoyant), Marilyn Rossner (graphologist)

A paranormal *Front Page Challenge* masterminded by writer, radio commentator, and occult investigator Spraggett (who claimed to be "as psychic as a carrot").

Psychic-powered panelists tried to guess the identity of a guest using astrological data, personal objects, palm prints, and handwriting samples. Hughes (who suffered from occasional "psychic blackouts") publicly charged that some panelists were spoon-fed answers in advance. The show started as a summer series, graduated to a full-fledged show, then wound up on weekday afternoons.

Mystery guests included: Buzz Aldrin, George Chuvalo, Chief Dan George, Abby

Hoffman, Tommy Hunter, and Alvin Karpis. Dull-witted viewers, thinking it was a live broadcast, complained that the psychics cheated by reading the guest roster in *TV Guide*.

Big City Comedy

CTV
Comedy
First Broadcast: Friday, September 26, 1980, 7:30 p.m.
Final Year Broadcast: 1981
Running Time: 30 min.
Host: John Candy
Regular Performers: Tino Insana, Tim Kazurinsky, Don Lamont, Audrie J. Neenan, Patti Oatman

After temporarily cutting ties with *SCTV*, John Candy struck out on his own with this disastrous sketch-comedy revue. Candy's characters included roving reporter Johnny Toronto and kids'-show host Uncle Silvo. The featured guest list looked like a mixture of inspired choice and bad joke: clever co-hosts Fred Willard and Martin Mull from U.S. cult comedy *Fernwood 2Night* in counterpoint to a wooden Margaret Trudeau. Many of the low-grade guest performers were lifted from U.S. programs: Conrad Bain, Rita Moreno, Marie Osmond, McLean Stevenson, and Jimmie Walker. Repertory player Kazurinsky graduated to a three-year stint on *Saturday Night Live*.

The Big Revue

CBC
Musical Variety
First Broadcast: Tuesday, September 9, 1952, 8:00 p.m.
Final Year Broadcast: 1953
Running Time: 30 min.

Hosts: Toby Robins, Budd Knapp, Peter Mews
Orchestra: Samuel Hersenhoren
Regular Performers: Phyllis Marshall, George Murray, John Aylesworth, Frank Peppiatt, The Revue Dancers, Terry and the Macs

Even network publicity material admitted: "Talent available in Canada for such a production is limited...." The fledgling network's first regular series was a dog-and-pony show performed live on cramped sets; an exercise in the logistics of moving massive props during commercial breaks. Peppiatt and Aylesworth provided filmed

Revue deluxe: A big dance production performed on a small stage, courtesy of *The Big Revue*.

comedy sketches to cover bigger set changes.

Sponsored by Westinghouse and booked solid with music, dance, novelty acts, and hoary comedy sketches, *Revue*'s tab came in at $10,000 per episode—big bucks for Canada, but a monthly cigar bill for U.S. rival Milton Berle. Live TV gaffes included torn clothing, collapsing sets, defecating animal acts, and a hypnotist who mesmerized performers and audience members into a stupor. *Revue* provided the forum for the television debut of Don Harron's Charlie Farquharson. Robins was billed as the show's "femcee." Norman Jewison directed. The program earns points for featuring Black performers, such as Marshall, without making a fuss about it.

The critics cheer: "…*Big Revue* does have variety, good sets, a lively band (socko trumpet)…." — Gordon Sinclair, *The Toronto Star*

The critics jeer: "…an amateur production…I find myself waiting impatiently for some of the performers to be dragged from the stage…a limp balloon…." — Hugh Garner, *Saturday Night*

Big Sound

Global
Comedy
First Broadcast: Monday, December 11, 2000, 9:30 p.m.
Final Year Broadcast: —
Running Time: 30 min.

Theme Music: The Jeff Healey Band, Moist
Cast:
Bill Sutton . . . . Greg Evigan
Gabe Moss . . . . David Steinberg
Nick Keester. . . . . Colin Cunningham
Phoebe Sutton. . . . . Meredith Henderson
Jessie Polt . . . . Deanna Milligan
Donna. . . . . Enuka Okuma
Artie . . . . Philip Maurice Hayes
Michelle . . . . Anne Marie Loder

Bill Sutton is manager of Big Sound, a record company beset by back-stabbing staffers and ego-driven musicians. The show's real producer Steinberg plays Big Sound's owner Moss. Musical guests who play themselves have included Jann Arden, Randy Bachman, Stewart Copeland, Thomas Dolby, Melissa Etheridge, M.C. Hammer, Chantal Kreviazuk, and Bif Naked.

CBC

The Billy O'Connor Show

CBC
Musical Variety
First Broadcast: Saturday, October 16, 1954, 11:10 p.m.
Final Year Broadcast: 1956
Running Time: 30 min.

Host: Billy O'Connor
Regular Performers: The Billy O'Connor Trio (Vic Centro, Kenny Gill, Jackie Richardson), Bill Isbister, Juliette, Jack Duffy

A northern take on *A Star Is Born*, which is remembered more for singer Juliette, who was introduced in 1955, than O'Connor. As cameras lingered lovingly on the female singing sensation, li'l Billy seemed to fray around the edges as he shot sarcastic barbs at his co-star. Juliette later stole the show and O'Connor's time slot. Also known as *The Late Show*.

Bim Bam Boom

CBC
Children's
First Broadcast: Friday, November 18, 1955, 4:30 p.m.
Final Year Broadcast: 1956
Running Time: 15 min.

Voice of:
Bim . . . . Rosemary Malkin
Bam . . . . Sam Payne
Cast:
Boom . . . . John Allen
Puppeteer: Kitty Dutcher

This obscure show, aimed at kids, featured fairy tales, two puppets (Bim and Bam), and a live clown, Boom.

Bizarre

CTV
Comedy
First Broadcast: Monday, September 22, 1980, 8:30 p.m.
Final Year Broadcast: 1984
Running Time: 30 min.

Host: John Byner
Regular Performers: Lally Cadeau, Jack Duffy, Jayne Eastwood, Bob Einstein, Tom Harvey, Saul Rubinek, Billy Van, Mike Walden, Steve Weston

Byner's program was broadcast in two versions: a raunchy series, replete with the "F-word," for U.S. cable network Showtime, and a CTV version, whose viewers were treated to expletives deleted, courtesy of conspicuous air horns, and video blackouts to disguise apparent nudity. Not so much bizarre as slightly off-colour and politically incorrect (one segment featured a family made up entirely of ethnic stereotypes trading racial slurs). Memorable skits include the San Francisco Straight Parade and Scared Thin, a social program run by the truly obese who try to steer kids away from junk food. Through sheer energy, volume of gags, and some dead-on impersonations, Byner managed to snag his share of laughs. Co-producer Bob Einstein expanded his continuing Super Dave Osborne act on the series, before launching his own *Super Dave* show.

Blackfly

CBC
Situation Comedy
First Broadcast: Thursday, January 4, 2001, 10:00 p.m.
Final Year Broadcast: —
Running Time: 30 min.

Cast:
Benny "Blackfly" Broughton . . . . Ron James
Corporal Entwhistle . . . . Colin Mochrie
Colonel Boyle . . . . Richard Donat
MacTavish . . . . James Kee
Lady Hammond . . . . Shauna Black
Misty Moon . . . . Cheri Maracle
Smack-Your-Face-In . . . . Lorne Cardinal
Ti-Jean . . . . Marcel Jeannin

A *Hatch's Mill* for the new millennium—an 18th-century sit-com, set in the fur-trading post of Fort Simpson-Eaton.

Follows the adventures of conniving Benny "Blackfly" Broughton, Scottish boss MacTavish, British officers Entwhistle and Boyle, saucy Lady Hammond, and Native barkeep Misty Moon. Sort of a *Blackadder* meets *F-Troop*, replete with anachronistic gags, assorted voyageurs, zany Jesuits, and wise-cracking Aboriginals. Trying mightily to please, *Blackfly* won audience favour, but was swatted by most critics.

The critics jeer: "It might be politely dubbed a 'classic' comedy; its style of humour is almost 40 years old." — Tony Atherton, *The Ottawa Citizen*

Black Harbour

CBC
Drama
First Broadcast: Wednesday, December 4, 1996, 9:00 p.m.
Final Year Broadcast: 1999
Running Time: 60 min.

Cast:
Katherine Hubbard . . . . Rebecca Jenkins
Tasha Haskell . . . . Melanie Foley
Ananda Haskell . . . . Barrett Porter
Frances . . . . Joan Gregson
Nick Haskell . . . . Geraint Wyn Davies
Mr. Haskell . . . . Leon Pownell
Mrs. Haskell . . . . Elizabeth Sheppard
Len Hubbard . . . . Joseph Ziegler
Paul Isler . . . . Alex Carter
Vicky Isler . . . . Rhonda McLean
Michael . . . . Simon Peter Duvall
Brenda Hubbard . . . . Carol Sinclair
Buddy Brigley . . . . Hugh Thompson
Walter Veinot . . . . Andy Jones
Kyle Duncan . . . . Graeme Millington
Darlene Duncan . . . . Nancy Beatty
Stan Landry . . . . Martin Julien
Aggie MacDuff . . . . Mary Colin Chisholm
Hughie Rudner . . . . Peter Richards
Andy Rudner . . . . Richard McMillan
Dan Christos . . . . Barry Dunn

Compared by some overwrought critics to U.S. cult drama *Twin Peaks* (please!), this prime time soap focused on the inhabitants of small-town Nova Scotia. Restaurateur Katherine, her husband Nick (a washed-up movie director), and two daughters (Tasha and Ananda) left L.A. for Black Harbour when Katherine's mother, Frances, became ill. Katherine encouraged Nick to buy the family boatyard from her resentful brother Len. Paul, the yard's master builder, was Katherine's ex-boyfriend, now married. Plot complications: Nick and Katherine split; Mom dies in a car accident; Paul proposes marriage; Nick returns to Hollywood; Katherine opens a restaurant; Nick's parents visit; and a hurricane hits the harbour. Dubbed "Bleak Harbour" by detractors.

The critics cheer: "Strong, intelligent drama...."—Tony Atherton, *Ottawa Citizen*

The critics jeer: "*Black Harbour* is all scenery and no action." — John Allemang, *The Globe and Mail*

Blue Murder

Global
Drama
First Broadcast: Wednesday, January 10, 2001, 10:00 p.m.
Final Year Broadcast: —
Running Time: 60 min.

Cast:
Inspector Victoria Castillo . . . . Maria del Mar
Detective Ed Oosterhuis . . . . Joel Keller
Detective Sergeant Jack Pogue . . . . Jeremy Ratchford
Deputy Chief Kay Barrow . . . . Mimi Kuzyk

Blue Murder is a special squad of Toronto police officers, charged with the duty of handling difficult, high-profile cases, some of which might be a tad embarrassing to the police force. Castillo heads the special unit, assisted by fashion victim Oosterhuis, his jaded partner Pogue, and hard-nosed Barrow. Loosely based on a 1997 CBC miniseries *Major Crime,* some of the scripts are based on real-life cases.

Bluff

CBC
Game Show
First Broadcast: Wednesday, October 6, 1976, 7:30 p.m.
Final Year Broadcast: 1977
Running Time: 30 min.

Host: Mike Darrow

Like the U.S. game show *Liar's Club,* contestants ferreted out lies in tall tales told by a panel of comedians, including Dave Broadfoot, Foster Brooks, Professor Irwin Corey, Norm Crosby, and Hart Pomerantz.

Bob and Margaret

Global
Animated
First Broadcast: Thursday, December 18, 1998, 9:30 p.m.
Final Year Broadcast: —
Running Time: 30 min.

Voice of:
Bob Fish . . . . Andy Hamilton
Margaret Fish . . . . Alison Snowden
Other Voices: Jonathan Aris, Peter Baynham, Susie Blake, Steve Brody, Rob Brydon, Amelia Bullmore, Steve Coogan, Trevor Cooper, Kevin Eldon, Chris Emmett, Simon Greenall, Sarah Hadland, Doon Mackichan, Enn Reitel, Meera Syal, Anna Wing

Bob's Birthday, an Oscar-winning NFB short, spawned this spinoff series about a boring British couple with a nasty streak and their dogs, William and Elizabeth. He's a London dentist, she's a podiatrist, and their lives consist of petty frustrations, half-expressed criticisms, and a dollop of misplaced self-congratulation. A homage to mediocrity? Not so, claim the show's creators, though they treat the title characters with more sympathy than they deserve. Episodes consist of simple plots like a trip to the supermarket, or a dental convention. A third season of episodes saw the Fish family—now misplaced Britishers—moving to Toronto to satisfy Canadian content regulations. Snowden is a co-creator. A British/Canadian co-production.

The Bobby Vinton Show

CTV
Variety
First Broadcast: Tuesday, September 9, 1975, 7:30 p.m.
Final Year Broadcast: 1978
Running Time: 30 min.

Host: Bobby Vinton

Hot on the heels of his fluky comeback hit, "Melody of Love" (which doubled, in polka-time, as the show's theme song), Vinton hosted this reasonably popular variety series shot in Toronto.

Guests who joined Vinton in musical and comedy sequences included Ted Knight, Loretta Swit, Barbara Walters, and all-round good guy, O. J. Simpson. Regular performers included comics Arte Johnson, Billy Van, Freeman King, and Jack Duffy.

KEEP FIT / BE HAPPY
with Bonnie Prudden

MUSIC BY OTTO CESANA

The Bob McLean Show

CBC
Variety
First Broadcast: Monday, September 1, 1975, 12:00 p.m.
Final Year Broadcast: 1981
Running Time: 60 min.

Host: Bob McLean

Vanilla square McLean interviewed celebrities, featured musical guests, and conducted cooking lessons, among other segments. Contributors included writer Gary Michael Dault, money manager Herman Smith, Walter Fox on criminal law, *Royal Canadian Air Farce*'s Roger Abbott and Don Ferguson, Howie Mandel, and Monica Parker. Keath Barrie (1975–76) and Don McManus (1976–77) provided songs. Resident musicians included Guido Basso and Moe Koffman. Produced in Toronto (subways rumbled on the soundtrack), Ottawa, Halifax, and Vancouver.

The Bonnie Prudden Show

CBC
Fitness
First Broadcast: Monday, November 15, 1965, 4:00 p.m.
Final Year Broadcast: 1968
Running Time: 30 min.

Host: Bonnie Prudden

Billed as "a grandmother with the body of a chorus girl," tough-as-nails American health maven Bonnie Prudden hosted this physical fitness program, seen in endless repeats through the 1980s. A mix of exercise techniques, lectures, and interviews, some of the programs were shot abroad, including Australia and the Far East. The show inspired a series of record albums.

Bordertown

CTV
Western
First Broadcast: Tuesday, September 12, 1989, 7:30 p.m.
Final Year Broadcast: 1993
Running Time: 30 min.

Cast:
Corporal Clive Bennett . . . . John H. Brennan
Marshal Jack Craddock . . . . Richard Comar
Dr. Marie Dumont . . . . Sophie Barjac
Jake Eppler . . . . Bill Pepperall
Otto Danzinger . . . . Fritz Bergold
Bruno Danzinger . . . . Wyatt Orr
Zachary Denny . . . . Duncan Fraser
Sally Duffield . . . . Beverly Elliott
Diane Denny . . . . Freda Perry
Willie Haddon . . . . Gregory Togal
Clara . . . . Kymberley Sheppard
Liam Gleeson . . . . Hagan Beggs
Wendell MacWherter . . . . Paul Batten
Domenic . . . . Domenico Fiore
Gabriel Couteau . . . . Patrice Valota

A Canadian-French co-production that literally straddled the border as Northwest Mounted Police Corporal Bennett and U.S. Marshal Craddock shared an office that sat smack dab on the international boundary line between Alberta and Montana in the dusty town of Pemmican. The 1880s Odd Couple (guess which one was the slob?), both played by Canadian actors, vied unsuccessfully for the affections of civic-minded Parisienne expatriate Dr. Dumont. Eppler looked after the office building; Otto was the town blacksmith. CTV temporarily suspended the series' run in the 1991–92 season. Seen concurrently on the U.S. Christian Broadcasting Network, despite a somewhat high body count.

The Buddies

CTV
Children's
First Broadcast: Saturday, September 9, 1967, 10:00 a.m.
Final Year Broadcast: 1968
Running Time: 30 min.

Cast:

Commander Bi Bi Latuque . . . . Peter Cullen
Space Cadet Wilbur . . . . Ted Zeigler

Two Canadian astronauts on a lonely refuelling station demonstrated bilingual tolerance—when they weren't hoarding food capsules and oxygen canisters or ejecting each other into airless space. Quebecois Latuque (who wore one) was a sentimental slob who melted when Mama Latuque made her weekly phone call ("Bi Bi…Bi Bi…do you love your mother, Bi Bi…?"). The Anglo, incompetent, rubber-faced Wilbur frequently crashed his bicycle on the way to the launching pad. The Buddies were also featured in episodes set in the Old West.

Bumper Stumpers

Global
Game Show
First Broadcast: Monday, September 14, 1987, 2:30 p.m.
Final Year Broadcast: 1990
Running Time: 30 min.

Host: Al Dubois
Announcer: Ken Ryan

A pretty lame game show, in which contestants tried to unscramble vanity licence plates into popular words or slogans. Champs got to play a "super stumper" at the show's end. Produced primarily for the USA network, whose viewers were apparently unaware they were watching Canadians vying for cash and merchandise prizes (the letter "zed" was pronounced "zee"). Cash prize values actually decreased during the show's three-year run. Dubois was a pleasant host.

Burns Chuckwagon from the Stampede Corral

CBC
Musical Variety
First Broadcast: Wednesday, November 3, 1954, 10:30 p.m.
Final Year Broadcast: 1955
Running Time: 30 min.

Regulars included comedian Barny Potts, singers Don Francks, Pat Kirkpatrick, and Lorraine McAllister, guitarist Arnie Nelson, and instrumental group The Rhythm Pals.

Produced in Vancouver, not Calgary, as the title might suggest. Based on a CBC radio show, *The Burns Chuckwagon*.

Butternut Square

CBC
Children's
First Broadcast: Monday, October 19, 1964, 11:30 a.m.
Final Year Broadcast: 1967
Running Time: 20 min. and 30 min.

Cast:

Mr. Dressup . . . . Ernie Coombs
Sandy . . . . Sandy Cohen
Music Man . . . . Donald Himes (1964–65)
Bob . . . . Bob Jeffrey (1965–67)
Puppeteer: Judith Lawrence

The beginning of a children's show dynasty, this program introduced Mr. Dressup and puppets Casey and Finnegan. Mr. Dressup play-acted in a shady town square, overlooked by the town clock tower, or created toys and crafts in his "Experiment-it" shop.

Sandy told stories in her See-Through House, while Music Man played piano and led kids in song. Bob visited twice a week with presents and surprises. Judith Lawrence's puppets, mischievous British schoolboy Casey, with a pasted-on grin, and mute canine pal Finnegan lived in a treehouse. Other puppets were two pandas, Alexander and Miranda, and Mrs. Trapeze.

Butternut Square was cancelled without fanfare in 1967, ostensibly to devote resources to coverage of the Centennial, but Coombs revived immediately as Mr. Dressup, along with fellow survivors Casey and Finnegan, in a more space-efficient setting. Misterogers (Fred Rogers) made guest appearances.

Butternut Squares: From left to right, Sandy Cohen, Ernie Coombs, and Donald Himes frame puppet pals Casey and Finnegan in *Butternut Square*.

Cal's Club

See: *Jazz With Jackson*

Camera 76

See: *Performance*

The Campbells

CTV
Drama
First Broadcast: Sunday, September 7, 1986, 7:00 p.m.
Final Year Broadcast: 1989
Running Time: 30 min.

Cast:
Dr. James Campbell . . . . Malcolm Stoddard
Neil Campbell . . . . John Wildman
Emma Campbell . . . . Amber-Lea Weston
John Campbell. Eric Richards
Housekeeper . . . . Rosemary Dunsmore
Captain Sims . . . . Cedric Smith

First seen in a series of four specials in January 1986, *The Campbells* turned into a gold mine for CTV. Dr. Campbell and his three bairns emigrated from Scotland to tough it out in 1830s Upper Canada, somewhere between Guelph and Cambridge. A Scottish-Canadian co-production. Audiences were much kinder to the series than some critics were.

The critics jeer: "…the scripts hop mindlessly all over the map—here a lacklustre try at farce, there an impoverished pass at pathos.…" — Rick Green, *The Globe and Mail*

Canada After Dark

CBC
Variety
First Broadcast: Monday, September 18, 1978, 11:45 p.m.
Final Year Broadcast: 1979
Running Time: 60 min.

Host: Paul Soles

A feeble phoenix rising from the cold ashes of *90 Minutes Live*, with Peter Gzowski, where cheerful Soles had guest hosted. No longer live, nor even 90 minutes, the late-night talk show featured guest appearances by CBC hacks and attracted savage critiques.

Producers tried to explain away low ratings (bottoming at 58,000 viewers nationwide) as "statistically insignificant," then blamed newspaper critics Dennis Braithwaite and Blaik Kirby for its demise the following January.

The critics jeer: "…a round-trip ticket on the *Titanic.*" — Bob Blackburn, *The Toronto Sun*

"…if [Johnny Carson is] bland, Soles is cornstarch pudding…full frontal tedium." — Dennis Braithwaite, *The Toronto Star*

Canada A.M.

CTV
Newsmagazine
First Broadcast: Monday, September 11, 1972, 7:00 a.m.
Final Year Broadcast: —
Running Time: 90 min. to 210 min.

Hosts: Elaine Callei, Helen Hutchinson, Dan Matheson, Linda McClennan, Deborah McGregor, Keith Morrison, Norm Perry, Valerie Pringle, J.D. Roberts, Percy Saltzman, Gayle Scott, Carole Taylor, Pamela Wallin, Nancy Wilson

A flagship CTV news program that gambled, at least initially, on the likability of Canada's favourite weatherman Percy Saltzman and co-host Carole Taylor. A genial mix of news, weather, sports, entertainment, and lifestyle features best watched in 15-minute chunks between breakfast, shower, and brushing of teeth. Though the studio is in Toronto, the producers make considerable effort to seek meaningful contributions from across the country. News readers have included Thalia

Assuras, Terrilyn Joe, Leslie Jones, Wally Macht, and Dennis McIntosh. Host Norm Perry holds the program's longevity record at 15 years, between 1975 and 1990. A one-hour Saturday version, *Canada A.M. Weekend*, was launched in January 1993. Moe Koffman wrote the show's original theme music.

The critics cheer: "...a seductive show—lazy, relaxed, informative in a pleasant, comfortable way, with just enough sleepy-eyed news to assure you that yesterday's world is still there, grinding along." — Heather Robertson, *Maclean's*

The Canadian Establishment

CBC
Documentary
First Broadcast: Sunday, September 21, 1980, 9:00 p.m.
Final Year Broadcast: 1980
Running Time: 60 min.

Narrator: Patrick Watson

These seven programs, based on Peter C. Newman's book of the same name, took a kindly look at the corporate establishment, circa 1980, including media mogul Conrad Black, shoe tycoon Thomas Bata, Paul Desmarais, chief of Quebec's Power Corporation, and Ian Sinclair, chairman of CPR. Other program subjects included department store competition and "new" money.

Canadian Short Stories

See: *Theatre Canada*

Canadian Superstars

CBC
Sports
First Broadcast: Sunday, January 15, 1978, 2:00 p.m.
Final Year Broadcast: 1981
Running Time: 60 min.

Hosts: Ernie Afaganis (1978–79), Tom McKee (1978–81), Don Wittman (1979–81)

Celebrity contestants chose seven sports from a roster of baseball, bicycling, bowling, gymnastics, obstacle course, rowing, soccer, swimming, tennis, weightlifting, 100-metre sprint, and half-mile run for a $46,400 prize. Contestants included Toller Cranston, Wayne Gretzky, Gordie Howe, Darryl

Sittler, Garry Unger, Brian Budd, Jamie Bone, and Gaetan Boucher. Winners graduated to the World Superstars competition.

Cannonball

CBC
Drama
First Broadcast: Monday, October 6, 1958, 9:30 p.m.
Final Year Broadcast: 1959
Running Time: 30 min.

Cast:
Mike "Cannonball" Malone . . . . Paul Birch
Jerry Austin. . . . . William Campbell
Mary Malone . . . . Beth Lockerbie
Ginny Malone . . . . Beth Morris
Butch Malone . . . . Steve Barringer
Harry Butler . . . . Howard Milsom

Canadian cool, thanks largely to a killer theme song (think "Mule Train" meets "Ghost Riders in the Sky"—"...the rumble of the diesel, the shiftin' of the gears..."). TV's first trucking show featured beefy working stiff Malone and eggheaded Jerry, sidetracked from college, pulling freight anywhere from Winnipeg to New York, encountering hijackers, protection rackets, assorted criminals, troubled travellers and such dreaded professional hazards as tunnel vision and driver fatigue. Featured great sequences like Mike piloting the brakeless rig down a hairpin turn at 80 mph while Jerry quotes Milton. The never-resolved cliffhanger had Jerry quit C&A Trucking to go back to college.

Mary was Mike's wife, Butch and Ginny their children; Harry was the dispatcher. Seen in the U.S., Australia, and Great Britain, and provided inspiration for 1970s U.S. copycat *Movin' On* with Claude Aikins and Frank Converse as the new truck jockeys.

Cannonball run: William Campbell (left) and Paul Birch face the perils of the open road as the hard-drivin' partners of C&A Trucking.

The critics cheer: "...better than most other adventure yarns and a lot easier to take than some of the family situation shows...." — Dennis Braithwaite, *The Toronto Star*

The critics jeer: "...you could knock out similar yarns with a home movie camera, one day's rental on a cloverleaf and some night school students." — Gordon Sinclair, *The Toronto Star*

Cariboo Country

CBC
Drama
First Broadcast: Saturday, July 2, 1960, 7:30 p.m.
Final Year Broadcast: 1967
Running Time: 30 min.

Cast:

Smith	David Hughes
Norah Smith	Lillian Carlson
Sherwood Smith	Greg Davies (1964), Alan Cherrier (1965–66)
Ken Larsen	Walter Marsh
Arch MacGregor	Ted Stidder
Henry James	Lloyd Cartwright
Morton Dillonbeigh	Buck Kindt
Mrs. Dillonbeigh	Rae Brown
Sarah	Jean Sandy
Phyllistine	Nancy Sandy
Ol' Antoine	Chief Dan George
Frenchie Bernard	Joseph Golland
Johnny	Paul Stanley

Dramatizations of Paul St. Pierre's stories, set in Namko, a fictional British Columbia community, originally produced for a Vancouver audience. Smith (no first name) his wife Norah, and their son Sherwood were dirt-poor ranchers, managing the province's smallest cattle herd into bankruptcy. The dramas were presented either as stories told by Arch MacGregor or told to him by other residents. An on-again, off-again series.

Cartoon Party

CBC
Children's
First Broadcast: Saturday, November 7, 1959, 5:30 p.m.
Final Year Broadcast: 1962
Running Time: 30 min.

Host: Malcolm the Dog
Puppeteer: John Keogh

A cartoon showcase hosted by puppet Malcolm.

Canada seen through soap: Volume Two of the Castle Zaremba study guide, created to accompany the soap opera series of the same name.

Castle
Zaremba
Volume Two

A Case For The Court

CBC
Drama
First Broadcast: Wednesday, July 6, 1960, 10:30 p.m.
Final Year Broadcast: 1962
Running Time: 30 min.

Host: Gil Christy

Actors plus real-life lawyers and judges engaged in mock trials. Christy introduced cases, then interviewed participants. A four-citizen panel discussed the case with a plain-clothes magistrate, who donned a robe for final judgment.

Castle Zaremba

OECA
Drama
First Broadcast: Tuesday, October 12, 1970, 10:00 a.m.
Final Year Broadcast: 1971
Running Time: 30 min.

Cast:

Kazimir Zaremba	Jan Rubes
Grandma	Nina Marrocco
Heinelore Gotthardt	Beate Hartig

Others: Eric House, Vladimir Valenta, August Schellenberg

An odd experiment in Canadian educational drama. The Toronto rooming house (77 Walker Avenue) of temperamental Colonel Kazimir Zaremba was the backdrop for a soap opera providing painless civics lessons for new Canadians. The plots involved searches for employment, romance, personal vendettas, shopping, family life, and a murderous gangster.

Some civics lessons were a little too frank. In one episode, Keith shows immigrant Ricardo how to avoid prosecution for failing to repay a loan. "Any time you see anybody coming up to you with a piece of paper you do the subpoena stomp," he advises, turning tail and running.

Episodes were seen twice weekly on OECA, the forerunner of TVO, and repeated on CBC stations.

A real Colonel Zaremba who turned up in Hamilton, Ontario, had to be convinced by producers that the program wasn't based on his life.

Catch Up

CBC
Musical Variety
First Broadcast: Monday, September 11, 1978, 4:30 p.m.
Final Year Broadcast: 1979
Running Time: 30 min.

Hosts: Margaret Pinvidic, Christopher Ward
Music: Christopher Ward Band

A kids' magazine with musical segments. Viewers submitted original lyrics for prizes in a contest segment.

CBC Concert Hour

CBC
Music
First Broadcast: Thursday, September 30, 1954, 8:30 p.m.
Final Year Broadcast: 1955
Running Time: 60 min.

Classical music and dance performances by noted artists, including Glenn Gould and Andres Segovia. A massive flop—ratings proved that even captive audiences in one-station cities like Winnipeg preferred a blank screen to an hour of classical music, opera, and ballet.

CBC Drama '73

CBC
Drama Anthology
First Broadcast: Sunday, September 30, 1973, 9:00 p.m.
Final Year Broadcast: 1973
Running Time: 60 min.

Filmed adaptations of literary works, including *More Joy in Heaven* by Morley Callaghan and *A Bird in the House* by Margaret Laurence.

CBC Film Festival

CBC
Film
First Broadcast: Tuesday, June 5, 1979, 9:00 p.m.
Final Year Broadcast: 1980
Running Time: 120 min.

A showcase of mainly Canadian feature films, including: *Kamouraska; Lies My Father Told Me; The Little Girl Who Lives Down the Lane; Skip Tracer;* and *Who Has Seen the Wind.* In 1979, the show included interviews with Hollywood directors including Sam Fuller, Martin Scorsese, and Don Siegel. Strange offerings included:

The Clown Murders (1975): Stephen Young, Al Waxman, John Candy, and *This is the Law*'s Susan Keller as a group of knuckleheads who accidentally kill someone during a party-gag kidnapping. They hide in a cottage, smoking and cussing as a masked butcher picks them off "Texas Chainsaw-style," while Candy (as Ollie) weeps, weeps, weeps.

Deadly Harvest (1972): A dreadful harvest—of bad acting. Stoic farmer Clint Walker defends his sappy family and cabbage patch from starving Torontonians through "the year where summer never came." For die-hard bad-film buffs only.

Love at First Sight (1974): Dan Aykroyd's first movie break, as a man blinded by staring into a solar eclipse. He's in love with Mary Ann McDonald and Kentucky Fried Chicken. Features Barry Morse, blind driving, and a cameo by Colonel Harland Sanders.

CBC Folio
See: *Folio*

CBC Playbill
See: *Playbill*

CBC Television Theatre

CBC
Dramatic Anthology
First Broadcast: Thursday, September 18, 1952, 8:30 p.m.
Final Year Broadcast: 1958
Running Time: 90 min. and 60 min.

Live and filmed dramas included: *Shadow of Suspicion* by Arthur Hailey; *Justice* by John Galsworthy; *An Enemy of the People* by Henrik Ibsen; *All My Sons* by Arthur Miller; *By Candlelight* by P.G. Wodehouse; *Candida* by George Bernard Shaw; *Othello* by William Shakespeare (starring Lorne Greene); and *One John Smith* by Lister Sinclair. Imported guest stars included future U.S. president Ronald Reagan. The series' defining moment was 1956's presentation of Arthur Hailey's *Flight Into Danger* about a flight crew poisoned by bad airline food and the fevered efforts of a nervous ex-pilot to guide

Flying out of danger: James Doohan takes the controls in the CBC production of *Flight Into Danger*.

CBC

a passenger plane to safety. Starring James "Scotty" Doohan and Corinne Conley, the teleplay proved so popular that it seems to have eclipsed all memories of Canadian television drama in that decade. ("So you think Canada can't produce world-class drama? Well what about *Flight Into Danger*?") The episode was sold internationally and adapted into Hailey's popular novel *Airport*, which begat the feature film, three sequels, and illegitimate comic offspring *Airplane* (not to mention the script adaptation studied in Canadian lit classes for decades). The program moved to Sundays for a few weeks, but competition from the popular U.S. program *$64,000 Challenge* relegated it to Tuesdays until the quiz show scandals made Sunday nights safe for Canadian drama.

The program's history was complicated by the backing of Ford, which sponsored one in four shows (including the premiere) under the banner *Ford TV Theatre*, while an unrelated program, also called *Ford TV Theatre*, showed half-hour filmed plays imported from the U.S. Also known as *General Motors Theatre*, when sponsored by GM between 1953 and 1956. Hour-long programs for the 1957-58 season were simply known as *Television Theatre*.

CBC Theatre

See: *CBC Television Theatre*

Ceilidh

CBC
Music
First Broadcast: Thursday, June 13, 1974, 8:30 p.m.
Final Year Broadcast: 1974
Running Time: 30 min.

Host: Alasdair Gillies
Regular Performers: The Cape Breton Fiddlers, The Ceilidh Dancers

A summer series from Halifax featuring Celtic, Scottish, Irish, and Canadian music. Pronounced *kay-lee*. John Allan Cameron appeared on a local version in 1973.

Celebrity Cooks

CBC
Cooking
First Broadcast: Monday, September 15, 1975, 3:30 p.m.
Final Year Broadcast: 1979
Running Time: 30 min

Host: Bruno Gerussi

Cooking and comedy featuring Gerussi and semi-celebrities from around the world, including Buffy Sainte-Marie (cod), a young David Letterman (inedible spinach noodles), well-sauced guests, and bizarre appearances by the likes of Margaret Trudeau and Alan Sues. William Hutt boycotted the series, which allegedly handed bigger pay cheques to U.S. guests than to home-grown cooks: $196 versus a princely $350.

The CGE Show

CBC
Musical Variety
First Broadcast: Monday, September 8, 1952, 9:00 p.m.
Final Year Broadcast: 1959
Running Time: 30 min.

Regular Performers: The Howard Cable Orchestra (1952–57), The Leslie Bell Singers (1952–54), Gladys Forrester, Jackie Kay, Charles Jordan, Joyce Sullivan, Elmer Eisler, Shirley Harmer, Don Garrard, Robert Goulet, Gloria Lambert

Back in the 1950s, sponsors named their own programs—in this case the sponsor was Canadian General Electric. A collection of songs, dances, and novelty acts (including one weird number: "Space Dance—a dance of the future") evolved from a radio program of the same name and appeared in TV listings under *The Leslie Bell Singers* while the act headlined. Bell left the show in 1954 over charges that singers forced to dance and perform comedy acts as well were overtaxed and that abysmal TV sound quality hurt performances. In a diatribe published in *Maclean's,* Bell referred to the program's indiscriminating audience as "half man and half chesterfield." Also known as *CGE Showtime.*

CGE Showtime

See: *The CGE Show*

Charlie Had One But He Didn't Like It, So He Gave It To Us

CBC
Comedy
First Broadcast: Wednesday, July 20, 1966, 11:40 p.m.
Final Year Broadcast: 1966
Running Time: 30 min.

Regular Performers: Barry Baldaro, Paul Soles

Boasting the longest title in Canadian television history (and almost subtitled: "And We Didn't Like It Either So We're Giving It Back to Charlie"), this program, a mixture of sketches and blackouts, was inspired by Britain's *The Goon Show* and Richard Lester's *Running, Jumping, Standing Still* film. Running gags featured an Olympic torch bearer (Soles) and a wheedling military officer (Baldaro) who negotiates with soldiers to perform dangerous missions. Female window dressing, used for sight gags, à la *Benny Hill,* included Sheila Rutanen, Dorothy Troll, and Anne Rohmer. Typical gag: a fisherman dumps his mermaid catch because he's a leg man.

Chairman of the Board

Syndicated: 1981
Drama
Running Time: 30 min.

Cast:

The Chairman........................ Stephen Young
Professor Hannah Cohen .... Jackie Burroughs
Paul Morel .... Cec Linder
Reverend Bruce Hardiman .... Dave Patrick
James Hale........................ Harvey Sokoloff
Others:
Claire Pimpaire, Ken Pogue, Jean Walker

A board of eight people, appointed by an unnamed government, decide how society will deal with contentious issues. A simple premise intelligently handled as academics, capitalists, socialists, unionists, the clergy, and assorted intellectuals hash out such issues as racism, transvestitism, and teenage crime. Does the board make bad decisions? Frequently—producer Jim Hanley intentionally allowed manipulative board members to lead audiences astray, supporting his premise that the public policy makers we trust are "whackos." Vignettes reveal skeletons in board members' closets: alcoholism, illicit affairs, and unresolved anger. A bizarre dramatic experiment, nicely scored, and unjustly ignored.

Check it Out!

CTV
Situation Comedy
First Broadcast: Saturday, September 21, 1985, 7:30 p.m
Final Year Broadcast: 1988
Running Time: 30 min.

Cast:

Howard Bannister........................ Don Adams
Edna Moseley........................ Dinah Christie
Jack Christian............................ Jeff Pustil
Marlene Weimaraner.................. Kathleen Laskey
Leslie Rappaport...................... Aaron Schwartz
Marvin .... Jason Warren (1985)
Alf Scully.................. Henry Beckman (1985–86)
Murray Amherst .... Simon Reynolds (1985–87)
Jennifer Woods.............. Tonya Williams (1985–86)
Mrs. Alfreda Cobb .... Barbara Hamilton (1985–86)
Viker .... Gordon Clapp (1986–88)
T. C. Collingwood .... Elizabeth Hanna (1987)

Beware show titles bearing exclamation marks! Would you believe Maxwell Smart heading north to take part in the not-terribly-funny adventures of a grocery store manager and his incompetent staff at Brampton's fictional Cobb's supermarket?

Most of the characters were stockboys and cashiers, with Leslie most prominent as a very stereotypically effeminate homosexual. Secretary Edna had a long-term, not-so-secret affair with Bannister. Jack was assistant manager, Alf was a security guard, and Viker was an inept handyman. In the final season, Cobb's was sold to Cendrax Corporation, introducing hard-driving executive Collingwood. Based on the British sitcom *Tripper's Day* and also seen on the USA network.

Chez Hélène

CBC
Children's
First Broadcast: Monday, October 26, 1959, 2:00 p.m.
Final Year Broadcast: 1973
Running Time: 15 min.

Host: Hélène Baillargeon
Cast:
Louise . . . . Madeleine Kronby
Voice of:
Susie the Mouse . . . . Charlotte Fielder
Others: Florence Schreiber, Jean-Louis Millette, Jean-Marie Lemieux

Host Hélène was a cross between your favourite public school teacher and a nice aunt from Montreal. Introducing each show with a cheerful "Bonjour mes petits amis," Hélène taught French to English-speaking pre-schoolers through games and French songs and stories, animated with paper cutouts. Based on the Tan-Gau theory of juvenile language instruction, which posits that children learn to speak a language in stages, rather than by stringing together words learned by rote. Cowardly CBC hacks cancelled the program, which still reached a half-million children daily, because it had "been on too long." While some viewers were undoubtedly inspired to seek rewarding bilingual government jobs in adulthood, lazy kids relied on co-stars Louise and puppet Susie the Mouse, who spoke English.

The critics cheer: "…the last of the jolly mamas, forcing the children into submission through sheer overpowering enthusiasm." — Heather Robertson, *Maclean's*

French on long-play: One of several record albums released to capitalize on the popularity of *Chez Hélène*.

▼

CAL-1072

Chez Hélène

RCA CAMDEN

Chez Nous

CBC
Children's
First Broadcast: Monday, October 21, 1957, 5:00 p.m.
Final Year Broadcast: 1957
Running Time: 30 min.

Hosts: Hélène Baillargeon, Alan Mills

A bilingual program set in a farmhouse with folk singer Mills and Baillargeon, test piloting for *Chez Hélène*. Shown on alternating weeks.

Children's Corner

See: *Small Fry Frolics*

Chrysler Festival

CBC
Variety
First Broadcast: Wednesday, November 14, 1956, 10:00 p.m.
Final Year Broadcast: 1957
Running Time: 60 min.

Hosts: Hume Cronyn, Elaine Grand

An occasional replacement for *Folio,* this expensive, glitzy broadcast came live from Toronto's Loew's Uptown Theatre. Headline guests included the Dave Brubeck Quartet, Canadian-born Percy Faith and His Orchestra, pianists Ferrante and Teicher, the Four Lads, Robert Goulet, Glenn Gould, Shirley Jones (later of *The Partridge Family*), Eartha Kitt, Liberace, the George Shearing Quintet, the Oscar Peterson Trio, Edith Piaf, Peter Sellers, and the Winnipeg Ballet.

Circus

CTV
Variety
First Broadcast: Friday, September 22, 1978, 7:30 p.m.
Final Year Broadcast: 1984
Running Time: 30 min. and 60 min.

Hosts: Cal Dodd, Sherisse Laurence (1978–83), Pierre Lalonde (1983–84)
Cast:
Rumpy the Clown . . . . Roger Prystanski

A *Circus* special begat this tatty big-top series featuring singing, plastic, wind-up hosts; clowns; jugglers; elephants; trapeze artists; and dancing Lippizanner stallions. Billy Van joined the regulars in the expanded second season. A *Sideshow* segment featured such freakish acts as the Jerk-Water People and Olga Perogy. Seen in more than 20 countries.

Rumpy the Clown?

Cities

CBC
Documentary
First Broadcast: Thursday, September 27, 1979, 9:30 p.m.
Final Year Broadcast: 1980
Running Time: 60 min

A neat idea: celebrities present their favorite cities. Anthony Burgess toured Rome; Glenn Gould promoted Toronto; Peter Ustinov performed his usual PR efforts for Leningrad; John Huston praised Dublin; Elie Wiesel presented Jerusalem; George Plimpton was guide for New York City; Germaine Greer introduced Sydney; and Melina Mercouri hosted "magnificently cursed" Athens. Seen in more than 30 countries.

Citizens' Forum

CBC
Discussion
First Broadcast: Tuesday, October 25, 1955, 10:00 p.m.
Final Year Broadcast: 1962
Running Time: 30 min.

Host: Gordon Hawkins

Based on a radio program, this public access show looked at social issues through panel discussions, team debates, dramatic sketches, studio audience involvement, and telephone call-ins. Typical topic: "Can prisons reform criminals?" Later morphed into *The Sixties.*

The City

CTV
Drama
First Broadcast: Sunday, March 7, 1999, 9:00 p.m.
Final Year Broadcast: 2000
Running Time: 30 min.

Cast:

Jack Berg	John Ralston
Katharine Strachan	Torri Higginson
Angie Hart	Robin Brule
Crispin St. James	Jody Racicot
Michael Croft	James Gallanders
Father Shane Devlin	Aidan Devine
Gabriel	Lorne Cardinal
Li Chen	Arthur Eng
Strachan Berg	Matthew Lemche
Mary Lamar	Shannon Lawson
Tyrone Meeks	Arnold Pinnock
Cassian McKeigan	Shawn Doyle
Milt	Michael Sarrazin
Radio Voice	Howard Glassman
City Councillor	Larrisa Laskin

More Canadian soap: behold The City, unnamed, shining urbanopolis with a dark, ugly side (it's Toronto we're talking about here fergoodness'sake!) The slate of stereotypical characters includes: greedy Jewish developer Berg and his long-suffering Gentile wife Katharine; single mom/prostitute Angie and her boyfriend Tyrone; cop McKeigan; troubled priest Devlin (he once had an affair with Katharine and fathered Strachan); St. James, an articulate drug dealer and street-lecturing economist; illegal immigrant Chen; Gabriel, a homeless Native guy with a nice motorbike (he's homeless, not poor); and Milt, the derelict.

In the second season Devlin was dropped, Mary became Katharine's secretary, and police detective Croft and a new city councillor were added.

CITY Lights

Syndicated: 1973
Interview
Running Time: 30 min

Host: Brian Linehan

Walking movie-star encyclopedia and obsequious host Linehan delighted in shocking celebrity guests like Warren Beatty, Jack Lemmon, George C. Scott, and Burt Reynolds with his broad knowledge of arcane biographical tidbits. Martin Short's *SCTV* parody character, Brock Linehan, offered similar detailed information—all of it wrong. Linehan returned to ask more four-minute questions in near-identical programs (*Linehan,* for example) on the WIC network and WTN.

Public access: A viewers' guide to participating in the CBC public affairs program *Citizens' Forum.*

CITIZENS' FORUM

Close-Up

CBC
Public Affairs
First Broadcast: Sunday, October 6, 1957, 10:00 p.m.
Final Year Broadcast: 1963
Running Time: 30 min. and 60 min.

Host: J. Frank Willis

"What happens here, happens as you watch it—it is all live": the opening announcement for this big-budget, in-your-face news program, produced by Ross McLean. Audiences loved the program's show biz savvy and cinéma-vérité-style, designed to inflame controversial issues (fall-out shelters, communism, homosexuality, beatniks) while CBC execs struggled with its popularity. Notable guests (Jack Benny, Anthony Eden, Aldous Huxley, Lucky Luciano, Somerset Maugham, Norman Vincent Peale, Ann Landers, Bertrand Russell, Joey Smallwood, Peter Ustinov, and Evelyn Waugh, to name but a few) were interviewed by the likes of Pierre Berton, Elaine Grand, Percy Saltzman, Dorothy Sangster, Charles Templeton, Patrick Watson, and Jack Webster.

A few notorious segments included a one-hour profile of Glen Exelby, an "unemployed" Hamilton worker, who, it turned out, had quit a comfortable job and turned down all offers of employment so he could earn $25 a day performing for *Close-Up* cameras. In a headline-grabber, the program also grilled a so-called "professional co-respondent" who later admitted she faked the interview. The program expanded to 60 minutes in 1961.

The critics cheer: "[Willis'] majestic face...rises above a size 16 collar like a crag hewn of salt sea spray and buffed by Maritime gales. He's a Bluenose, this one; and it's downright difficult to find anything more Canadian than that." — Ron Poulton, *Toronto Telegram*

Club 6

CBC
Music
First Broadcast: Tuesday, October 18, 1960, 6:15 p.m.
Final Year Broadcast: 1962
Running Time: 30 min.

Hosts: Bob Willson, Mike Darrow

A Canadian *Bandstand,* hosted each week at a different high school. Student interviews, dancing, and music by regulars including Tommy Ambrose and Pat Hervey, the Mickey Shannon combo, the Walter Boys, and Darrow himself. Dance prizes included sets of encyclopedia.

The critics cheer: "...the kind of teenage show that even a mother could love. Music is muted, the young singers keep their voices down, and there is an air of good works about the whole deal...." — Dennis Braithwaite, *The Toronto Star*

The critics jeer: "...[the hosts] conduct some dull interviews while some dull youngsters dance around in the background to some dull music." — Bob Blackburn, *The Toronto Star*

CODCO

CBC
Comedy
First Broadcast: Thursday, October 13, 1988, 9:30 p.m.
Final Year Broadcast: 1993
Running Time: 30 min.

Regular Performers: Andy Jones, Cathy Jones, Greg Malone, Tommy Sexton, Mary Walsh

A groundbreaking, satirical, sketch-comedy series that marked a broader Canadian acceptance of Maritime-based humour (the series actually scored decent ratings in western provinces). The CODCO company had existed as a live performing unit since the early 1970s, and had already been presented on television twice in two CBC series: *The Wonderful Grand Band* and *The S&M Comic Book.*

Popular repeat features on the show included: the *Monty Python*-esque St. John's Street Talk Ladies; the pathetically dateless Friday Night Girls, Mona and Matilda, bitching while bouncing on beds and making plans for an evening at the Avalon Mall; the Loud Feminists; manic Nervous Rex; the two "happy homos," Duncan and Jerome: Queen's Counsellors-at-large; Frank Arsenpuffen, host of *Frank Talk;* home improvement cable TV series *Newfoundland Indoors;* televangelists Byna and Lawton Swerdlow; and news program *The Jugular.*

Popular characters and impressions included: Malone's Warren Beatty, the Duke of Windsor, and Barbara Frum; Walsh's Nan Budgell (of the Newfoundland slumlord Budgells); Jones' VJ Erica Emm and hirsute Love Murphy; and Sexton's Linda Evans, Barbara Walters, Pee-Wee Herman, and newscaster Dawn Day, host of *Hard Facts.* The series' most bizarre and ambitious sketch? A 1950s-style black-and-white film spoof, *I Am Beano Ballicator*, about the forbidden Irish vice of foot-sniffing.

Andy Jones left the show briefly in protest when his 1990 sketch, *Pleasant Irish Priests in Conversation*, about sexual deviancy among priests, was cut by the CBC in the wake of the Mount Cashel orphanage sex scandal. The sketch eventually aired in 1993, along with other banned or blue-pencilled sketches, when the program was shifted to an 11:00 p.m. time slot.

The similarly satirical *This Hour Has 22 Minutes* was a sequel of sort, reuniting Walsh and Cathy Jones.

The critics cheer: "…by turns, bleak, avant garde, vulgar, poetic, inspired and sometimes breathtaking in its daring." — John Haslett Cuff, *The Globe and Mail*

The critics jeer: "The Newfoundland comics aren't blessed with the outrageous inventiveness of the Python crew or the comic consistency of SCTV. At its best, *Codco* is sublimely silly. At its worst, the show is plain dumb." — Mike Boone, Montreal *Gazette*

The Cold Squad

CTV
Drama
First Broadcast: Friday, January 23, 1998, 10:00 p.m.
Final Year Broadcast: —
Running Time: 60 min.

Cast:

Sergeant Ali McCormick	Julie Stewart
Detective Tony Logozzo	Michael Hogan
Jill Stone	Joy Tanner
Detective Nick Gallagher	Paul Boretski
Inspector Vince Schneider	Jerry Wasserman
Sam Fisher	Jay Brazeau
Sergeant Lloyd Mastrowski	Paul Coeur
Detective James Kai	Hiro Kanagawa
Police Coroner Christine Liu	Linda Ko
Inspector Simon Ross	Peter Wingfield
Detective Jackie Cortez	Lori Triolo
Eddie Carson	Bob Frazer
Sergeant Frank Coscarella	Stephen McHattie
Detective Mickey Kollander	Tamara Craig-Thomas
Detective Nicco Sevallis	Gregory Calpakis
Larry Iredell	Eli Gabay
Bernice Boyle	Sharon Alexander
Manny Needlebaum	Richard Ian Cox
Christine	Joely Collins

Hot pursuit: *Cold Squad*'s Julie Stewart (left) and Michael Hogan cuff a suspect on CTV's popular police drama.

Hot murder files mean a warm body, a suspect, an opportunity, and a motive, while harder-to-solve cases are booted down to the police department basement to be handled by the Cold Squad, a holding pen for has-been cops, keeners, and authority bashers. Sgt. McCormick is head of Vancouver's Cold Squad; Logozzo is a burnt-out vet who doesn't like to work under a dame; Stone performs research and psychological profiling; Inspector Schneider is head of Homicide; and Fisher is head of the Forensic Unit.

Ratings dipped in the second season with new Homicide chief (and Ali's love interest) Inspector Ross replacing Schneider, and the additions of Detective Cortez and rookie cop Carson.

The third season, featuring grittier story lines, saw Ali transferred and the rest of the cast reassigned; Logozzo and Ross were spared until the season's second episode.

The critics cheer: "…tight plotting, crisp dialogue and sharply delineated characters." — Henry Mietkiewicz, *The Toronto Star*

The critics jeer: "…it's an open and shut case…. Change the channel and watch the genre at its most well-done, *Homicide: Life on the Street*." — Claire Bickley, *Toronto Sun*

The Collaborators

CBC
Drama
First Broadcast: Sunday, December 16, 1973, 9:00 p.m.
Final Year Broadcast: 1974
Running Time: 60 min

Cast:

Detective Sergeant Jim Brewer	Michael Kane
Detective Sergeant Richard Tremblay	Donald Pilon (1974)
Dr. Charles Erickson	Paul Harding (1973)
Liz Roman	Toby Tarnow
Detective Quinn	Lawrence Benedict
Detective Kaminski	Les Carlson

Forensic scientists Dr. Charles Erickson and assistant Liz Roman "collaborated" with wise-cracking, hard-headed Toronto cop Detective Brewer to solve crimes. Kane and Harding left the series, leaving stoic Detective Sergeant Tremblay to collaborate with Liz. Detective Brewer's disappearance was unexplained.

Two weird episodes: the collaborators get the goods on an insane homosexual Nazi motorbike gangster; they battle a voodoo cult in another segment. The pilot was called *Matter of Fact*.

Comedy Café

CBC
Comedy
First Broadcast: Saturday, February 4, 1970, 10:15 p.m.
Final Year Broadcast: 1970
Running Time: 30 min.

Regular Performers: Barrie Baldaro, Dave Broadfoot, Peter Cullen, George Carron, Joan Stuart, Ted Zeigler

A sketch comedy series capitalizing on French/English tension, based on radio program *Funny You Should Say That*. Taped live at Montreal's Windsor Hotel, regular features included: *L'Anglaises*, with Stuart and Carron as a French/English couple whose "entente" had lost its "cordiale." Other characters included Jerry Atrix, leader of the Age Rebellion, David Broadfoot as "the Member for Kicking Horse Pass," and a hippie surgeon. Typical sketch: two WASPs in a futuristic Quebec try to avoid language police while piloting a Trojan Horse to Ontario; they take a wrong turn and win first prize in a St. Jean Baptiste parade.

The program, cancelled in six weeks, had previously been broadcast in Montreal. Reincarnated as *Comedy Crackers*.

The critics jeer: "…Comedy Café, with its first edition alone, has set TV humor all the way back to the Stone Age.…
— Patrick Scott, *The Toronto Star*

Comedy Crackers

CBC
Comedy
First Broadcast: Wednesday, February 4, 1970, 10:30 p.m.
Final Year Broadcast: 1970
Running Time: 30 min.

Regular Performers: Barrie Baldaro, Dave Broadfoot, George Carron, Joan Stuart, Ted Zeigler
Announcers: Alec Bollini, Stanley Gibbons
Music: The Harry Marks Orchestra

A direct descendant of the briefly seen *Comedy Café*, produced in Montreal and trading largely on skits based on French/English tensions. Regular features included: *L'Anglaises*—Stuart and Carron as a mixed-language couple; Stuart as baby Sweetie; and *The B&B Pub*, with co-owners Jean-Guy Brisebois (Carron) and Bert Bromhead (Baldaro) embroiled in intercultural tension. Carron died before the final program aired.

The critics jeer: "A stupid name for a stupid show." — Bob Blackburn, *The Globe and Mail*

Comedy Factory

CTV
Comedy
First Broadcast: Thursday, June 27, 1985, 7:30 p.m.
Final Year Broadcast: 1985
Running Time: 30 min.

Regular Performers: Geoffrey Bowes, Susan Hogan, Mary Long, Mary Ann McDonald, Derek McGrath, Denis Simpson

In this oddball concept, a troupe of actors performed a single episode of a brand new sitcom each week, backing an alleged guest star imported from the U.S. (Bill Daily, Max Gail, Pat Harrington, Jr., Avery Schreiber). Shows were taped live in front of a studio audience, without the benefit of a laugh track. Shown as a summer series on ABC in the U.S. Production notes indicate that a post-*WKRP in Cincinnati* Jan Smithers was supposed to have participated.

Come Fly With Me

CBC
Musical Variety
First Broadcast: Tuesday, June 24, 1958, 8:00 p.m.
Final Year Broadcast: 1958
Running Time: 30 min.

Host: Shane Rimmer
Music: The Don Wright Singers, The Rudy Toth Orchestra

The CBC showed off its microwave transmission technology (and little else) while earnest, winsome bachelor Rimmer engaged in tame travelogues and introduced acts from various world capitals in Canada, the U.S., and Europe in this summer series. Rimmer once formed one-third of the musical group The Three Deuces with Paul Summerville and someone named Johnny Wacko.

The critics jeer: "Crashed as a flaming bore only minutes after it had cleared the field..." — William Drylie, *The Toronto Star*

Coming Up Rosie

CBC
Comedy/Children's
First Broadcast: Monday, September 15, 1975, 4:30 p.m.
Final Year Broadcast: 1978
Running Time: 30 min.

Cast:

Rosie Tucker	Rosemary Radcliffe
Dudley Nightshade	Barrie Baldaro
Ralph Oberding	Dan Hennessey
Mona Swicker	Fiona Reid
Myrna Wallbacker	Catherine O'Hara
Dwayne Kramer	John Stocker
Wally Wypyzypychwk	John Candy
Purvis Bickle	Dan Aykroyd

Second City alumnus Radcliffe played a documentarist housed in the basement of 99 Sumach Street. Resident loons, portrayed largely by Second City grads and future *Saturday Night Live/SCTV* stars, included assistant at Zonk Productions Dudley Nightshade; Neva Rust storm door salesman Ralph Oberding; Mona and Myrna, operators for the Ringading Answering Service; elevator operator Dwayne; Wally of Sleep-Tite Burglar Alarms; and Purvis Bickle, janitor. The television acting debut for Aykroyd, who broke his leg on the first day of filming. Series creator Trevor Evans envisioned the show as a vehicle to promote a Canadian star system; when the CBC pulled the budget plug, the future stars scattered to the four winds. Seen up to three days per week. Rerun in 1984 to capitalize on the later success of its cast.

Communicate

CBC
Game Show
First Broadcast: Monday, October 3, 1966, 4:00 p.m.
Final Year Broadcast: 1967
Running Time: 30 min.

Hosts: Tom Harvey (1966), Bill Walker (1966–67)

A pale weekday imitation of *Password:* team members supplied one-word clues to guess a person, place, or thing for cash prizes. Players were teamed with marginal celebrities, including future host Walker. The sole big-shot guest, Cliff Robertson, probably fired his agent over the booking.

The critics jeer: "...it's a mess...it's simply being ineptly handled and it's difficult for the viewer to know or care what's going on." — Bob Blackburn, *Toronto Telegram*

CBC

Rosier than thou: *Coming Up Rosie*'s cast of characters included several future stars. Top, from left to right: Barrie Baldaro, Dan Aykroyd, Fiona Reid, John Candy. Bottom, from left to right: Rosemary Radcliffe, Dan Hennessey, John Stocker, Catherine O'Hara.

Corwin

CBC
Drama
First Broadcast: Sunday, October 5, 1969, 9:00 p.m.
Final Year Broadcast: 1971
Running Time: 60 min.

Cast:

Dr. Greg Corwin	John Horton
"Doc" James	Alan King
Mrs. "Mac" Mackie	Ruth Springford
Sergeant Bromley	Robert Warner

Canada's first mini-series featured Greg Corwin, a psychiatrist who doffs his job to work for Doc James in an inner-city practice. The two-part opener featured Margot Kidder as Corwin's patient and fiancée (professional ethics anybody?)

Life imitated art when Horton admitted to being depressed about the series, which concentrated on everything but his inexplicably peripheral title character. An expensive critical disaster, but moderately popular with audiences.

The critics cheer: "...settling down as a soundly written, professionally executed series." — Douglas Marshall, *Maclean's*

The critics jeer: "A glossy bomb...but a bomb nonetheless....an overblown, overdrawn melodramatic potboiler beset by a tedious script, cliché-ridden dialogue and, worst of all, a lot of truly appalling acting." — Patrick Scott, *The Toronto Star*

Country hospitality: *Country Canada* host Sandy Cushon (left) and Karen Webb, circa 1975.

CBC

Counterstrike

CTV
Drama
First Broadcast: Saturday, November 2, 1991, 10:00 p.m.
Final Year Broadcast: 1994
Running Time: 60 min.

Cast:

Alexander Addington	Christopher Plummer
Peter Sinclair	Simon MacCorkindale
Nikki Beaumont	Cyrielle Claire (1991–92)
Luke Brenner	Stephen Shellen (1991–92)
Gabrielle Germont	Sophie Michaud (1992–94)
Hector Stone	James Purcell (1992–94)
Suzanne Addington	Laurence Ashley-Taboulet (1991–92)
Helene Previn	Patricia Cartier (1992–94)
J. J. Johnson	Andre Mayers
Bennett	Tom Kneebone

From his Paris headquarters, Canadian billionaire Addington finances a private force to free his kidnapped wife, then turns his attention to combating world terrorism. Sinclair was a Scotland Yard inspector/freelance cop, Beaumont was a con artist, and Brenner was a mercenary. When Beaumont married and Brenner was killed in the line of duty, second-season replacement team members were ex-CIA agent Stone and ex-journalist Germont. Suzanne was Addington's computer-savvy daughter; Helene, his secretary; Bennett, his butler. A Canada/France co-production.

The critics jeer: "Implausible, preposterous and shallow...." — Greg Quill, *The Toronto Star*

Country Calendar

CBC
Agriculture
First Broadcast: Sunday, October 31, 1954, 1:00 p.m.
Final Year Broadcast: —
Running Time: 30 min.

Contributors: Hal Andrews, Garnett Anthony, Bob Hutt, David Quinton

A long-running show about Canadian agriculture, with considerable urban appeal. Typical episode: Harold Dodds reviews egg prices; Jim Ross discusses wood lots; Earl Cox talks about tropical plants. Not really one show, but several regional programs with interchangeable features. When the program's name changed to *Country Canada* in 1971 it continued to cover farm news, but also aimed for urban relevance.

Hosts of the program have included Norm Garriock, Earl Cox, Johnny Moles, Jim Ross, John Foster, Bob Carbert, Laurie Jennings, Ron Neily, John O'Leary, Glen Powell, George Atkins, Karen Webb, and, most recently, Sandy Cushon. Switched to an evening time slot in 1998.

Country Canada

See: *Country Calendar*

Country Hoedown

CBC
Musical Variety
First Broadcast: Saturday, June 20, 1956, 9:00 p.m.
Final Year Broadcast: 1965
Running Time: 30 min.

Host: Gordie Tapp
Performers: King Ganam and his Sons of the West, The Haymes Sisters (Marjorie, Norma, Jean), The Hoedowners, The Singing Swinging Eight, Lorraine Foreman, Tommy Hunter, Tommy Common, Lloyd Cooper, Johnny Davidson, Al Cherney, Mary Frances, Pat Hervey, Wally Traugott

A corn pone country show set in a barnboard shack with phony, painted-on floorboards. Viewers were welcomed to "Come right in, it's *Country Hoedown* time!" Fiddler Ganam punctuated each number with a wink to the audience. Folksy Gordie Tapp "Aw shucks"-ed his way through the show, making "friends and neighbours" welcome ad nauseam and portrayed dandified Gaylord and resident hick Cousin Clem (who wound up transplanted wholesale to the U.S. *Hee-Haw* show).

Tommy Hunter, a member of Ganam's band, rose in popularity, crooning ballads like Hank Williams' "Cold, Cold Heart" (he eventually inherited *Hoedown*'s slot with *The Tommy Hunter Show*). Ameen "King" Ganam left the show in 1959 over a contract dispute. Guests included Jim Reeves and Red Foley.

A ratings winner, the show also featured musical competitions, with champs and challengers squaring off for top spot. The last number performed on each program was "Love Is the Only Thing." Norman Jewison sometimes directed.

Country Hoedown **time:** Gordie Tapp (foreground) as Cousin Clem mugs for (from left to right): Tommy Common, The Haymes Sisters, Lorraine Foreman, and (rear) Tommy Hunter.

Country Joy

CBC
Soap Opera
First Broadcast: Monday, November 19, 1979, 12:30 p.m.
Final Year Broadcast: 1980
Running Time: 30 min.

Cast:
Dick Brugencate	Howard Dallin
Joy Burnham	Judith Mabey
Pam Brugencate	Debra Au Coin
Rob Brugencate	Jim Calderbank
Helen Brugencate	Vernis McQuaig
Andy Mallory	Brian Taylor
John Morgan	Wally McSween
Tom Breckin	Stephen Walsh
Bill Chapman	John Juliana
Carol Mannering	Pamela Boyd
Alan Gamble	Jack Wyntars

Prairie suds set in fictional Coronet, Alberta, where widowed real estate agent/mayor Dick Brugencate married Joy Burnham (get the title?) from the hospital building committee. Not so thrilled were Dick's mother Helen and teenaged kids Pam and Rob. Series highlights: Pam has an affair with farmer Andy; Rob is falsely accused by no-account Tom of a hit-and-run; Joy has second thoughts about ex-lover Bill Chapman, Assistant Deputy Director of Hospitals; Dr. Gamble drinks too much; and rich-bitch Carol meddles in everyone's business. Produced in Edmonton.

Country Music Hall

CTV
Musical Variety
First Broadcast: Monday, September 7, 1964, 9:00 p.m.
Final Year Broadcast: 1966
Running Time: 30 min.

Host: Carl Smith
Regular Performers: Diana Leigh, Chuck Stewart, Cy Anders, Jean Carignan, The Maple Creek Boys

Smith was a twangy Nashville import who performed and hosted Canadian and U.S. country acts, including the likes of Tex Ritter. Closing titles included a credit for cowboy boots.

Country Roads

CBC
Musical Variety
First Broadcast: Friday, August 19, 1973, 9:00 p.m.
Final Year Broadcast: 1973
Running Time: 60 min.

Host: Ronnie Prophet
Regular Performers: The OK Chorale, Gwen Neighbours, The Peaches, Joey Tardiff, Dave Woods and the Country Roads Brass
Puppeteers: Alison Vandergun, John Vandergun

A summer country series. Musical segments included: *It's Cryin' Time Again* (sad songs); *The Grease Spot* (rockabilly); and *The New Song Spot* (brand new country). Comedy was provided by Granny Slanders (Neighbours), and puppets Yackie Duck and Harold the Frog (Prophet).

Countrytime

CBC
Musical Variety
First Broadcast: Saturday, February 28, 1970, 10:30 p.m.
Final Year Broadcast: 1974
Running Time: 30 min.

Hosts: Don Tremaine (1970–73), Mike Graham (1973–74)
Regular Performers: Myrna Lorrie, Vic Mullen and the Hickorys

To placate the former audience of *Don Messer's Jubilee*, this down-east music fest, taped live in the Dartmouth Senior High School auditorium, brought back Messer alumni Mullen and Tremaine. Guests included Wilf Carter, Stompin' Tom Connors, The Mercy Brothers, and the Allan Sisters.

The critics jeer: "…another bad-music show without a hint of comedy, conscious or otherwise, to redeem it." — Patrick Scott, *The Toronto Star*

Cross-Canada Hit Parade

CBC
Musical Variety
First Broadcast: Wednesday, October 19, 1955, 9:00 p.m.
Final Year Broadcast: 1960
Running Time: 30 min. and 60 min.

Hosts: Austin Willis (1955–58), Wally Koster (1958–59), Bill Walker (1959–60)
Orchestra Leader: Bert Niosi
Regular Performers: Joyce Hahn, Wally Koster, Bert Niosi Orchestra, Robert Goulet, Phyllis Marshall, Adam Timoon, The MCs, The Gino Silvi Singers (1959–60), The Hit Parade Dancers (1959–60)

Based on popular U.S. programs like *Your Hit Parade*, the set piece for this musical was a "futuristic" control panel featuring a map of Canada (minus P.E.I.), inset with cheap flashing light bulbs representing major cities. Votes were tabulated to determine the top songs in Canada that week, while regulars performed cover versions of winners, including watered-down renditions of raucous rock hits like Elvis Presley's "All Shook Up."

Acts occasionally performed their own hits (Bill Haley and His Comets played "Rock Around the Clock" to widespread adult disapproval). Each song inspired new choreography, even if it returned week after week. Result: 18 productions for 18 renditions of "Green Door." In a guest segment, radio DJs predicted future hits.

Middle-of-the-road performers became increasingly uncomfortable with a Top 10 list that forced them to chew on the likes of "Purple People Eater." The 1958-59 program alternated rock'n'roll broadcasts (Paul Anka) with more mushy fare, then returned in 1959 as the even less rocky *Hit Parade*, whose guests included the Everly Brothers, Mitch Miller, and Pete Seeger. Spoofed by Wayne and Shuster as "Cross-Canada Hoke Parade." Also known as *Music '60 Presents The Hit Parade*.

The critics jeer: "There is, about this show, a peculiar kind of stiffness that it never manages to shake. Part of it is due to Austin Willis, whose forced grins and ponderous manner could annoy anyone." — Robert Fulford, *Toronto Telegram*

Crossword Quiz

CBC
Game Show
First Broadcast: Friday, December 26, 1952, 9:00 p.m.
Final Year Broadcast: 1953
Running Time: 30 min.

Moderators: Kim McIlroy (1952–53), Morley Callaghan (1953)
Panel: Ralph Allen, James Bannerman

Two guests and two regulars answered questions based on crossword clues. Allen was editor of *Maclean's*. Unlikely game-show host Callaghan ushered the program into oblivion.

Custard Pie

CBC
Situation Comedy
First Broadcast: Tuesday, September 20, 1977, 7:30 p.m.
Final Year Broadcast: 1977
Running Time: 30 min.

Cast:
Sheila Ann Murphy . . . . Kate Lynch
Maggie Tuckle . . . . Nancy Dolman
Harvey Douglas . . . . Derek McGrath
Leo Strauss . . . . Peter Kastner
Aldo Ludwit . . . . Les Carlson
Vicie DeMarco . . . . Vivian Reis

Custard Pie was the name of a musical group featuring: aspiring actress Sheila Ann Murphy, singer Maggie Tuckle (who waited on tables at a restaurant/gas station called Aldo's); Harvey Douglas, "the guy with the van"; and manager Leo Strauss (Peter Kastner, star of ABC's gender-bending sitcom *The Ugliest Girl in Town*). Vicie DeMarco was the group's landlady. Self-described as "crazy" and "zany," the seemingly bewildered cast performed a group face-plant after 13 episodes.

Based on a superior pilot, *The Rimshots*, starring Andrea Martin, Catherine O'Hara, Dave Thomas, and Saul Rubinek.

The critics jeer: ". . .four young people who do silly things that are supposed to be funny, always at the highest pitch of hysteria." — Blaik Kirby, *The Globe and Mail*

Television Comes to Winnipeg

On the first day we owned a television set (the first home on our street to have one), in the first year of TV in Canada, 1953, the neighbourhood kids gathered round to watch. In that era of the half-channel universe (CBC didn't begin broadcasting until after school), we'd watch pretty much anything.

The first show that held us six-to-eight-year-olds in thrall was *Roy Rogers*. I loved the wide-openness of it all; I loved the fact the good guys always won fairly (although I would have liked to see the occasional baddy actually bite the dust; even at seven, I was suspicious of the clutch-chest-and-topple, bloodless school of screen death). Most of all, I loved the fact that everything had a name: not just Roy and Dale Evans and sidekick Pat Brady, but dog Bullet, horse Trigger, and even Jeep Nellybelle.

In those very early days, the distinctions of border did not loom large. What was Canadian and what was other, i.e., American, was more or less indistinguishable. (To me, "Canadian" was essentially a British-American consortium—with hockey.) Until, that is, Canada began to emerge as an independent entity via the tube. There were several shows then that helped forge the feeling about home as a place larger than one's living room, one's street, one's neighbourhood or, for the more worldly, one's town.

There was, of course, *Hockey Night in Canada*. Now, it's an institution. Then, it was simply an unexpected treat, a visual extension of radio. The fact that for many years the broadcast began only in the second period (or at the end of the first, if there'd been some brawls) gave it the veneer of a guilty, serendipitous pleasure. Only two of the six teams were Canadian, and even the Montreal Forum and Maple Leaf Gardens had the aura of exotic, faraway places we could never hope to visit outside TV-land. (And what the heck was a gondola anyway?) But what gave *HNIC* its most distinct aura of Canadianness were the single-sponsor commercials from Esso and their spokesperson, Murray Westgate. "When your motor's humming and your car da da...when the dee-da-da-da, da-da-da-dee-da..." It brought us to the sign of happy motoring. "Esso," we felt, now that's *Canadian!* Murray Westgate, pumping gas for the good of the nation; now he's *Canadian!* So *HNIC* did give us some sense of a larger society, a larger country out there.

What made me begin to feel Canadian, or at least feel that Canada extended farther than I had yet conceived, was a modest show called *The Plouffes*. I barely remember it, other than as a series of grainy images and vignettes depicting the lives of an ordinary—I assumed they were ordinary—Quebec family. The show's relentless domesticity began to assume the lineaments of a shadow daily life for me. I remember *Les Plouffes* as boring, but I think that was part of its fascination. When you watched it for a while, you became aware that these people, speaking a different language, living in a distinct society (long before that term had any political currency), were neighbours and, you hoped, friends of a sort. I had the feeling that they were people one could possibly know, and that we'd have something to talk about—hockey, for instance, or the travails of school, which seemed to be no less burdensome in French.

By then, I imagined a triumvirate of Canadianness: hockey, Eaton's (for some, it was The Bay), and *Les Plouffes*. Together, they were just about enough to make a kid think that he lived in a real country.

—Martin Levin

Danger Bay

CBC
Drama
First Broadcast: Monday, October 18, 1984, 8:30 p.m.
Final Year Broadcast: 1990
Running Time: 30 min

Cast:

Dr. Grant Roberts	Donnelly Rhodes
J.L. Duvall	Susan Walden
Jonah Roberts	Christopher Crabb
Nicole Roberts	Ocean Hellman
Dr. Donna Chen	Michele B. Chan
Joyce Carter	Deborah Wakeman
Dr. George Dunbar	Hagan Beggs
Adam Berman	Michael Fantini
Lars Johnson	Tom Heaton
Dennis	Kyle Skinner
Uncle Charles	Roy Vickers

Dr. Grant was the crusading curator of marine mammals at the Vancouver Aquarium, devoted to rescuing endangered animals—anything from narwhals to poisonous toads—along the B.C. coast. Assisting were his environmentally savvy kids, Jonah and Nicole, and helicopter pilot Joyce Carter. Dr. Chen was a fellow biologist; Beggs played real-life aquarium director Dunbar. Carter disappeared after the first season, replaced by new Harbour Air owner, J.L. Duvall. J.L. and Grant tied the knot in 1988, though the wedding was delayed by a family of ailing seals in distress. Co-produced with The Disney Channel, U.S. investors insisted on adding streetsmart Chicago teen Adam Berman.

Dateline

CBC
Drama
First Broadcast: Friday, October 7, 1955, 8:00 p.m.
Final Year Broadcast: 1956
Running Time: 30 min.

Canadian dramas, long on historical accuracy and short on the jingoistic fun that boosted American pioneer hokum (*Davey Crockett*) to TV popularity. Some episodes were based on events of the Battle of the Plains of Abraham, the Riel Rebellion, and the search for the North Magnetic Pole. Filmed in English and French (*Je me souviens* was the French title) and shown every other week.

The David Steinberg Show

CTV
Comedy/Variety
First Broadcast: Friday, September 24, 1976, 7:30 p.m.
Final Year Broadcast: 1977
Running Time: 30 min.

Host: David Steinberg
Cast:

Johnny Del Bravo	Martin Short
Raymond J. Johnson Jr./Vinnie	Bill Saluga
Kirk Dirkwood	Joe Flaherty
James MacGregor	Dave Thomas
Spider Reichman	John Candy
Julie Liverfoot	Andrea Martin
Bambi Markowitz/Margi	Trudy Young

Booga-Booga! Steinberg's homage to Jack Benny was a show-within-a-show, most of it taking place backstage before the "actual" program, and in the restaurant across the street, the Hello Deli (har!).

Steinberg made heavy use of Second City troupers before their first series debuted on Global in 1976. Del Bravo was Steinberg's cousin, the world's worst singer, Dirkwood was the stage manager, MacGregor was a security guard, Reichman was a musician, and Liverfoot was a hippie singer. Bambi was an actress, and Margi was the Deli's waitress. Saluga ("You can call me Ray, and you can call me Ray J...") kept showing up at random through the show, asking for directions and inexplicably winding up on Ossington Avenue, when he wasn't doubling as Vinnie, the deli's owner.

Da Vinci's Inquest

CBC
Drama
First Broadcast: Wednesday, October 7, 1998, 9:00 p.m.
Final Year Broadcast: —
Running Time: 60 min.

Cast:

Dominic Da Vinci	Nicholas Campbell
Sunita (Sunny) Raman	Sue Mathew
Detective Leo Shannon	Donnelly Rhodes
Angela Kosmo	Venus Terzo
Detective Mick Leary	Ian Tracey
Patricia Da Vinci	Gwynyth Walsh
Dr. James Flynn	Robert Wisden
Sergeant Sheila Kurtz	Sarah-Jane Redmond
Joe Da Vinci	Robert Clothier
Portia Da Vinci	Joy Coghill
Danny Leary	Max Martini
Gabriella Da Vinci	Jewel Staite
Helen	Sarah Strange

Canada revisits *Wojeck* territory, as an ex-narc/ex-alcoholic becomes Vancouver's combative coroner and perennial pain in the ass to Chief Coroner Flynn. Leary, Kosmo, and Shannon are cops; Raman, a pathologist. Ex-wife Patricia is the chief pathologist and Flynn's current lover.

The critics cheer: "Storylines are unflinching and compelling." — Claire Bickley, *The Toronto Sun*

The critics jeer: "Let's hear no more about this being the best show on television. *Da Vinci's Inquest* isn't even close." — John Allemang, *The Globe and Mail*

Work with me baby: Nicholas Campbell emotes to a corpse as the combative coroner of *Da Vinci's Inquest*.

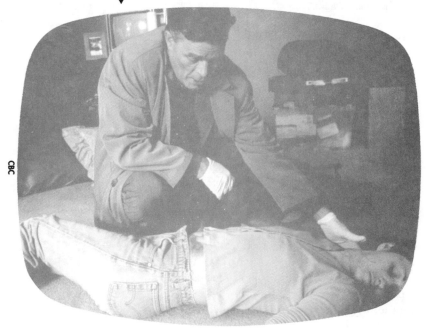

CBC

Definition

CTV
Game Show
First Broadcast: Monday, September 9, 1974
Final Year Broadcast: 1990
Running Time: 30 min.

Hosts: Bob McLean (1974–75), Jim Perry (1975–90)
Announcer: Dave Devall

Long-running game show based on the word game Hangman, as contestant teams tried to guess a blanked-out mystery word through clues and letter hints. After heavily retreading minor guest stars, the program relied solely on amateur talent in its final years. McLean was the show's first host, though it seems like genial Perry was actually there from the start. The memorable theme music was Quincy Jones' "Soul Bossa Nova," though a later recording by rappers The Dream Warriors added lyrics to pay homage to the show ("My definition…my definition is this…"). Seen at various times on different CTV affiliates.

Degrassi High

CBC
Children's
First Broadcast: Monday, November 6, 1989, 8:30 p.m.
Final Year Broadcast: 1991
Running Time: 30 min.

Cast:

Joey Jeremiah	Pat Mastroianni
Derek (Wheels) Wheeler	Neil Hope
Snake	Stefan Brogren
Caitlin	Stacie Mistysyn
Michelle	Maureen Mackay
Spike (Christine Nelson)	Amanda Stepto
Lucy	Anais Granofsky
Kathleen	Rebecca Haines
Heather	Maureen Deiseach
Erica	Angela Deiseach
Dwayne	Darrin Brown
L.D.	Amanda Cook
Casie	Andrew Lockie
Dale	Cameron Graham
Yick Yu	Siluk Saysanasy
Tessa Campanelli	Kirsten Bourne
BLT (Bryan Lester Thomas)	Dayo Ade

Hot'n'heavy teen issues (sex, drugs, rock-'n'roll, and relationships), as the *Degrassi Junior High* folks grow up a little—but just a little. Many cast members were holdovers from *Junior High.* Among the series' highlights: pro-lifer Erica becomes pregnant; Joey's band, The Zit Remedy, records a rock video; Michelle's parents split; L.D. gets cancer; and Joey walks naked through the cafeteria to raise money for a car.

This series ends at the grad dance, and the school is shut down for repairs. But wait! A follow-up 1991 film, *School's Out! The Degrassi Feature,* reveals that, in the ensuing summer, Tessa becomes pregnant by Joey. Caitlin and Joey are engaged. Tessa has an abortion. Caitlin dumps Joey and goes to college, but—let bygones be bygones—they remain friends. In a sub-plot, Wheels drives drunk and is imprisoned for criminal negligence causing death.

The end of the *Degrassi* saga? See *Degrassi Talks* and watch for a proposed CTV series *Degrassi: The Next Generation,* slated for 2001.

The critics cheer: "The most astonishing teen TV series ever produced in North America..." — Sid Adilman, *The Toronto Star*

Degrassi Junior High

CBC
Children's
First Broadcast: Sunday, January 18, 1987, 5:00 p.m.
Final Year Broadcast: 1989
Running Time: 30 min.

Cast:

Joey Jeremiah	Pat Mastroianni
Derek (Wheels) Wheeler	Neil Hope
Snake	Stefan Brogren
Spike (Christine Nelson)	Amanda Stepto
Caitlin	Stacie Mistysyn
Arthur Kaye	Duncan Waugh
Shane	Bill Parrott
Alexa	Irene Courakos
Heather	Maureen Deiseach
Erica	Angela Deiseach
Simon	Michael Carry
Karen	Anais Granofsky
Stephanie Kaye	Nicole Stoffman
Yick Yu	Siluk Saysanasy
Liz	Cathy Keenan
Voula	Niki Kemeny
Rick Munro	Craig Driscoll
Mr. Garcia	Robert Montgomery
Ms. Avery	Michelle Goodeve
Emma Nelson	Samantha Morrison (baby)/Ashlee Hendricks (toddler)

A sorta sequel to *Kids of Degrassi Street.* Yes, the street remains the same, and some of the actors have returned, but not as their original characters. With a cast of hundreds (no complete cast and credits lists seem to exist) the program was seen 'round the world. Aimed primarily at a teen audience who liked to watch sex-obsessed peers wringing their hands about major social issues like sex, drugs, venereal disease, wet dreams, eating disorders, and suicide. Spike's pregnancy and motherhood (the baby's name is Emma), struck a chord with viewers. Joey's band (with Wheels and Snake) is The Zit Remedy. The school catches fire during the graduation dance, clearing the way for *Degrassi High.* Some foreign markets refused to show controversial episodes and edited others. A documentary, *Degrassi: Between Takes,* narrated by Peter Gzowski, aired in 1989.

Degrassi Talks

CBC
Children's
First Broadcast: Monday, February 24, 1992, 8:30 p.m.
Final Year Broadcast: 1992
Running Time: 30 min.

Hosts: Rebecca Haines, Neil Hope, Pat Mastroianni, Stacie Mistysyn, Amanda Stepto

Ten *Degrassi* actors interviewed teens across the country about some of the issues they dramatized on the myriad *Degrassi* shows: addiction, pregnancy, abusive relationships, and homosexuality among them.

Delilah

CBC
Situation Comedy
First Broadcast: Thursday, October 4, 1973, 9:00 p.m.
Final Year Broadcast: 1974
Running Time: 30 min.

Cast:

Della	Terry Tweed
Aunt Peggy	Barbara Hamilton
T.J.	Eric House
Franny	Peter Mews
Frances	Kay Hawtrey
Mavis	Joyce Gordon
Isabel	Paulle Clark
Vincent	Miles McNamara
Mr. Kennaway	Arch McDonnell

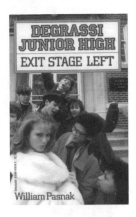

William Pasnak

The lit of Degrassi Street: One in a series of paperbacks based on the popular *Degrassi* series.

Citified Della returns to small-town Egerton to run a heavily mortgaged barber shop (named Delilah, after Samson's biblical barber), left in trust to her "super hip" teenage brother Vincent. This massive bomb featured assorted "zany" characters including local newspaper editor T.J., meddling Aunt Peggy, and Della's best friend Franny (who was probably gay) and his pet plant Bruce. Some critics preferred *The Trouble With Tracy*.

The critics jeer: "I was really so appalled, I don't know what to say…it is not enough to simply dismiss it as awful." — Bob Blackburn, *The Toronto Sun*

"…the season's most dismal failure." — Sid Adilman, *The Toronto Star*

Denny's Sho*

CBC
Music
First Broadcast: Thursday, June 1, 1978, 9:00 p.m.
Final Year Broadcast: 1978
Running Time: 30 min.

Former lead singer for the Mamas and the Papas, Denny Doherty returned to Halifax to welcome musical guests including Salome Bey, Gloria Kaye, Moe Koffman, Murray McLauchlan, Original Caste, John Sebastian, and Ken Tobias. The opener served as a post-Mama Cass reunion of the Mamas and the Papas.

The Denny Vaughan Show

CBC
Musical Variety
First Broadcast: Wednesday, June 16, 1954, 8:00 p.m.
Final Year Broadcast: 1957
Running Time: 30 min.

Host: Denny Vaughan
Regular Performers: The Mello-aires, The Add-Fours, The Bobolinks, Charles Calmers, The Diamonds, Don Wright Singers, Joan Fairfax, Don Hewitt, Glenna Jones, Mitch Nutick

Slick singer/pianist/accordionist Vaughan led his orchestra, the Mello-aires, through this series that grew from a radio program and summer TV time slot. The Diamonds, performing such stellar material as "Ka Ding Dong," alternated with The Add-Fours. Known in Britain as "The English Sinatra," Vaughan lost his toupée on the show's live opener.

Destiny Ridge

Global
Drama
First Broadcast: Monday, November 29, 1993, 9:00 p.m.
Final Year Broadcast: 1995
Running Time: 60 min.

Cast:

Anna	Elke Sommer
Chief Warden Don Jenkins	Richard Comar
Sam Whitehorse	Raoul Trujillo
Darlene Kubolek	Laurie Holden
Julie Fryman	Nancy Sakovich
Linda Hazelton	Rebecca Jenkins
Clay Roberts	Kavan Smith
Peter	Arnold Brauss
Jack Kilbourne	Scott Hylands
Walt	Michael Tayles
Rich Dearden	Shaun Johnston
Molly Dearden	Cheryl Wilson
Merle Owen	Esther Purves-Smith
Frank Kubolek	Philip Granger
Constable Jerry McNeal	Peter Yunker
James Hazelton	Ken Camroux

As a German-Canadian co-production, this series about life in Canada's north looked like a nature tour. When the Germans pulled out (taking the inappropriately cast Elke with them) the series morphed into a steamy soap opera—a *Chippendales* meets *North of 60* as oversexed characters spent much of their time in bed, trying to get each other into bed, or fantasizing about taking each other to bed (sometimes while lying in bed). Set in the fictional town of Argent, Alberta. A CBC pilot show was called *High Country*.

The critics jeer: "All this is supposed to get viewers snorting like a hot-blooded moose in season…." — Liam Lacey, *The Globe and Mail*

Detective Quiz

CBC
Game Show
First Broadcast: Wednesday, September 10, 1952, 9:30 p.m.
Final Year Broadcast: 1952
Running Time: 30 min.

Host: Morley Callaghan

"Investigator" Callaghan challenged viewers to identify a criminal using on-screen clues. A first-month CBC flop.

Diamonds

Syndicated: 1987
Mystery
Running Time: 60 min.

Cast:

Mike Devitt .... Nicholas Campbell
Christina Towne .... Peggy Smithhart
Darryl .... Alan Feiman
Lt. Lou Gianetti .... Tony Rosato
Rene .... Roland Magdane

Another made-in-Canada filler for U.S. TV (CBS and USA). Married actors Mike and Christina perform on a program called *Diamonds*. The program is cancelled and so is their marriage, leaving the hapless couple to join forces as a real-life detective team, the Two of Diamonds Agency. Darryl was a special effects expert who rigged costumes and props. Lt. Gianetti was Mike's helpful cousin. Rene was added in the second season, to placate French financiers. Seen irregularly on Global in Canada.

The Diane Stapley Show

CBC
Music
First Broadcast: Friday, January 22, 1976, 7:30 p.m.
Final Year Broadcast: 1976
Running Time: 30 min.

Host: Diane Stapley

After an ill-considered whirlwind press tour and impossible-to-follow network promotional build-up, Stapley (rhymes with haply) performed middle-of-the-road material and show tunes in a shoestring effort produced in a minuscule Winnipeg studio. Guests included Dinah Christie, Tom Gallant, and Gordon Pinsent.

The critics jeer: "...the tackiest piece of entertainment to come down the pipe in some time...The whole sorry mess looks like it cost $1.95 to produce." — Ron Base, *Maclean's*

D'Iberville

CBC
Drama
First Broadcast: Monday, October 7, 1968, 4:30 p.m.
Final Year Broadcast: 1969
Running Time: 30 min.

Cast:

Pierre Lemoyne d'Iberville .... Albert Millaire
Paul Lemoyne, Sieur de Maricourt .... Jean Besre
Jacques Le Ber .... Alexandre Rigneault
Sieur de LaBarre...................... Jacques Monod
Charles Lemoyne .... Francois Rozet
Marquis de Denonville .... Gilles Pelletier
Chevalier de La Salle.................. Yves Letourneau
Chevalier de Troyes........................ Leo Ilial

One of Canada's few swashbucklers, *D'Iberville* was shot in French, then badly dubbed into English.

The Belgian/Swiss/Canadian co-production was set against the 17th-century rivalry among the French, English, and Dutch for control of the fur trade, and based on the life of Pierre Lemoyne, Sieur D'Iberville—lover, fighter, naval commander, and explorer.

Key events included: Pierre's romance with Genevieve Picote du Belestre; Pierre's part in De Troyes's expedition to Hudson's Bay, and the exploration of Newfoundland.

The series boasted more than 175 actors, including French imports Rigneault and Monod, in addition to the English actors who dubbed the series: Arch McDonnell, Len Carlson, Leslie Yeo, Jack Scott, Peggy McNamara, Sandra Scott, Frank Perry, Sandy Webster, and Murray Westgate. Shot in colour on sets built near Quebec City. A full-scale replica of D'Iberville's ship, *The Pelican*, was altered 28 times to represent various vessels.

A documentary, *This is D'Iberville*, followed.

Variety on a budget: Diane Stapley hosts the self-titled *Diane Stapley Show*.

CBC

Discoveries

CBC
Children's
First Broadcast: Friday, February 8, 1957, 5:00 p.m.
Final Year Broadcast: 1959
Running Time: 15 min.

Hosts: Dick Sutton, Dr. R.P. Coats, "Uncle Stan" Westaway, Rod McKenzie

Amateur TV personalities took turns hosting this educational program. Sutton, curator of the Manitoba Museum, covered nature and history; Coats handled communications; Westaway discussed plants; McKenzie dealt with electricity.

Don Messer's Jubilee

CBC
Musical Variety
First Broadcast: Friday, August 7, 1959, 9:30 p.m.
Final Year Broadcast: 1969
Running Time: 30 min.

Host: Don Messer
Announcer: Don Tremaine
Regular Performers: The Islanders, Charlie Chamberlain, Cec MacEachern, Warren MacRae, Waldo Murdo, Duke Nielsen, Marg Osburne, Rae Simmons, Ray Calder, Catherine McKinnon, Johnny Forrest, The Gunter Buchta Dancers

Paradise for fans of Maritime and folk music, hell for highbrows, *Don Messer's Jubilee* started life as a summer replacement for the popular *Country Hoedown*. Produced

Friday night Jubilee: Don Messer delighted audiences for a decade until CBC executives purged their television schedule of most of countrified fare.

in Halifax, where fiddler Messer and his Islanders were already a big act on tour, radio, and local television. On air, Messer all but disappeared, preferring to let his fiddle do the talking. The more popular Islanders were: Chamberlain as a swaggering lumberjack; Duke Nielsen (reportedly a fire eater and bear wrestler) playing any of 22 musical instruments; and stately vocalist Marg Osburne.

Critics savaged the show for its high glucose content, amateurish feel, and stingy budget; rural audiences loved its down-home sincerity and folksy devotion to all things Canadian. The program became so popular in its niche market that it peaked at 96 per cent of Maritime viewing audiences. Though the show stiffed in some major urban centres, a healthy rural audience pushed viewership higher than three million—beating some *Hockey Night in Canada* broadcasts, and pleasing sponsors Pillsbury and Massey-Ferguson no end, as sales of cake mixes and tractors soared.

In a deliberate attempt to squash what it called "geriatric fiddlers" the CBC killed the program in its tenth year in search of younger audience demographics. Protesters slammed the decision as elitist, immoral, and anti-Canadian. Newspapers ran scathing editorials and offered mail-in protest cards. Fiddlers and square dancers demonstrated on Parliament Hill. MP John Diefenbaker decried the cancellation in the House of Commons. The CBC remained silent. In the network's defence, Messer's Friday-night ratings had slipped from Top Ten to a less comfortable twenty-second spot, shattering the self-perpetuated Messer myth that he was assassinated at the height of popularity.

Messer returned to syndicated television (through Hamilton's CHCH-TV) in 1970, cast intact, with Sandy Hoyt as announcer. A smattering of the CBC-produced programs were syndicated in the U.S. Followed by a 1985 stage show of the same name. Typical episode: Marg Osburne performs "Dear Hearts"; the Islanders perform "Grandma's Chickens" and "Dominion Reel."

The critics jeer: "[A] perennial horror program. Last night they had a fellow scratching away on grandmother's scrub board.... Surely Nova Scotia should not be represented to the rest of the nation on the CBC by this sad country music show." — Roy Shields, *The Toronto Star*

"An amateur presentation on a professional medium such as television is not cute, but vulgar." — Hugh Garner, *Toronto Telegram*

"...this drab, colorless, lifeless figure obviously fills a real need in our compulsive quest for Canadian identity." — Patrick Scott, *The Toronto Star*

The critics cheer: "They believe in the worth of what they are doing and though their range is small, within it they have achieved an excellence and serenity that touch the viewer." — Dennis Braithwaite, *The Toronto Star*

Double Exposure

CTV
Comedy
First Broadcast: Saturday, November 27, 1997, 7:00 p.m.
Final Year Broadcast: —
Running Time: 30 min.

Regular Performers: Linda Cullen, Bob Robertson

Based on the CBC radio program, with Cullen and Robertson (they're married) performing stand-up satire and employing their talents for impersonation to dub new dialogue into actual news footage.

Double Up

CBC
Game Show
First Broadcast: Monday, July 1, 1974, 9:30 p.m.
Final Year Broadcast: 1974
Running Time: 30 min.

Host: Hart Pomerantz
Announcer: Warren Davis

Three sets of contestants with unusual hobbies doubled up to play for up to 800 bucks in prize money in this popular summer series. A spoof on quiz shows, Pomerantz's questions were beside the point, tucked between valiant attempts to control star-struck contestants (a celebrity toothpick collector/a woman who paints on eggs) blinded by their five minutes of fame. Champs could return to double their piddling winnings.

Double Your Money

CTV
Game Show
First Broadcast: Friday, September 11, 1964, 10:00 p.m.
Final Year Broadcast: 1964
Running Time: 30 min.

Host: Hughie Green

A direct copy of Green's British series, which had run in England for nine years under the same name. Contestants doubled their loot by answering skill-testing questions until they reached the staggering sum of $100 in prize money. A segment of each show was filmed in England.

Down Home Country

CBC
Musical Variety
First Broadcast: Friday, July 11, 1975, 9:00 p.m.
Final Year Broadcast: 1975
Running Time: 60 min.

Host: Tom Gallant
Regular Performers: Blue Jane, Nancy White

This summer series' guests included Chad Allan, Jessi Coulter, Waylon Jennings, Kenny Rogers, "Diamond" Joe White, Sneezy Waters, Myrna Lorrie, and the Good Brothers. Harvey Atkin did comedy bits as "get-along-gourmet" Chuck Wagon, to Peter Cullen's off-key musician, Luke Warm.

Dracula: The Series

Syndicated: 1990
Horror
Running Time: 30 min.

Cast:
Alexander Lucard . . . . Geordie Johnson
Gustav Helsing . . . . Bernard Behrens
Klaus Helsing . . . . Geraint Wyn Davies
Max Townsend . . . . Jacob Tierney
Chris Townsend . . . . Joe Roncetti
Sophie Metternich . . . . Mia Kirshner
Eileen Townsend . . . . Lynne Cormack

Alexander Lucard. Could it be—Dracula spelled sideways? In this campy series, the Armani-clad Count planned world domination through his multinational corporation, Lucard Industries. On his trail: Gustav Helsing, a descendant of the original vampire hunter, and Sophie and her nephews Max and Chris. Klaus, Gustav's son, was a vampire victim. Plots involved vampire-killing laser guns, curse cures, and frequent bouts of vampirism among the living cast. Best episode title: "I Love Lucard." Davies played another vampire in the Canadian series *Forever Knight*. Filmed in Luxembourg.

Pose cool kids: The *Drop-In* gang is photographed at an impromptu lakeside rap session.

Susan Conway

included "teen-age magician" Doug Henning and Prime Minister Pierre Trudeau. Musical guests included Copperpenny, Perth County Conspiracy, and Shirley Eikhard. Guest hosts represented various regions of Canada. Seen Mondays, Wednesdays, and Fridays. Pilot series: *Dress Rehearsal.*

Drop-In

CBC
Children's
First Broadcast: Monday, September 28, 1970, 4:30 p.m.
Final Year Broadcast: 1974
Running Time: 30 min.

Hosts: Rex Hagon (1970–73), Susan Conway (1970–74), Pat Rose, Susan Anderson
Reporters: Jeff Cohen, Lynne Griffin
Puppeteer: Nina Keogh
Music: Ron Nigrini's Gentle Rock Band

"*Stop in...Drop-In!*" Life after *The Forest Rangers* for the two hosts in this vaguely psychedelic, loosely formatted program for young teens, offering interviews, music, and comedy sketches by the Drop-In Little Theatre performed by actors including John Candy, Eugene Levy, and Doug McGrath. Guests

Drop the Beat

CBC
Drama
First Broadcast: Monday, February 7, 2000, 8:30 p.m.
Final Year Broadcast: —
Running Time: 30 min.

Cast:
Dennis	Merwin Mondesir
Jeff	Mark Taylor
Mega	Omari Forrester
MC Divine	Michie Mee
DJ Craft	Shamann
Kat	Jennifer Baxter

Earnest (perhaps *too* earnest) series about two DJs programming a hip-hop show at a campus radio station. While pursuing their musical goals, the boys illuminate important societal issues, including racism and freedom of speech.

Guest recording artists, some of them playing themselves, have included Bishop, Citizen Kane, Choclair, Chuck D, DJX, Ghetto Concept, High and Mighty, Infinite, Jemeni, Kardinal Offishall, Kid Kut, Maestro Fresh Wes, Rahzel, Red1, Singlefoot, Subliminal, and Tara Chase. Program spin-offs include CDs and show gear.

The critics jeer: "The music is a welcome addition to tube time, but *Drop the Beat* would be easier to take if the characters could calm themselves occasionally." — Pat St. Germain, *Winnipeg Sun*

Dr. Simon Locke

Syndicated: 1971
Drama
Running Time: 30 min.

Cast:
Dr. Simon Locke	Sam Groom
Dr. Andrew Sellers	Jack Albertson
Nurse Louise Wynn	Nuala Fitzgerald
Chief Dan Palmer	Len Birman

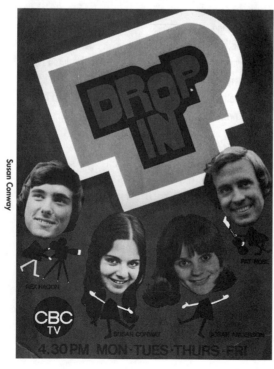

Susan Conway

CTV loved the idea of earning Canadian content points with a doctor series starring two Americans. When the CRTC relaxed Cancon rules, the network dropped out, leaving American producers stranded in East York to finish the show. Set in the small town of Dixon Mills, typical episodes featured xenophobic residents trying to kick Dr. Locke's citified ass out of town, while he and crusty Dr. Sellers locked horns over patient care. Each episode began with a bizarre nonsequitur featuring Groom scuttling across a snowy landscape, with a helicopter in hot pursuit. Caught in the chopper's spotlight a megaphoned voice blared the program's title: "Dr. Locke! Dr. Simon Locke!"

This miserable, low-budget mess (with guest stars borrowed from CBC's megabomb *Jalna*) actually turned a first-year profit and earned respectable audience shares when U.S. sponsor Colgate-Palmolive offered it *free* to NBC affiliates, though Albertson left from embarrassment by year's end. How low-budget? Groom was apparently forced to make costume changes in the bushes, and numerous guest appearances by the boom microphone almost warranted separate billing. Followed by a sorta sequel, *Police Surgeon*.

The critics jeer: "...sub par, make that sub-sub-par in every ingredient...unbelievable in every connotation of that word...bad dialogue, terrible supporting acting, overly bright set lighting and incoherent continuity gave the half hour the look and sound of a local station soap opera of about 20 years ago."
— *Variety*

Dr. Zonk and the Zunkins

CBC
Children's
First Broadcast: Monday, September 23, 1974, 4:30 p.m.
Final Year Broadcast: 1975
Running Time: 30 min.

Cast:
Billy Meek. . . . . Robin Eveson
Voice of:
Zooey . . . . Trevor Evans
Dunkin . . . . John Stocker
Regular Performers: John Candy, Dan Hennessey, Robert McKenna, Rosemary Radcliffe, Gilda Radner, Fiona Reid
Puppeteers: Nina Keogh, John Stocker

"Hey listen to that plunkin'
Bringin' love in a chunk in
It's Zooey and Dunkin
Our computer Zunkins."

Young Billy Meek imagines such characters as Dr. Bob, Miss Lonelykid, Lovestory Man, Ms. A. Vaughn, Goomba, Honest Ralph the salesman, and the Wilkins, assisted by computer-puppet Zunkins: Zooey and Dunkin. Lots of pre-famous supporting players, movie stills, burlesque, and music. Dr. Zonk, of the program's title, was a never-seen comic book character. *Coming Up Rosie* was a partial sequel. Seen on Mondays, Wednesdays, and Fridays.

Due South

CTV
Drama
First Broadcast: Saturday, April 23, 1994, 9:00 p.m
Final Year Broadcast: 1998
Running Time: 60 min.

Cast:
Constable Benton Fraser . . . . Paul Gross
Detective Ray Vecchio . . . . David Marciano (1994–96)
Angie Vecchio . . . . Katayoun Amini
Mr. Vecchio . . . . David Calderisi (1994–96)
Lieutenant Harding Welsh . . . . Beau Starr
Detective Louis Guardino . . . . Daniel Kash (1994–96)
Detective Jack Huey. Tony Craig
Elaine Besbriss . . . . Catherine Bruhier
Diefenbaker . . . . Lincoln (1994–96), Draco (1996–98)
Detective Stanley Raymond Kowalski . . Callum Keith Rennie (1996–98)
Stella Kowalski . . . . Anne Marie Loder (1996–98)
Detective Thomas E. Dewey . . . . . . Tom Melissis (1996–98)
Inspector Margaret Thatcher . . . . . Camilla Scott (1995–98)
Sergeant Robert Fraser . . . . Gordon Pinsent
Francesca Vecchio . . . . Ramona Milano
Constable Renfield Turnbull . . . Dean McDermott (1995–98)
Dr. Mort Gustafson. . . . . Jan Rubes (1996–98)

Constable Benton Fraser is everything a good Mountie should be: brave, honourable, dependable, kind to cats, and devastatingly shy around women.

In this tongue-in-cheek series, straightlaced Fraser is assigned to the (fictitious) Canadian Consulate in Chicago, where he assists wisecracking Vecchio on local cases.

The first Canadian series to appear on full network U.S. prime time, CBS actually cancelled the series twice, though it continued on CTV and in syndication, supported by its European success ("Thank you kindly").

The revived program brought changes. New sets were blamed on a fictional fire. Cast shifts included the disappearance of

Due for re-run heaven: *Due South*'s dynamic duo, Paul Gross as Constable Fraser, and faithful pooch Dief.

Vecchio, who went undercover to impersonate a mobster (though he made occasional guest appearances), and the addition of Kowalski. Guardino was killed by a car bomb. Besbriss, a civilian aide, became a police officer in the third season. Angie was Vecchio's ex-wife (the actress was his real wife), and Francesca was Ray's sister. Sergeant Fraser was Benton's father, a by-the-book ghost, who provided him with advice; Vecchio's father, also a ghost, occasionally appeared to heap derision on his son.

Cultural in-jokes abound, though they're not very tricky and largely limited to character names (Stanley and Stella Kowalski, Margaret Thatcher, and three cops named Huey, Dewey, and Louis). Myriad Canadian references include a reporter named Mackenzie King and, of course, Dief, a Siberian Husky who played Benton's lip-reading wolf pet. Leslie Nielsen guest starred as Sgt. Duncan "Buck" Frobisher. A genuine cult item, the series boasts dozens of Web sites, volumes of fan fiction, and merchandise including sound track albums, program guidebooks, T-shirts, mousepads, and a desk clock.

While the series was ushered into existence on April 23, 1994 by a two-hour TV movie, the regular season began on Saturday, September 22 at 9:00 p.m.

Earth: Final Conflict

See: *Gene Roddenberry's Earth: Final Conflict*

Ed and Ross

CBC
Children's
First Broadcast: Thursday, July 4, 1957, 5:00 p.m.
Final Year Broadcast: 1959
Running Time: 30 min.

Hosts: Ed McCurdy, Ross Snetsinger

Singer McCurdy and guitarist Snetsinger lived in adjacent apartments in a magical house with puppet pal Foster. Other characters included a talking (dubbed) parrot. Snetsinger boasted a huge collection of electric trains, seen on the show.

The critics cheer: "...one of the more amiable children's shows around." — Robert Fulford, *Toronto Telegram*

The Edison Twins

CBC
Children's
First Broadcast: Monday, January 3, 1983, 4:30 p.m.
Final Year Broadcast: 1987
Running Time: 30 min.

Cast:

Tom Edison	Andrew Sabiston
Annie Edison	Marnie McPhail
Paul Edison	Sunny Besen Thrasher

A latter-day *Hardy Boys* with a dash of science and history, as smarty-pants Edison twins, a brother and sister team, used scientific principles and book learning to solve crimes, foil bullies, and influence people. Precocious little brother Paul tagged along for the ride. The well-done series was smartly written and entertaining. Many episodes featured the twins slurping down a cornucopia of gooey desserts. Also seen on The Disney Channel. Title song by Bob Segarini.

Ed McCurdy

See: *Uncle Ed's Party*

Ed's Night Party

CITY-TV
Talk Show
First Broadcast: Friday, February 10, 1995, 10:30 p.m.
Final Year Broadcast: —
Running Time: 30 min.

Co-hosts: Howard Glassman, Harland Williams, Craig Campbell, and many others

"If you don't have something nice to say, say it often."

— Ed the Sock

Ed is a foul-mouthed, cigar-chomping sock puppet with green hair, host of Canada's longest-running late-night talk show. Ed abuses guests, both famous and not-so-famous, as dancers gyrate in the background. Is Ed actually funny? Let's just say he was more amusing in his Rogers Cable days, when guests like Robert Vaughn didn't know what kind of hell they'd been booked into (Ed grilled him about the Helsinki Formula for hair growth that Vaughn had recently plugged). Literate comedian Eric Tunney, the only co-host capable of holding his own against Ed's tirades— even reducing the Yarn Boy to sputtering silence—didn't make the transition to commercial television, where the Sock consumes weak-kneed co-hosts with a voracious appetite. While this is billed as adult entertainment, audience shots reveal Ed's most ardent supporters—pimply-faced adolescent males (sans dates) who guffaw and chortle with the precision of a laugh track. Ed's best character: Eddo the Magnificent, a take on Johnny Carson's mind-reading Carnack. The program changed its name to *Ed the Sock* in its fourth year, returning to a less glitzy set in an effort to help recapture Ed's grittier early years.

Ed's identity is a not-very-closely guarded secret; everyone suspects the man behind the sock (80% cotton, 20% polyester) is Joel Kerzner. *Saturday Night Live* briefly plagiarized the format in a short-lived skit. Seen in Australia and New Zealand.

Ed's Place

See: *Uncle Ed's Party*

The Elephant Show

CBC
Musical Variety/Children's
First Broadcast: Monday, October 8, 1984, 4:30 p.m.
Final Year Broadcast: 1988
Running Time: 30 min.

Hosts: Sharon Hampson, Lois Lilienstein, Bram Morrison

Billed as Canada's first weekly variety show for children, this effort featured popular singing act Sharon, Lois and Bram romping with kiddies, introducing guests, then performing songs in concert. Elephant (someone in an elephant suit) and Eric Nagler were regular guests. Also frequently appearing were Fred Penner, Ann Mortifee, Bob Schneider, Circus Smirkus, Bob Berkey, and The Whole Leaf Theatre. Also known as *Sharon, Lois & Bram's Elephant Show.*

Emily of New Moon

CBC
Drama
First Broadcast: Sunday, January 4, 1998, 7:00 p.m.
Final Year Broadcast: —
Running Time: 60 min.

Cast:

Emily Starr	Martha MacIsaac
Aunt Laura	Sheila McCarthy
Aunt Elizabeth	Susan Clark
Cousin Jimmy	Stephen McHattie
Uncle Malcolm Murray	John Neville
Aunt Isabel Murray	Linda Thorson
Ilse Burnley	Jessica Pellerin
Perry Miller	Kris Lemche
Douglas Starr	Michael Moriarty
Maisie Adams	Maisie Jenkins
Lofty John	Maury Chaykin

Another dip into the Lucy Montgomery files—sort of a *Road To Avonlea: the Dark*

Salter Street Films

Side. After Emily's father dies, she's forced to stay with sourpuss Aunt Elizabeth (later, Scottish Aunt Isabel) who loses a draw to keep the orphaned girl. Ilse is Emily's best friend. Cousin Jimmy is mentally disabled (Aunt Elizabeth pushed him down a well as a youth). There isn't anything very nice about 1890s P.E.I. in this show. Good people die, bad people live, and Emily spends considerable time communing with the spirits of the departed, though the producers "nicened" the series a notch as it progressed. Filmed in P.E.I.

The critics cheer: "A sadistic pedagogue, a thieving servant, a snooty town gentry, a bunch of cruel classmates—there's something nearly Marxist in the show's depiction of those who represent the status quo." — Richard Corliss, *Time*

E.N.G.

CTV
Drama
First Broadcast: Friday, October 26, 1990, 9:00 p.m.
Final Year Broadcast: 1994
Running Time: 60 min.

Cast:

Anne Hildebrandt	Sara Botsford
Jake Antonelli	Mark Humphrey
Mike Fennell	Art Hindle
Eric "Mac" MacFarlane	Jonathan Welsh
J.C. Callahan	Neil Dainard
Dan Watson	Karl Pruner
Terri Morgan	Cynthia Belliveau
Seth Miller	James H. Millington
Bobbi Katz	Mary Beth Rubens
Kyle Copeland	George R. Robertson
Jane Oliver	Sherry Miller
Marge Atherton	Theresa Tova
Clarke Roberts	Clark Johnson
Janice Roberts	Rachael Crawford
John Elman	Eugene Clark
Barbara Cole	Barbara Eve Harris
Adam Hirsch	Victor Garber
Tessa Vargas	Andrea Roth
Kelly Longstreet	Lisa La Croix
Bruce Foreman	David Cubitt

E.N.G. stands for electronic news gathering, the topic of this dramatic series set in the television newsroom of fictional Channel 10. Anne Hildebrandt was an executive producer and acting news director of the news until by-the-book director Mike Fennell breezed into town. Hildebrandt was having an affair with cameraman Antonelli, though audiences were waiting for Mike and Anne to hit it off. Unfortunate assignment editor Callahan was first depicted as a recovering alcoholic and then confined to a wheelchair before being killed off in 1993. Morgan was a calculating reporter, and Copeland was the wishy-washy station manager. MacFarlane was a producer who came out of the closet.

Mike and Anne resigned in the final episode after saving the station from switching to a lifestyle format. Mike was offered a position in Tokyo and Anne intended to join him—until she was offered a job at a rival station. That storyline, sans Mike, was the springboard for a never-produced series, tentatively titled *The Cutting Edge*.

Very popular in Britain, though the series didn't fare so well in the U.S., where the Lifetime network picked it up for only a few months.

Excuse My French

CTV
Situation Comedy
First Broadcast: Thursday, September 12, 1974, 7:30 p.m.
Final Year Broadcast: 1976
Running Time: 30 min.

Cast:

Peter Hutchins	Stuart Gillard
Marie-Louise	Lisa Charbonneau
Charles Philip Hutchins	Earl Pennington
Gaston Sauvé	Paul Berval
Mrs. Sauvé	Pierrette Beaudoin
Sauver's daughter	Isabelle Lajeunesse
Jean-Guy Sauvé	Daniel Gadouas

What happens when strait-laced anglo law student Peter marries sexy francophone waitress Marie-Louise? Their stereotypical families, each headed by its own homegrown Archie Bunker, restage the Battle of the Plains of Abraham on a weekly basis. The first episode set the tone for the series: Charles visits his secretly married son at school and finds a wig and red dress in the closet. That's bad: McGill has a reputation for "turning people gay." But wait, the wig belongs to a French woman! "That's good," says Charles, "a French mistress!" Mais non, a French wife! "That's bad," screams Dad as he storms out of the room. Jean-Guy was a raving separatist, played by a real-life separatist. Many scripts were written by

Americans, one of them a 19-year-old college student who churned out scripts on his summer vacation. A salve for hand-wringing, bleeding-heart anglos who thought this sitcom might help unite the nation. Alas, the program wasn't even broadcast in French.

The critics jeer: "The comic situations are trifling, the jokes stuck in like pears in aspic, the characters one-dimensional and not even likeable." — Blaik Kirby, *The Globe and Mail*

Evil Touch

Syndicated: 1973
Dramatic Anthology
Running Time: 30 min.

Host: Anthony Quayle

Almost forgotten supernatural series featuring Quayle, replete with swirling fog, introducing tales of comeuppance for featured evil-doers. The strangest episodes involved a man who tried to silence a parrot, the blabby witness to a murder he committed, and a greedy land developer transformed into a circus geek for trying to shut down a tatty big top. A U.S./Australia/Canada co-production.

Eye Bet

CTV
Game Show
First Broadcast: Monday, September 11, 1972, various
Final Year Broadcast: 1975
Running Time: 30 min.

Host: Jim Perry

Contestants watched sequences from old movies, then tried to recall minute details for prizes. The program ceased production when copyright owners became more sticky about the use of film clips.

Fables of La Fontaine

CBC
Musical Variety
First Broadcast: Thursday, January 2, 1958, 5:15 p.m.
Final Year Broadcast: 1958
Running Time: 15 min.

Fables featuring live animal "actors," based on stories by 17th-century poet and libertine La Fontaine. Producers struggled with a rabbit who wouldn't vacate a toy jeep, and an escaped monkey who swung through the studio's wire-studded rafters.

La Famille Plouffe

See: *The Plouffe Family*

Family Court

CTV
Drama
First Broadcast: Monday, September 20, 1971, various
Final Year Broadcast: 1972
Running Time: 30 min.

Cast:

Judge Carlton	Bill Kemp (1971–72)
Judge Alan Cameron	Alan Mills (1972)
Mrs. Scott	Mignon Elkins
Court Clerk	Walter Massey
Court Psychiatrist	David Phillips (1972)

A hybrid of soap opera and public service announcement. This weekday program dramatized court cases and how personal conflicts could be worked out in the family court system. Unlike most daytime dramas, the stories tended to wind down after two or three episodes. Mrs. Scott was the probation officer.

Famous Jury Trials

CTV
Soap Opera
First Broadcast: Monday, September 13, 1971, 2:30 p.m.
Final Year Broadcast: 1972
Running Time: 30 min.

Regular Performers: Donnelly Rhodes, Tim Henry, George Raymond, Joanna Noyers, Cec Linder

Ostensibly about famous *Canadian* jury trials, this sudsy monstrosity bucked its Canadian content promises and focused almost exclusively on U.S. trials. Brothers Rhodes and Henry played brother lawyers, appearing at every famous jury trial in recent history. Linder played a prosecuting attorney.

A ratings topper in some U.S. cities, though Rhodes once admitted: "I don't understand how it can be Number One in anything." Rhodes was a veteran of *The Young and the Restless*. Based on a U.S. series of the same name, which was seen on the defunct DuMont network in 1949.

The critics jeer: "…the acting is atrocious and the awesome aura of cheapness is so overwhelming that it is the only prepackaged TV series…in which an actor blows his lines twice in one segment, actually peeks at the cameras to check if they're still rolling and gives it another try…." — Patrick Scott, *The Toronto Star*

Fantastica

CTV
Children's
First Broadcast: Saturday, September 15, 1973, various
Final Year Broadcast: 1975
Running Time: 30 min.

Host: Tom Kneebone

A weird show featuring black-light images, animated clothing, friendly fish, puppet performers, and dance numbers. A novel presentation for its day.

Festival

CBC
Dramatic Anthology/Music
First Broadcast: Monday, October 10, 1960, 9:30 p.m.
Final Year Broadcast: 1969
Running Time: 90 min.

Notable productions of this filmed and taped arts showcase included: a Stratford production of *HMS Pinafore*, directed by Tyrone Guthrie; *The Pirates of Penzance*; Giuseppe Verdi's *Othello*; Henrik Ibsen's *The Wild Duck*; W.O. Mitchell's *The Devil's Instrument*; the National Ballet's performance of *Giselle*; a program featuring Glenn Gould and Yehudi Menuhin, and occasional episodes of *Cariboo Country*. Extremely popular, with as many as 900,000 homes tuning in. A production of *A Scent of Flowers* won an Emmy in 1969.

the fifth estate

CBC
Public Affairs
First Broadcast: Tuesday, September 16, 1975, 9:00 p.m.
Final Year Broadcast: —
Running Time: 60 min.

Estate of the art: One of the many incarnations of the *fifth estate* news team. From left to right, Ian Parker, Adrienne Clarkson, and Eric Malling.

Hosts: Stevie Cameron, Adrienne Clarkson, Gillian Findlay, Hana Gartner, Bob Johnstone, Linden MacIntyre, Sheila MacVicar, Victor Malarek, Eric Malling, Bob McKeown, Ian Parker, Francine Pelletier, Peter Reilly, Warner Troyer, Trish Wood

Canada's answer to *60 Minutes*—a quality investigative hour featuring a slate of journalists with impressive credentials. Its guiding statement: "If everyone believes it to be true, it probably isn't." Troyer resigned in 1976, and Reilly died in 1977. Three documentaries, including *Four Women* and *To Sell a War*, won Emmies. *Just Another Missing Kid*, about the disappearance of an Ontario teen in the U.S., won an Oscar as Best Feature Length Documentary in 1983. *The fifth estate* also *made* news; a 1985 report on rancid tuna led to the resignation of federal Fisheries Minister David Collenette. Program segments have been picked up by news magazines around the world. The term "fifth estate" refers to electronic media.

55 North Maple

CBC
Talk Show/Situation Comedy
First Broadcast: Monday, September 7, 1970, 1:30 p.m.
Final Year Broadcast: 1971
Running Time: 30 min.

Hosts: Max Ferguson, Joan Drewery

This novel failure was Canada's first sitcom/talk show. Ferguson played a writer who lived with his sister Joan and a neverseen brother-in-law. They entertained talkshow guests like visitors to the fictional address (Claire Mowat dropped in to show slides from her trip to Siberia, and Max showed a pal how to make carrot whiskey). The series was created entirely on the basis of audience market research.

The co-hosts were dropped for the final four installments, to be replaced by Kate Reid(?!)

Fighting Words

CBC
Game Show
First Broadcast: Wednesday, November 4, 1953, 8:30 p.m.
Final Year Broadcast: 1962
Running Time: 30 min.

Host: Nathan Cohen

"A program in which four people first try to identify the author of a controversial quotation and then engage in a spontaneous and unrehearsed give and take of opinion about the merits of that quotation."

— Opening narration, *Fighting Words*

Legend has it that a TV exec handed someone the program's title, then asked them to build a program around it. Following a bizarre animated opening sequence featuring battling stick men, this highbrow game show got down to business as guests and panelists (including Morley Callaghan, Robert Fulford, and Irving Layton) guessed the quotation's author (with the help of clues and visual hints by illustrator Gert Pollmer). Ensuing discussions resulted in explosions of intellectual mayhem, occasionally moderated by drama critic Cohen. Viewers, of course, were slavering for uncontrolled outbursts rather than rational discourse. Bounced around the dial, the show was cancelled in 1955, but revived after a write-in campaign. Viewers sent in quotations as quiz fodder, hoping for book and record prizes (one LP if the panel guessed correctly; two if they didn't). Later programs in the series were criticized for their lack of chaos.

Revived twice for CHCH-TV, by Cohen, briefly, in 1970, and by Peter Gzowski, disastrously, in 1982.

The critics cheer: "…one of the most interesting [shows] on TV. Certainly the best by far in Canada…. Its discussions made interested viewers think, and that in itself is a rare achievement…." — Ron Poulton, *Toronto Telegram*

The critics jeer: "…don't expect too much of it unless you happen to be an egg-head who lives in an ivory tower…." — Gordon Sinclair, *The Toronto Star*

The First Wave

Syndicated: 1998
Science Fiction
Running Time: 60 min.

Cast:
Cade Foster . . . . Sebastian Spence
Crazy Eddie Nambulous . . . . Rob LaBelle
Joshua . . . . Roger Cross
Colonel Grace . . . . Dana Brooks
Jordan Radcliffe . . . . Traci Lords
Hannah Foster . . . . Stacy Grant

CBC

"In 1564 Nostradamus predicted the destruction of Earth in three terrifying waves. The first wave is here."

— Opening narration, *The First Wave*

As Test Subject 117, Cade Foster is framed for the murder of his wife Hannah by a nasty group of alien invaders known as the Gua. It's all been predicted by Nostradamus, you see, so much of the series is based on quatrains from the prophet's original predictions.

The aliens are everywhere in human form, but dissolve in a spectacular puddle of green fluorescent slime when killed. Assisting Foster in exposing the alien conspiracy is nutty techno-whiz/conspiracist Crazy Eddie, who publishes an on-line journal called *The Paranoid Times*. Joshua is an elite alien troubleshooter who has some niggling doubts about the Gua invasion. Colonel Grace is a military type who wants to capture Foster, and his journals, ostensibly to defeat the aliens, though her connections with a strange underground organization may indicate that she's an undercover alien. Jordan is the leader of elite military force Raven Nation, dedicated to destroying the invaders, particularly an "Antichrist" alien leader named Mabus, predicted by Nostradamus.

Unlike most foreign-funded productions filmed in Canada, lead actor Spence is Canadian. A neat series with some outstanding music. Seen on Canada's Space Channel. Francis Ford Coppola produces.

Flappers

CBC
Situation Comedy
First Broadcast: Friday, September 21, 1979, 7:30 p.m.
Final Year Broadcast: 1981
Running Time: 30 min.

Roaring at the Twenties: Susan Roman played Prohibition's perpetual comic victim on CBC's *Flappers.*

Cast:

May Lamb	Susan Roman
Yvonne Marie	Andrée Cousineau
Francine	Denise Proulx
Andy	Michael Donaghue
Oscar	Victor Desy
Uncle Rummy	Edward Atienza (1979–80)
Robert	Robert Lalonde
Bunny	Gail Dahms

Unfunny sitcom set in the Roaring Twenties and made worse by a particularly annoying laugh track. May owns a Montreal nightclub, Le Club, staffed by "zany" employees: bootlegging chef Oscar; Francophobes Uncle Rummy and maitre d' Robert; wisecracking bandleader Andy; cigarette girl Yvonne Marie; cook Francine; and dancer Bunny. Guests included Dawn Greenhalgh, Derek McGrath, and Jonathan Welsh.

Flashback

CBC
Game Show
First Broadcast: Sunday, September 23, 1962, 7:30 p.m.
Final Year Broadcast: 1968
Running Time: 30 min.

Hosts: Paul Soles (1962–63), Bill Walker (1963–66), Jimmy Tapp (1966–68)
Panelists: Allan Manings (1962–66), Alan Millar (1962–64), Maggie Morris (1962–68), Larry Solway (1966–68), Elwy Yost (1964–68)

A *Front Page Challenge* clone: four panelists identified a person, place, event, or thing, then interviewed a related mystery guest. Viewers got $25 for submitting quiz items; $50 if the panel was stumped. A bizarre, short-lived choice for panelist was CBC research assistant Donnalu Wigmore. Publicity material for Solway was so spare, it was padded with descriptions of his home (central air, panelled rec room). Ford spokesman Walker left after Chrysler became the sponsor. When three guests—Adolphe Menjou, Zasu Pitts, and Glen Gray—died shortly after appearing on the program, *Flashback* became known as a curse to guests, as well as critics.

The critics jeer: "…the resemblance to [*Front Page Challenge*]…is nothing short of shocking…. I'm afraid all I can be is shocked and indignant." — Bob Blackburn, *Toronto Telegram.*

Fleurs d'amour

CBC
Music
First Broadcast: Sunday, June 16, 1968, 9:37 a.m.
Final Year Broadcast: 1968
Running Time: 30 min.

Hosts: Nanette Roman, Tony Roman

A self-billed "psychedelic show," featuring musical guests.

Floor Show

CBC
Musical Variety
First Broadcast: Monday, June 22, 1953, 9:00 p.m.
Final Year Broadcast: 1953
Running Time: 30 min.

Host: Monty Hall
Orchestra Leaders: Bobby Gimby, Art Hallman, Mart Kenney

A summer variety program set in a nightclub. *Let's Make a Deal*-er Hall's first TV series. Alan Lund was a featured dancer. Hall also co-hosted *Matinee Party,* an afternoon show (1953–54), from Toronto's Eaton's Auditorium.

Fly by Night

Syndicated: 1991
Drama
Running Time: 60 min.

Cast:

Sally "Slick" Monroe	Shannon Tweed
Mack Shepperd	David James Elliott
Jean-Phillipe Pasteur	François Guteray
Berry	Ian Tracey

Playboy centrefold Shannon Tweed burst onto the Canadian television scene as the owner of cash-strapped Slick Air, a one-plane airline flying out of Vancouver. Another program created primarily for CBS, though seen briefly on CTV, with pilot Mack commuting from Seattle to give U.S. viewers someone to identify with. The character of co-pilot Jean-Phillipe was added to please French investors. Clients who chartered the company's 727 jet usually entangled the staff in adventures on the wrong side of the law. Some episodes were filmed in France.

Folio

CBC
Dramatic Anthology
First Broadcast: Sunday, September 25, 1954, 10:00 p.m.
Final Year Broadcast: 1959
Running Time: 60 min. and 90 min.

Host: Clyde Gilmour (1958–59)

A showcase for dramas, featuring Canadian performers and/or writers, including: *Macbeth,* starring Barry Morse; W.O. Mitchell's *The Black Bonspiel; Take to the Woods,* a musical comedy by Eric Nicol, featuring Robert Goulet; Stratford Festival's production of *Oedipus Rex; The Nutcracker,* performed by the National Ballet; and the musical adaptation of Lucy Maud Montgomery's *Anne of Green Gables,* by Don Harron and Norman Campbell. Frequently decried by audiences as too highbrow, the program earned no fans for pre-empting an NHL hockey playoff game. Replaced by *Ford Startime* for one season, then reworked as the more popular *Festival.* Also known as *CBC Folio.*

Foolish Heart

CBC
Drama
First Broadcast: Monday, September 6, 1999, 9:00 p.m.
Final Year Broadcast: 1999
Running Time: 60 min.

Cast:
Peter/George Findlay . . . . Ken Finkleman
Barbara/Kate . . . . Sarah Strange
Jean-Pierre . . . . Patrick Olafson-Henault
Louisa . . . . Claire Sims

This mini-series examined broken hearts, while actors played dual roles in show-within-a-show ambiguity. One episode involved a Kafka-esque trial over the indiscretions of two married people; another took on the tone of a 1940s romantic comedy. Finkleman also revealed his own true love here: his *Newsroom* character, George Findlay, parachuted into the proceedings as a director who awards himself the role of Peter.

Ford Startime

CBC
Dramatic Anthology/Music
First Broadcast: Tuesday, October 6, 1959, 9:30 p.m.
Final Year Broadcast: 1960
Running Time: 90 min.

Ford Motor Company sponsored a U.S. program under this title on NBC, while Ford of Canada sponsored the Canadian counterpart. Presentations included Arthur Miller's *The Crucible,* with Leslie Nielsen; Terence Rattigan's *The Browning Version;* Sir Arthur Sullivan's *Pineapple Ball,* performed by the National Ballet; and James Thurber's *The Thirteen Clocks,* starring Robert Goulet and Kate Reid. Some presentations were imports from the U.S. series. Also known as *Startime.*

Ford TV Theatre

See: *CBC Television Theatre*

Foreign Affairs

Global
Soap Opera
First Broadcast: Tuesday, September 15, 1992, 2:00 p.m.
Final Year Broadcast: 1992
Running Time: 30 min.

Cast:
Gwen Copeland . . . . Anne Curry
Jan Van Velsen . . . . Rene Frank
Audrey Blackburn. . . . . Deborah Wakeman
Miranda de Mers . . . . Michele Duquet
? . . . . Stephen Young

Big TV bomb—international style. Canada, Argentina, and the Netherlands teamed up to crush the soap opera world with this series set in Buenos Aires. Copeland was a Canadian ambassador; Van Velsen was her

Forest flyer: A promotional, fold-it-yourself *Forest Rangers* desk calendar for the year 1965.

Fire extinguishers: From left to right, Ralph Endersby, Peter Tully, Susan Conway, and Rex Hagon battle fires, felons, and ill-mannered campers in *The Forest Rangers.*

ex-lover; Blackburn was a nasty U.S. trade official; Young's character managed a night-club where international diplomats mingled.

The critics jeer: "…an enigma. It looks and feels dumb and clumsy. It's hard to tell…whether this is a poor attempt at surreal humor or a serious effort to push the soap envelope."— Greg Quill, *The Toronto Star*

The Forest Rangers

CBC
Children's
First Broadcast: Saturday, December 7, 1963, 5:00 p.m.
Final Year Broadcast: 1966
Running Time: 30 min.

Cast:

Peter Keeley	Rex Hagon (1963–1965)
Mike Forbes	Peter Tully (1963–66)
Chub Stanley	Ralph Endersby (1963–66)
Zeke	Paul Tully (1963–64), Ron Cohoon (1964–65)
Gaby LaRoche	Syme Jago (1963–64)
Ted	George Allen
Kathy	Susan Conway (1964–66)
Ranger George Keeley	Graydon Gould
Joe Two Rivers	Michael Zenon
Sergeant Brian Scott	Gordon Pinsent (1963–65)
Sergeant Stewart	Larry Reynolds
Aggie Apple	Barbara Hamilton
Steve	Don Mason
Denise	Barbara Pierce
Uncle Raoul LaRoche	Rolland Bedard
Mr. McGregor	Joe Austin

Relentlessly cheerful theme music introduced members of the Junior Rangers Club, three boys and a girl, who lived in a ramshackle fort near Indian River, Ontario, apparently without parental supervision. The kids assisted the real Forest Rangers and RCMP under the guidance of de facto leader Peter Keeley (the guy with the ham radio). Chub was a troubled city boy known, according to promotional material, for his "…ravenous appetite and 'kookie' attitude." Kathy was "…official secretary and 'big sister.' Although just tolerated by the boys, she can handle a canoe, portages, snow shoes, fish worms and horses just as well as the boys." Zeke was resident nerd/genius, a Latin-spouting bird-watcher. Peter's older brother, Ranger Keeley, made feeble efforts to discourage Junior Ranger assistance. Ted was Ranger Keeley's nephew. Sergeant Scott was an RCMP officer in full regalia; Joe Two Rivers was a smooth-talkin' Métis fur trapper who occasionally helped the kids; and crazed, alcoholic prospector McGregor led the kids into danger. Ex-Plouffe, Uncle Raoul, supplied French-Canadian witticisms and performed jolly antics with a comical moose.

Animal pals included Chub's horse Charlie, a great dane, Topper, Spike the Husky, and a bear named Carol.

The Rangers captured international spies, humbled juvenile delinquents, confounded beaver poachers, fought fires, and sniffed out a Wendigo, while suffering painful lessons in TV-land morality ("We can't keep the reward money—it wouldn't be right.") Only occasionally did the show delve into the Rangers' personal lives; one episode, for example, revealed that Chub's parents were divorced. No fan of dramatic licence, the Ontario Department of Lands and Forests lambasted the series, since Ontario's real Junior Ranger program discouraged its members from firefighting.

The series started as *Razzle Dazzle With the Forest Rangers,* with host Alan Hamel, and was serialized in six-minute chunks on *Razzle Dazzle.* Filmed north of Toronto near Kleinburg. One of Canada's most widely syndicated programs, it was seen in more than 40 countries, including France, West Germany, Australia, and Norway (try pronouncing *Skogwokterklubben*).

The critics cheer: "…a rainbow-hued cake with adventure and conservation lessons as its main ingredient." — Gordon Froggatt, *The Globe and Mail*

Forever Knight

Syndicated: 1992
Horror/Police
Running Time: 60 min.

Cast:

Detective Nicholas Knight	Geraint Wyn Davies
Detective Don Schanke	John Kapelos
Natalie Lambert	Catherine Disher
Captain Joseph Stonetree	Gary Farmer (1992–93)
Lucien Lacroix	Nigel Bennett
Janette Ducharme	Deborah Duchene
Captain Amanda Cohen	Natsuko Ohama (1993–94)
Detective Tracy Vetter	Lisa Ryder (1994–95)
Captain Reese	Blu Mankuma (1994–95)
Javier Vachon	Ben Bass (1994–95)

A rarity: a filmed-in-Canada series that didn't pretend it was set somewhere else. Each episode of this vampire drama featured prominent scenes of the Toronto skyline—even in the opening credits.

Nicholas de Brabant visits Paris in the year 1228. On a drunken binge, he's introduced to the ranks of the undead by Janette who introduces Nick to his new master, Lacroix, a powerful vampire. Nick took victims, but also "did good" on occasion. Flashbacks trace his history through eight centuries: he meets Joan of Arc, travels to the American Colonies, encounters Jack the Ripper, faces a McCarthy hearing, and works as a medic during the Vietnam War. Along the way he's dogged by Lacroix and sometime-girlfriend, Janette.

The 1990s sees Nick as a vampire police officer, working the night shift in a Toronto homicide department; he's determined to pay for his past crimes.

He has exceptional strength and hearing, the powers of flight (but not as a bat), and infrared vision, but prefers bottles of cow's blood to human vintages. He holes up during the day, sometimes in the trunk of his 1962 Cadillac (Ontario plates, 35H MV6). Natalie, a pathologist, works to cure him.

In the second season, Nick and souvlaki-eating Detective Schanke are transferred from Captain Stonetree's 27th Precinct (yes, we know Toronto has no precincts) to Captain Cohen's 96th Precinct. Cohen and Schanke die in a plane crash at the end of the second season. Captain Reese heads the 96th Precinct in season three, and Nick takes a new partner, Tracy Vetter, who knows nothing about Nick's secret, but has a thing for another vampire, Javier, who protects her.

Janette operates a Toronto nightclub known as The Raven. Lacroix, a late-night radio DJ on station CERK, saves his "son" from precarious situations, but torments him with criminal behaviour and taunts him to sample human blood. In season three, Lacroix buys the nightclub and broadcasts his program from there.

The series, co-produced with Germany, was based on a pilot film, *Nick Night,* set in the U.S. and starring singer Rick Springfield as the vampire detective. The show was first seen in 1992 in CBS's late-night slot, and cancelled after the second year. Fan support kept the program alive in first-run syndication.

Series spinoffs include paperback novels, a sound track album, and plenty of fan-written fiction.

For The Record

CBC
Docudrama
First Broadcast: Sunday, January 16, 1977, 9:00 p.m.
Final Year Broadcast: 1986
Running Time: 60 min. and 90 min.

This successor to *Performance* attempted to combine journalism with drama by plucking inspiration for its stories from newspaper headlines. Notable productions included: *Someday Soon* by Rudy Wiebe and Barry Pearson; *An Honourable Member* by Roy MacGregor, starring Fiona Reid; *Seer Was Here* by Don Bailey and Claude Jutra; *The Winnings of Frankie Walls* by Rob Forsyth, starring Al Waxman; and *Snowbirds* by Margaret Atwood. *The Tar Sands,* by Peter Pearson, Peter Rowe, and Ralph Thomas, about negotiations over the Athabasca tar sands, led to a successful lawsuit by Alberta premier Peter Lougheed over his portrayal (and comments he allegedly made) by Kenneth Welsh. Claude Jutra directed several segments.

4 on The Floor

CBC
Comedy
First Broadcast: Thursday, January 16, 1986, 7:30 p.m.
Final Year Broadcast: 1986
Running Time: 30 min.

The Frantics: Paul Chato, Rick Green, Dan Redican, Peter Wildman

For some reason, this program featuring comic troupe The Frantics was named *4 on the Floor* (a lame publicity release suggests the "antics" of the group had left the producer lying on the floor).

After many years on CBC radio, the gang finally introduced television audiences to such stalwarts as crime-fighting master of disguise Mr. Canoehead (looks like he sounds), Mr. Interesting, Quenelle and Mary, and The Evil Ultramind.

The show's opening credits feature The Frantics driving around in an erstwhile Monkeemobile—a pink 1957 Chrysler Saratoga with the top chopped off. Reruns still play on Canadian television, while cuts from The Frantics' 1984 album, *A Boot to the Head,* continue to receive airplay on North American radio, particularly the U.S. program *Dr. Demento.*

Export versions of the program seen on PBS in the U.S. were known, more sensibly, as *The Frantics.*

Fraggle Rock

CBC
Children's
First Broadcast: Sunday, January 13, 1983, 5:30 p.m.
Final Year Broadcast: 1987
Running Time: 30 min.

CBC

Cast:
Doc. . . . . Gerard Parkes
Voices:
Gobo . . . . Jerry Nelson
Boober . . . . Dave Goelz
Red . . . . Karen Prell
Wembley . . . . Steve Whitmore
Mokey. . . . . Kathryn Mullen
Junior Gorg. . . . . Richard Hunt

Muppeteer Jim Henson dabbled in Canadian content with this musical series, introducing viewers to three new Muppet species: Fraggles, Doozers (miniature industrialists), and Gorgs (a dopey ruling class of giants). In the Fraggle camp were: Gobo, the head Fraggle, who ventured through a tunnel to the workshop of Doc, eccentric inventor and the series' only human character; Red, Gobo's klutzy female friend; Boober, a pessimistic fear-monger who lived to do laundry; Wembley, a smaller Fraggle who idolized Gobo and imitated a siren for the Fraggle Rock Fire Department; and Mokey, a female Fraggle, the group's philosopher and artist. Junior Gorg (15 times taller than the average Fraggle) was an intellectual piker, heir apparent to the Throne of the Universe, now held by Mom and Pop. Other characters included Doc's dog, Sprocket, Marjory the Trash Heap, and Traveling Uncle Mat. The series spawned books, toys, videos, and calendars and won an International Emmy award in 1983, though some critics wondered why the hell Henson was allowed to use taxpayer-subsidized CBC to produce this Muppetfest.

The Frankie Howerd Show

CBC
Situation Comedy
First Broadcast: Thursday, February 26, 1976, 9:00 p.m.
Final Year Broadcast: 1976
Running Time: 30 min.

Cast:
Frankie . . . . Frankie Howerd
Mrs. Otterby . . . . Ruth Springford
Mrs. Otterby's Son . . . . Gary Files
Wally Wheeler . . . . Jack Duffy
Denise. . . . . Peggy Mahon

A merciful last-minute decision prevented this debacle from airing as *Oooh, Canada.* In scripts penned with the blunt end of a toilet brush, vulgar comedian Howerd played a lazy British immigrant injecting chaos into cherished Canadian institutions. Dubbed King Leer, Howerd lived in Mrs. Otterby's crumbling rooming house, with reclusive Wally Wheeler and model/dancer Denise, who provided fodder for mammary gags. An embarrassed network killed the program, which drew in more viewers than the popular *King of Kensington*. Ken Finkleman was a writer.

The critics jeer: "…inexcusable…forcing Frankie Howerd on us comes close to being a national insult…[an] oafish, slack-mouthed fugitive from those atrocious *Carry On* movies." — Dennis Braithwaite, *The Toronto Star*

The Frantics

See: *4 on The Floor*

Friday Island

CBC
Children's
First Broadcast: Friday, October 19, 1962, 5:30 p.m.
Final Year Broadcast: 1963
Running Time: 30 min.

Cast:

Mum Granger	Lillian Carlson
Dad Granger	Walter Marsh
Stephen Granger	Mark de Courcey
"Tadpole" Granger	Kevin Burchett
Grandpa Granger	James Onley
Aunt Sophie	Rae Brown
Aunt Vi	Mildred Franklin
Annabelle	Barbara Tremain
Archie	Robert Clothier

An Ottawa family, the Grangers, open a lodge on fictional Friday Island, off the B.C. coast. Stephen and Tadpole were the kids. Feuding eccentrics Annabelle the postmistress and Archie the grocer shared a store split down the middle by a fence.

Friday Night with Ralph Benmergui

CBC
Variety/Talk Show
First Broadcast: Friday, October 30, 1992, 9:00 p.m.
Final Year Broadcast: 1993
Running Time: 60 min.

Host: Ralph Benmergui
Music: The Look People

Perhaps Canadian television's most ill-considered hour. Take nobody's favourite television personality, darling of CBC execs, and use him to replace popular Tommy Hunter. A major embarrassment for the network, the program failed to capture even half of Hunter's audience. Undaunted, the CBC rescheduled the program to 11 p.m.; *Friday Night*'s viewers deserted in even greater numbers. A new studio, new format, new producer (Yuk Yuks' Mark Breslin), a staff of ten writers, and bloated budgets failed to turn the tide as critics delivered merciless hammer-blows to poor Benmergui, who was, after all, only playing himself.

The network's explanation of why it pulled the plug: Canadians are actually incapable of creating successful talk shows. An issue of *TV Guide*, featuring a defiant Benmergui on its cover, appeared on newsstands days after his cancellation.

Friday the 13th

Syndicated: 1987
Horror
Running Time: 60 min.

Cast:

Micki Foster	(Louise) Robey
Ryan Dallion	John D. LeMay (1987–89)
Jack Marshack	Chris Wiggins
Johnny Ventura	Steven Monarque (1989–90)
Lewis Vendredi	R.G. Armstrong
Lloyd	Barclay Hope

"Lewis Vendredi made a deal with the devil, to sell cursed antiques. But he broke the pact, and it cost him his soul. His niece Micki, and her cousin Ryan, have inherited the store, and with it, the curse."
— Opening narration, *Friday the 13th*

Micki and Ryan teamed up with Jack Marshak, a retired magician/occult expert. Re-opening the store as Curious Goods (address: 666 Druid Avenue), the team sets out on a gory antique hunt to save unfortunates whose lives are threatened by demonic artifacts. Nasty Uncle Lewis made guest appearances, while Micki's fiancée Lloyd soon dropped out of the picture. The third season kicked off with a spooky, handsomely filmed episode, shot around Quebec City, as the intrepid trio confronted Asteroth, a demon who was busy cleaning house in preparation for Lucifer's arrival. The episode marked the departure of Ryan, who transformed into his 10-year-old self and went home with Mother. Johnny Ventura appeared in subsequent episodes. Best episode title? "My Wife as a Dog."

What does the program have to do with Paramount's *Friday the 13th* films? Absolutely nothing, though actor LeMay starred in 1994's *Jason Goes to Hell: The Final Friday*. Even the title's "Friday" refers to the Vendredi character. Produced in Canada, but shown primarily on the U.S. FOX network, the program was very popular in Mexico and Japan. Eventually seen in Canada on Global.

Chris Wiggins on *Friday the 13th*:

"It was a very strange experience. People assume you must be into all the weird things going on in the series—para-psychology and demonology. I was end-lessly asked: 'Have you always been very interested in the occult?'

"I complained about the violence in some of the episodes—one was gory to the point of vomiting. Then they pulled out a response form; the three shows I most complained about rated highest on the audience enjoyment index.

"We were going to do a fourth season, but a minister in the U.S. Midwest launched a huge complaint. A hundred and fifty thousand people signed a pledge against this 'satanic' program. He went straight to the sponsors, and FOX executives, brave corporate souls that they are, folded the show in two days."

A very friendly giant: Bob Homme (centre) played the simply named Friendly Giant, flanked by puppet pals Jerome (left) and Rusty (right).

The Friendly Giant

CBC
Children's
First Broadcast: Tuesday, September 30, 1958, 4:30 p.m.
Final Year Broadcast: 1984
Running Time: 15 min.

Cast:
The Friendly Giant . . . . Bob Homme
Voice/Puppeteer:
Rusty the Rooster, Jerome the Giraffe . . . . . Rod Coneybeare
Rusty's Harp Performances: . . . . John Duncan
Theme Music: "Early One Morning"

"Once upon a time, not long ago, not far away," began this gentle program set in a medieval castle. Next, a seasonal descrip-tion of activities in the surrounding coun-tryside, and then the familiar show-opening ritual of setting out furniture for guests as a large hand offered "a little chair for one of you and a bigger chair for two to curl up in—and for someone who likes to rock, a rocking chair in the middle." Finally: "Look up: look way-y-y-y up," as the camera raised its sights to the full height of the Friendly Giant himself.

How tall was Friendly? A lot taller than falsetto-voiced Rusty the Rooster, a little, hatchet-faced bantam puppet who lived in a polka-dotted book bag, hung on the castle wall. And he was even taller than Jerome, a purple-spotted giraffe with an easy-going manner and the mellow tones of a 1920s dance band vocalist.

Segments included book readings, with selections from Rusty's book bag, or musical performances featuring Friendly on recorder, pennywhistle, and clarinet, Rusty on guitar, harp, and accordion, and Jerome providing harmonica accompaniment, vocals, and dance numbers. Concert days, set in the castle's conservatory, featured an expanded ensemble including cats Angie (on harp) and Fiddle (on bass fiddle), and raccoons Patty and Polly on woodwinds.

Friendly debuted in Madison, Wisconsin, in May 1954 at 6:45 p.m., the bedtime of its intended audience. That explains why the closing credits for a CBC morning show fea-tured Friendly's castle at night, the draw-bridge rising and a cow jumping over a full moon (occasionally, a wooden shoe carried Winkin', Blinkin', and Nod across the sky). In Canada, Friendly made a guest appearance on *Junior Magazine* in 1958, before earning a daytime slot. He also hosted *Children's Cinema*, a series of films airing between 1969 and 1975, and made guest appearances on Christmas editions of the *Juliette* show.

Seen on U.S. educational television, the Canadian giant became an unlikely icon of New York City's homosexual subculture, where the program, screened in gay bars in the early '70s, was greeted with wild applause.

In typically courageous fashion, CBC hacks cancelled the still-popular Giant after more than 25 years of service, with nary a public handshake, giant gold watch, or gargantuan set of golf clubs to mark his impeccable service record. But, as loyal viewers know, Friendly, Rusty, and Jerome continue their quiet conversations, book readings, and weekly concerts somewhere—just out of television camera range. And though his castle may be difficult to locate, travellers on isolated back roads swear they've heard the gentle lilt of an oversized recorder and pint-sized harp wafting through lonely valleys and echoing back from the mountains.

The critics cheer: "In a medium dominated by hard-driving men, he is notably easygoing and gentle...his show is popular because it is unchanging and tranquil." — Leslie Millin, *The Globe and Mail*

Bob Homme on *The Friendly Giant*

"When we moved the program to Canada, I carried everything across the border in my station wagon, including the props. Customs held us up to check the castle's plastic vines—they thought it was an exotic plant, until I broke off a leaf for them.

"The program was paced slowly to help build children's attention spans. I was just doing on the show what I did with my own youngsters—talking to them as adults. Our manner was our message. The characters were considerate, they appreciated each other."

Rod Coneybeare on *The Friendly Giant*

"The program started out with another puppeteer. This man was not tall. He didn't have a long enough arm to make Jerome appear as a giraffe. Jerome would come up to the window, slump down, and look more like a horse or a cow.

"We used two puppeteers, until I took over for Rusty as well. At that point Bob and I realized we could ad lib the program and dispensed with scripts, which gave the show a different ambience."

Frigidaire Entertains

CBC
Musical Variety
First Broadcast: Friday, October 1, 1954, 8:30 p.m.
Final Year Broadcast: 1955
Running Time: 30 min.

Hosts: Frosia Gregory, Byng Whittaker
Performers: Bert, Joe, and Johnny Niosi
Orchestra Leader: Jimmy Namaro

A musical program staged like a masquerade ball; guests were unmasked as they were introduced.

Front Page Challenge

CBC
Game Show
First Broadcast: Monday, June 24, 1957, 9:30 p.m.
Final Year Broadcast: 1995
Running Time: 30 min.

Hosts:
Win Barron (1957), Alex Barris (1957), Fred Davis (1957–95)
Announcer .... Bernard Cowan
Regular Panelists: Pierre Berton (1957–95), Gordon Sinclair (1957–84), Toby Robins (1957–61), Betty Kennedy (1961–95), Allan Fotheringham (1984–95), Jack Webster (?–95)
Guest panelists included: Dick Beddoes, Jacques Bergerac, Roy Bonisteel, David Brinkley, Ed Broadbent, Bennett Cerf, Adrienne Clarkson, Rod Coneybeare, Walter Cronkite, Bruno Gerussi, Don Harron, Juliette, Judy LaMarsh, Lord Athol Layton, Johnny Lombardi, Hugh MacLennan, Howie Meeker, W.O. Mitchell, Barry Morse, Angelo Mosca, Gordon Pinsent, Jacques Plante, Morley Safer, Alex Trebek, Mike Wallace, Patrick Watson, Al Waxman, Johnny Wayne, Austin Willis, Elwy Yost, Moses Znaimer

Starting as a mere summer replacement, this game show has been both celebrated as the height of intellectual populism and damned as the worst of the genre—hoary, elitist, and slug-paced.

With a format lifted from *What's My Line*, the familiar premise involved four panelists who quizzed a sometimes concealed figure about his or her involvement with a news headline. The headline was revealed either by the panel's laser-like questioning, or by the announcer after a suitable period of misfires. An interview followed.

Early reviews were savage. *The Toronto Star* referred to the program as a "corpse" kept on the air for "autopsy purposes." The *Telegram* compared the show's pacing to "a tortoise in full flight."

While the program ran through a roster of hundreds of permanent and guest panelists, the most memorable were: author and bow-tied "intellectual" Pierre Berton; boorish, hircine media figure Gordon Sinclair, known for a line of insensitive questioning (How much money did guests earn? Did swimmer Elaine Tanner train while menstruating?); demure radio broadcaster Betty Kennedy; and affable actress Toby Robins who remained on the program while pregnant and raised the eyebrows of oversensitive viewers by wearing a blonde wig.

The host would tip the panel on whether the headline was national or international, then leave them to a glorified game of "twenty questions." Headlines could be current or historical, and identifying the guest wouldn't provide an automatic link to the headline. Boris Karloff, for example, represented the 1912 cyclone that struck Regina while he was there, and Jayne Mansfield stood for "Conservatives win U.K. election." Producers occasionally slipped in a trick guest, such as panelists Berton or Sinclair.

As the program dragged on for more than 30 years, the public divided itself into

three camps: a small, devoted group of fans, mostly seniors; weary viewers demanding a mercy-killing; and those who developed a grudging respect for the freakish longevity of the program, not unlike 100-year-old lobsters spared from the dinner table at seafood restaurants. The weary viewers won, as the program finally concluded its run in 1995.

The Daytime Challenge, an afternoon spinoff also hosted by Davis, debuted in 1982, concentrating on people and entertainment rather than headlines.

Some of *Front Page Challenge*'s more notable guest challengers included:

Harold Ballard	Punch Imlach
Menachem Begin	Irish Rovers
Mrs. L. Berton	Fergie Jenkins
(Pierre's mom)	Christine Jorgensen
Marilyn Bell	Juliette
Jean Beliveau	Alvin Karpis
Tony Bennett	Martin Luther King
Big Bird	Timothy Leary
Bonhomme Carnival	Gypsy Rose Lee
Dr. Joyce Brothers	Jack Lemmon
Helen Gurley Brown	René Lévesque
Morley Callaghan	Rich Little
Frank Capra	Mickey Mantle
Bennett Cerf	Groucho Marx
Uncle Chichimus	Marshall McLuhan
George Chuvalo	Butterfly McQueen
Joe Clark	Ethel Merman
Alex Colville	Charles Mingus
Tom Connors	Farley Mowat
(Stompin')	Malcolm Muggeridge
Jacques Cousteau	Bridey Murphy
Walter Cronkite	Ralph Nader
Ann B. Davis	Jesse Owens
Yvonne DeCarlo	Lester Pearson
Jack Dempsey	Mary Pickford
John Diefenbaker	Jacques Plante
Roger Doucet	Francis Gary Powers
Duke Ellington	Otto Preminger
Max Ferguson	Vincent Price
Ella Fitzgerald	Nelson Riddle
Errol Flynn	Cliff Robertson
Stan Freberg	Eleanor Roosevelt
David Frost	Louis St. Laurent
Zsa Zsa Gabor	Eddie Shack
Indira Gandhi	Frank Shuster
Igor Gouzenko	Dr. Benjamin Spock
Nancy Greene	Ed Sullivan
Germaine Greer	Alvin Toffler
Arthur Hailey	Margaret Trudeau
Foster Hewitt	Pierre Trudeau
Thor Heyerdahl	Peter Ustinov
Sir Edmund Hillary	Baroness Von Trapp
Gordie Howe	Johnny Wayne
Bobby Hull	Malcolm X

Funny Farm

CTV
Musical Comedy
First Broadcast: Thursday, September 12, 1974, 7:00 p.m.
Final Year Broadcast: 1975
Running Time: 30 min.

Host: Blake Emmons
Music: Maple Street
Regular Performers: Valri Bromfield, John Evans, Ben Gordon, Monica Parker, Linda Renhoffer, Jank Zajfman

A country music program apparently designed to offend almost everyone—including country music fans. A bald-faced *Hee-Haw* rip-off offering less music and more comedy: country drunks, gay cowboys, village idiots, and Yiddish farmers. Cartoon one-liners added to the fun.

The critics jeer: "…frequently slips over the line from slapstick into bad taste." — Jack Miller, *The Toronto Star*

Fun Time

CBC
Children's
First Broadcast: Thursday, July 5, 1956, 5:30 p.m.
Final Year Broadcast: 1956
Running Time: 30 min.

Cast:
Captain Frank . . . . Frank Heron
Children . . . . Alan Jack, June Mack, Tom Auburn
Matey the parrot

Fun and games aboard the Fun Time Showboat, featuring guest acts, filmed segments, magician Auburn, and Elmer the Safety Elephant.

The Galloping Gourmet

CBC
Cooking
First Broadcast: Monday, December 30, 1968, 4:00 p.m.
Final Year Broadcast: 1972
Running Time: 30 min.

Host: Graham Kerr
Assistants: Patricia Burgess, Wilemina Meerakker

Originating on Australian television, the Galloping Gourmet found international fame in Canada. On the surface, it was a cooking show, but discriminating viewers realized Kerr was engaged in a bizarre sort of lovemaking—with his audience, his food, his cooking

utensils, and even himself. For this culinary Caligula, skinning an eel took on a subtle context that had censors champing at the bit.

Programs began with a gag—Kerr as a big game hunter peering from behind potted plants, for example—then a frantic sprint to the kitchen to wild applause and catchy theme music by Champ Champagne. Kerr introduced the dish and tacky travelogues of himself and wife Treena (the program's producer) partaking of foreign cuisine.

Recipes tended toward the rich, creamy, and decadent. Preparation was punctuated by copious applications of booze, which wound up, by thirds, in the dishes, on the floor, and inside Kerr; his secret code: a "short slurp" was a fluid ounce, and a "glug" was one-and-a-half.

Low humour included audio cues before and after commercials: screaming chimps, blaring klaxon horns, and flushing toilets.

In each program's climax, Kerr presented the finished dish on a dining room table, replete with candelabra, and selected an audience member to sup with him. With soft piano accompaniment, Kerr sampled the dish in close-up, as unctuous moans and stray food oozed from between pursed lips.

Kerr left the series after suffering back injuries. As a Christian convert, his later programs (*Take Kerr* and *Graham Kerr*) emphasized low-fat, healthy dishes. Unfortunately, a happier, healthier Kerr creating a "biteables box" of carrot and celery snacks was not the stuff of continued cult celebrity.

Widely syndicated in the U.S. and other countries, program spinoffs included a radio program and best-selling cookbooks.

The critics jeer: "Mr. Kerr's dubious prominence on TV is not so much to be found in his sauces as in his cultivation of a suffocating demeanor of haughty cuteness." — *New York Times*

"I have been unable to eat since I started to watch it…. He manages to make a stove resemble a bed and meatloaf a sexual adventure…. He burps and slurps and talks with his mouth full, all the while rolling his tongue and eyes around with equal suggestiveness." — Patrick Scott, *The Toronto Star*

General Motors Presents

CBC
Dramatic Anthology
First Broadcast: Tuesday, October 5, 1954, 10:00 p.m.
Final Year Broadcast: 1961
Running Time: 60 min.

Another early failure to export Canadian drama to a U.S. market. CBC execs patted each other on the back over initial news that ABC had signed on, under the banner *Encounter*, for 39 weeks of simulcasting at $35,000 a pop. The U.S. program was cancelled five weeks later. The broadcast featured a wide selection of plays by Canadian writers. Among the productions: *The Flower in the Rock* by Joseph Schull; *The Oddball* by Bernard Slade; *The Apprenticeship of Duddy Kravitz*, written and adapted by Mordecai Richler; *Shadow of a Pale Horse* by Bruce Stewart; as well as adaptations of Somerset Maugham's *The Land of Promise*, and Ibsen's *Hedda Gabler*. Notable actors included Barry Morse and Patrick Macnee. The series ended its run by repeating a British series, *Interplay*.

General Motors Theatre

See: *CBC Television Theatre*

Gene Roddenberry's Earth: Final Conflict

Syndicated: 1997
Science Fiction
Running Time: 60 min.

Cast:

William Boone	Kevin Kilner
Liam Kincaid	Robert Leeshock
Captain Lili Marquette	Lisa Howard
Agent Ronald Sandoval	Von Flores
Da'an	Leni Parker
Marcus "Augur" Deveraux	Richard Chevolleau
Jonathan Doors	David Hemblen
Dr. Belman	Majel Barrett Roddenberry
Zo'or	Anita La Selva
Kee'sha	Stavroula Logothettis
Claude Bertrand	Raymond Accolas
Randy/Ha'gel	Graeme Millington
Siobahn Beckett	Kari Matchett
Morovsky	John Evans
Renee Palmer	Jayne Heitmeyer
Joshua Doors	William DeVry
J Street	Melinda Deines

The bald, sexless Taelons have come to Earth as saviours, bringing new technology and medical treatments with them. Unfortunately, there's a catch: our Taelon friends have trouble breeding and would like to see humans used as soldiers in a galactic conflict. At the centre of the drama is the Earth Resistance movement, headed

Beware aliens bearing gifts: Da'an (Leni Parker, left) and Zo'or (Anita La Selva, right) have unpleasant plans for Earthlings in *Gene Roddenberry's Earth: Final Conflict.*

Alliance Atlantis

by industrialist Jonathan Doors and supported by a roster of undercover agents including Taelon shuttle captain Marquette and Dr. Belman. Chief conspirator is Boone, a security agent ostensibly working for the Taelons after it's revealed that his wife was killed by the aliens.

In a first season climax, Boone is injured in a battle with an alien life form, the Ha'gel, then taken off life support by the Taelons. His replacement with the Resistance is the offspring of the Ha'gel alien who conveniently hijacked some human DNA just before his death. Newly christened Liam Kincaid grows to maturity in hours and is discovered to be part of a race that has a bone to pick with the Taelons. After rescuing Da'an from a precarious situation, Liam is chosen as his personal protector.

A clever series with neat technology (particularly the insectoid alien shuttles), lots of complex political interplay between Resistance and Taelon factions, nasty infighting, treachery, and great theme music. Actress Roddenberry was the driving force behind the series, created from notes and outlines left by her husband.

Seen on Canada's Space Channel and irregularly on CTV stations.

George

CTV
Situation Comedy
First Broadcast: Thursday, September 21, 1972, 7:00 p.m.
Final Year Broadcast: 1973
Running Time: 30 min.

Cast:

Jim Hunter	Marshall Thompson
Frau Gerber	Erna Sellmer
Helga	Trudy Young
Freddie	Volker Stewart
Walter Clark	Fred Mullaney

Dreadful family comedy featuring George, a slobbering St. Bernard who wreaked havoc in the Swiss town of Grindelwald (a thinly disguised collection of British Columbia chalets) while fetching dates for his master, Hunter (Thompson had recently played an animal medico in the U.S. series *Daktari*). Freddie and his aunt (Young) lived in the chalet next door. Frau Gerber was Hunter's stereotypical frantic housekeeper, resigning twice per episode over some entirely predictable canine calamity. Based on a full-length 1970 film also starring creator/producer Thompson on behalf of Thompson International.

The critics jeer: "They are supposed to be German and Swiss...but they speak English with pure North American accents. Bottom-of-the-barrel children's shows are like that." — Blaik Kirby, *The Globe and Mail*

A Gift To Last

CBC
Drama
First Broadcast: Sunday, January 22, 1978, 7:00 p.m.
Final Year Broadcast: 1979
Running Time: 60 min.

Cast:

Sergeant Edgar Sturgess	Gordon Pinsent
Harrison Sturgess	Alan Scarfe
Clara Sturgess	Janet Amos
Clement Sturgess (young)	Mark Polley
Clement Sturgess (old)	Syd Brown
Jane Sturgess	Kate Parr
Lizzy Sturgess	Ruth Springford
James Sturgess	Gerard Parkes
John Trevelyan	John Evans
Sheila	Dixie Seatle
Willie Sutcliffe	R.H. Thomson
Nancy	Trudy Young

CBC

Turn-of-the-century drama: Gruff Edgar Sturgess (Gordon Pinsent, right) levels with young Clement (Mark Polley, left) in *A Gift To Last.*

Spawned by a 1976 Christmas special starring Melvyn Douglas as elderly Clement Sturgess looking back at life in turn-of-the-century Tamarack, Ontario; in particular at his uncle, iconoclastic Sergeant Edgar Sturgess of the Royal Canadian Regiment, owner of the local hotel, the Mafeking House.

The series begins with the death of Harrison Sturgess in 1899 and concentrates on family survivors: wife Clara, children Clement and Jane, mother Lizzy, and brothers James and Edgar.

Series highlights: Edgar fights in the Boer War, later marries the Sturgess maid Sheila (whose no-goodnik husband Willie conveniently dies), and joins the local militia; Edgar and Sheila's baby dies at birth; Clara marries John Trevelyan, owner of the general store, has a child, and contracts consumption; John establishes the J. Trevelyan Footwear Company; and James becomes the mayor of Tamarack and runs for Parliament. The series ended when writer Pinsent withdrew the gift of his presence, leaving viewers up in the air after a fire (occurring in 1905) destroyed the footwear factory, the town's major employer. Pinsent sang the show's closing theme song.

Followed by a stage play and a stage musical. Seen in the U.S., Belgium, Australia, Ireland, and South Africa.

The critics cheer: "...[Pinsent] has a true feeling for bringing out the nuances of the characters, providing them with a depth and scope seen too rarely on television." — Bruce Blackadar, *The Toronto Star*

GM Theatre

See: *CBC Television Theatre*

Going Great

CBC
Magazine
First Broadcast: Wednesday, October 13, 1982, 4:30 p.m.
Final Year Broadcast: 1984
Running Time: 30 min.

Host: Chris Makepeace
Contributors: Darcelle Chan, Keanu Reeves

Fresh from his successes in the films *Meatballs* and *My Bodyguard*, Makepeace hosted this program aimed at teens. Makepeace's laconic interviewing style ("Really? Great.") caught on with the show's intended audience. The show won the Children's Broadcast Institute Award in 1983 for Best Network Television Program. Interview subjects were often teen athletes and performers, including a young Celine Dion. Also shown on the U.S. Nickelodeon network. Yes, *that* Keanu Reeves.

Good Eating

See: *Hans in the Kitchen*

Goosebumps

YTV
Children's
First Broadcast: Tuesday, October 31, 1995, 7:30 p.m.
Final Year Broadcast: 1999
Running Time: 30 min.

A TV version of kid-lit phenomenon R.L. Stine's *Goosebumps* series. The episodes featured tweenagers caught in a scary dilemma that usually resolved itself in a twist ending. No blood, guts, gore, or violence. Episode titles include: "The Cuckoo Clock of Doom," "Go Eat Worms," Let's Get Invisible," and "How I Got My Shrunken Head."

Grand Old Country

CTV
Musical Variety
First Broadcast: Wednesday, September 8, 1975, 10:00 p.m.
Final Year Broadcast: 1981
Running Time: 60 min.

Host: Ronnie Prophet

This country music show made an effort to showcase Canadian guest musicians, including The Peaches, Zeke Sheppard, and Lucille Starr. The program's title was changed, simply, to *Ronnie Prophet* in 1980.

Graphic

CBC
News Magazine
First Broadcast: Friday, March 2, 1956, 9:00 p.m.
Final Year Broadcast: 1957
Running Time: 30 min.

Host: Joe McCulley
Announcer: Rex Loring

A news magazine format featuring live interviews, lavishly budgeted at $20,000 per broadcast. Features included interviews with Yousuf Karsh, breakfast at home with Maurice "Rocket" Richard, and a segment pitting the sports smarts of Foster Hewitt and five other sportscasters against an early IBM computer. The very particular McCulley claimed he couldn't perform without having a special office chair carted in for each broadcast. Almost billed *Ford Graphic*, after the show's sponsor.

The Great Canadian Culture Hunt

CBC
Documentary
First Broadcast: Wednesday, March 10, 1976, 8:30 p.m.
Final Year Broadcast: 1976
Running Time: 60 min.

Host: Gordon Pinsent

What do you get when you cram interviews with Margaret Atwood, Bruce Cockburn, Greg Curnoe, Robert Fulford, Ted Kotcheff, Irving Layton, Murray McLauchlan, Anne Murray, Peter C. Newman, Michael Ondaatje, and Michel Tremblay into six one-hour documentaries about the state of Canadian culture? Lots of hand-wringing and public clawing at hair shirts. Come to think of it, maybe that's what Canadian culture is really all about.

The Great Debate

Global
Debate
First Broadcast: Thursday, January 10, 1974, 9:30 p.m.
Final Year Broadcast: 1983
Running Time: 60 min.

Moderator: Pierre Berton

A pretty interesting debate show, with guest debaters ranging from rabid Canadian nationalist Mel Hurtig, Gloria Swanson, and Malcolm Muggeridge to *Chariots of the Gods* oddball Erich Von Daniken (who claimed to gather evidence of alien landing by mental telepathy). Debate topics included the acceptable use of violence as an ideological weapon, and the workability of Canadian bilingualism (featuring university professor

Jacques Parizeau on the negative side). When producers teetered on the brink of bankruptcy, Berton dug deep into his own pockets to pay guests who were offered a paltry 25 cents on the dollar for appearing. Briefly revived on CHCH-TV in 1983 after a few years hiatus.

The Great Detective

CBC
Drama
First Broadcast: Wednesday, January 17, 1979, 8:00 p.m.
Final Year Broadcast: 1982
Running Time: 60 min.

Cast:

Inspector Alistair Cameron	Douglas Campbell
Dr. Chisholm	Sandy Webster
Prudence	Tracy Brett
Mrs. Lutz	Kay Hawtrey
Sergeant Striker	Jim Dugan
Willie	Roy Wordsworth (1981–82)

Based on the memoirs of John Wilson Murray, appointed Ontario's first provincial detective in 1875 (though only two episodes were based on real cases from the original detective's files).

Fictional Inspector Alistair Cameron was a bachelor Scot with a penchant for booze. Prudence was Cameron's helpful niece; Chisholm his forensic-scientist friend, and Mrs. Lutz was the chambermaid. Beefcake Sgt. Striker was added to boost the series'

action quota. Willie was an underworld informer. A first shot at the series failed in 1976, after ACTRA complained about the choice of a British actor, Ian Cuthbertson, for the lead. Murray's real-life granddaughter went on record to say she didn't approve of Campbell's portrayal of Grandfather, particularly his TV counterpart's appreciation for alcoholic beverages.

The critics cheer: "…[tells] a whacking good tale…worth watching." — William Casselman, *Maclean's*

The critics jeer: "…a superhuman effort required to stay awake…a meticulous bore…like watching grass grow." — Mike Boone, Montreal *Gazette*

The Great Outdoors

See: *The Red Fisher Show*

Gullage's

CBC
Situation Comedy
First Broadcast: Wednesday, October 2, 1996, 9:00 p.m.
Final Year Broadcast: 1998
Running Time: 30 min.

Cast:

Calvin Pope	Bryan Hennessey
Dolly Pope	Elizabeth Pickard
Angora Pope	Janis Spence
Iris Hussey	Brenda Devine
Pis Parsons	Michael Wade
Eugene "Nuts" O'Neil	Jody Richardson
Bert	Philip Dinn
Russell	Brian Best
Little Jimmy Gullage	Frank Barry
Mrs. Clancy	Mercedes Barry
Mr. Clancy	Ray Guy

"Ahhh! Another glorious St. John's day!" Gullage's Cab Company is a St. John's taxi firm chockablock with "zany" employees. Cabbie Pope lives in a cramped bungalow with his mother Angora, daughter Dolly, and an old man who never speaks; ex-significant other Iris, Dolly's mother, lives next door. Gullage's new owner is Pis (it's pronounced *Piz*, wise guy!) Fellow cabbies include Nuts, Bert, and Russell. Bizarre plots involved Pis's attempts to breed wolverines, a naked parachutist, and a camp-out at the gravel pits. Guest appearances included *CODCO*'s Andy Jones as con artist Stumpy Parsons, and Brian Dunn as Zabo Vazaline.

A great detective: Inspector Alistair Cameron (Douglas Campbell) sniffs out a bogus medium (Barbara Hamilton) in *The Great Detective.*

CBC

Half the George Kirby Comedy Hour

CTV
Variety
First Broadcast: Thursday, September 14, 1972, 9:00 p.m.
Final Year Broadcast: 1973
Running Time: 30 min.

Host: George Kirby
Regular Performers: Julie Amato, Jack Duffy, Joey Hollingsworth, Connie Martin, Steve Martin, The Walter Painter Dancers

Another faux Canadian program featuring Kirby, an American singer-dancer-comic-pianist-impressionist who favoured U.S. guests (e.g., Arte Johnson, Henry Mancini). Slim Canadian content provided by Amato, Duffy, and Hollingsworth. Yes, *the* Steve Martin.

Hammy Hamster

Syndicated: 1972
Children's
Running Time: 30 min.

Voice of:
Hammy Hamster/G.P., Matthew Mouse . . . . Paul Sutherland

This second series of *Riverbank* tales followed more than ten years after *Tales of the Riverbank*. It featured the same setting as the original, but the half-hour episodes were more plot-heavy. Other changes were made

to appease U.S. distributors: Roderick Rat became Matthew Mouse for fear of offending inner-city audiences presumably plagued by large rodents; Guinea Pig's name was shortened to G.P., because "Guinea" is an obscure insult demeaning to Italians. The hamster became something of a cult item in universities, with Hammy Fan Clubs springing up on campuses across the country. Shot on the Isle of Wight, the dialogue was looped in Canada.

Undisciplined animal actors frequently engaged in random activity, smoothed over by additional dialogue. Hammy (fidgeting at the window while waiting for a snowmobile ride): "I'm so excited, I must rearrange the curtains!" Seen primarily on the Global network.

Paul Sutherland

Producer Paul Sutherland on *Hammy Hamster:*

"Casting is simple: the animal has to look right and can't be too crazy or wild. Acting talent doesn't figure into it—you can't teach them how to act. We've never been accused of being mean to the actors—we treat them with kid gloves. They only work for a few minutes at a time. If G. P. sneezes he gets immediate medical attention. We have veterinarians on duty at the set. One day we thought Hammy might be having heart problems, so the vet gave him a hamster ECG, and prescribed him some heart medication."

Hangin' In

CBC
Situation Comedy
First Broadcast: Wednesday, January 7, 1981, 7:30 p.m.
Final Year Broadcast: 1987
Running Time: 30 min.

Cast:
Kate Brown . . . . Lally Cadeau
Michael DiFalco . . . . David Eisner
Doris Webster . . . . Ruth Springford
Rosanna . . . . Gina Wilkinson (1986–87)

Trials and tribulations of workers at a youth counselling centre—the simple formula that kept this comedy (with occasional dramatic interludes) on the air for six years.

Kate headed the centre, assisted by young, idealistic Michael and hard-nosed receptionist Mrs. Webster. (Luba Goy played Webster, then named Primrose, in the series' 1980 pilot).

Teen problems included such serious fare as birth control, homosexuality, teen pregnancy, and attempted suicide. Michael married high school sweetheart Rosanna in the sixth season. Kate Reid and Chris Wiggins made occasional appearances as Kate's parents.

The critics cheer: "…somehow it works, with the occasional foray into adolescent drama serving to balance the lighter dialogue and lend credibility to the premise." — Randall McIlroy, *Winnipeg Free Press*

Hans in the Kitchen

CBC
Cooking
First Broadcast: Thursday, January 22, 1953, 10:30 p.m.
Final Year Broadcast: 1954
Running Time: 30 min.

Host: Hans Fread

A cooking show featuring continental chef Hans Fread, who also ran a Toronto restaurant, The Sign of the Steer. "Live well. Be happy." Also known as *Good Eating*.

The Hardy Boys

See: *Nancy Drew*

The Hart and Lorne Terrific Hour

CBC
Variety
First Broadcast: Sunday, October 4, 1970, 9:00 p.m.
Final Year Broadcast: 1971
Running Time: 60 min.

Terrific comedy: Hart Pomerantz (left) and Lorne Michaels (right) performed highbrow shtick on *The Hart and Lorne Terrific Hour.*

CBC

Hosts: Hart Pomerantz, Lorne Michaels
Regular Performers: Jackie Burroughs, Paul Bradley, Marvin Goldhar, Sylvia Lennick, Andrea Martin, Nicole Morin, Alan Price, George Raymond, Bill Reiter, Carol Robinson, Steve Weston

Following the joke title, each episode began with a psychedelic animated opening before settling into family-friendly sketches by the Canadian comedy team. Typical set-ups had Michaels interviewing Pomerantz as a wide variety of characters, including Ed Feigelman of myriad vocations (Ed Feigelman—Mountie, Ed Feigelman—mountain climber, etc.).

Most popular was Pomerantz's turn as The Beaver, a fur-clad *castor canadensis* who embarrassed the network by becoming a temporary pop-culture icon. The Beaver ran for Prime Minister, passing out thousands of Beaver Power buttons to adoring fans.

Hart Pomerantz on *Hart and Lorne:*

"Lorne and I became partners in radio in 1967, doing sketches on *The Russ Thompson Show.* Through my contacts we were hired to do *The Beautiful Phyllis Diller Show* in 1968. Lorne and I transplanted ourselves and our wives, Rosie and Nancy, to Hollywood. The show ran about three months. I walked into my office one day and everything was gone—they'd put the staff of *The Jerry Lewis Show* there. Nobody bothered to tell me that the program had been cancelled. I walked down the hall, hunched over and dejected, and was knocked down by Dan Rowan and Dick Martin. They were worried that they'd injured me, so we talked awhile and they asked me to send some of our radio tapes. We were hired to do *Laugh-In*'s opening dialogues for a year—we even received an Emmy nomination. We also wrote stand-up material for Woody Allen. When we became tired of making other people appear funny, we returned to Canada to do the *Terrific Hour.* It was rather psychedelic—hippies were still running the country. The CBC never saw our material before we went to air because we wrote until the last second. They hated the 'Beaver Power' campaign—they couldn't stand anything so popular.

"Eventually, Lorne went to seek his fortune in New York, working behind the scenes, while I stayed to do *This Is the Law.*"

Series' best moments: Baffin Island declares its independence and creates a new national anthem, featuring only the words "Baffin Island" sung to the tune of "O Canada"; a mockumentary examining the agricultural pestilence Dutch Puck Disease, which is devastating Canada's most important crop. Features scenes of Welland puck farmers inspecting their withered crop, and hockey legend King Clancy in a trumped-up public service announcement. Musical guests included Lighthouse, Melanie, Murray McLauchlan, Cat Stevens, and James Taylor.

Hatch's Mill

CBC
Comedy-Drama
First Broadcast: Tuesday, October 24, 1967, 9:00 p.m.
Final Year Broadcast: 1967
Running Time: 60 min.

Cast:

Noah Hatch	Robert Christie
Maggie Hatch	Cosette Lee
Saul Hatch	Marc Strange
Silence Hatch	Sylvia Feigel
Fred Hill	Jonathan White
Big Kurt	Kurt Schiegl

It was "All in the Family Compact" in this heavy-handed comedy set near Toronto of the 1830s. Moderately popular with audiences, critics opened fire at this ten-episode failure (though a Calgary reviewer launched a *Hatch* fan club).

Appearing in prototype as *The Road*, on CBC's *The Serial*, the series was ballyhooed a year before it appeared, raising viewer expectations beyond hope of consummation. "A series of this importance merits a place in the forefront of the new season," said one press release.

Unlike the solemn pilot (in which Hatch's wife dies) the new Noah Hatch was a pioneer card—a town magistrate who ran the general store, inn, and mill with a jolly, rock 'em sock 'em attitude. His new wife Maggie and children Saul and Silence helped to portray pioneer life as a string of boozing, carousing, kick-ass adventures. Contrary to established patriotic notions, press releases called Canadians of the period: "an astonishing lot—wild, reckless, insolent, arrogant, indifferent to authority and niceties."

Plagued by mosquitoes, the series was filmed on old *Forest Rangers* sets, in Black Creek Pioneer Village, and on a sprawling pioneer town set, constructed north of Toronto. The first CBC drama shot in colour. Many cast members wound up on *Strange Paradise*.

The critics jeer: "It's worse than *Seaway*, and I didn't think that was possible.... [Executive producer Ron] Weyman pleads artistic license; if so, it's a license to insult the intelligence of a good many of us." —Douglas Marshall, *Maclean's*

"You can always add a bit more violence to any show. It's much more difficult, however, to add another jolly." — Roy Shields, *The Toronto Star*

Haunted Studio

CBC
Musical Variety
First Broadcast: Thursday, July 22, 1954, 10:30 p.m.
Final Year Broadcast: 1954
Running Time: 30 min.

Host: Barry Morse
Regular Performers: Joanne Bernardi, Jean Cavall, Esther Gahn, The Esquires, Doug McLean, Don Parrish, Margaret Stilwell
Orchestra Leader: Jack Groob

An experiment in minimalism (or perhaps just a low-budget filler) featuring a near-empty set, punctuated by a few sticks of furniture. Jerry Hicks played the Theremin, coolest of electronic instruments.

Hawkeye

See: *Last of the Mohicans*

Headline Hunters

CTV
Game Show
First Broadcast: Tuesday, September 20, 1972, 7:30 p.m.
Final Year Broadcast: 1983
Running Time: 30 min.

Host: Jim Perry
Announcer: Dave Devall

Genial Perry hosted this more palatable version of *Front Page Challenge*, with headline clues, set to a noisy teletype backdrop, helping contestants to identify a person place, thing, or special guest (often a hockey jock, or someone appearing in a current CTV program).

Here Comes The Wolfman

See: *The Wolfman Jack Show*

Here Come The Seventies

CTV
Documentary
First Broadcast: Monday, September 17, 1970, 9:30 p.m.
Final Year Broadcast: 1973
Running Time: 30 min.

Narrator: Harry Ramer

Exploration of Mars by the year 2000? Increased use of performance-enhancing drugs in competitive sports? Full public nudity as office fashion? Two out of three ain't bad, as this program attempted to predict events of the next decade and beyond. The opening credits featured a naked woman walking into the water. Repackaged for U.S. consumption as *Towards the Year 2000* (minus the naked woman). Somebody rerun this time capsule! Followed by a sorta sequel, *Target The Impossible.*

Here's Duffy

CBC
Musical Variety
First Broadcast: Saturday, June 21, 1958, 10:30 p.m.
Final Year Broadcast: 1959
Running Time: 30 min.

Host: Jack Duffy
Regular Performers: Jill Foster, The Crescendos, Ed Karam Orchestra, Alfie Scopp, Larry Mann, Doug Romaine

Comedian Jack Duffy as a versatile Sinatra-esque singer? Yep. He even looked the part and he used to sing with the Tommy Dorsey Orchestra, Sinatra's old gig. Romaine

Billy Van

performed a "drunk" act. In a this-could-only-happen-in-the-fifties turn, Duffy was blasted in the House of Commons for a skit portraying an American tourist as "brassy," possibly offending the visiting head of the U.S. Rotary Club.

The critics cheer: "Duffy is droll, but with a sad smile that sometimes lights his features...probably one of mankind's funniest comedians on underplaying." — McStay, *Variety*

He Shoots, He Scores

CBC
Drama
First Broadcast: Tuesday, September 23, 1986, 9:00 p.m.
Final Year Broadcast: 1988
Running Time: 60 min.

Cast:
Pierre Lambert	Carl Marotte
Denis Mercure	Jean Harvey
Maroussia Lambert	Macha Méril
Ginette Letourneau	Marie-Chantale Labelle
Linda Hébert	Sylvie Bourque
Marc Gagnon	Marc Messier
Marilou	Sophie Renoir
Gilles Guilbeault	Michael Forget
Jacques Mercier	Yvan Ponton
Lucien Boivin	Denis Bouchard
Lucy	France Zobda
Suzie Lambert	Marina Orsini
Nicole	Lise Thouin
Paul Couture	Jean Deschênes
Maryse	Annette Garant

Lambert was a rookie with fictional NHL team the Quebec Nationals. His dream of a glorious stint in the major leagues was tarnished by team infighting and romantic complications.

Denis was Pierre's hockey buddy; Gagnon was a treacherous veteran player. The women in Pierre's life were sad-faced mama Maroussia; fashion-model sister Suzie; hometown girlfriend Ginette; urban girlfriend Lucy; and sports reporter Hébert. A Quebec production, filmed in French and English, then partially dubbed—some actor voices were inexplicably replaced to eliminate Quebec accents.

More explicit sex scenes, broadcast in Quebec, were snipped for English viewing. Some of the actors, including Méril, were imported from France to please French investors.

Known as *Lance et Compte* on the French network. A sequel, dubbed *Lance et Compte: The Next Generation,* and starring Marotte, Messier and Orsini is scheduled for Quebec broadcast in 2002.

The critics cheer: "…packaged slickly with authentic looking action sequences." —Jim Bawden, *The Toronto Star*

The critics jeer: "…wooden acting, bad writing and an atrocious sound track." —Les MacPherson, *Saskatoon Star-Phoenix*

Hey, Taxi!

CBC
Situation Comedy
First Broadcast: Thursday, July 6, 1972, 7:30 p.m.
Final Year Broadcast: 1972
Running Time: 30 min.

Cast:
? . . . . Terry David Mulligan
Henri le Champignon, et al . . . . Bill Reiter

Pitiful comedy: Mulligan played a Vancouver university student who won a taxi cab licence for his Austin Mini in a game of Scrabble; Bill Reiter played a succession of unamusing characters, including the above-mentioned French mechanic, a Japanese bartender, a traffic cop, and a pizza chef.

The critics jeer: "… [a] shameful half hour. This is as low as television can get." — Kaspar Dzeguze, *The Globe and Mail*

Hidden Pages

CBC
Children's
First Broadcast: Wednesday, June 16, 1954, 5:00 p.m.
Final Year Broadcast: 1958
Running Time: 15 min. and 30 min.

Host: Beth Gillanders

Gillanders, a librarian for the Vancouver Public Library, would spotlight a book, dramatize scenes, then tell kiddies how to borrow it from the library, where a stampede of junior viewers competed for the title. Gillanders briefly hosted a similar afternoon series, *Story Book.*

Hi Diddle Day

CBC
Children's
First Broadcast: Friday, November 7, 1969, 4:30 p.m.
Final Year Broadcast: 1976
Running Time: 30 min.

Cast:
Durwood's Music Teacher . . . . Wyn Canty
Mr. Post . . . . Bob Gardiner
Puppeteers and Voices: Noreen Young, Bob Dermer, Johni Keyworth, Stephen Braithwaite

A local Ottawa show debuting in 1966, this puppet series, set in Crabgrass, Ontario, featured brassy mayor Gertrude Diddle. Puppets who lived in her Victorian home included: Granny Diddle; prize beagle Basil; Durwood, a 900-year-old dragon; Wolfgang Von Wolf; Chico the Crow; Ti, a French-Canadian moose; Sebastian the cat; Madame ESP, a psychic; Sam Cletcher; Baby Swartze; Lucy Goose; Spilmilk, an alien; and a puppetized Pierre Elliott Trudeau.

The critics cheer: "…delightful, clever, engaging and imaginative…." — Ohio State Award for Excellence judging committee

The critics jeer: "…the most offensive show on TV…an appalling half hour with a cast of grotesque puppets starring a hideous old bag…." — Heather Robertson, *Maclean's*

High Hopes

CBC
Soap Opera
First Broadcast: Monday, April 3, 1978, 3:00 p.m.
Final Year Broadcast: 1978
Running Time: 30 min.

Cast:
Dr. Neal Chapman . . . . Bruce Gray
Jessica Chapman . . . . Marian McIsaac
Meg Chapman . . . . Doris Petrie
Paula Myles . . . . Nuala Fitzgerald
Trudy Bowen . . . . Barbara Kyle
Louise Bates . . . . Jayne Eastwood
Helen . . . . Candace O'Connor
Walter Telford . . . . Colin Fox
Evelyn Telford . . . . Deborah Turnbull
Mike Stewart . . . . Gordon Thomson
Michael Stewart, Sr. . . . . Michael Tait
Norma Stewart . . . . Vivian Reis
Amy Sperry . . . . Gina Dick
Dr. Dan Gerard . . . . Jan Muszynski

An American-produced soap set around Delaney College in Cambridge and its suburb, Cambridgeport, in that amorphous country that is neither wholly the U.S. nor Canada. Centred around Dr. Neal Chapman, a family counsellor, and the women in his life: teen daughter Jessica, mother Meg (who "seizes life and squeezes it for joy"), bitchy ex-wife Helen, sister-in-law Paula, talk-show host Trudy, whom he chases, and real estate agent Louise, who chases him. Lawyer Walter is Neal's friend; colleague Dr. Gerard is a lonely bachelor. Jessica's best friend is Amy, the sexpot. Major plot complications: when Jessica learns she's Paula's daughter, she develops a sexual fascination for ex-father, Michael Stewart (who still sees Paula), though she seems to have a thing for new dad as well; Michael's son Mike pursues Amy *and* his half-sister; Meg heads for a retirement home. U.S. soap vet, Winnifred Wolfe, was head writer. Seen on 20 American stations, *Peyton Place* actress Dorothy Malone appeared in the final episodes in a last-ditch effort to win U.S. viewers.

The critics jeer: "Canadian soap [is] 99 44/100 per cent pure American crud." — Diahne Martindale, *Halifax Chronicle-Herald and Mail-Star*

"Maybe *Modest Hopes*...." — Jack Miller, *The Toronto Star*

Highlander

Syndicated: 1992
Adventure
Running Time: 60 min.

Cast:

Duncan MacLeod . . . . Adrian Paul
Tessa Noel . . . . Alexandra Vandernoot (1992–93)
Richie Ryan . . . . Stan Kirsch
Randi McFarland . . . . Amanda Wyss (1992–93)
Darius . . . . Werner Stocker (1992–93)
Joe Dawson . . . . Jim Byrnes
Charlie DeSalvo . . . . Philip Akin (1993–95)
Maurice . . . . Michael Modo (1994)
Dr. Anne Lindsey . . . . Lisa Howard (1994–95)
Amanda . . . . Elizabeth Gracen
Sergeant Powell . . . . Wendell Wright
Methos . . . . Peter Wingfield
James Horton . . . . Peter Hudson

Based on a spate of *Highlander* films, this series explored the continuing saga of the immortals—human beings who could live forever, if not for other immortals who behead them (always off-screen) and rob them of their awesome energies in a pyrotechnical display known as "the quickening." Ultimately, only one immortal will survive to rule the universe. Duncan MacLeod is a 400-year-old immortal Vancouverite (though characters seem to refer to the city as "Seacouver") who is introduced by his film counterpart Connor MacLeod (Christopher Lambert) in the first instalment. None of the proceedings, however, gel with either the previous films or the concurrently produced animated series. Episodes involve MacLeod's dealings with immortals, both nasty and not, and frequent flashbacks with historical themes. Tessa was MacLeod's girlfriend, murdered by a foe's henchmen; pal Richie was also apparently killed, but discovered he was immortal too. Randi was a suspicious TV reporter. Charlie ran a martial arts studio owned by MacLeod (Akin and Paul overlapped by one episode as regulars in the Canadian series *War of the Worlds*) but was later killed by an immortal. Dr. Lindsey was another love interest. Dawson was head of a secret group known as The Watchers, who tried to weed out evil immortals; his brother, James, was a rebellious "Hunter" who preferred immortals dead. Darius was an immortal priest, and Amanda was MacLeod's immortal, but only occasional, lover. A Canada-France co-production, characters frequently leave "Seacouver" for Paris (no pseudonym), then decide they like things better in pseudo-Canada. In reality, this was part of a production deal that saw half the episodes filmed in each country for the show's six seasons. Theme music by Queen. Duncan and Connor were reunited in the 2000 follow-up film *Highlander: Endgame*. Television sequel: *Highlander II: The Raven*.

Highlander II: The Raven

Syndicated: 1998
Adventure
Running Time: 60 min.

Cast:

Amanda . . . . Elizabeth Gracen
Nick Wolfe . . . . Paul Johannson
Lucy Becker . . . . Patricia Gage
Bert Myers . . . . Hannes Jaenicke
Basil Morgan . . . . Julian Richings

A successor to the immensely popular *Highlander* series, with its occasional character Amanda taking the helm as a 1200-year-old immortal in this sequel.

After a mortal sacrifices herself to save Amanda's life, Amanda abandons years of thievery and chicanery to develop a conscience, teaming up with ex-cop Wolfe to fight crime. Lucy was Amanda's bookkeeper; Bert ran a security agency, relying on Nick and Amanda for assistance; Basil was a roguish immortal who made money dealing in stolen goods. A Canada-France co-production.

The Hilarious House of Frightenstein

Syndicated: 1971
Children's
Running Time: 60 min.

Cast:

The Resident Spectre . . . . Vincent Price
Count Frightenstein, Griszelda The Ghastly Gourmet, The Librarian, The Oracle, Doctor Pet Vet, The Wolf Man, The Ping-Pong Ball Ape, Bwana Clyde Battie, Sergeant Goodie . . . . Billy Van
The Mosquito/Super-Hippie . . . . Mitch Markowitz
Igor . . . . Fishka Rais
The Vapid Vampire . . . . Guy Big
Professor Julius Sumner Miller . . . . Himself
Harvey C. Wallbanger, The Gronk, The Grammar Slammer . . . . Joe Torbay
Fangs: Dr. E.C. Cooperman, D.D.S.

This subversive children's series was produced by Hamilton's CHCH studios to help boost Canadian content. A surprise success, it was syndicated in the U.S. and continues in reruns 30 years later. Meet Count Frightenstein, green-faced 13th son of the original Transylvanian Count, exiled to Frightenstone, Canada, for failing to revive Brucie, a Frankenstein-like monster. The show featured the Count's efforts to revive Brucie, assisted by family retainer Igor, an overweight incompetent, and a three-foot-tall mini-count. Each episode featured recitation of the Count's pledge and a rendition of his country's national anthem: *Gory, Gory Transylvania*. Vincent Price introduced regular segments in rhyme, mugging heavily as he toyed with skulls and shrunken heads. Notable segments:

The Wolf Man: A werewolf DJ (at radio station WDOG) doing a Wolfman Jack impression spins records and plays air guitar to Igor's capering, in what may be Canada's first psychedelic rock videos. In a stroke of genius, then-current hit singles by the Rolling Stones or Tony Orlando and Dawn were dubbed Golden Oldies to avoid dating the program. Theme song: "I Want to Take You Higher," by Sly & the Family Stone.

The Grammar Slammer: Negating everything *Sesame Street* stood for, The Grammar Slammer, an eight-foot monster, emerges to pound Igor to a pulp if he can't correct a grammatical error. Catch phrase: "Hammer, slammer, bammer Igor now?"

The Professor: Wild-haired U.S. physicist Professor Julius Sumner Miller, veteran of *The Mickey Mouse Show* (Professor Wonderful), provided legitimate science lessons while striving gamely to play along with the Frightenstein scenario: "We do physics here...in this place...this very, very strange place."

This was not a great show—perhaps not even a good one—but *Hilarious House* possessed what many kiddie programs lack: considerable chutzpah. And its pseudo-educational content was a nice touch to deflect uneasy parents who otherwise kept their kids away from programs featuring Rolling Stones records and jokes about cannibalism.

The critics jeer: "A Canadian *Sesame Street* it ain't." — Roy Shields, *Toronto Telegram*

"Some of the lines were in questionable taste—as when the ghoul stood over the coffin, shouting at the corpse 'Are you going to lie around all day?'"— Jack Miller, *Toronto Telegram*

Fangs a lot: A cast of characters from *The Hilarious House of Frightenstein*, most of them played by Billy Van. Clockwise from top left: The Wolfman, The Librarian, Brucie (a prop), The Count, Griszelda, and Igor (Fishka Rais).

Billy Van

The Hitchhiker

First Choice
Fantasy
First Broadcast: 1983, various times
Final Year Broadcast: 1989
Running Time: 30 min.

Cast:
The Hitchhiker . . . . Nicholas Campbell/Page Fletcher

Dreadful, dreadful fantasy series that typified the worst of early pay television. Inane storylines, terrible direction, and overblown acting conspired to sink this to the bottom of the genre. Pointless introductions featured the laconic Hitchhiker, neither mysterious nor frightening, traipsing through an unnamed American desert, offering simple-minded moralizations about the show's goings-on. Worst episode: an evil, eavesdropping husband is killed by the amplified sounds of his adulterous wife's lovemaking. Also seen on the U.S. HBO network.

The Hit Parade

See: *Cross-Canada Hit Parade*

Country cookin':
Country Hoedown sponsor Aylmer prepared this recipe book, including instructions on how to prepare such culinary delights as Dude Pie.

Hobby Workshop

CBC
Children's
First Broadcast: Monday, October 19, 1953, 5:15 p.m.
Final Year Broadcast: 1955
Running Time: 15 min.

Hosts: Tom Martin, Ross Snetsinger

Simple projects for kiddies, using Dad's tools. Snetsinger replaced Martin.

Holiday Edition

See: *Junior Magazine*

Holiday Ranch

CBC
Musical Variety
First Broadcast: Monday, July 20, 1953, 9:00 p.m.
Final Year Broadcast: 1958
Running Time: 30 min.

Hosts: Cliff McKay, Fran Wright
Regular Performers: Monique Cadieux, Percy "Duke" Curtis, Matt "Happy Face" de Florio, Ralph "Flying Fingers" Fraser, Anne Gable, "Smiling" Al Harris, Norma Hutton, Don "Shy Guy" Johnson, Doug "Hap" Master, Lorraine McAllister, "Dapper" Don McFarlane, "Bouncing" Billy Richards

"We'd like to tell you, friends and neighbours, that the good times are at Holiday Ranch."
—Introduction to *Holiday Ranch*

Host McKay's response to the show's musical request to "Tell us where the good times are" kicked off one of Canada's top-rated programs. McKay was a holdover from radio's *The Happy Gang* and oversaw this cotton-pickin' country program (with a side order of jazz), produced on a shoestring and broadcast from a cheesy ranch set (the Bar M Holiday Ranch) replete with BBQ pit.

Cheerful idiot ranch manager, Doug "Hap" Master, provided introductions for a musical cast composed almost entirely of people with nicknames. McKay recorded on his own *Holiday Ranch* record label. Comedian Libby Morris was booted off the show, for fear of offending sponsor Aylmer with an unintentional plug for its competitor's beans.

Four Aylmer tomato juice labels and two bucks netted viewers a nifty junior cowboy outfit. Each broadcast featured a "thought for tomorrow" from McKay and a safety spot for kids. Though it premiered on a Monday, the program settled comfortably in a Saturday evening slot for most of its run. Revived briefly on Hamilton's CHCH-TV in 1961.

The critics jeer: "...it ought to be mercifully snuffed out before it dies a lingering death right on our TV screens...deadly dull." — Jerry Walmsley, *Winnipeg Free Press*

Home Fires

CBC
Drama
First Broadcast: Sunday, November 9, 1980, 9:00 p.m.
Final Year Broadcast: 1984
Running Time: 60 min.

Cast:
Dr. Arthur Lowe........................ Gerard Parkes
Anna Lowe .... Kim Yaroshevskaya
Terry Lowe........................... Wendy Crewson
Sidney Lowe .... Peter Spence
Terry's Sweetheart....................... Jeff Wincott
Bruce McLeod......................... Booth Savage
Jakob... ?

The story of the Lowes, a Toronto family, during World War II. Dr. Lowe, his wife Anna, and children Terry and Sidney lived in a modest house where he ran a family practice. Terry married a soldier who was killed at Dieppe, then worked at an aircraft factory and married war correspondent McLeod. Sidney signed up for the Air Corps, was reported missing in action, then returned with a British wife, who was pregnant.

Hot Shots

Syndicated: 1986
Drama
Running Time: 60 min.

Cast:
Amanda Reed........................ Dorothy Parke
Jason West........................... Booth Savage
Nicholas Broderick .... Paul Burke
Al Pendleton .... Clark Johnson
Cleo .... Heather Smith
Receptionist .... Mung Ling

Two rival reporters (Amanda and Jason) for *CrimeWorld* magazine deny their mutual attraction while scaring up scoops. Nicholas was the magazine's publisher, Al his researcher, Cleo his secretary. More Canadian fodder for CBS's late-night line-up, but at least the leads were Canadian. Eventually seen on Global in Canada.

House of Pride

CBC
Drama
First Broadcast: Thursday, September 19, 1974, 7:30 p.m.
Final Year Broadcast: 1976
Running Time: 30 min.

Toronto Cast:
Ross Pride .... Budd Knapp
"Old" Daniel Pride .... George Waight
Daniel Pride .... Murray Westgate
Andrew Pride........................... Cec Linder
Hester Pride........................... Angela Clare
Irwin Fisher .... George R. Robertson
Rico................................... John Evans

Vancouver Cast:
Mary Kirby .... Charmion King
Jim Dowhan.......................... Neil Dainard
Carol Dowhan........................ Shirley Milliner
Calvin Kirby .... David Stein

Montreal Cast:
Lili Fortin .... Amulette Garneau
Claude Fortin........................ Pierre Dufresne

Halifax Cast:
Bernice Pride...................... Florence Patterson
Dan Pride .... Colin Fox

Winnipeg Cast:
Arthur Boychuk .... Steve Pernie
Jenny Boychuk .... Julie Amato

When former MPP "Old" Daniel Pride died, a developer offered a million bucks for the property. That's the pivotal opening of this short-lived series (dubbed *Son of Jalna*) that tried to squeeze the story of five branches of the Pride family—Toronto, Vancouver, Halifax (the Prides), Winnipeg (the Boychuks), and Montreal (the Fortins)—into a half-hour program.

Trying to keep storylines and 24 characters straight (including *three* Daniel Prides) required a guidebook. Series highlights: Daniel Pride and daughter Hester want to farm the homestead instead of becoming fabulously wealthy; brother Andrew claims he holds the deed to the land; Hester becomes pregnant by illegal immigrant farmhand Rico and runs for office against her kin, MPP Ross Pride; Arthur's gas station is crushed in the grip of the Energy Crisis, while daughter Lucy is diagnosed with a learning disability, and Jenny goes to work in a seedy nightclub.

In season two, the Vancouver and Montreal houses were cut from the picture entirely, although divorcée Mary Kirby fled B.C. for the old Toronto homestead. The series helped foster the notion that most WASPS are "Yuke-er-ainian"-hating bastards.

Howdy Doody

CBC
Children's
First Broadcast: Monday, November 15, 1954, 4:30 p.m.
Final Year Broadcast: 1959
Running Time: 30 min.

Cast:

Timber Tom	Peter Mews
Cap'n Scuttlebutt	Larry Mann
Clarabell	Alfie Scopp
Princess Pan of the Forest	Maxine Miller Gerrard/Toby Tarnow
Princess Haida	Caryl McBain
Mendel Mantelpiece Mason	Drew Thompson
Willow	Eric House/Barbara Hamilton
Papa La Touke	Jean Cavall
Trapper Pierre	Robert Goulet

Voices of:

Howdy Doody	Claude Rae/Jacqueline White
Phineas T. Bluster, Mr. X	Claude Rae
Prunella Bluster	Donna Miller
Dilly Dally, Percival Parrot, Hista the Snake, etc.	Jack Mather
Heidi Doody	Norma Macmillan/Donna Miller
Flub-a-dub	Larry Mann/Jack Mather

Puppeteers: Hal Marquette, Renee Marquette, Marilyn Marquette

CBC

Some Canadian kids never realized they were watching two *Howdy Doodys*—an American production and a Canadian mirror-image that ran on Mondays, Wednesdays, and Fridays. CBCers found the U.S. program overcommercialized and violent, so they commissioned a wholesome home-grown Doodyville. Royal Canadian Howdy didn't differ from the U.S. version as much as, say, the good and evil Captain Kirks differ from each other. There was a larger educational component, a safety club, and less rough-and-tumble fun—beatings, explosions, silent movie slapstick, and puppet hysteria.

Both programs started on radio. The Canadian version held on to a few characters: Clarabell Clown, yellow-striped Cap'n Windy Scuttlebutt, and puppets Phineas T. Bluster, Doodyville's misanthropic mayor (and his sister, Prunella), Dilly Dally, a lazy-ass carpenter, Flub-a-dub (with a duck's head, spaniel's ears, giraffe's neck, dachshund's body, seal's flippers, pig's tail, cat's whiskers, and an appetite for spaghetti and meatballs), and Heidi Doody, Howdy's sister. Canadian creations included Willow the Witch and Mr. X, an embryonic Dr. Who, who traversed time and space in his "whatsis box," until parents complained he was too scary for kids.

Absent was "Buffalo" Bob Smith, replaced with wholesome forest ranger Timber Tom. James "Scotty" Doohan was hired for the post, but held out for more cash. Mews replaced him, but failed to show up for the first few programs. Subbing for Mews was none other than Doohan's *Star Trek* captain William Shatner as clean-cut Ranger Bob. Robert Goulet also subbed for Mews as fur trapper Lucky Pierre.

Thirty live kids were penned up in the Peanut Gallery to warble the familiar "It's Howdy Doody Time" theme song, with Tom encouraging kids from various Canadian cities to join the ruckus. Actor Barry Morse once snuck into the Gallery to prove to his children that he really was a TV star.

Howie Mandel's Sunny Skies

CBC
Comedy
First Broadcast: Wednesday, October 11, 1995, 8:30 p.m.
Final Year Broadcast: 1995
Running Time: 30 min.

Host: Howie Mandel
Regular Performers: Tim Bagley, Jennifer Butt, Rob Cohen, Steven Furst, Deborah Theaker

"Over the top and off the wall… A cross between Monty Python's Flying Circus *and* Bob Vila's This Old House.*"*

— CBC press release

More like a cross between the *Titanic* and the *Hindenberg*, with the CBC yanking the program after only five episodes. Among the few segments aired: Howie played a Hebrew magician and hosted a program called Sensitive Guys.

The critics jeer: "I am, for once in my life, incapable of articulating how dreadful this alleged comedy is." — John Haslett Cuff, *The Globe and Mail*

Howie Meeker's Hockey School

CBC
Sports
First Broadcast: Wednesday, September 19, 1973, 7:30 p.m.
Final Year Broadcast: 1977
Running Time: 15 min.

Host: Howie Meeker

All-round hockey icon, commentator, player, and coach Meeker carved out a niche as a TV hockey coach for juniors, stressing skills development and yelling at kid players when they screwed up. "Practise, kids! Practise! Practise! Practise!"

Hudson's Bay

Syndicated: 1958
Drama
Running Time: 30 min.

Cast:
John Banner . . . . Barry Nelson
Regular Performer: George Tobias

This series brings new meaning to the word "forgotten"; the few references to this 39-episode adventure program about 18th-century fur trappers suggest it was planned but never made. Nelson has the distinction of being the first actor to play James Bond—in a 1954 TV adaptation of Ian Fleming's *Casino Royale*. The palisade appearing in the series apparently doubled as the fort in *The Forest Rangers*.

Hymn Sing

CBC
Music
First Broadcast: Sunday, October 3, 1965, 5:30 p.m.
Final Year Broadcast: 1995
Running Time: 30 min.

Hosts: Hector Bremner, Don Brown, Sharon-Ann Evans, Barry Stilwell, Claude Dorg, Ken Smutylo, Judy Pringle, Cynthia Laird
Musicians: Mitch Parks, Paul Olynyk

This Winnipeg staple featured old-time hymns and spirituals, performed by an evolving chorus of robed singers, usually no older than 25.

So popular, its ratings once rivalled *This Hour Has Seven Days.* The chorus was directed by Eric Wild to 1978, and then Winnifred Simm, the original organist.

Hymn Sing concentrated on traditional numbers; "How Great Thou Art" and "Abide With Me" were the show's two most popular selections.

The critics cheer: "*Hymn Sing* turned out to be a pleasant, crisply produced, entirely musical hour of singing by a fine choir." — Frank Penn, *Ottawa Citizen*

Hymn singers: The clean-cut gang from *Hymn Sing* performed traditional hymns in a long-running TV series and a passel of record albums.

In Opposition

CBC
Situation Comedy
First Broadcast: Tuesday, October 24, 1989, 7:30 p.m.
Final Year Broadcast: 1990
Running Time: 30 min.

Cast:

Karen Collier	Kathleen Laskey
Tom Sheridan	Peter Keleghan
Joe Reynolds	Lawrence Dane
MacGilvary	Damir Andrei
Mary Margaret McCarthy	Jennifer Dale
Grace Kiley	Judy Marshak

The CBC's feeble apology for another unfunny political comedy *Not My Department* a few years earlier. Collier was the MP representing Moncton Macquedewawa South for the fictional Dominion Party. Sheridan was a shifty backbencher, Reynolds was party leader, MacGilvary was House leader, and Kiley was a veteran secretary. Closer to home, McCarthy was Collier's pesky neighbour who hosted a TV show for seniors. Based on a 1988 pilot featuring David McIlwraith in Keleghan's role. Ratings for the series were so low that CBC execs started looking more fondly at the network's other dreadful sitcom, *Mosquito Lake*.

The critics jeer: "The jokes range fom the unexpected crudity of a woman sneezing on everyone to the stupidity of the line 'alien beings have been opening my mail.'" — John Haslett Cuff, *The Globe and Mail*

Inspector Gadget

Syndicated: 1986
Animated
Running Time: 30 min.

Voices of:

Inspector Gadget	Don Adams
Penny	Cree Summer (1984–85), Holly Berger (1985–86)
Brain/Dr. Claw/MAD Cat	Frank Welker
Chief Quimby	Maurice LaMarche
Capeman	Townsend Coleman (1985–86)

"Go, go, gadget legs!"

The body of bumbling cyborg detective Inspector Gadget housed an array of devices—springs, extensible claws, and propellers, to name but a few—he used to fight criminals, particularly Dr. Claw, evil genius and director of enemy agency MAD (Mean And Dirty).

While Gadget meant well, niece Penny and dog Brain did all the dirty work, unknown to the oblivious agent. Quimby was Gadget's boss.

To help balance Gadget's mayhem, the inspector provided an incongruous safety lesson at the end of each episode. The series was broadcast on Global in Canada.

A live action film, based on the character, was released in 1999.

Irish Coffee

CBC
Discussion
First Broadcast: Wednesday, September 24, 1969, 10:30 p.m.
Final Year Broadcast: 1970
Running Time: 30 min.

Hosts: Fred Davis, Paul Kligman, Paul Soles, Bill Walker

This bomb collected groups of people with similar interests or backgrounds (clergymen, aviators, politicians, actors, musicians, and Scots, to name but a few) at a (heavily plugged) Toronto restaurant, Julie's, and broadcast their after-dinner conversations. Guests of the boring gabfest included Gordie Tapp, Ben Wicks, Peter Worthington, and Anna Cameron.

A *Toronto Star* critic suggested the program might have been more palatable if the entire meal had consisted of Irish coffee.

The Irish Rovers

CBC
Musical Variety
First Broadcast: Monday, April 5, 1971, 7:30 p.m.
Final Year Broadcast: 1975
Running Time: 30 min.

The Irish Rovers: George Millar, Joe Millar, Will Millar, Jimmy Ferguson, Wilcil McDowall

The Irish Rovers parlayed their surprise number one worldwide hit, "The Unicorn," into a popular TV series that included dubious sketch comedy and big-name acts, including Johnny Cash. Most programs featured a segment in which the Rovers, dressed in leprechaun costumes, were chroma-keyed into a cheap, oversized set. Some programs were taped in Ireland. The Irish Rovers returned in 1980 with their overhyped *Irish Rovers Comedy House Superspecial*.

The critics jeer: "The Irish Rovers are terrible…[they] only know one tune, which they play very enthusiastically, as if to make up for it." — Heather Robertson, *Maclean's*

It's Happening

CTV
Musical Variety
First Broadcast: Thursday, September 7, 1967, 8:30 p.m.
Final Year Broadcast: 1969
Running Time: 30 min.

Host: Jungle Jay Nelson
It's Happening Dancers: Linda Shenkin, Linda Christopher, Claudette Houchen (1967–68), Leeyan Granger, Janis Goodman, Anne Steele, Candy Turner (1968–89)

Host Robbie Lane and his musical Disciples (Doug Riley, Bill Cudmore a.k.a. Wicked William, Bert Hermiston, Kirk Shearer, Gene Trach, and Terry Bush) inherited the remnants of *A Go Go '66* and attracted up to a million viewers per week. The series spawned an album of the same name, recorded by Lane.

CBC

It's Your Choice

CBC
Game Show
First Broadcast: Monday, April 5, 1976, 5:00 p.m.
Final Year Broadcast: 1977
Running Time: 30 min.

Host: Bill Lawrence
Team Captains: Juliette, Don McGill

"Crazy cut-ups! Daffy definitions! Wacky wordage!" beamed the network in this TV adaptation of the game Dictionary, with celebrity teams bluffing each other about obscure word definitions. The network promised a quiz show "that isn't full of Hollywood hoopla, hucksters, dash or greed." Translation: No prizes, no contestants—just well-worn, mugging pseudo-celebs (including columnist Gary Lautens and interior decorator Roy Staples) with nothing at stake.

It's Your Move

CTV
Game Show
First Broadcast: Monday, September 14, 1964, various
Final Year Broadcast: 1978
Running Time: 30 min.

Hosts: Paul Hanover, George Balcan

Weekday charades for cash, taped in Montreal. Teams "bid" to complete a charade in

Luck of the Irish: The Irish Rovers spun their novelty hit "The Unicorn" into worldwide fame and a CBC variety show.

A brand new appliance!: Paul Hanover, host of *It's Your Move*, presents a winning contestant with an exciting photo of her prize: a state-of-the-art (1966) Maytag washer.

CFCF-TV

the least time possible; if they failed, the opposing team took the point. Three points netted team members (mostly husbands and wives) moderate prizes like cameras and small appliances.

I Was a Sixth Grade Alien

CTV
Children/Drama
First Broadcast: Tuesday, September 14, 1999, 6:30 p.m.
Final Year Broadcast: —
Running Time: 30 min.

Cast:

Pleskit Ventraa	Ryan Cooley
Tim Thomkins	Daniel Clark
Blur	Leah Cudmore
Robert McNally	Panou
Ms. Weintraub	Jennifer Wigmore
Ms. Buttsman	Gina Clayton
Meenom	Julian Richings
Principal Grand	C. David Johnson

Pleskit is a purple-skinned alien with something that looks like blue sage grass growing out of his head.

His dad, Meenom, is a native of planet Hevi-Hevi, ambassador to Earth from the League of Galactic Bodies. Entering sixth grade like other Earth kids is a bit of a trial for young Pleskit, who can levitate, loves homework, and belches when he greets someone. Tim is Pleskit's best friend, Ms. Weintraub is the teacher, and Grand is principal of Coville Elementary. McNally is Pleskit's UN-appointed bodyguard, and Ms. Buttsman is a Protocol Secretary assigned to Pleskit.

Based on a series of popular books by Bruce Coville. "Gripnik!"

Jack London's Tales of the Klondike

CBC
Drama
First Broadcast: Sunday, May 16, 1981, 8:00 p.m.
Final Year Broadcast: 1981
Running Time: 60 min.

Narrator: Orson Welles

Six dramas based on the stories of Jack London, including: *The One Thousand Dozen,* starring Neil Munro; *In A Far Country,* with Scott Hylands and Robert Carradine; *Scorn Of Women,* starring Eva Gabor; and *The Unexpected,* with John Candy and Cherie Lunghie. It's a well-known fact that Canadians are genetically incapable of being narrators, so Orson Welles was used instead.

Jackpot

Global
Game Show
First Broadcast: Monday, September 30, 1985, 7:30 p.m.
Final Year Broadcast: 1988
Running Time: 30 min.

Host: Mike Darrow

Awful game show based on a 1975 U.S. show of the same name. A massive rack of 15 contestants vied for a chance at the podium to answer a dopey riddle. Answer the question, and you kept the dollar value assigned to that riddle; blow a question, and you lost your precious perch to the asker. Find the special "Jackpot" question, and you shared a bigger wad of cash with the questioner.

One of the show's problems: mumble-mouthed contestants couldn't pronounce simple words, so host Darrow often repeated the entire riddle. Even if players came up with better answers than the arbitrary scripted ones, Darrow cheerfully robbed intelligent contestants of their winnings. Contestants were apparently chosen for their ability to scream "Jackpot!"

Jake and the Kid (1961–63)

CBC
Drama
First Broadcast: Tuesday, July 4, 1961, 8:30 p.m.
Final Year Broadcast: 1963
Running Time: 30 min.

Cast:

Jake Trumper	Murray Westgate
The Kid	Rex Hagon
Ma	Frances Tobias
MacTaggart	Bob Christie
Repeat Golightly	Eric House
Sam Gatenby	Alex McKee

W.O. Mitchell's stories about a handyman, a widow, and her son, were popular in *Maclean's* and on CBC radio, but failed miserably on television. Canadian producers waited in the wings while U.S. producers mulled over the possibility of their own *Jake* series, tentatively starring Burgess Meredith.

When the Americans declined, the NFB announced that it would produce a TV series starring John Drainie (he played Jake on radio and in one appearance on *Folio*) and Tony Haig. Only one NFB episode was produced. For better or worse (worse, said Mitchell), this became the definitive TV version of tales set in Crocus, Saskatchewan, on the banks of the Brokenshell River. Canadians took another stab at the series in 1995.

The critics jeer: "…I can only report that the show is a catastrophe. It simply enrages people who knew and loved the [radio] version." — Nathan Cohen, *The Toronto Star*

Jake and the Kid (1995–97)

Global
Drama
First Broadcast: Saturday, December 16, 1995, 7:00 p.m.
Final Year Broadcast: 1997
Running Time: 60 min.

Narrators: Joe-Norman Shaw (1995), Henry Ramer (1996–97)

Cast:

Jake Trumper	Shaun Johnston
Ben Osborne	Ben Campbell
Julia Osborne	Patti Harras
Moses Lefthand	Lorne Cardinal
Albert Rickey	Brian Taylor
Emily Henchpaw	Julie Khaner

Yet another go-round at dramatizing W.O. Mitchell's stories set in the fictional town of Crocus, Saskatchewan, with Jake now more of a hayseed hunk than country handyman. The program died when the Alberta government phased out the Alberta Motion Picture Development Corporation, leaving producers stuck without cash.

The critics cheer: "…palatable TV treacle with safe, G-rated humour, all beautifully shot under the big prairie sky amid a warm, hospitable western ambiance…." — Grant McIntyre, *Broadcast Week*

Jalna

See: *The Whiteoaks of Jalna*

Jazz With Jackson

CBC
Musical Variety
First Broadcast: Saturday, January 10, 1953, 8:00 p.m.
Final Year Broadcast: 1955
Running Time: 30 min.

Host: Dick MacDougal

Music with pianist Cal Jackson, a big band, and guests. Jackson called his piano style "painting with music." Though jazz was the grist for Jackson's TV mill, he favoured Rachmaninov off-camera. Jackson, who was Black, typified the CBC's commitment to a racially diverse slate of performers. Norman Jewison produced.

Jellybean Comedy Clubhouse

CTV
Children's
First Broadcast: Wednesday, September 12, 1962, 4:30 p.m.
Final Year Broadcast: 1967
Running Time: 30 min.

Cast:

Johnny Jellybean	Ted Zeigler

Johnny Jellybean aired for four years in New York City before moving to Montreal. As manic Johnny, rubber-faced Zeigler appeared in an oversize polka-dotted bow tie and beanie topped by a trademark jelly bean. Live audiences sported the official hat, while home viewers could buy the beanie, badge, and official membership card.

Zeigler portrayed a slate of characters including Hemlock Bones, Uncle Schnitzel, Polo the Clown, Enzio Pesta, 142-year-old Morrie the Mailboy, the Ole Wrangler and Speedy Sam the Newspaper Man. Kids encouraged Johnny to obliterate a talking "squawkbox" with either the Masher, Basher, or Smasher, progressively larger sledgehammers (guess which one he used?) and watched faux commercials for McGarry Sausages and Puff Grass ("Puff Grass, Puff Grass, chock full of vitamins and chlorophyll too!")

Zeigler, who started his children's programming career in Australia, later appeared on the Sonny and Cher program. Seen in Toronto as a segment of *Professor's Hideaway*. Also known as *Lunchtime Little Theatre*.

This one?: Ted Zeigler as Johnny Jellybean asks the juvenile studio audience if he should smash his suspended "Squawkbox" with a Masher, Smasher, or Basher on *Jellybean Comedy Clubhouse.*

▼

CFCF-TV

The Jerry Lester Show

CTV
Variety
First Broadcast: Monday, September 21, 1963, 10:00 p.m.
Final Year Broadcast: 1964
Running Time: 60 min.

Host: Jerry Lester

Jerry Lester was NBC's first late-night emcee on *Broadway Open House.* Of course, that was in 1950 when competition was light. A borscht-belt comic with a resemblance to Mickey Rooney, Lester was imported to provide pratfalls and wild audience participation stunts—unfortunately to cool TV-land response. Singer Richard Hayes was a semi-regular. Syndicated in some U.S. cities.

The critics cheer: "[Lester] is a hard-working comic who wants to amuse you." — Pierre Maple, *TV Guide*

The critics jeer: "Jerry Lester was definitely a child of his time—and that time was not A.D. 1962." — Hale Erickson, *Syndicated Television: The First Forty Years*

The Joan Fairfax Show

CBC
Musical Variety
First Broadcast: Monday, July 6, 1959, 8:30 p.m.
Final Year Broadcast: 1960
Running Time: 30 min.

Host: Joan Fairfax
Regular Performers: The Van Dorn Sisters

Smiley singer Fairfax and her 11-piece "all-woman" orchestra moved from summer replacement to regular program. Viewers may have wondered why the program hyped the female aspect of the orchestra, since it was rarely seen, conducted off-screen by Samuel Hersenhoren. Musical guests included Wally Koster, Bobby Gimby, and Roger Doucet, later famous for his rendering of the national anthem at NHL hockey games.

The critics cheer: "It is encouraging…to see a show standing on its own Canadian feet…warm and tuneful.…" — Elwy Yost, *The Toronto Star*

The critics jeer: "…this series is the lame duck of the current variety schedule and badly needs help.…" — Dennis Braithwaite, *The Toronto Star*

The John Allan Cameron Show

CBC
Musical Variety
First Broadcast: Friday, June 29, 1979, 9:00 p.m.
Final Year Broadcast: 1980
Running Time: 30 min.

Host: John Allan Cameron
Music: Cape Breton Symphony

In this summer series, musician Cameron made a valiant attempt to extend his musical repertoire, mugging as Dr. Jekyll, The Phantom of the Opera, Errol Flynn, Charlie Chaplin, and Rudolph Valentino, or matching hockey skills with Eddie Shack. The comedy team of Hughie and Allen performed "news from home." Musical guests included Bruce Cockburn, Valdy, Mason Williams, the Good Brothers, Will Millar, Denny Doherty, Roger Whittaker, Murray McLauchlan, Ian Tyson, and Ronnie Prophet. Dance numbers by the John Allanettes. From Halifax.

John Woo's Once a Thief

CTV
Comedy/Drama
First Broadcast: Monday, September 15, 1997, 10:00 p.m.
Final Year Broadcast: 1998
Running Time: 60 min.

Cast:

Mac Ramsey	Ivan Sergei
Victor Mansfield	Nicholas Lea
Li Ann Tsei	Sandrine Holt
The Director	Jennifer Dale
Dobrinsky	Howard Dell
Jackie Janczyk	Vicky Pratt
Camier	Julian Richings
Murphy	Greg Kramer

Two criminals in love (Ramsey, Tsei) flee the Hong Kong crime boss who trained them in the martial arts when he tries to force Tsei to marry his son. In Canada they join forces with an ex-cop (Mansfield) to fight crime as part of an elite law enforcement agency answering to "The Director." The three leads were apparently killed in this action/comedy series' final episode, remaining deceased in the absence of a second season. Action director Woo was executive producer here, though he directed the TV movie pilot seen in 1996. Lea portrays popular "rat boy" Krycek on *The X-Files.*

Julie

CTV
Variety
First Broadcast: Tuesday, September 21, 1973, 9:30 p.m.
Final Year Broadcast: 1974
Running Time: 30 min.

Host: Julie Amato

Julie sang, danced, and performed comedy sketches.

Juliette

CBC
Musical Variety
First Broadcast: Saturday, October 27, 1956, 11:10 p.m.
Final Year Broadcast: 1966
Running Time: 30 min.

Host: Juliette
Announcer: Gil Christy
Regular Performers: Bobby Gimby, George Murray
(1956–57), Roy Roberts (1957–58), Ken Steele (1958–59),
The Romeos (1959–65), The Four Mice (1960–64), The Art
Hallman Singers (1966)
Theme Song: "Love and Marriage"

While it's no "Just the facts, ma'am," the program's opening announcement to "Meet, and greet, your pet...Juliette," was probably Canada's only TV-inspired catch phrase of the 1950s.

Juliette Augustina Sysak wasn't a catchy stage name. Neither was married name Juliette Sysak Cavazzi so this star lived by Juliette alone. Popular on radio in *Here's Juliette*, the blonde singer caught fire on TV's *Billy O'Connor Show*, where she became more popular than the show's star. When the CBC canned O'Connor, it promoted Juliette to a new program—in O'Connor's old time slot after *Hockey Night in Canada*.

In a living room set, Juliette held court in the easygoing manner of a northern Dinah Shore. The hunks, Roberts and Steele ("C'mon boys"), escorted Juliette to minimalist sets—a vaselined lens, fake pine tree, and artificial snow, for example. Guests included Canadians (like Don Messer's Marg Osburne) and international stars, including Jack Jones and *Hogan's Heroes'* Bob Crane. Christmas specials featured musical appearances by Friendly Giant, Jerome, and Rusty the Rooster.

One of the CBC's few stars, Juliette was treated shabbily by a network that appeared to dote on producers and dismiss talent. Criticized by enemies as a bitchy neatnik and backstage control freak (musician Bobby Gimby left the show in a huff after a nasty blow-up), critics branded her a hokey showbiz phoney. But while a hockey lead-in helped viewer numbers considerably, audiences developed a genuine affection for the blonde chanteuse, who got the last laugh by taking home an Order of Canada in 1975.

"Good night, Mom."

The critics cheer: "...high on talent and low on frills...undoubtedly the most refreshing musical program available...pleasant in its simplicity and happy in its choice of music." — *Winnipeg Free Press*

The critics jeer: "...sick...from an overdose of bad writing and enfeebling coziness...it isn't so much a program as it is an afterthought.... Juliette deserves a better fate." — Ron Poulton, *Toronto Telegram*

Juliette and Friends

CBC
Discussion/Variety
First Broadcast: Monday, September 17, 1973, 2:00 p.m.
Final Year Broadcast: 1975
Running Time: 30 min.

Host: Juliette
Co-Hosts: Larry Solway, Bill Lawrence, Doug Lennox

Juliette's stab at a daytime talk show—an uneasy mixture of music, glamour, and household tips. The series' most controversial moment (pre-dating Oprah Winfrey's cattle crisis): Juliette tells the audience that "beef is expensive"; a cattle rancher visits a few days later to prove she's wrong. Solway, Lawrence, and Lennox served as second bananas.

Canada's pet: Juliette belts out a Gay '90s number on her popular self-titled variety show.

CBC

Junior Magazine

CBC
Children's
First Broadcast: Sunday, December 4, 1955, 2:00 p.m.
Final Year Broadcast: 1962
Running Time: 60 min.

Hosts: John Clark (1955–58), Roberta Maxwell (1957–58), Garrick Hagan (1959–60), Ross Snetsinger (1960–62), Norman Welsh (1961–62)
Contributors: Louis Applebaum, Leslie Bell, Lorraine Green, Hank Hedges, Doug Maxwell, Frank Rodwell

A cornucopia of local and international features, including talent shows, and U.S. dramas *Treasure Island* and *Long John Silver*, fresh from the Disney studios. Applebaum and Bell provided music education, Green was a dancer, Hedges covered nature, and Maxwell, sports. Rodwell was an impressionist. Paul Saltzman (Percy's kid) and Patrick Watson occasionally hosted. Fred Rogers, in pre-*Neighborhood* days, was a guest puppeteer. A summer version, *Holiday Edition*, (1959–61) featured Clark (1959–60), Snetsinger (1960–61), and Toby Tarnow (1960–61) as hosts, and magician Michael Roth (1960–61). Kids wrote in to receive *Junior Magazine* Reporter ID cards.

Junior Roundup

CBC
Children's
First Broadcast: Monday, October 17, 1960, 4:45 p.m.
Final Year Broadcast: 1961
Running Time: 45 min.

Host: Murray Westgate

Esso spokesguy Westgate hosted this weekday program that offered viewer mail and hobby segments and a new educational theme each day. The opening line-up included:
Monday: Dave Broadfoot and Jean Templeton overseeing games and contests with the studio audience, and a telephone quiz.
Tuesday: Percy Saltzman on space travel, and John Lund of the Royal Ontario Museum.
Wednesday: country and folk music from Winnipeg with Stu Phillips, and a Halifax segment on Native people. Phillips went on to write theme music for popular U.S. programs, including *Battlestar Galactica* and *Quincy: M.E.*
Thursday: drama, concerts, and ballet.
Friday: *Your World This Week*, a news show for kids.

The 15-minute segment preceding the program, known as *Bantam Roundup*, was filled by repeats of *Friendly Giant, Maggie Muggins, Just Mary*, and *The Children's Corner*, with Fred Rogers (*Misterogers*).

Just Ask, Inc.

CBC
Children's
First Broadcast: Wednesday, February 4, 1981, 4:00 p.m.
Final Year Broadcast: 1981
Running Time: 30 min.

Host: David Suzuki
Cast:
Lustra . . . . Joan Stuart
Ami . . . . Luba Goy

With the aid of robots Lustra and Ami, Dr. Suzuki examined science questions, some of them supplied by children. Suzuki had appeared with Ami the year before on CBC's *W.O.W.* (Wonderful One-of-a-Kind Weekend). Among the subjects tackled: why people snore, why stars twinkle.

Just Mary

CBC
Children's
First Broadcast: Thursday, April 7, 1960, 4:30 p.m.
Final Year Broadcast: 1960
Running Time: 15 min.

Regular Performers: Joe Austin, Alex Barringer, Sid Brown, Winnifred Dennis, Gillie Fenwick, Barbara Hamilton, Syme Jago, Merle Salsberg, Toby Tarnow, Sandy Webster
Puppet Voices: Winnifred Dennis, Doug Master, Jack Mather, Roberta Maxwell, Douglas Rain, Pauline Rennie, Ruth Springford
Puppeteers: John Keogh, Linda Keogh

Writer Mary Grannan narrated her *Just Mary* stories, largely about children and animals, while puppets and actors performed them. Originally a radio series, the program became part of *Junior Roundup*'s *Bantam Roundup* in October 1960.

Katts and Dog

CTV
Drama
First Broadcast: Friday, September 16, 1988, 8:00 p.m.
Final Year Broadcast: 1993
Running Time: 30 min.

Cast:

Officer Hank Katts	Jesse Collins
Rudy	Rudolph Von Holstein III
Alice	Sharon Acker
Maggie Davenport	Cali Timmins
Stevie Katts	Andrew Bednarski
Captain Colin Murdoch	Ken Pogue
Sergeant Callahan	Peter MacNeill
Sergeant Lou Adams	Dan Martin
Officer Renee Daumier	Denise Virieux
Officer Leah McCray	Nancy Anne Sakovich
Officer Ron Nakamura	Denis Akayama
Officer Dennis Brian	Brian Kaulback
Officer Connie	Corrine Koslo
Lieutenant Logan	Chuck Shamata
Sergeant O.C. Phillips	Phil Jarrett

K-9 Corps officer Katts has a secret weapon: Rudy, the German shepherd who can sniff out assorted bombs, punks, and clues while felling armed tough guys with his mighty forepaws. Maggie was Hank's widowed sister-in-law; Stevie, her son. Don't you hate corny show titles like this? So did the U.S. Family Channel, which gave the series an even more pointless name: *Rin Tin Tin K-9 Cop.* A Canada/France co-production.

Keith Hampshire's Music Machine

CBC
Variety
First Broadcast: Saturday, September 22, 1973, 6:30 p.m.
Final Year Broadcast: 1975
Running Time: 30 min.

Host: Keith Hampshire

Singing host Keith ("The First Cut," "Daytime-Nighttime") Hampshire performed his own material and cover versions of current hits. Hampshire was backed by Dr. Music and regular vocal group Soul Company. Comedy troupe the Zoo Factory (Harriet Cohen, Bruce Gordon, Dan Hennessey, Jerelyn Homer, John Stocker) were canned after two weeks of unfavourable audience reaction. When the program moved to evenings, it added a vocal group, Liberation, and encouraged Hampshire to sing a golden oldie medley. Guest acts included April Wine, Copperpenny, Downchild, Fludd, Andy Kim, Lighthouse, Ian Thomas, and Valdy. The first program featured the Rolling Stones in a performance of "Angie," taped exclusively for the show. A slightly revamped version of *Music Machine.*

Kiddo the Clown

CFTO-TV
Children's
First Broadcast: Monday, September 10, 1962, 8:00 a.m.
Final Year Broadcast: 1965
Running Time: 30 min.

Cast:

Kiddo	Trevor Evans

Kiddo the clown was a building superintendent who lived in a vile basement apartment strewn with detritus. Mrs. Clavicle, who lived upstairs, dumped dirty laundry into Kiddo's suite through an open chute. Nasty General Grump hurled insults through a heating duct. Milton the mouse provided Kiddo's only company, typing messages to him on a miniature typewriter. A meagre sign read Home Sweet Home.

Signature gags: an icebox blasted Arctic gales, and a furnace boiler contained a rehearsing orchestra. A suspiciously adult voice (Evans provided all of them) interrupted Kiddo with: "Hey, Mister, can you come out and play?" Preoccupied Kiddo always begged off with, "Not today, Billy," until on one program Kiddo left his skid-row apartment to join Billy in an off-screen game of catch.

Later episodes were set at a fleabag hotel known as the Wiltin' Hilton.

Kiddo was born on *Sunbeam Birthday Party* seen locally on CHCT in Calgary in 1956. Evans carried the act to Edmonton and Red Deer, finally settling in Toronto where Kiddo became so popular that he hosted three daily Toronto kiddie series—including *Kiddo Cartoons*—at once! The flagship *Kiddo the Clown* show was syndicated in other major Canadian cities. Evans went on to direct *Coming Up Rosie, Dr. Zonk and the Zunkins,* and Wayne and Shuster comedy specials.

The critics cheer: "The most imaginative and creative [program] now being produced in Canada…I am captivated by Kiddo." — Ross McLean, *Toronto Telegram*

Kids in the Hall

CBC
Comedy
First Broadcast: Thursday, September 14, 1989, 9:30 p.m.
Final Year Broadcast: 1995
Running Time: 30 min. & 60 min.

The Kids in the Hall: David Foley, Bruce McCulloch, Kevin McDonald, Mark McKinney, Scott Thompson

This live-performing comedy troupe adapted itself to television sketch comedy in this uneven mixture of brilliant material and self-indulgent, land-with-a-thud duds.

Some of the sketches used repeat characters and scenarios: the two laconic Cherry Beach police officers; the head-crusher (a moron who pretends to pinch human heads between thumb and forefinger); a trio of gay guys discussing life on "The Steps"; two bored streetwalkers; Thompson's gay-bar entrepreneur, Buddy Cole; office schlepp Idiot Boy; and the well-meaning, obnoxious Dar*ill* ("Not Darryl!"). The Kids' "fifth Beatle": series writer Paul Bellini, who developed a cult following by wandering into scenes wearing only a towel.

The program's funniest bits, though, were often one-offs: *Chalet 2000,* a full show devoted to the budding romance between Queen Elizabeth II (Thompson) and an oversized beaver (McCulloch); a visit with the misfit (McDonald) of a Polynesian tribe

who refuses to accept that reciting popular trivia is not a sufficient ritual of tribal manhood; a simple-minded Santa Claus (McKinney) slides down the chimney to convince a "selfish" childless couple to procreate ("If you don't have any children, who will the other children play with?"); the tale of a man (Thompson) devastated by news of his own kidnapping (he reads about it in the newspaper); an axe murderer (Foley) holds a pleasant conversation with a knife sharpener.

Some bits were merely dark: *Love and Sausages,* a short film about a repressed sausage-factory worker, for example, is cleverly filmed and devastatingly dismal. Unfortunately, the targets of the program's admirably cruel humour were often easy game: social rejects, nebbishes, and the mentally challenged.

The kick-ass twangy guitar intro performed by Shadowy Men on a Shadowy Planet is obviously the best Canadian theme song ever. Come to think of it, it vies with themes from *The Munsters* and *The Prisoner* for coolest of all time. (The Shadowy Men appear in the opening segment in later seasons.)

Co-produced by Lorne Michaels. A slightly racier version of each episode appeared on HBO, though a move to CBS in the series' final season resulted in greater restrictions on language and subject matter.

In the program's final episode, the Kids, and their series, were buried in a mass grave. The series' title refers, apparently, to wannabe writers for *The Jack Benny Show,* who waited outside Benny's office to pitch him lines.

Just kidding: Trevor Evans as Kiddo the Clown checks the weather outside his dismal basement apartment.

Clown mail: Kiddo the Clown sent thousands of these postcards to eager kiddie viewers who wrote in.

The Kids of Degrassi Street

CBC
Children's
First Broadcast: Wednesday, September 12, 1979, 4:30 p.m.
Final Year Broadcast: 1986
Running Time: 30 min.

Cast:

Billy Martin.	Tyson Talbot
Benjamin Martin	Chris Charlesworth
Lisa Canard	Stacie Mistysyn
Noel Canard	Peter Duckworth-Pilkington II
Casey Rothfels	Sarah Charlesworth
Robin "Griff" Griffiths	Neil Hope
Duke Griffiths.	Dave James
Connie Jacobs.	Danah Jean Brown
Karen Gillis.	Anais Granofsky
Rachel Hewitt.	Arlene Lott
Pete Riley	John Ioannou
Chuck Riley.	Nick Goddard
Martin Schlegel	Jamie Summerfield
Leon Schlegel	Shane Toland
Squeeze.	Shawn Biso
Tina Sheldon	Lisa Barry
Irene.	Nancy Lam
Ida Lucas.	Zoe Newman
Fred Lucas	Allan Melusi
Catherine "Cookie" Peters	Dawn Harrison
Sophie Brendakis	Stacey Halberstadt
Dodie.	Heather Wall
Norman	Jason Lynn

The first series in the Degrassi Street dynasty began as the short film *Ida Makes a Movie* in 1979. The show looked at the world of elementary school children with a certain unabashed realism, avoiding the traps of presenting youngsters as too nice, too sweet, or too pretty. Typical episodes: the kids try to put together a school yearbook; Lisa and Griff form a shaky dating relationship; Rachel and Billy oppose each other in a school election; and a local gang, the Pirates, try to muscle in on Degrassi territory.

Though only 26 episodes were produced, the series achieved widespread popularity, especially in the U.S. on the Disney Channel. The series' final episode, "Griff Gets a Hand," won an International Emmy. Followed by *Degrassi Junior High*, which featured many of the same actors in new roles.

The critics cheer: "…the art behind *The Kids of Degrassi Street* is to make you think you're eavesdropping on actual people…." — Jim Bawden, *The Toronto Star*

The King Kong Show

ABC
Animated
First Broadcast: Saturday, September 10, 1966, 10:00 a.m.
Final Year Broadcast: 1969
Running Time: 30 min.

Voices of:

Bobby Bond	Billie Mae Richards
Susan Bond.	Susan Conway
Professor Bond/Tom	Carl Banas

Other Voices: John Drainie, Alfie Scopp, Paul Soles

A U.S. cartoon featuring a Canadian cast. Bobby Bond befriended a toned-down version of the towering simian on Mondo Island, and occasionally battled the villainous Dr. Who. Spawned an awful live-action film, *King Kong Escapes*. Included a second feature, *Tom of T.H.U.M.B.* (Tiny Humans Underground Military Bureau) about a miniature secret agent and his Asian sidekick Swinging Jack who fought against the villainous M.A.D. (Maladjusted, Anti-social, Darn Mean).

King Of Kensington

CBC
Situation Comedy
First Broadcast: Thursday, September 25, 1975, 9:00 p.m.
Final Year Broadcast: 1980
Running Time: 30 min.

Cast:

Larry King	Al Waxman
Cathy King.	Fiona Reid (1975–78)
Gladys King	Helene Winston
Tony "the Duke of Milan" Zarro	Bob Vinci (1975–78)
Nestor "the Jester" Best	Ardon Bess (1975–78)
Max Harris	John J. Dee (1978–80)
Tina Olsen.	Rosemary Radcliffe (1978–80)
Jack Soble	Peter Boretski (1978–80)
Gwen Twining	Jayne Eastwood (1979–80)
Ron Bacon.	Robert Haley (1979–80)
Dorothy	Linda Rennhofer (1979–80)

An antimatter Archie Bunker—meddlesome blimp Larry King owned a seedy variety store in Toronto's Kensington Market.

From Polish-Jewish stock (his ancestral name is Kinitsky), Larry lived above the store with his ex-suburbanite WASP-y wife, Cathy, and his mother, Gladys.

King gambled and kibbitzed with regulars

Max the variety store assistant; Tony "the Duke of Milan" Zarro, a cab driver; and mailman Nestor "the Jester" Best, in "the Club," a basement room between Manny's Strictly Kosher Butcher's and Da Silva's Portuguese Fish Market.

When Reid left in 1978 (King was *so* helpful that Cathy couldn't stand him anymore), the show changed format to target a younger audience, dropping Tony, Nestor, and Max in the process and adding girlfriend Tina. King became athletic director of the Kensington Community Centre and married Tina in 1979, leaving his variety store to the management of Gladys and boyfriend, Jack Soble, pharmacist at Soble's Drug Mart.

New characters from the Centre included: manager Gwen Twining; maintenance man Ron Bacon; and dance instructor Dorothy. In the final episode, King sells the store, Tina agrees to marry him, and Jack and Gladys move to Florida. A rumoured Jack and Gladys spinoff never materialized.

So popular that it held its own against big-time competition like *The Six Million Dollar Man*, though a brief U.S. syndication effort didn't generate much heat. Deliberate "contemporary" references to Canadian news items and politics have transformed the series into a weird time capsule. Waxman, who claimed he *lost* 40 pounds to play the overweight King, grew up in the Kensington area. A 1974 pilot featured Paul Hecht and Sandra O'Neill.

The critics cheer: "...Al Waxman and Fiona Reid are becoming more compatible, interesting and likeable every week." — Sid Adilman, *The Toronto Star*

The critics jeer: "...a genuine, solid-state, radio-passive, 25-megagroan bomb." — Douglas Marshall, *TV Guide*

The King Whyte Show

CBC
Sports
First Broadcast: Saturday, October 29, 1955, 10:45 p.m.
Final Year Broadcast: 1962
Running Time: 15 min.

Host: King Whyte

Toronto Star columnist, radio commentator, hunter, and fisher Whyte presented films and interviews on outdoor sports, hunting, fishing, and boating.

CBC

Klahanie

CBC
Nature
First Broadcast: Thursday, March 2, 1967, 6:00 p.m.
Final Year Broadcast: 1978
Running Time: 30 min.

Hosts: Bob Fortune (1967–72), Don White (1972–78)

Klahanie is a Chinook word meaning "the great outdoors," the subject of this long-running wilderness program produced in Vancouver.

Krazy House

CBC
Comedy
First Broadcast: Wednesday, January 12, 1977, 10:30 p.m.
Final Year Broadcast: 1977
Running Time: 30 min.

A mishmash of on-off comedy pilots. The series was most notable for bringing radio's *Dr. Bundolo's Pandemonium Medicine Show* to TV with radio regulars Norman Grohman, Bill Reiter, and Bill Buck assisted by Nancy Dolman, Barbara Barsky, Susan Wright, and Ross Petty portraying Vic Vaseline, Latoque, the Lone Deranger and his faithful companion, Toronto.

Other pilots featured Billy Van, Dave Broadfoot, Vanda King, Bonnie Brooks, Luba Goy, Harvey Atkin, and Charles Kirby.

Last of The Mohicans

CBC
Drama
First Broadcast: Friday, September 27, 1957, 8:00 p.m.
Final Year Broadcast: 1958
Running Time: 30 min.

Cast:
Nat "Hawkeye" Cutler...................... John Hart
Chingachgook .... Lon Chaney, Jr.
Calhoun Brent .... Ben Lennick
Others: George Barnes, Beryl Braithwaite, Lloyd Chester, Don
Cullen, Larry Mann, Joan Root, Powys Thomas, Hugh Watson

Hart, a former *Lone Ranger* on U.S. television, was imported as Hawkeye, along with famous wolfman Lon Chaney, Jr. as his aging (and unconvincing) "Indian sidekick." Loosely based on the James Fenimore Cooper novel set in 1757 during the colonial wars between the French-Indian alliance and the English.

Perhaps politically problematic for historically savvy Canadian kids encouraged to root for early American Hawkeye, whose kind kicked British colonial butt a mere decade later.

Not a bad little drama of its sort, though, and the tom-tom theme music was catchy. Syndicated worldwide. Also known as *Hawkeye* and *Hawkeye and the Last of the Mohicans*.

The Late Show
See: *The Billy O'Connor Show*

Learning the Ropes

CTV
Situation Comedy
First Broadcast: 1988
Final Year Broadcast: 1988
Running Time: 30 min.

Cast:
Robert Randall .... Lyle Alzado
Mark Randall .... Yannick Bisson
Ellen Randall...................... Nicole Stoffman
Carol Dixon...................... Cheryl Wilson
Bertie Baxter........................ Grant Cowan
Principal Whitcomb Mallory .... Richard Farrell
Beth........................... Jacqueline Mahon
Cheetah......................... Jefferson Mappin

The wafer-thin premise of this wretched presentation: the vice-principal of a co-ed private school can't make ends meet, so he takes an evening job wrestling as the Masked Maniac. To avoid embarrassment, Pop has to keep girlfriend Carol and his two kids in the dark. Produced with the blessings of the National Wrestling Alliance.

The critics jeer: "If Alzado's timing as a defensive end for the Denver Broncos…had been as bad as his delivery on this show, he would have ended up playing touch football."
— *TV Guide*

Leo And Me

CBC
Situation Comedy
First Broadcast: Friday, May 29, 1981, 2:30 p.m.
Final Year Broadcast: 1981
Running Time: 30 min.

Cast:
Leo................................ Brent Carver
Jamie .... Mike Fox
Leo's sister .... Shirley Milliner
Leo's sister's husband.................. Mina E. Mina
Others: Guy Bannerman, Colin Vint, Simon Webb

This short-lived sitcom sat on the shelves for a couple of years before receiving this bottom-of-the-barrel afternoon berth. The adventures of troublemaking Leo and his smarter, younger, nephew Jamie, who lived in a boat off the coast of Vancouver. Notable for early appearances of Brent Carver and Mike Fox (a.k.a. Michael J. Fox).

The Leslie Bell Singers

See: *The CGE Show*

Let's Call the Whole Thing Orff

CBC
Comedy
First Broadcast: Saturday, September 18, 1971, 7:00 p.m.
Final Year Broadcast: 1972
Running Time: 30 min.

Regular Performers: Barrie Baldaro, Andrée Boucher,
    Yvon Ducharme, Wally Martin, Terrence G. Ross
Music: France Castel, Peggy Mahon

Subtitled *An Arawak Named Urn* (something to do with a link between ancient Egyptian and South American civilizations), this fast-paced sketch comedy series milked Canada's biculturalism with one-liners and black-outs. The bastard son of a long line of failed efforts (*Comedy Café, Comedy Crackers, Zut!*) to produce a program popular enough to suit two distinct cultures (let alone one). The show's title was credited to a *Toronto Telegram* TV critic who used the phrase.

Let's Go

CBC
Musical Variety
First Broadcast: Monday, October 2, 1967, 5:30 p.m.
Final Year Broadcast: 1968
Running Time: 30 min.

The ghost of *Music Hop,* this low-budget series took the name of its predecessor's Vancouver segment. Programs had local hosts and originated from different cities each day:
Monday: Halifax, with host Frank Cameron, featuring Anne Murray and Doug Billard.
Tuesday: Montreal, with host Robert Demontigny.
Wednesday: Toronto, with Diane Miller, formerly of the Girlfriends, sax player Don "D.T." Thompson, Jay Jackson and the Majestics, the 5D, the Out Crowd, and Norman Amadio and the New Sounds band.
Thursday: Winnipeg, with host Chad Allan.
Friday: Vancouver, with host Mike Campbell, followed by Tom Northcott, introducing acts including Patty Surbey, Joani Taylor, and Ed Whiting.

— *With notes from Blaine Allan*

CBC

Let's Go to the Museum

CBC
Children's
First Broadcast: Tuesday, October 5, 1954, 5:00 p.m.
Final Year Broadcast: 1956
Running Time: 30 min.

Host: Robert MacNeil

Programs produced in the National Museum in Ottawa. The same MacNeil of PBS's *The MacNeil-Lehrer Report.*

Let's Make a Deal

Syndicated: 1980
Game Show
Running Time: 30 min.

Host: Monty Hall

Let's Make a Deal returned from a two-year hiatus from U.S. television. This time the program, in which costumed contestants traded cash and consumer goods for hidden prizes, came from Vancouver. Conspicuously absent: copious quantities of American greenbacks, replaced—probably due to some obscure Canadian content ruling—by "Monty Money," featuring the host's smiling visage.

Let's Make Music

CBC
Children's
First Broadcast: Tuesday, September 27, 1953, 5:00 p.m.
Final Year Broadcast: 1954
Running Time: 30 min.

Host: David Ouchterlony

In Canada's first music show for kids, Ouchterlony demonstrated musical instruments from around the world and taught music appreciation. A slightly retooled version of the program was entitled *Mr. O*, presumably to spare young viewers from having to strain their tiny tonsils on "Ouchterlony."

Let's See

CBC
Information
First Broadcast: Monday, September 6, 1952, 7:15 p.m.
Final Year Broadcast: 1954
Running Time: 15 min.

Host: Percy Saltzman
Voices of:
Uncle Chichimus/Holly Hock . . . . John Conway
Puppeteer: John Conway
Regular Performer: Larry Mann

Back in the early days of television, Canadian viewers were imprinted with this program, which appeared first thing each day, seven days a week. Designed to alert viewers to the programs they'd see that night, it featured weatherman Percy Saltzman, while puppets Uncle Chichimus and Holly Hock provided comedy. Saltzman concluded each forecast with his special signature—catching a piece of chalk thrown in the air—while viewers waited breathlessly for the occasional fumble. Chich

sassed Saltzman during forecasts and interfered with production (he sold Saltzman's anemometer for 25 cents). Chich also created special features, including a production in which he played Romeo to a Juliet played by a dog named Skunky. Raspy, nasal-voiced, pot-bellied Chich was created for puppeteer John Conway's touring show, *Dragon Ho!* A green face and frock coat went unappreciated by viewers who saw him in black and white. Chich was assisted by yellow-faced Holly Hock, his niece and housekeeper, an aspiring actress who was described by Hugh Garner as sporting "the hatchet-shaped visage of a retired private secretary and a horsetail hairdo made from a string mop." A sassy boy puppet named Pompey aggravated Chich.

Chich made front-page headlines in 1954, when Conway's puppets were "kidnapped" from his unlocked car. Mann, who supplied regular comedy bits, stalled for time as new puppets were manufactured, investigating the crime until he was "gunned down" before revealing the culprit—who was never caught.

Ultimately, Conway called the show quits for a self-imposed sabbatical, though Chich and company continued long after *Let's See* bit the dust, as host of numerous kid shows (variously known as *The Adventures of Chich, Uncle Chichimus,* and *Uncle Chichimus Tells a Story*) and guest on *Front Page Challenge.*

Though lovingly remembered by those who experienced those heady days of pioneer television, this early exercise in program filler may leave contemporary viewers scratching their heads.

Let's Sing Out

CBC/CTV
Musical Variety
First Broadcast: Friday, October 11, 1963, 9:30 p.m.
Final Year Broadcast: 1967
Running Time: 30 min.

Host: Oscar Brand

This folk-song fest was a northern *Hootenanny*, though its producers considered the U.S. program cheap vaudeville. Concerts were recorded at Canadian university campuses and featured performances by guests including Gale Garnett and the Tarriers, David Campbell, Eric Andersen, and Brand himself (who graced vinyl with such memorable fare as "Blinded by Turds"). The program jumped from CTV to CBC in 1966. Seen in England, Scotland, Australia, and New Zealand.

Puppet people:
Uncle Chichimus (left) and niece Holly Hock (right) used voices provided by puppeteer John Conway to harass weatherman Percy Saltzman on *Let's See.*

CBC

Lexx

Syndicated: 1997
Science Fiction
Running Time: 60 min.

Cast:

Stanley Tweedle	Brian Downey
Xev	Xenia Seeberg
Kai	Michael McManus
Zev	Eva Habermann
790	Jeff Hirschfield

Voice of:

The Lexx	Tom Gallant

Science fiction that masquerades as postmodernism by being a little vague about itself (where? when? why?).

A cowardly security guard (Tweedle) teams up with an intergalactic sex slave (Zev), a lustful robot's head (790: he just wants to live inside Zev's pants), and an ancient assassin (Kai) who happens to be dead. Together they steal a talking, insect-shaped spacecraft/superweapon known as the Lexx, then hightail it from the dark dominion of galactic dictator, His Divine Shadow, to zoom around an alternate universe, The Dark Zone, getting into trouble and destroying things—like entire planets, even.

Dubbed *Lust in Space* by detractors, the show features campy comedy, some overt sexuality, and more than moderate violence.

Some special effects are well done, and the series doesn't shy away from pushing the computer graphics envelope—if the script describes it, they'll show it.

The program first appeared as a series of four TV movies (*The Dark Zone Stories*), then graduated to a regular hour-long series in 1998. Xev replaced Zev (same pronunciation) a few episodes into the regular TV series.

This Canadian-German co-production, seen in over a hundred countries, proved that Americans will watch a series featuring Canadian actors.

Possible cult fodder here.

The critics jeer: "Violent and gory, there are also so many gross scenes of human vivisection, decapitation, severed limbs, etc. that you begin to wonder if this isn't entertainment for people who pull the wings off bugs. . .I only fear that I'm making it sound better than it is. " — Claire Bickley, *Toronto Sun*

Salter Street Films

The Lexx files: Canadian cult sci-fi, delivered by (from left to right) Xenia Seeberg, Brian Downey, Jeff Hirschfield (the voice of computerized head 790), and Michael McManus.

Liberty Street

CBC
Drama
First Broadcast: Wednesday, January 11, 1995, 8:30 p.m.
Final Year Broadcast: 1996
Running Time: 30 min.

Cast:

Frank Pagnozzi	Pat Mastroianni
Drive Home Dave	Reiner Schwarz
Mack Fischer	Joel Bissonnette
Christine	Melissa Daniel
Janet Beecher	Kimberly Huie
Annie Hamer	Henriette Ivanans
Stuart	Dean Paras
Teena Siracus	Jhene Erwin
Nathan Jones	Billy Merasty
Marsha Velasquez	Marcia Laskowski
Lucille Trudeau	Katherine Ashby
Ernie Kravitz	Richard Zappieri
Wade Malone	L. Dean Ifill
Cynthia	Nahanni Johnstone (1995–96)
James	Keith Knight (1995–96)
Ben	Hamis McEwan (1995–96)
Lionel	Jim Codrington (1995–96)

Meet the hip folks who live on Liberty Street. The coy, over-produced opening sequence featured a flower pot falling in slow-mo past the cooler-than-thou cast of characters.

A series so earnest it hurt, with a brace of politically correct tenants crammed into a prime time civics class majoring in New Age etiquette. Pagnozzi was a wannabe musician and superintendent of a warehouse converted into apartments (The Pit); Teena was his clingy girlfriend, Dave was his radio-host uncle. Other denizens of the Pit: ex-drug addict Fischer; idealistic Annie; Janet, a single mom from the Maritimes; and Nathan, a gay Cree. Lucille and Ernie ran The Wreck Room, a retro diner. Theme music by the Cowboy Junkies. Based on a 1994 TV movie, *X-Rated* (Generation-X, that is).

The Little Revue

CBC
Musical Variety
First Broadcast: Monday, May 25, 1953, 9:30 p.m.
Final Year Broadcast: 1953
Running Time: 30 min.

Host: Monty Hall

The flip side of *The Big Revue* featured guest singers and dancer Alan Lund. Another early appearance by game-show favourite Monty Hall.

The Littlest Hobo

CTV
Children's
First Broadcast: Tuesday, September 24, 1963, 7:00 p.m.
Final Year Broadcast: 1985
Running Time: 30 min.

Cast:
Hobo . . . . London

*"You know I hunger to be free,
Roamin's the only life for me."*

— From *The Littlest Hobo* theme song

Chuck Eisenmann

Canine crusader: The Littlest Hobo, a nosy German shepherd, travelled the world looking for problems to solve.

Based on a 1958 U.S. film of the same name, this series featured the adventures of a roving German shepherd who stayed in one place just long enough to help a troubled-human-of-the-week. Featured a great theme song and moody black-and-white location photography. Most guests were U.S. actors, including Keenan Wynn, Pat Harrington, Jr., and *Laugh-In*'s Henry Gibson. An appearance by ventriloquist Edgar Bergen and puppet Charlie McCarthy was one of several failed attempts to create series spinoffs.

Publicity promised anything from "Hitchcock suspense to Lucy-type humor," and claimed that London's four stand-ins could understand a combined total of 4,700 words and three languages. Some of Hobo's more outlandish antics included taking the witness stand in a court case and uncovering a plot to train a look-alike shepherd as an international assassin. Production was briefly suspended during a lawsuit over who owned the "London" trademark.

The first show ran until 1966 and was revived by CTV in 1979, this time in colour. A two-dimensional effort (both in its unoriginal storylines and flat-looking shot-on-video photography), the new series was more popular than the original, running until 1985 and seen internationally. Although one of the dogs playing the lead in the new series was named London, most of the on-screen time went to a dog named Bo.

The critics cheer: "…far superior to run-of-the-kennel dog shows on TV." — John Ruddy, *Toronto Telegram*

The critics jeer: "Hobo is a German shepherd…pawing around the country bailing out human beings who get into trouble. Whoever thought up this too-cute title could use his services." — Pierre Maple, *TV Guide*

Live a Borrowed Life

CBC
Game Show
First Broadcast: Wednesday, July 1, 1959, 8:30 p.m.
Final Year Broadcast: 1962
Running Time: 30 min.

Host: Charles Templeton
Announcer: Bill Walker
Panelists: Anna Cameron (1959–60), Bill Walker, Elwy Yost

In this TV adaptation of a radio program, three panelists and a guest played Twenty Questions to uncover the identity of three mystery characters, represented by guest contestants. Guests earned money for each minute they stalled the panel, but, in a cruel twist of fate, lost the cash winnings in a second segment if they failed to answer panelists' questions about their own mystery identities. Panelists were criticized as stiff know-nothings who pulled their questions and answers from prepared scripts.

Producer Jim Guthro was suspended for two weeks after booking contestant George Rolland, a white supremacist, who portrayed Abraham Lincoln as a flaming racist. The concept, though not the program, was sold to British television. Written by Bernard Slade.

The critics jeer: "*Live a Borrowed Life* wasn't even good enough for radio and turned up a fat ZERO in my own book ...the format (everybody's dead) can't ever promise anything first rate...a bush league *Front Page Challenge*...the only movement is Elwy Yost's eyebrows...." — Bill Drylie, *The Toronto Star*

Live it Up!

CTV
Consumer Affairs
First Broadcast: Thursday, September 21, 1978, 9:00 p.m.
Final Year Broadcast: 1990
Running Time: 30 min.

Hosts: Dianne Buckner, Ron Carlyle, Alan Edmonds, Mary Lou Finlay, Liz Grogan, Jack McGaw, Jonathan Rudin, Sharon Seto, Tracie Tighe

A brash, fast-paced consumer program featuring happy hosts investigating the important issues surrounding herbal remedies, circumcision, disposable lighters, and the health benefits of kosher chicken soup. Lawyer Rudin was the program's Legal Beagle, checking the legal aspects of consumer questions. Ron Carlyle was The Watchdog, who sniffed out upcoming consumer issues.

Edmonds and McGaw remained with the series for most of its run.

Lonesome Dove: The Series

CTV
Western
First Broadcast: Saturday, October 15, 1994, 9:00 p.m.
Final Year Broadcast: 1996
Running Time: 60 min.

Cast:

Newt Call	Scott Bairstow
Colonel Francis Clay Mosby	Eric McCormack
Kelly Rowan	Mattie Shaw
Austin Peale	Paul Johansson
Amanda	Tracy Scoggins
Josiah Peale	Paul LeMat
Un-Bob	Frank C. Turner
Hannah Peale Call	Christianne Hirt
Ida Grayson	Diahann Carroll
Sheriff Owen Kearney	Denny Miller

A western series based on Larry McMurtry's novel *Lonesome Dove* and two previous miniseries which had run on CBS. Adventures were set in the town of Curtis Wells in the Dakota Territory (though shot in Alberta) of the 1870s. The stories were the recollections of now-elderly Newt. Hannah was Newt's wife; Mosby was a former Confederate soldier who also loved her. The show switched gears in its second season with the death of Hannah.

Changing its name to *Lonesome Dove: The Outlaw Years*, and pushing the series two years into the future, Newt was now a dark-hearted bounty hunter, crossing swords with Mosby, whose nasty influence now dominated the good citizens of Curtis Wells.

McCormack went on to greater fame in his popular NBC sit-com *Will & Grace*.

Long Shot

CBC
Variety
First Broadcast: Sunday, June 28, 1959, 10:30 p.m.
Final Year Broadcast: 1959
Running Time: 30 min.

A weird, amorphous concoction featuring music, sketch comedy, guest hosts such as wooden hockey broadcaster Ward Cornell and cellist Olga Kwasniak, and a cast of semi-regulars (Don Francks, Larry Solway, Peter Whittall).

An eclectic guest roster included Bob and Ray, Jonathan Winters, Stan Freberg, Elaine May and Mike Nichols, Shari Lewis and Lambchop, and Boxcar Betty. One episode featured five wrestlers (Lord Athol Layton and Gene Kiniski among them) discussing the problems of mid-20th century humanity. More than just a few decades ahead of its time.

Love Handles

Global
Game Show
First Broadcast: Monday, April 29, 1996, 11:30 a.m.
Final Year Broadcast: 1998
Running Time: 30 min

Host: Stu Jeffries

In a thinly disguised *Newlywed Game,* couples answered questions about their relationships. Some viewers complained about programs in which contestants appeared to be gay. The elusive grand prize was a $100,000 bond. Winners received trips and the like, while losers went home with a sack of sausages.

Luncheon Date

CBC
Interview
First Broadcast: Monday, October 14, 1963, 12:00 p.m.
Final Year Broadcast: 1975
Running Time: 30 min., 60 min., and 90 min.

Host: Elwood Glover

A "soft" interviewer, Glover schmoozed with—but never ruffled—guests, who often had something to plug. Broadcast from Toronto's Four Seasons Hotel, parts of the program were seen only in Toronto. Expanding to an hour in 1965, the show was split in two, sandwiching an hour of soap operas. In 1970, the show expanded to 90 minutes, added a musical trio headed by Sonny Caulfield, and introduced Merle Shain, Bernadette Andrews, Henry Morgan, and Al Boliska in a Friday satirical news segment. In November 1971, the show returned to 60 minutes and Bruce Marsh often filled in for Glover.

The Ontario Liquor Licensing Board killed the show's ambience in 1975 by banning minors from the set and prohibiting audiences, who were dining at the hotel, from consuming alcohol on air.

One of Glover's most popular broadcasts was the on-air marriage of Stompin' Tom Connors and Lena Walsh on November 2, 1973.

Glover resigned in 1975 because of a hearing problem. In a letter to *The Globe and Mail,* he wrote: "As for the book-plugging, self-plugging guests, we had the best. The TV-watching public loves the faces of the famous and we showed them with dignity and class."

The critics cheer: "...the CBC can't be all bad...because it has Elwood Glover." — Bill Drylie, *Toronto Telegram*

The critics jeer: "Puffery is inevitable on this kind of show...there is no law, however, that says [guests] have to be smothered in melted butter, as Elwood does...." — Blaik Kirby, *The Globe and Mail*

"A series of little commercials for books and movies.... It should not be broadcast to the rest of the country." — Heather Robertson, *Maclean's*

Lunchtime Little Theatre
See: *Jellybean Comedy Clubhouse*

Canadian TV Sports

Sports on Canadian television is as old as the medium itself. The two longest-running network shows on Canadian TV both began in 1952: *Hockey Night in Canada* and *CFL Football*. The latter, despite the vagaries that have escorted it with regularity to death's door, including ratings that sometimes sank lower than the *Edmund Fitzgerald*, has always managed to survive in one form or another. Once it was a titan, a TV staple, and the Grey Cup was perhaps the country's most popular event, even outside sports. In later years, though, the CFL broadcast has been a bit of an orphan, variously adopted by CTV/Baton and The Sports Network (TSN). It even had a brief, fruitless flirtation with U.S. television, and with U.S. expansion.

Televised NHL hockey, on the other hand, seems invincible, even as teams endure a slow death in some Canadian cities. Despite expansion, dilution in the quality of play, growing Americanization of both team and theme, and the loss of franchises, hockey's position as sporting king of Canadian TV seems unassailable. There's a reason CBC routinely postpones news during Stanley Cup season: it's called ratings. Even when ratings flatten, as they have done during the Maple Leafs' long somnolence, about 900,000 viewers still tune in; as for TSN, virtually any playoff game will pull in 200,000–300,000 viewers.

From the day the Montreal Expos opened against the New York Mets on April 8, 1969 (the Expos won 11-10), baseball has found a fairly regular home on the Canadian tube. For eight years, the Expos were Canada's TV team, often ragtag, but usually entertaining. That changed in 1977 when the Toronto Blue Jays entered the scene. The first televised Jays game: April 7, 1977, at a cold and snowy Exhibition Stadium in Toronto. Score: Blue Jays 9, Chicago White Sox 5. The Jays replaced the Expos in many Canadian hearts. Part of the rise was attributable to the growth of the cable sporting giant TSN, a Toronto-based outfit that began broadcasting in 1984 and has televised many more Blue Jays than Expos games. By the 1990s, Expo fans found fewer than 30 games a year on the box, while Jays supporters had at least 125. Visibility has a powerful way of creating, and maintaining, loyalties.

Curling is arguably *the* Canadian game. Despite the hordes of people who find it as dull as a federal leadership convention, televised curling—at least the annual Labatt Brier for men and the Scott Tournament of Hearts for women—draws hundreds of thousands of loyal viewers. Curling was first televised in the 1950s and has been a TV staple ever since.

Canada's love affair with the televised Olympics shows no sign of abating. CBC generally devotes hundreds of hours to the Summer Olympics. And it's universally acknowledged (outside New York and Los Angeles) that Canadian Olympic coverage is fairer, broader, and less jingoistic than that of U.S. networks.

The Winter Olympics are a bit different. Since there are fewer sports than in the Summer Olympics, the amount of time CBC devotes here is questionable. Huge blocks of air time are filled with peripheral interviews, repetitive looks at the host city, and interminable "humorous" fillers as we wait for the events.

The Olympics have also generated spinoff sports broadcasts that regularly garner high ratings. For example, many viewers just can't get enough figure skating. In 1998, for instance, CTV devoted 19 hours to covering the world championships in Minneapolis, Minnesota. After the 1976 Montreal Olympics, where Romanian athlete Nadia Comenici made such a showing, gymnastics ascended to enormous television popularity.

After years of contenting ourselves with National Basketball Association coverage on U.S. networks, we finally had two Canadian (if not made in Canada) basketball teams, the Vancouver Grizzlies and the Toronto Raptors, who won their TV debuts in 1995. Pro roundball is having a tough time, though, establishing itself as a TV sport. Low ratings for NBA games show that the game's appeal to Canadians is still limited.

As for college basketball—sheesh! Canadians are quite keen on the U.S. college telethon known as March Madness, the annual 64-team, three-weekend quest for the right to shriek "We're number 1!" while leaning from dormitory windows. But we're...let's say, indifferent, to the Canadian version. —*Martin Levin*

The Mad Dash

Syndicated: 1979
Game Show
Running Time: 30 min

Host: Pierre Lalonde
Announcer: Nick Hollinrake

Humans were reduced to the level of pawns on a giant game board in this long-running show. Teams of two would roll dice and answer questions to add meagre prizes ($10 to $50, or small merchandise items) to their collective kitties. Some board spaces netted advantages (Roll Forward), while others delivered penalties (Go Broke, Roll Backward.) Another space forced players to switch places. Contestants had to land on the "Win" space by an exact number of moves—or invoke the show's title by landing on the "Breakaway" space, throwing a die and dashing across the board surface for one to five seconds (no sixes—one face of the die netted a $10 prize.) Seven wins netted lucky contestants the grand prize. Polish viewers enjoyed *Duety Do Mety,* an adapted version of the game.

Made in Canada

CBC
Satire
First Broadcast: Monday, October 5, 1998, 8:30 p.m.
Final Year Broadcast: —
Running Time: 30 min.

Cast:

Richard Strong	Rick Mercer
Veronica Miller	Leah Pinsent
Alan Roy	Peter Keleghan
Victor Sela	Dan Lett
Raymond Drodge	Ron James
Lisa Sutton	Janet Kidder
Siobahn Roy	Emily Hampshire
Michael Rushton/Parson Hubbard/Damocles	Alex Carter
Captain McGee	Maury Chaykin
Wanda	Jackie Torrens
Walter Franklin	Gordon Pinsent

Television often bites the hand that feeds it (albeit feebly). This satirical look at program production features Richard Strong, boy script-reader, who connives his way to the top of Pyramid Productions, producer of low-budget TV shows, including *Sword of Damocles* and *Beaver Creek.* Recurring characters include: company execs Alan (the boss), Veronica, and Lisa (she's axed in season two); Siobahn, Alan's daughter; butt-kisser Victor; and Raymond, Richard's nice-guy brother-in-law. Captain McGee is a lecherous kiddie show actor; Alex Carter plays *Sword of Damocles'* beef-witted star and doubles as militant homosexual Hubbard. Features walk-on bits by real-life entertainment figures (Peter Gzowski, Evan Solomon, Sarah Polley, Moses Znaimer) and some parallels to real-life industry blather, but treads lightly on the toes of its originating network ("I'm not a fool," says Mercer). Mercer produced this show as a side-project to his other CBC series, *This Hour Has 22 Minutes.* Seen in the U.S. as *The Industry,* the show's original title.

Salter Street Films

Madison

Global
Drama
First Broadcast: Tuesday, September 21, 1993, 8:00 p.m.
Final Year Broadcast: 1998
Running Time: 30 min.

Cast:

Rachael	Joely Collins
Tom	Chad Willett
Penny	Michelle Beaudoin
Tia	Stacy Grant
R.J.	Jonathan Scarfe
Jamie	Chris Martin
Derek	William Sasso
Carol	Sarah Strange
Kevin	Peter Stebbings
Sherry	Enuka Okuma

Looking at the lives and loves of the kids at Madison High, this popular series aimed at teens was bounced around the dial and TV schedule. Filmed in Vancouver, the show was vague about its Canadian setting. The final two years of the program followed the kids beyond high school.

Magee and Company

TVO
Comedy/Public Affairs
First Broadcast: Monday, September 20, 1976, 6:45 p.m
Final Year Broadcast: 1978
Running Time: 15 min.

Regular Performer: Michael Magee

This biting weekday satire featured Michael Magee as a dozen characters, each with his own spin on daily events and issues, to give viewers some ideas about how news is created and manipulated. The program's other aim: to help Canadians develop their sorry sense of humour. The program was funny and outrageous. The cast of characters included:

Constable George Blow: a veteran police officer.

Fred C. Dobbs: Magee's oldest character, on radio since 1956. A cranky curmudgeon, Dobbs had solutions for everything wrong with Canada.

Reginald Hardcastle: A lawyer and a spokesman for a hemorrhoid product, available in a tube or "new, handy spray." Inevitably, Reg's hemorrhoids acted up during interviews, as he'd gently rise out of camera frame to deal with his discomfort.

Gaston de B. Hatfield: A gay drama critic who had trouble keeping food, particularly eggs, out of his shaggy red beard.

Harst Holman: Beer company spokesman and Montreal Olympics supporter who once filmed a promotional Olympic spot while using an outhouse.

Jay Carter Hughs: Chief Executive Officer of Dominion Gas and Screw, Hughs had twice run unsuccessfully for Parliament as a Tory.

The Ombuddysboy: A pint-size version of CBC's *Ombudsman*, Robert Cooper, who sat on his desk, feet swinging aimlessly, while agreeing whinily with everything ("Yes-s-s-s-s! Yes-s-s-s-s-s!").

The Pastor: Armed with dark glasses and a glass of carrot juice, this televangelist was head of the Church of the Winnebago.

Mario Sartorio: Ex-BBC producer, writer, director, and performer, he originated the "one camera, one chair on a riser" style of programming so popular in Canada.

Baunston Tudball: A one-time private-school master, an ex-sergeant major, and a contender in the international Stationary Bicycle Competition. His philosophy: "squeeze and release."

The best segment was *Reach For the Bottom*, a game show in which Magee played all eight contestants and the host. Characters interacted with one another, trading insults from top to bottom, or arguing from side to side.

TVO, which Magee referred to disparagingly as TV Zero, took a chance on Magee and came up with a memorable winner.

TVO

Squeeze and release: was the simple philosophy of *Magee and Company*'s stationary bike champion Baunston Tudball (Michael Magee).

CBC

Maggie Muggins

CBC
Children's
First Broadcast: Thursday, September 29, 1955, 4:45 p.m.
Final Year Broadcast: 1962
Running Time: 15 min.

Cast:
Maggie Muggins . . . . Beth Morris (1955–56), Deanne Taylor
  (1956–59), Mary Long (1959–62)
Mr. McGarrity . . . . . . John Drainie (1955–56), Frank Peddie
  (1956–59), Doug Master (1959–62)
Voices of:
Fitzgerald Fieldmouse . . . . Norma Macmillan
Grandmother Frog . . . . Margo Christie
Other Voices: Alice Hill, Linda Keogh, Beth Lockerbie, Peggi
  Loder, Robin Paul, Pauline Rennie, Ruth Springford
Puppeteers: John Keogh, Linda Keogh

Based on the books and radio plays by
writer Mary Grannan about Maggie
Muggins, a freckle-faced redhead with pig-
tails.

Though she narrated on radio, Grannan
was uncomfortable with TV appearances, so
she gave her blessing to this dramatization
of her Maggie stories. The leisurely paced
show consisted of puppet adventures,
lessons in manners, and songs. Maggie
greeted neighbour McGarrity at the top of
each show, before escaping to a puppet fantasy world populated by the likes of

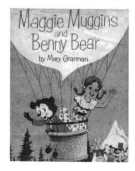

Fitzgerald Fieldmouse, Grandmother Frog,
Benny Bear, Big Bite Beaver, Chester Pig,
Fluffy Squirrel, Greta Grub, Henrietta Hen,
Leo Lion, and Reuben Rabbit. Typically, the
show was cancelled by the CBC while still
very popular.

The Magic Lie

CBC
Children's
First Broadcast: Wednesday, January 26, 1977, 4:30 p.m.
Final Year Broadcast: 1979
Running Time: 30 min

Host: W.O. Mitchell

These short films produced across the
country were based on short stories that
would appeal to children. Films included: *A
Horse For Running Buffalo* from a story by
Madeline Freeman; *Boy On Defence* by Scott
Young; *The Infinite Worlds of Maybe* by Lester
Del Rey; *A Bird in the House* by Margaret
Laurence; and *Emily of New Moon* from Lucy
Maud Montgomery's novel. Michael J. Fox
appeared in the futuristic tale *The Master* by
T.H. White. Mitchell appeared on-screen to
help young viewers find books in their local
libraries.

Magistrate's Court

CTV
Drama
First Broadcast: Monday, September, ?, 1963, various
Final Year Broadcast: 1972
Running Time: 30 min.

Cast:
Judge Jacques. . . . . Roy Jacques

*"Boom-boom-boom…A case of larceny…Boom-
boom-boom…"*

Each case on this *People's Court* precursor
was introduced by a solemn announcer and
sombre drum beat. Presiding over the case-
load, supposedly mined from actual court
files, was dimple-chinned judge Roy
Jacques, handing out judgments "to help
citizens become more familiar with the laws
of the land."

Actors were given case details and then
ad libbed for added realism. Stern Judge
Jacques tolerated no nonsense, demanding

respect and order from a cast of hippies, low-lifes, nasty old ladies, dishonest businessmen, and young punks.

Toronto Telegram reporter Pat Annesley appeared as a thief who pinched a traffic sign to impress her daughter. Judge Jacques intended to let her off with a $25 fine, until she answered the unrehearsed question: "What does your husband do?" "He's a lawyer...." she ad libbed. Judge Jacques exploded. "Do you mean to say that a member of the bar, a man who…" By tirade's end, the judge had bumped the fine to $100 and dispensed a warning never to darken his courtroom again. Nobody crossed Judge Jacques.

Make a Match

CBC
Game Show
First Broadcast: Saturday, November 6, 1954, 7:00 p.m.
Final Year Broadcast: 1955
Running Time: 30 min.

Seen every other week, this bizarre game show involved a panel of four people (a married couple and two singles) who questioned a mixed group of seven men and women in hopes of matching each to their real-life spouses. Fouling the waters were disguised "ringers" who weren't married to anybody.

— *With notes from Blaine Allan*

Man Alive

CBC
Public Affairs
First Broadcast: Sunday, October 1, 1967, 5:00 p.m.
Final Year Broadcast: —
Running Time: 30 min.

Hosts: Roy Bonisteel (1967–89), Peter Downie (1989–96), R.H. Thomson (1996–)

This series examines the issues surrounding human faith. The title for the series was derived from a quote by St. Irenaeus, Bishop of Lyons, who wrote, "The glory of God is man fully alive." Though mistaken as a church promotion (many viewers believed Bonisteel was a minister), the program rarely mentioned God. "But though He's not named, He's there, because if you approach programs with integrity and love

of God, and your fellow men, it shows," said Rev. Brian Freeland, CBC's assistant supervisor of religious broadcasts, about the show. Among the subjects covered: capital punishment, exorcism, and abortion. Interview subjects included: the Dalai Lama, Chief Dan George, Billy Graham, Germaine Greer, Dr. Stephen Hawking, Margaret Mead, Malcolm Muggeridge, Camille Paglia, Mother Teresa, and Elie Wiesel. The program occasionally featured dramas, among them plays about the battle between Oliver Cromwell and King Charles I, the assassination of Thomas Beckett and the Reformation of Martin Luther, with Bonisteel interviewing the characters. Bonisteel left the program in 1989, citing a CBC muzzling policy that prevented him from speaking out on public issues.

Man of the cloth?: Long-time *Man Alive* host Roy Bonisteel was so strongly associated with the religious series, viewers often mistook him for a minister.

The Man From Tomorrow

CBC
Children's
First Broadcast: Monday, July 7, 1958, 5:00 p.m.
Final Year Broadcast: 1958
Running Time: 15 min.

Cast:
Melpar .... Ted Greenhalgh
Nick .... Michael Morrow
Sam .... Stefan Gair

Melpar came from the future to take two "modern-day" boys on adventures, including a trip to Mars. Produced in Vancouver.

Maniac Mansion

YTV
Situation Comedy
First Broadcast: Monday, September 17, 1990, 78:30 p.m.
Final Year Broadcast: 1993
Running Time: 30 min.

Cast:

Fred Edison	Joe Flaherty
Casey Edison	Deborah Theaker
Tina Edison	Kathleen Robertson
Ike Edison	Avi Phillips
Turner Edison	George Buza
Idella Orkin	Mary Charlotte Wilcox
Harry Orkin	John Hemphill

Crazed inventor Fred tormented his loving family and the world at large with bizarre inventions. Casey was his wife; Ike, Tina, and Turner (yeah, yeah) were his kids. Fred had accidentally turned brother-in-law Harry into a fly with a human head (he seemed to prefer it), though it was even more unsettling to watch four-year-old Turner transformed into a hulking 40-year-old man. Wilcox's character, Harry's wife, was an *SCTV* refugee—essentially Melonville's own ladies' lounge manager Idela Voudry with a new last name.

Innovative and often funny, the series opened with its own tenth anniversary special. Other novel ventures: a "live" show, and spoofs of TV's *Twin Peaks* and the film *Misery.*

Named by *Time* as one of the ten best shows of 1990, the program's unwillingness to conform to traditional sitcom standards confused too many viewers. Talented Flaherty, too often overlooked, was at least given a starring role here.

Based, very loosely, on a George Lucas computer game. Theme song by Jane Siberry.

The critics cheer: "...a delightful comedy confection, with often sad emotional overtones, that challenges and energizes the intellect." — Greg Quill, *The Toronto Star*

The Manipulators

CBC
Drama
First Broadcast: Wednesday, January 28, 1970, 8:30 p.m.
Final Year Broadcast: 1971
Running Time: 30 min. and 60 min.

Cast:

Rick Nicholson	Marc Strange
Maggie Campbell	Roxanne Erwin
Maggie's son	Gregory Nash
Bill	Al Kozlik
Clem	Anthony Holland
Staff psychologist	Dorothy Davies

Filmed in Vancouver, this popular drama about parole officers and their charges is probably best remembered for a single scandalous scene featuring actress Linda Goranson, who removed her top on the tube, ostensibly to help her husband—a drug addict—pull himself together.

Probation officers Nicholson and Campbell worked with senior officers Bill and Clem and a staff psychologist to keep remorseful cons out of trouble. Guest stars included Margot Kidder and Chief Dan George. The pilot was called (more sensibly) *The Clients.* Strange went on to create *The Beachcombers.*

The critics cheer: "...tougher and truer than the best the Americans can offer." — Douglas Marshall, *Maclean's*

Mantrap

Syndicated: 1971
Discussion
Running Time: 30 min.

Host: Alan Hamel
Panelists: Selma Diamond, Margot Kidder, Phyllis Kirk, Sue Lyon, Meredith MacRae, Pamela Mason, Jaye P. Morgan, Stefanie Powers, Suzanne Sommers, Carol Wayne

Three semi-famous women, usually actresses, gang up on a sorta-famous guy who may have made a public statement that outrages them. Briefly cool, even in the U.S., where Dick Cavett made frequent reference to it. Male guests included Paul Lynde and Harlan Ellison. Opening graphics featured three chattering circles stomping on a triangle, followed by a sultry female voice-over: "Mannnn-trap!" Seen on CTV stations in Canada.

The critics cheer (sort of): "...employs the services of literate, witty and obviously intelligent women...here is a show that is genuinely fascinating, yet it seems to me an essentially unhealthy premise...gratuitously [widening] the artificial gap between men and women." — Harlan Ellison, *Los Angeles Free Press*

The Marion Clarke Show

CBC
Interview
First Broadcast: Monday, May 24, 1954, 10:40 p.m.
Final Year Broadcast: 1954
Running Time: 20 min.

Host: Marion Clarke

A three-day fiasco hosted by Clarke, winner of a *Chatelaine* beauty contest.

Marketplace

CBC
Consumer Affairs
First Broadcast: Thursday, October 5, 1972, 10:00 p.m.
Final Year Broadcast: —
Running Time: 30 min.

Hosts: George Finstad (1972–77), Joan Watson (1972–83), Harry Brown (1977–78), Bill Paul (1978–95), Christine Johnson (1983–87), Norma Kent (1987–91), Jacquie Perrin (1991–), Jim Nunn (1995–)
Theme song: "Marketplace," performed by Stompin' Tom Connors

The staff of *Marketplace* investigates product claims, frauds, misleading advertising, and other consumer issues. Entertaining and informative—but why'd they drop Stompin' Tom's great theme song? U.S. satirist Marshall Efron made early appearances on the show.

The critics jeer: "…snaffles on essentially trivial grievances like an overpriced macrame kit and belabors them with righteous indignation." — Heather Robertson, *Maclean's*

The Marvel Superheroes

Syndicated: 1966
Animated
Running Time: 30 min.

Captain America Cast:
Captain America/Bucky Barnes . . . Bernard Cowan, Paul Soles
Red Skull . . . . Paul Kligman
Incredible Hulk Cast:
Bruce Banner/Hulk/Rick Jones . . . Bernard Cowan, Paul Soles
Betty Ross . . . . Peg Dixon
General Ross . . . . Paul Kligman
Major Talbott. . . . . John Vernon

Iron Man Cast:
Tony Stark/Iron Man . . . . John Vernon
Virginia "Pepper" Potts . . . . Peg Dixon
Harold "Happy" Hogan/Mandarin. . . Bernard Cowan, Paul Soles
Sub-Mariner Cast:
Sub-Mariner (Prince Namor) . . . . John Vernon
Lady Dorman . . . . Peg Dixon
Lord Bashty . . . . Bernard Cowan, Paul Soles
Mighty Thor Cast:
Thor/Donald Blake . . . . ?
Jane Foster . . . . Peg Dixon

This Canadian production marked the entry of Marvel Comics characters into animation. Featured characters, each with his own theme song, included: Captain America ("When Captain America throws his mighty shield…"); the Incredible Hulk ("He's Bruce Banner, belted by gamma rays…"); Iron Man ("He's the coolest guy, with the hottest steel…"); Mighty Thor ("Across the Rainbow Bridge of Asgaard…"); and Sub-Mariner ("Namor, Namor, prince of the sea…"). Animation was so limited that some scenes consisted entirely of the camera panning across original comic art panels, or an oddly mobile arm twisting feebly on an otherwise still picture.

Material World

CBC
Comedy/Drama
First Broadcast: Monday, February 5, 1990, 7:30 p.m.
Final Year Broadcast: 1993
Running Time: 30 min.

Cast:
Kitty Reeves . . . . Laura Bruneau
Popsi Abrahams . . . . Jack Kruschen (1990–91)
Virginia . . . . Linda Sorenson
Bernice . . . . Jayne Eastwood (1990–92)
Yvonne . . . . Suzanne Coy
Tim Lyons . . . . Chris Potter
Angela. . . . . Angela Dohrmann (1991–93)
Martin Weinstock . . . . James Kee (1991–93)

Aspiring fashion designer Kitty tries to revive grandfather Popsi's ailing clothing business (he's the King of Polyester). "Zany" characters included: man-hungry mother Virginia; bookkeeper Bernice; model Yvonne; and nice-guy love interest Tim. The program ceased production after three episodes and returned with Kitty as the new head of debt-ridden Classy Fashions (Popsi retires to Florida, where he dies) to focus on serious issues like AIDS and serial rapists(!) Third season changes: new business partner Weinstock and neighbour Angela; Bernice departs; Kitty opens her own clothing store. Critics were hard on the program's frequent shifts in format, from comedy to drama to an uneasy mixture of both.

Matrix

CTV
Drama
First Broadcast: Saturday, October 30, 1993, 10:00 p.m.
Final Year Broadcast: 1994
Running Time: 60 min.

Cast:
Steven Matrix . . . . Nick Mancuso
Billy Hicks . . . . Phillip Jarrett
Liz . . . . Carrie-Anne Moss
Narrator: John Vernon

After a quick trip to Hell (known as The City In-Between), assassin Steven Matrix decided he'd better mend his ways and start helping people instead of blowing them away; messengers from Beyond told him what he had to do to redeem himself. Billy, a former partner-in-crime, decided to help; Liz was a love interest who managed Matrix's gym, the Silver Flex.

The critics cheer: "…morally reprehensible but nonetheless engaging…." — Greg Quill, *The Toronto Star*

Matt and Jenny

Global
Children's
First Broadcast: Sunday, October 21, 1979, 7:00 p.m.
Final Year Broadcast: 1980
Running Time: 30 min.

Cast:
Matt Tanner . . . . Derrick Jones
Jenny Tanner . . . . Megan Follows
Dr. Adam Cardston . . . . Neil Dainard
Kit . . . . Duncan Regehr

In 1850, Matt, Jenny and their mother leave Bristol, England, to find their Canadian uncle; mom dies en route. The search takes the orphaned kids from Halifax to Vancouver in 26 episodes, with Kit and the mysterious Dr. Cardston tagging along to keep them out of trouble. Seen in Holland, Germany, and a handful of other countries. Also known as *Matt and Jenny on the Wilderness Trail.*

Max Glick

CBC
Drama
First Broadcast: Monday, November 5, 1990, 9:00 p.m.
Final Year Broadcast: 1992
Running Time: 30 min.

Cast:
Maximilian Glick . . . . Josh Garbe
Sarah Glick . . . . Linda Kash
Henry Glick . . . . Alec Willows
Byrna Glick . . . . Susan Douglas Rubes
Augustus Glick . . . . Jan Rubes
Celia . . . . Melyssa Ade
Rabbi Teitelman . . . . Jason Blicker

The story of a 13-year-old smarty-pants Jewish kid, set in 1963 Beausejour, Manitoba. His opinionated family included parents Sarah and Henry (they ran a furniture store), and live-in grandparents Byrna and Augustus. Celia was Max's dream girl. Based on *The Outside Chance of Maximilian Glick*, a novel by Morley Torgov, and a feature film of the same name. Detractors accused the program of consciously imitating U.S. series *The Wonder Years.*

The critics cheer: "I'm tempted to say that *Max Glick* is the best sitcom ever produced by the CBC…." — Tony Atherton, *Ottawa Citizen*

Max, the 2,000-Year-Old Mouse

Syndicated: 1967
Animated
Running Time: 5 min.

Narrator: Bernard Cowan

Max, an insufferably wimpy white rodent in a vest, added the only animation to these 104 still-frame historical cartoons. "Ask me…I was there. Yeah, me, Max, the 2,000-year-old mouse." The series (and its companion, *The Wonderful World of Professor Kitzel*) were greedily sucked up by TV stations eager to defend themselves against charges that their programming lacked educational content. A Max doll appeared briefly in stores. Dubbed into Spanish.

McQueen

CBC
Drama
First Broadcast: Tuesday, September 23, 1969, 9:00 p.m.
Final Year Broadcast: 1970
Running Time: 30 min.

Cast:
McQueen .... Ted Follows
Natasha............................... Jan Goldin
Denise.............................. Daphne Gibson

McQueen was a newspaperman known as The Actioneer, after his daily consumer-action column. Based on *Toronto Telegram* reporter Frank Drea's "Action Line," the program was partially shot in *Telegram* news-rooms. Natasha and Denise were McQueen's assistants, and Margot Kidder made appearances as Jenny, a newspaper staffer. A minor-league crusader, McQueen (no first name) tackled vanity-publishing scams, baldness-cure peddlers, phony talent agencies, and a nasty furniture salesman who sold a broken vacuum cleaner to a nice old lady. Occasionally McQueen sniffed out meatier fare, like trouble involving U.S. draft dodgers. Drea reportedly liked the series, which received disastrous reviews. Seen in England and Scotland.

The critics cheer: "*McQueen* is entertainment, the kind you can't get anywhere else…it's a lot of fun, especially listening to some creep howl that using a handmade bug is illegal, unethical and un-Canadian." — Douglas Marshall, *Maclean's*

The critics jeer: "…some of the most puerile dialogue ever to disgrace a television screen…rubbish." — Leslie Millin, *The Globe and Mail*

Me and Max

Syndicated: 1985
Situation Comedy
Running Time: 30 min.

Regular Performers: Dave Smith, Max Smith, Morag Smith, Steve Smith

Steve Smith starred his real-life family in this ambitious domestic comedy produced on a shoestring. A follow-up to the *Smith and Smith* variety program and notable for early appearances of the family's eccentric Uncle Red— Red Green that is, of current cult TV fame.

The Actioneer: Ted Follows (left) played *McQueen*, a crusading newspaper columnist. Looking shifty is guest star Bruno Gerussi.

The Mike Neun Show

CBC
Musical Variety
First Broadcast: Monday, September 21, 1970, 7:30 p.m.
Final Year Broadcast: 1971
Running Time: 30 min.

Host: Mike Neun

Mike who? A satire musical with musician-comedian Neun and guests including Pat Hervey, Eleanor Collins, Chief Dan George, and Terry David Mulligan. Typical segment: Mike interviews a tree propper-upper. Hastily replaced by *The Irish Rovers*.

The critics jeer: "The CBC has finally admitted defeat in the case of Mike Neun, a defeat so complete the network is scrapping his Vancouver-produced variety show in mid-season…." — Blaik Kirby, *The Globe and Mail*

Misterogers

CBC
Children's
First Broadcast: Monday, October 15, 1962, 1:30 p.m.
Final Year Broadcast: 1964
Running Time: 15 min.

Host: Fred Rogers

A two-year dry run for Fred Rogers' *Misterogers' Neighborhood.* Daniel S. (Striped) Tiger, X the Owl, Henrietta Pussycat, Cornflake S. Pecially, Collette de Tigre, and King Friday XIIIth, monarch of Calendarland, strutted their puppet stuff with the off-screen assistance of Ernie Coombs (*Mr. Dressup*) who had left Pittsburgh with Rogers.

Rogers' familiar puppets had previously appeared on the *Children's Corner* segment

CBC

of *Junior Roundup*. The show was the genesis of Rogers' trademark trolley car, although a beaver puppet, who provided Canadian content, failed to make the transition to the U.S. series.

Moment of Truth

CBC
Soap Opera
First Broadcast: Monday, December 28, 1964, 4:00 p.m.
Final Year Broadcast: 1965
Running Time: 30 min.

Cast:

Dr. Robert Wallace	Douglas Watson
Nancy Wallace	Louise King
Johnny Wallace	Michael Dodds
Sheila Wallace	Barbara Pierce
Walter Leeds	Robert Goodier
Wilma Leeds	Lynne Gorman
Carol Williams	Toby Tarnow
Jack Williams	Stephen Levy
Dr. Russell Wingate	Ivor Barry
Monique Wingate	Fernande Giroux
Dr. Gil Bennett	John Bethune
Dr. Vincent Conway	Peter Donat
Dean Hogarth	Cec Linder
Olivia Hogarth	Billie Tyas
Barbara Harris	Mira Pawluk
Linda Harris	Anna Hagan
Kathy	Anne Collings
Arthur	Alan Blye
Lila Bowen	Sandra Scott
Diane Bowen	Anne Campbell
Eric Brandt	John Horton
Dexter Elliott	Chris Wiggins

Billed as "more than a soap opera," this daily sudser was taped in Toronto and sold to NBC television, where it ran from January to November, 1965. Watson and King were marginal American actors; Canadians filled the other slots.

Dr. Robert Wallace was a psychology professor at an unnamed university in either the American Midwest or Ontario—viewers filled in their own blanks, allowing CBC to claim local content.

Nancy was Wallace's wife, and Johnny and Sheila were their children. Dr. Wallace also ran a private practice, which gave him insight into the problems and infidelities of other characters.

Among the exciting plot twists in the soap's short run:
- Diane is branded a nymphomaniac.
- Dr. Wallace is charged with murder.
- Monique becomes attracted to Dexter.
- Dr. Conway reveals a secret marriage; Linda Harris secretly pines for him.
- Walter jumps off a bridge; wife Wilma is carted to a mental institution.

The critics jeer: "The pace is agonizingly slow, the dialogue padded and cliché-ridden, the action minimal. The story line is rehashed continually and moves ahead hardly at all...."
— Bob Blackburn, *Toronto Telegram*

Mom P.I.

CBC
Drama
First Broadcast: Saturday, October 13, 1990, 7:30 p.m.
Final Year Broadcast: 1992
Running Time: 30 min.

Cast:

Sally Sullivan	Rosemary Dunsmore
Ray Sullivan	Shane Meier
Marie Sullivan	Emily Perkins
Bernie Fox	Stuart Margolin
Johnny Beaumont	Blu Mankuma
Nadine Beaumont	Freda Perry
Books Monahan	Robert Ito

Self-billed "family-noir" finds mom, Sally, teaming up part time with ailing detective Fox; she also keeps her job at the Pacific Cafe, owned by the Beaumonts. Kids Ray and Marie get involved in cases.

Nice to see *The Rockford Files*' Angel Martin (Margolin) in anything. Filmed in Vancouver.

The critics jeer: "...a lame, badly acted piece of regional fluff...infantile ersatz Americana." — John Haslett Cuff, *The Globe and Mail*

More Tears

CBC
Drama
First Broadcast: Monday, March 30, 1998, 9:30 p.m.
Final Year Broadcast: 1998
Running Time: 30 min. and 90 min.

Cast:

George Findlay	Ken Finkleman
Diane	Leah Pinsent
Shaffik	Hrant Alianak
The Artist	Larissa Laskin
Nikki	Lou Thornton
Andrea	Arsinée Khanjian
Chambermaid	Cristina Vasquez

"More tears" is what news director George Findlay wants from interview subjects on his sensation-mongering news program. Series creator Finkleman set out to show that news is manipulated by hacks with showbiz sensibilities. In the series finale Finkleman takes another frame out of Fellini (as he does in *all* his shows) as Findlay makes a film, *George II*, about a documentarian who manipulates the news. Shaffik is a blathering philosopher, Diane is a news anchor, Andrea is George's wife, Nikki and The Artist are mistresses. A four-part sequel to *The Newsroom*. Sequel: *Foolish Hearts.*

Mosquito Lake

CBC
Situation Comedy
First Broadcast: Sunday, October 8, 1989, 9:30 p.m.
Final Year Broadcast: 1989
Running Time: 30 min.

Cast:

Bob Harrison	Mike MacDonald
Rita Harrison	Mary Long
Tara Harrison	Tara Charendoff
Brian	Bradley Machry
George	Dan Redican
Ramona	Maria Vacratsis
Kenny	Eric Keenleyside

Not as bad as *Not My Department*—merely the second-worst CBC sitcom of the 1980s. Math teacher Bob moved his family to cottage country for the summer. Rita was his long-suffering wife; Tara and Brian his smart-ass kids. George was Bob's idiot neighbour, and Ramona ran the local marina with her socially challenged big brother Kenny.

The critics jeer: "...it's not good at all. It's not even funny...." — Greg Quill, *The Toronto Star*

Mr. Chips

CBC
Home Improvement
First Broadcast: Friday, June 1, 1973, 7:30 p.m.
Final Year Broadcast: 1979
Running Time: 15 min. and 30 min.

Hosts: Don McGowan (1973–79), Bronwen Mantel (occasional)
Cast:
Mr. Chips ... Bill Brown (1973–78), Jon Eakes (1978–79)

Home repairs with an emphasis on carpentry, seen on local Montreal television beginning in 1967.

Mr. Dressup

CBC
Children's
First Broadcast: Monday, February 13, 1967, 11:00 a.m.
Final Year Broadcast: 1996
Running Time: 30 min.

Cast:

Mr. Dressup	Ernie Coombs

Puppeteers: Judith Lawrence (1964–90), Karen Valleau (1990–96), Nina Keogh (1990–96), Cheryl Wagner (1990–96), Jani Lauzon (1990–96)

Coombs, an American, was a puppeteer on Fred Rogers' Canadian series, *Misterogers.* That led to an on-screen spot on *Butternut Square*, which was axed in 1964. Thanks to copious viewer mail, Mr. Dressup survived. With a Tickle Trunk (originally, the Tinker Trunk) packed with costumes, and shelves crammed with storybooks, construction paper, bits of yarn, crayons, and bottle caps, mild-mannered Mr. Dressup became a Canadian TV icon, presiding over a land of crafts, music, and make-believe without a hint of condescension. Mr. Dressup's cast of puppet characters included: four-year-old, rosy-cheeked Casey, an occasionally naughty British schoolboy, and his pantomime dog Finnegan (both *Butternut* holdovers) who lived in a tree house; the

CBC

"And me...Mr. Dressup": Children's TV icon Ernie Coombs as Mr. Dressup, surrounded by puppet friends Miss Biss-Bird (left), Casey (top), and Finnegan (bottom).

Wise Old Owl ("Tuh-with-tuh-whoooo"); Alligator Al; eccentric Aunt Bird, a sassy ostrich; Miss Biss-Bird; Hat-Rack Moose; and Hester. Regular visitors included Susan Marcus, Beth Anne Cole, and a mime known as Poko, played by Adrian Pecknold. Puppeteer Lawrence retired in 1990, leaving enough footage to get children used to the idea that Casey had finally, after 25 years of pre-school, entered Kindergarten. Replacing those puppets were Lorenzo the raccoon, Chester the crow, a creature named Truffles, Annie (and her Granny), Little Alex, and a girl named Lisa.

In 1996, after 4,000 episodes, the show was retired, though Coombs still made personal appearances.

The critics cheer: "...probably the best show for small children on TV...I like Mr. Dressup because he's quiet, honest, innocent. He treats children with respect.... He's not trying to sell them Crispy Critters or Fruit Loops [sic]; best of all, he's not trying to educate them." — Heather Robertson, *Maclean's*

Mr. Fixit

CBC
Home Repair
First Broadcast: Saturday, October 8, 1955, 6:30 p.m.
Final Year Broadcast: 1966
Running Time: 15 min.

Host: Rex Loring
Cast:
Mr. Fixit . . . . Peter Whittall

Mr. Fixit explained simple home repair and building projects that could be demonstrated in a short, short program. Host Loring acted as a surrogate audience. Whittall, a former CBC producer, stopped taping after a stroke. The series spawned a passel of books, and Mr. Fixit promoted various tool products at trade shows and in store displays.

Mr. O

CBC
Children's
First Broadcast: Thursday, April 5, 1956, 4:30 p.m.
Final Year Broadcast: 1957
Running Time: 15 min

Cast:
Mr. O . . . . David Ouchterlony
Puppet Voices: Len Davidson, Bill Needles, Peggi Loder
Puppeteers: John Keogh, Linda Keogh

Mr. O, on piano, was assisted by puppet characters, including Chelli the violoncello, Clarence the clarinet, Manley, and Whisper, in introducing kids to music.

Mr. Piper

CBC
Children's
First Broadcast: Thursday, October 3, 1963, 4:00 p.m.
Final Year Broadcast: 1965
Running Time: 30 min.

Cast:
Mr. Piper. . . . . Alan Crofoot

Once a professional wrestler known as the Singing Lifeguard, heavyweight opera tenor Crofoot played jovial Mr. Piper, who told stories or mined a polka-dotted "musical-magical bag of tricks" that gave him supernatural powers, often revealing a suppressed megalomania. A filmed segment, *Animal Farm*, featured Rupert the cat, Bessie the bunny, Calvin Coon, Charlotte Cow, Freddie Frog, Harriet Hen, Kookie Kitten, and a rat. Seen in the U.K., Australia, and New Zealand.

Mr. Showbusiness

CBC
Musical Variety
First Broadcast: Monday, October 4, 1954, 9:30 p.m.
Final Year Broadcast: 1955
Running Time: 30 min

Announcer: Elwood Glover
Regular Performers: Jack Arthur, Sheila Billing, Robert Christie, Terry Dale, Doreen Hume, Wally Koster, Ben Lennick, Johnny Moreland, Sammy Sales, Alfie Scopp, Joyce Sullivan
Orchestra Leader: Howard Cable

A live show-within-a-show, featuring songs, dance, and comedy loosely built around a vaudeville stage.

Arthur, a vaudeville veteran who began the show on radio, was, presumably, one of many self-billed Mr. Showbusinesses, but the only one who received the Order of the British Empire, for entertaining troops during WWII.

Mr. Wizard

CBC
Children's
First Broadcast: Monday, September 6, 1971, 5:00 p.m.
Final Year Broadcast: 1975
Running Time: 30 min.

Cast:
Mr. Wizard . . . . Don Herbert
Assistants: Andrew Galbreath, Margaret Kelly

"Gee, Mr. Wizard!" In its endless quest for Canadian content, the CBC imported U.S. educator Don Herbert, whose *Mr. Wizard* program was an American TV fixture from 1951 to 1965. Using household materials to demonstrate scientific principles and astound junior assistants and viewers, the Canadian series appeared in NBC's Saturday morning line-up in the 1971–72 season.

In a bizarre turnabout, NBC quashed the CBC's effort at creating artificial Americana by promoting the kids' Canadian citizenship. Herbert outlived this program, returning to Nickelodeon with *Mr. Wizard's World* until 1991.

Musicamera

CBC
Drama/Documentary
First Broadcast: Wednesday, November 23, 1973, 9:00 p.m.
Final Year Broadcast: 1979
Running Time: 60 min. and 90 min.

This long-running music series focused on Canadian performers, music, and musical productions. Programs featured Glenn Gould, Maureen Forrester, Sylvia Tyson, the Royal Winnipeg Ballet's production of *Klee Wyck: A Ballet For Emily Carr,* and the National Ballet's Emmy-winning broadcast of *Sleeping Beauty* featuring Rudolf Nureyev and Veronica Tennant.

Music Hop

CBC
Music
First Broadcast: Thursday, October 3, 1963, 5:30 p.m.
Final Year Broadcast: 1967
Running Time: 30 min.

Hosts: Alex Trebek (1963–64), Dave Mickie (1964–67)

Music Hop began in Toronto, featuring host Trebek, house sextet Norm Amadio and the Rhythm Rockers, and a regular trio, the Girlfriends. Guest acts included Bobby Curtola and Pierre Lalonde. Dancer Lorraine Green demonstrated new steps like the Monkey, the Slop, and the Prince Philip Walk. In the second season, pompadoured Dave Mickie, a CKEY disc jockey, replaced Trebek, and the program became an umbrella for five weekday music programs:
• **Monday:** *Let's Go,* from Vancouver, with DJs Fred Latremouille and Red Robinson, a sextet called the Classics, and teen fashion expert Randi Conlin. Guests included musicians Mike Campbell, Bobby Faulds, and Susan Pesklevits. (In 1967, the program moved to Tuesday with host Howie Vickers, the Let's Go band, Patty Surbey, Bruce Bissell, Mark Midler, and go-go dancer Toni Sinclair).
• **Tuesday:** *Jeunesse Oblige,* from Montreal, hosted by Jean-Pierre Ferland in 1964, Pierre Lalonde in 1965, and Chantal Renaud in 1966 (it occasionally featured fashion shows).
• **Wednesday:** *Hootenanny,* from Winnipeg, hosted by singer Ray St. Germain ("a junior

Tele-ballet: Karen Kain performs in *Giselle* on CBC's popular arts series *Musicamera.*

CBC

111

Jimmy Dean"), and featuring jazz guitarist Lenny Breau.

- **Thursday:** the original *Music Hop*, from Toronto.
- **Friday:** *Frank's Bandstand*, a dance party from Halifax, hosted by Frank Cameron, with regulars Patricia Anne McKinnon, Karen Oxley, D.J. Jefferson, and Brian Ahern and the Brunswick Playboys.

At the peak of its popularity, one million viewers tuned in at least once a week. Trebek, no rock fan, told the *Toronto Telegram*: "I'm not trying to be a swinger.... When the kids in the studio get unruly, I can tell 'em to shut up."Succeeded by *Let's Go*, based on the Monday segment.

—With notes from Blaine Allan

The critics cheer: "...one whacking popular success...[the] variety program which has passed unnoticed by everyone except its rabid teenaged fans and their TV-trapped families." — Frank Moritsugu, *The Toronto Star*

The Music Machine

CBC
Variety
First Broadcast: Sunday, June 21, 1970, 7:00 p.m.
Final Year Broadcast: 1970
Running Time: 30 min.

Host: Bob Francis

A squarish, middle-of-the-road summer series featuring Moe Koffman, singing group The Machinery, and Hamilton rockers Tranquility Base. Percy Neeps provided record reviews. Koffman had been going "mod" with recent albums *Moe Koffman Goes Electric* and *Curried Soul*. Guests included Mother Trucker's Yellow Duck. Later revived as the slightly rockier *Keith Hampshire's Music Machine*.

CBC

Music maker: Jack Kane, backed by his orchestra, was the star of a raft of CBC musical series, including *Music Makers '58/'59*.

Music Makers '58/Music Makers '59

CBC
Music
First Broadcast: Thursday, October 31, 1957, 9:30 p.m.
Final Year Broadcast: 1961
Running Time: 30 min. and 60 min.

Host: Bill Walker
Regular Performers: Jack Kane and his Music Makers, Sylvia Murphy (1957–60), The Music Makers

Big-band music relying heavily on guest stars (often American), including Peter Appleyard, Cab Calloway, Oscar Peterson, Gene Krupa, Steve Lawrence, Mel Torme, Artie Shaw (who banned women performers from the broadcast) and singing wrestler Frank "Farmer Boy" Townsend. Kane, who refused to play rock'n'roll or "hillbilly music" died in March 1961, and the program finished its run under the title *Music Makers* with guest hosts, including trumpeter Maynard Ferguson.

One of the Music Makers was flautist Moe Koffman who once played "Swingin' Shepherd Blues" to oscilloscope accompaniment, helping viewers adjust their TV audio for optimum "hi-fi" satisfaction. Check out Kane's music in his U.S. LP, *Kane is Able*. A direct descendant of the summer series *Summertime '57*.

The program was retitled every year and known as *The Jack Kane Hour*, *The Jack Kane Show*, and *Music '60 Presents The Jack Kane Show* (which alternated every other week with *Cross-Canada Hit Parade*).

The critics cheer: "One of the most exciting chunks of musical entertainment yet whipped up by the CBC." — Alex Barris, *Toronto Telegram*

The critics jeer: "...little originality or Canadianism and no thought whatever for the program as a whole." — Gordon Sinclair, *The Toronto Star*

The Music of Man

CBC
Documentary
First Broadcast: Wednesday, October 24, 1979, 9:00 p.m.
Final Year Broadcast: 1979
Running Time: 60 min.

Host: Yehudi Menuhin

A series of eight programs in which host Yehudi Menuhin (who also co-wrote) explored the development of music from prehistoric times to modern Western society. Featured performers included Judy Collins, Karen Kain, Maureen Forrester, Glenn Gould, Oscar Peterson, Ravi Shankar, and Frank Sinatra. A Canada-U.S. co-production.

Music '60 Presents The Hit Parade

See: *Cross-Canada Hit Parade*

Music '60 Presents The Jack Kane Show

See: *Cross-Canada Hit Parade*

My Secret Identity

CTV
Children's
First Broadcast: Monday, September 16, 1988, 7:30 p.m.
Final Year Broadcast: 1991
Running Time: 30 min.

Cast:

Dr. Jeffcoate	Derek McGrath
Andrew Clements	Jerry O'Connell
Stephanie Clements	Wanda Cannon
Erin Clements	Marsha Moreau
Kirk Stevens	Christopher Bolton
Mrs. Shellenbach	Elizabeth Leslie

A sweet-natured comedy: Andrew's a normal 15-year-old who's accidentally given super powers by eccentric neighbour, Dr. Jeffcoate. The doc wants Andrew to keep his powers under wraps until he can effect a cure; all Andrew wants to do is watch bullets bounce off his chest and clean his room at superspeed. Stephanie was Andrew's mom and Erin was his sister. O'Connell later found hunky fame in FOX network's sci-fi series *Sliders*.

Mysterious Island

Syndicated: 1995
Science Fiction
Running Time: 45 min.

Cast:

Captain Cyrus Harding	Alan Scarfe
Jack Pencroft	C. David Johnson
Joanna Pencroft	Colette Stevenson
Gideon Spilett	Stephen Lovatt
Herbert Pencroft	Gordon Michael Woolvett
Neb Brown	Andy Marshall
Captain Nemo	John Bach

Based on Jules Verne's sequel to *20,000 Leagues Under the Sea*, this adventure series follows the exploits of six inmates who escape from a Confederate prison during the U.S. Civil War in 1865.

Taking flight in a hot air balloon, they crash land on a Pacific island, there to endure the manipulations of the brilliant but mad Captain Nemo. Unengaging fare, re-syndicated in half-hour chunks. Filmed in New Zealand.

Canadian Cult: Home-Grown Shows Deserving Cult Status

We all know someone who fits the definition of a pop cultist. We mean friends who've told us they've seen *Star Wars* 20 times or watched the same rerun of *The Prisoner* twice in a row, on different channels. (Although a true cultist would have it on DVD.) Film critic Andrew Sarris says a cultist loves the cult object "beyond all reason."

Canadian cultists have largely had to be content with foreign cult programs, such as *Star Trek*, or *The Avengers*, or *The X-Files*. The fact that Canada hasn't been recognized for producing its own cult television is a historical error we'll do our small part to begin righting here. We've identified a number of Canadian TV shows that we think are worthy of cult status. What follows is in no way a definitive list—cult can never be that. It's just a way of inspiring Canadians to start thinking about their own esoteric TV heritage.

1. Cult Comedies

Let's mention the obvious right off—those shows, in this case all comedies, that have a cult following, but also have considerable popularity. I mean the brilliant *SCTV*, *Wayne and Shuster* in their various incarnations, *The Kids in the Hall*, *CODCO*, *This Hour Has 22 Minutes*, and *Royal Canadian Air Farce*. A special case is the work of Ken Finkleman, the producer-writer-director of a number of oddball series featuring cinéma vérité and Fellini-like structures: *The Newsroom*, a biting satire about Televisionland Canada; *More Tears*, a four-episoder that covered much of the same turf, but was darker and more self-absorbed; and *Married Life*, a mixture of reality and illusion, life and art.

2. This Hour Has Seven Days, 1964–66

This show lasted just two seasons, but what seasons they were! It's still the best, and probably the most popular, public-affairs program Canada has ever produced. It mixed a bit of entertainment, investigative journalism, and commentary with some free-wheeling interviews, like the one with American Nazi George Lincoln Rockwell—who, between puffs on a corncob pipe, calmly and dispassionately announced the inferiority of Blacks and Jews. At its peak, the show was seen by as many as 3.25-million viewers. Naturally, the CBC killed it. Alas, producer-host Patrick Watson (with co-host Laurier Lapierre) and producer Douglas Leiterman had rocked the bureaucratic boat just a little too much.

3. Don Messer's Jubilee, 1959–69

Here's one sure way to identify a cult show: The CBC cancels it when it's doing well. This straightforward, hokey, down east music show was shot down by Corps brass in 1969 for reasons that remain shadowy even today. The Maritime music of fiddler Messer and singer Marg Osburne drew over three million viewers weekly at its peak, and was rarely out of the top ten during its ten-year run. Maybe it was just too unsophisticated. Viewers didn't think so, though. The cancellation occasioned Parliament Hill protests, thousands of angry and hurt letters, and a speech in the House from member of Parliament John Diefenbaker—all to no avail.

4. Fighting Words, 1952–62

TV for people with brains. Drama critic Nathan Cohen hosted this show, in which a panel—frequent guests included writers Irving Layton and Morley Callaghan—tried to identify the source of a controversial quote, and then debated its meaning. The show was cancelled in 1955, but a write-in vote rescued it—CBC must have listened more carefully in its earlier years. Two attempts to revive the series, with Cohen in 1970 and Peter Gzowski in 1982, failed.

5. Coach's Corner

A show within a show, sometimes more popular than its *Hockey Night in Canada* framework. The popularity resides entirely with Don Cherry, "Grapes," with his trademark three-inch collars, plaid jackets of colours unknown in nature, Canadian boosterism, xenophobia, and penchant for on-ice mayhem. Cherry loves toughness, kids, and any player from Kingston, Ontario (Doug Gilmour, Kirk Muller). He's an ultranationalist hoser curmudgeon, who often sprinkles his hockey views with ill-considered or just plain silly social opinion. Nonetheless, he remains somehow engaging. Proof of cult status: the advent of university courses deconstructing Cherry's cultural meaning.

6. The Red Fisher Show, 1968–90

This show consisted mostly of Red's chit-chat with cronies in Scuttlebutt Lodge, his studio cabin set, accompanied by grainy film of people sitting in boats and occasionally hauling in their lines. The program was cultish enough to have been lampooned by *SCTV*—John Candy, as Gil Fisher, would retreat to his remote cabin with such unlikely guests as the punk group The Tubes for fishing and sushi.

7. Party Game, 1969–80

Of all the cheesy Canadian game shows (and that's pretty much all of them), this was the cheesiest, and maybe the most fun. It was produced at the independent station CHCH in Hamilton, and syndicated nationally. Basically, it was Charades with sexual undertones and single entendres as the regular team of Dinah Christie, Billy Van, and the leering Jack Duffy would take on a team of three celebrity guests, with much inane, but oddly compelling hilarity ensuing.

8. The Best (and Worst) of Cable

Local free-access cable is where Ed the Sock got his start, with *Ed's Night Party*, a genuine cult show featuring a cigar-chomping, sexist, grumpy sock puppet. This was a Puppet with Attitude, paired with an amusing host, comedian Eric Tunney, and interviewing surprising and often bewildered guests such as Tony Randall. When the program moved from cable to regular TV (on Toronto's CITY), the show began to falter. But what we could use for our cult vaults is either a series of videotapes, called "The Best of Cable" or, better, "The Worst of Cable," ransacking the vaults of local cable outfits across the country. In Winnipeg, for instance, Videon's cable access channel produced such classics in the mid-1980s as *The Ronnie and Natalie Show,* in which local entertainers Ronnie and Natalie Pollock, with complete lack of self-consciousness, interviewed themselves, danced awkwardly, committed stunning non sequiturs, hauled guests off the street, orchestrated pointless discussions, and generally pretended to be hip rock 'n' rollers. Every city in Canada must have produced similar fare, which would make for a TV show that would definitely deserve cult status.

— Martin Levin

Nancy Drew/The Hardy Boys

Syndicated: 1995
Drama
Running Time: 60 min.

Nancy Drew Cast:
Nancy Drew...........................Tracy Ryan
Bess Marvin...........................Jhene Erwin
George Fayne.........................Joy Tanner
Seymour.......................Conrad Bergshneider

The Hardy Boys Cast:
Joe Hardy...........................Paul Popowich
Frank Hardy...........................Colin Gray
Kate Craigen...........................Fiona Highet

An updated version of the popular books, with Nancy and the Hardys alternating weeks. The characters are a little older here, weighing in at twenty-something. Nancy now lived in a big city and had a boyfriend; Frank Hardy was a newspaper reporter at *The Eagle,* and Joe studied criminology, using a computer to track down crooks. French investors co-produced this single-season effort.

Nashville North

CTV
Music
First Broadcast: Monday, September 14, 1970, 8:00 p.m.
Final Year Broadcast: 1975
Running Time: 30 min.

Host: Ian Tyson

The self-consciously titled effort featured the musical couple and Tyson's back-up band The Great Speckled Bird. To further confuse U.S. viewers, the title was changed to *Nashville Now,* and then *The Ian Tyson Show.* Sylvia Tyson appeared in about half the programs. Guests included Stompin' Tom Connors, Murray McLauchlan, Van Morrison, Anne Murray, and Conway Twitty.

The Nature of Things

CBC
Documentary
First Broadcast: Sunday, November 6, 1960, 5:30 p.m.
Final Year Broadcast: ——
Running Time: 30 min. and 60 min.

Hosts: Donald Crowdis, Patterson Hume, Donald Ivey, Lister Sinclair, David Suzuki

Canada's most successful science series has a deserved reputation for providing lucid, fascinating investigations into scientific knowledge. Now so identified with host Dr. David Suzuki, its prior 20 years are almost forgotten.

Original hosts Professors Ivey and Hume hailed from the University of Toronto, Crowdis from the Nova Scotia Science Museum, and producer/broadcaster Sinclair was a CBC regular. Program topics in the early period included future moon landings, schizophrenia, a demonstration of brain activity using an ordinary flashlight, and guest host Isaac Asimov in a satiric investigation of science-fiction themes. Series shown under the *Nature* umbrella included *Animals and Man, Galapagos,* and *The Ages of Man.*

When geneticist Suzuki assumed host duties in 1980, the program became closely identified with its scientific superstar, and changed its title to *The Nature of Things, With David Suzuki.* Suzuki had a knack for explaining complex scientific matters, describing, with equal aplomb, how HIV works and why chickens develop dark meat.

Nellie, Daniel, Emma, and Ben

CBC
Situation Comedy
First Broadcast: Friday, January 4, 1980, 7:30 p.m.
Final Year Broadcast: 1980
Running Time: 30 min.

Cast:
Nelly . . . . Alicia Ammon
Daniel . . . . Roy Brinson
Emma. . . . . Barbara Tremain
Ben . . . . Jack Ammon
Jennifer . . . . Lani Ashenhurst

Four seniors decide to leave Shady Oaks nursing home to take care of themselves, indulging in Little League baseball, disco dancing, and latter-day dating. Two pilots for the program aired in 1978. Alicia was Jack's real-life mother.

Neon Rider

CTV
Drama
First Broadcast: Saturday, September 29, 1990, 10:00 p.m.
Final Year Broadcast: 1995
Running Time: 60 min.

Cast:
Dr. Michael Terry . . . . Winston Rekert
Vic . . . . Samuel Sarkar
C.C. Dechardon . . . . Alex Bruhanski
Fox Devlin. . . . . Antoinette Bower
John Philip Reed III. . . . . William S. Taylor
Pin . . . . Peter Williams
Rachel Woods. . . . . Suzanne Errett-Balcom
Eleanor James . . . . Barbara Tyson
Kevin. . . . . Jim Byrnes
Walt . . . . Philip Granger

A family drama with its heart in the right place, based on a 1988 pilot film. After writing a bestseller about teenage behaviour problems, ex-alcoholic and University of Toronto professor Dr. Terry buys a ranch in the Rockies, which he turns into a camp for troubled youth. Stories involved the kids who visit the ranch. Dr. Terry worked closely with: 1117, a Vancouver youth organization (where Rachel worked); Reed, a helpful police officer; and Pin, a street contact. Ranch staff included: C.C., the cook; Vic, a Native ranch hand; and Devlin, a previous ranch manager. Danny Virtue, the series' co-creator with Rekert, occasionally appeared on-screen as a horse trainer. Some scripts were based on stories recounted by young people visiting Vancouver Eastside Youth Activities, a real-life agency on which 1117 was based. The programs featured public service announcements telling troubled kids where to find help—Rekert was an advocate

Nellie, Daniel, etc.: (Clockwise from top left) Jack Ammon, Lani Ashenhurst, Roy Brinson, Alicia Ammon, and Barbara Tremain as denizens of the Shady Oaks nursing home.

CBC

and spokesman for many Canadian youth organizations. Though popular, the program was cancelled by CTV in 1992, then revived by YTV and a consortium of individual stations until 1995.

Network

CTV
Musical Variety
First Broadcast: Monday, September 24, 1963, 10:55 p.m.
Final Year Broadcast: 1964
Running Time: 25 min.

Hosts: Bill Brady, Denyse Ange
Music: Peter Appleyard

CTV's first shot at a variety showcase featured segments originating from different cities each night, while the hosts, Brady and singer Ange, remained in Toronto introducing guests, movie clips, and talent show contestants. Jimmy Tapp performed nightly from Montreal, and regulars included singers Jackie and Roy, The Colonials, the Brian Browne Jazz Trio, singer Eleanor Collins, and a slate of Australians discovered by producer Ross McLean: Rolf "Tie Me Kangaroo Down, Mate" Harris, who played his wobble board twice a week from Vancouver; American comedian Dick Curtis (discovered in Australia); writer/performer Chris Beard; and singing twins Tom and Ted LeGarde. Guests included Bob and Ray, Phyllis Diller, Victor Borge, Liberace, Mel Torme, Oscar Peterson, Dave Broadfoot, and the cast of *Beyond the Fringe*. The off-hour schedule was meant to snatch CBC's 11 p.m. national news audience.

A pilot version featured newscasts by Peter Jennings.

The critics jeer: "...[Brady and Ange] go together like oysters and chocolate sauce." — Bob Blackburn, *The Toronto Star*

The New Adventures of Pinocchio

Syndicated: 1961
Animated
Running Time: 30 min.

Voices of:

Pinocchio	Joan Fowler
Crick	Jack Mather
Gepetto	Stan Francis
Foxy Q. Fibble	Larry Mann
Cool S. Cat	Paul Kligman

From the people who brought you *Tales of the Wizard of Oz*, this was a crass update of the Pinocchio story, filmed in Animagic, a stop-motion process. Gone was Pinocchio's nose as moral compass—instead, "Crick" induced the puppet to lie on cue so his elongated nose could be used to pick a lock or vault a canyon. There was some narrative flow, but many outlets showed the program out of sequence in five-minute chunks, obscuring the fact that Pinocchio never finds the Blue Fairy, who was supposed to turn him into a real boy. Recurring villains included the Wicked Witch of the North, and Foxy Q. Fibble, a vulpine con man, and his beatnik accomplice Cool S. Cat. "Pin" also met up with a wimpy singing cowboy and his sassy horse, private eye Pedro Pistol, dog detective Simoro, the Loch Ness monster, and the cast of a monster sitcom-within-a-cartoon that predated *The Munsters*. Narrated by Gepetto.

www.rankinbass.com

The New Avengers in Canada

Syndicated: 1976
Adventure
Running Time: 60 min.

Cast:

John Steed	Patrick Macnee
Mike Gambit	Gareth Hunt
Purdey	Joanna Lumley

The New Avengers was a sorry sequel to the incredibly cool 1960s series, *The Avengers*. Retaining only Patrick Macnee, the British series featured agents Mike Gambit and Purdey (Lumley of *Absolutely Fabulous* fame). Four Canadian episodes (and three filmed in France) were shown as part of the series' irregular run on CTV stations. Episodes dubbed *The New Avengers in Canada* involved: an enemy agent who turns out to be a super-intelligent building security system; a training camp for assassins hidden north of Toronto (the Avengers crack the case with the assistance of a typical Canadian hillbilly moonshiner played by George Chuvalo); a secret Russian base located under Lake Ontario; and a chase through the rural back roads of suburban Toronto, replete with local gun-toting egg farmers.

The Newcomers

CBC
Drama
First Broadcast: Sunday, November 20, 1977, 8:00 p.m.
Final Year Broadcast: 1979
Running Time: 60 min.

Imperial Oil sponsored these seven films, inexplicably scattered over two-and-a-half years, on Canada's immigrants. Programs featured: *1740*—settlers of New France (Michel Cote, Donald Pilon); *1832*—the Scottish (Kenneth Welsh, Susan Hogan); *1847*—the Irish (Linda Goranson, David McIlwraith); *1911*—the Danish (R.H. Thomson); *1927*—Ukrainians (Duncan Regehr, Susan Roman) in the prairies; and *1978*—Italians (Bruno Gerussi, Martha Henry) in "contemporary" Toronto. Filmed in French and English. A prologue, starring Chester McLean, was devoted to Canada's original Native inhabitants. Timothy Findley and Alice Munro wrote some episodes. The series spawned a spinoff book.

News From Zoos

CBC
Children's
First Broadcast: Monday, October 20, 1981, 4:00 p.m.
Final Year Broadcast: 1981
Running Time: 30 min.

Voice of:

Charlie	Carl Banas

Narrator: Sandy Hoyt

An utterly cheesy half-hour, with a lo-o-o-o-n-g intro featuring pseudo-host Charlie the Chimp rushing to get to the studio. The set-up was a cheat: Charlie hung around for about a minute and a half, then shut up to watch cheap, canned zoo footage narrated by Hoyt. Hoary theme and incidental music appeared to be borrowed from 1950s educational films.

The Newsroom

CBC
Situation Comedy
First Broadcast: Monday, October 21, 1996, 9:30 p.m.
Final Year Broadcast: 1997
Running Time: 30 min. and 60 min.

Cast:

George Findlay	Ken Finkleman
Jeremy	Jeremy Hotz
Mark	Mark Farrell
Audrey	Tanya Allen
Jim Walcott	Peter Keleghan
Bruce	Dave Huband
Karen	Karen Hines
Gillian Soros	Elisa Moolecherry
Dodie Graham	Nancy Beatty
Kris	Lisa Ryder
Sandra	Kay Valley
Dernhoff	Julie Khaner
Rani Sandhu	Pamela Sinha

George Findlay is a cowardly news director obsessed with preferential parking spots, cafeteria muffins, and which hiring decisions might net him a roll in the hay.

His staff consists of: anchorman Walcott, a Ted-Baxterish blowhard; butt-kissing producers Mark and Jeremy; and Audrey, an intern. Second season changes: Jeremy is replaced by Karen; Gillian becomes the new regional programming head.

Other new characters: Bruce the weatherman and Dodie a broadcasting exec.

The self-indulgent series occasionally broke stride: a three-parter, with Fellini-esque overtones, featured Findlay's musings while he planned news coverage of a possible nuclear meltdown; in the hour-long series finale Findlay managed Walcott's campaign for a seat in the House of Commons after they were both fired "after the collapse of public broadcasting."

Guest appearances on the program (they played themselves) included Angelo Mosca, Pamela Wallin, Eddie Shack, David Cronenberg, Hugh Segal, Bob Rae, and John Haslett Cuff.

Working titles for the show included: *1,500 Buried Alive, Dead Woman Kept 73 Cats,* and *Film at 11.* A book of *Newsroom* scripts was published. Sequels: *More Tears, Foolish Hearts.*

The critics cheer: "…the funniest, freshest, most original sitcom to air here this season." — Howard Rosenberg, *Los Angeles Times*

"…a sharp riff on feeble-mindedness, deceit and dishonesty,"— Alex Strachan, *The Vancouver Sun*

The critics jeer: "…Findlay's…adventures have all the lingering resonance of a test pattern." — Henry Mietkiewicz, *The Toronto Star*

Nic and Pic

CBC
Children's
First Broadcast: Wednesday, September 10, 1975, 5:00 p.m.
Final Year Broadcast: 1977
Running Time: 30 min.

Voices of:

Nic	Joan Stuart
Pic	Madeleine Kronby

Puppeteers: Michel Frechette, Pierre Regimbald

A Quebec series dubbed into English, with puppet mice Nic and Pic travelling around the world in their hot air balloon. Kronby had earlier appeared in the flesh on *Chez Hélène.*

Two French mice: Nic and Pic pack for another hot air balloon trip on their self-titled series. ▼

CBC

Nicknames of Fame

CTV
Game Show
First Broadcast: Wednesday, July 12, 1961, 10:30 p.m.
Final Year Broadcast: 1962
Running Time: 30 min.

Host: Rick Hart
Panelists: Dofy Skaith, Dodie Dale-Harris, Brigadier Claude Dewhurst

A slate of panelists, teamed with audience members, tried to guess the nickname of a person, place, object, event, or mystery guest.

Nightcap (1953-54)

CBC
Musical Variety
First Broadcast: Wednesday, October 21, 1953, 10:30 p.m.
Final Year Broadcast: 1954
Running Time: 30 min.

Host: Alan Mills
Cast:
The Waiter.................... William Robert Fournier
Regular Performers: Gilberto Assais, Nina Dova

A boozy, schmoozy musical with smooth-talkin' host Mills circulating among a real-life audience in a phony cabaret to find transparently placed celebrities, then cajoling them onto the stage.

The *Nightcap* gang: Belying the show's modest budget, the cast of *Nightcap* goes upscale for the camera.

Billy Van

Nightcap (1963-67)

CBC
Satire
First Broadcast: Wednesday, October 2, 1963, 11:37 p.m.
Final Year Broadcast: 1967
Running Time: 60 min. and 45 min.

Hosts: Alan Hamel, Billy Van
Regular Performers: June Sampson, Bonnie Brooks, Jean Christopher (1963–65), Vanda King (1965–67), Chris Beard, Guido Basso
Music: The Rubber Band, with Guido Basso

A leering, sex-obsessed late-night satire, self-promoted as "the worst TV show in the world," and so popular it often beat Johnny Carson's *Tonight Show* in the ratings. Originally seen just in Toronto, then expanded to the full network in 1966. Billy Van (originally billed Billy Van Evera) sang, as well as hosted. Written by Terry Kyne and Chris Beard. Under heavy budget pressure, the el cheapo revue budget was shaved from shoestring to gossamer thread by CBC execs, who cut Beard's on-camera appearances to save $100 a week and shaved 15 minutes from the show in 1966. The network tried to control bawdy and political content, warning the staff, for example, not to mention the Gerda Munsinger spy scandal (they devoted a full hour to it) or trying (but failing) to bar *Nightcap* from its Ottawa affiliate to avoid political flak.

A regular sketch, *Flemington Park*, was spun off in 1966 into a six-episode series, *Flemington Park—A Cesspool of Desire in the Heart of Suburbia*. It involved young Dr. Carson (Van), the object of lust for three women: Selena Carpenter (Sampson); Jane Morton Murdock (Christopher, who subbed for King), daughter of millionaire Merton Morton Murdock; and Natalie Nolan (Brooks), "a 16-year-old schoolgirl with the body of a woman."

A hoped-for U.S. breakthrough never materialized; neither did a planned movie, to be filmed in Spain. A brief long shot of a topless woman made the newspapers, after a local critic suggested it was the next logical step in low-brow programming.

Though cancelled in 1967, *Nightcap* refused to die:
• An album of unaired sketches, *Canada Observed*, was released post-mortem.
• Extremely popular in New York state, WCBS-TV ordered a single episode of

Nightcap Looks at New York, in 1968.
• Global television taped a single reunion (minus Hamel) in 1976.

Night Heat

CTV
Crime Drama
First Broadcast: Tuesday, September 10, 1985, 10:00 p.m.
Final Year Broadcast: 1989
Running Time: 60 min.

Cast:

Tom Kirkwood	Allan Royal
Detective Kevin O'Brien	Scott Hylands
Detective Frank Giambone	Jeff Wincott
Nicole "Nickie" Rimbaud	Susan Hogan
Detective Freddie Carson	Stephen Mendel
Detective Colby Burns	Eugene Clark
Liutenant Jim Hogan	Sean McCann
Whitey Low	Tony Rosato
Prosecutor Elaine Jeffers	Deborah Grover
Prosecutor Dorothy Fredericks	Wendy Crewson (1985)
Detective Fleece Toland	Lynda Mason Green (1985)
Detective Stephanie "Stevie" Brody	Louise Vallance (1985–86)
Detective Dave Jefferson	Clark Johnson (1986–88)
Detective Christine Meadows	Laura Robinson (1987–89)

Cops O'Brien and Giambone of the Mid-South Precinct team up with newspaperman Kirkwood to cover the town (an anonymous North American town) after sunset. The series was named after Kirkwood's newspaper column. Nickie was O'Brien's girlfriend and owner of Nicole's, a cop hangout. Informant Whitey was a streetwise weasel. The final episode suggested that the precinct would be shut down. This was the first of a raft of Canadian programs to be imported into CBS's late-night schedule as relatively cheap, first-run filler.

Night Walk

Global
?
First Broadcast: Sunday, May 4, 1986, 4:00 a.m.
Final Year Broadcast: 1993
Running Time: 60 min.

Bizarre filler. A night-time point-of-view walk down a Toronto street, set to a jazz score. Only one walk was featured, then repeated endlessly for years. A companion program was called *Night Ride*—no description necessary.

Nikita

CTV
Crime Drama
First Broadcast: Monday, February 24, 1997, 10:00 p.m.
Final Year Broadcast: 2000
Running Time: 60 min.

Cast:

Nikita Samuelle	Peta Wilson
Michael	Roy Dupuis
Operations	Eugene Robert Glazer
Walter	Don Francks
Birkoff	Matthew Ferguson
Madeline	Alberta Watson
Carla	Anais Granofsky

Nikita was a junkie, wrongly convicted of murder, who was kidnapped and rehabilitated by secret agency Section One, then forced to take part in anti-terrorist police work as a professional assassin. Glazer ran Section One, Michael was her trainer, Madeline was a strategist, Birkoff a computer genius, and Walter the company gadget maker.

Based on the gutsier 1991 French film *La Femme Nikita,* in which Nikita happened to be a hard-assed cop killer.

90 Minutes Live

CBC
Talk Show
First Broadcast: Monday, April 19, 1976, 11:22 p.m.
Final Year Broadcast: 1978
Running Time: 90 min.

Host: Peter Gzowski

Although this show was extensively tested in various cities, popular CBC radio host Gzowski withered before TV cameras in a two-year debacle that was supposed to establish a beachhead in late-night Canadian programming. Inexplicably renewed for a second season, the program's starting time was shifted to 11:35, just past Johnny Carson's opening monologue on the *Tonight Show,* after which Canadians were presumably free to turn to Gzowski.

Regulars included Danny Finkleman, Allan Fotheringham, John Kastner, Flo & Eddy, Michael Magee, Rick Moranis, Valri Bromfield, Clemence Desrochers, and John Harvard.

A grateful Gzowski left the show, commenting: "We should not have had a studio audience, and if we did, I should not have been host." Repackaged as *Canada After Dark*.

The critics jeer: "Gzowski is gauche, erratic, inattentive, irrelevant, often rude, often sycophantic, coy, dull...." — Bob Blackburn, *The Toronto Sun*

The critics cheer: "...we were very close to watching...the perfect TV talk show...." — Jack Miller, *The Globe and Mail*

Norman Corwin Presents

CBC
Anthology
First Broadcast: Monday, July 7, 1972, 8:30 p.m.
Final Year Broadcast: 1973
Running Time: 30 min.

Host: Norman Corwin

Radio icon Norman Corwin wrote many of this program's weird teleplays ranging from comedy and drama to science fiction and fantasy. Highlights included: *You Think You've Got Troubles?*, with Michael Dunn as a shipwrecked Martian; *Aunt Dorothy's Playroom*, with Diane Baker and Fred Gwynne taking part in a TV show in which children are adults; *The One Man Group*, with Don Harron as a man possessed by the spirits of historical figures; and *Two Gods on Prime Time*, a TV talk show featuring Mars and Venus.

Other episodes featured Stan Freberg and his space-guy puppet Orville, and Milton Berle in a musical, as a judge presiding over the trial of a renegade molecule. Actors included: Diane Baker, Beau Bridges, Hume Cronyn, Frank Converse, Gale Garnett, Paul Kligman, David McCallum, Barry Morse, Leslie Nielsen, Franz Russell, William Shatner, Donald Sutherland, Rip Torn, Forrest Tucker, and Cicely Tyson.

The series bombed when syndicated in the U.S., but ran longer here.

North of 60

CBC
Drama
First Broadcast: Thursday, December 3, 1992, 9:00 p.m.
Final Year Broadcast: 1998
Running Time: 60 min.

Cast:

Eric Olssen	John Oliver (1992–94)
Michelle Kenidi	Tina Keeper
Sarah Birkett	Tracey Cook
Chief Peter Kenidi	Tom Jackson
Trevor "Teevee" Tenia	Dakota House
Corporal Brian Fletcher	Robert Bockstael
Constable James Harper	Peter Kelly Gaudreault
Rosie Deela	Tina Louise Bomberry
Betty Moses	Tantoo Cardinal
Joey Small Boat	Mervin Good Eagle
Hannah Kenidi	Selina Hanuse
Andrew One Sky	Michael Horse
Leon Deela	Erroll Kinistino
Gerry Kisilenko	Lubomir Mykytiuk
Albert Golo	Gordon Tootoosis
Nathan Golo	Michael Obey
Elise Tsa Che	Wilma Pelly
Rosemary Fletcher	Julie Stewart
Sylvie LeBret	Michelle Thrush
Harris Miller	Tim Webber
Lois Miller	Willene Tootoosis
Harry Dobbs	Art Hindle
Joe Gomba	Jimmy Herman
Bertha	Lori Lea Okemaw

Sixty degrees latitude, that is, in the isolated community of Lynx River, N.W.T., where a white RCMP corporal, Olssen, learns he can't impose by-the-book authoritarianism on the predominantly Native community (the previous officer had a breakdown). The extensive cast featured a slate of major characters: Native Constable Michelle Kenidi, nurse Birkett, and Band leader Peter Kenidi.

When Olssen died, he was replaced by new Mountie Fletcher, who was replaced later in the series by Constable Harper. While the program's wide story arcs and soap opera sensibilities defy a neat synopsis, suffice it to say that plots included relationships, political in-fighting, domestic violence, housing shortages, natural resources development, and nasty bootlegger Albert Golo.

The series was cancelled in 1998, but returned as TV movies *In The Blue Ground* (1999) and *Trial by Fire* (2000) with more films promised. Filmed in Bragg Creek, Alberta.

The critics cheer: "...a great show with superb talent...." — John Copley, *Alberta Native News*

The critics jeer: "... reeks of superior attitude...it's politically correct propaganda." — John Doyle, *The Globe and Mail*

Northwood

CBC
Drama
First Broadcast: Monday, March 4, 1991, 8:30 p.m.
Final Year Broadcast: 1994
Running Time: 30 min.

Cast:

Maria Giovanni	Brigitta Dau
Michael Thomas	Gabe Khouth
Jason Williams	Lochlyn Munro
Brian Potter	Darrell Dennis
Valerie Andersson	Frances Flanagan
Peter Andersson	Trevor Hughes
Karin Andersson	Tamsin Jones
Mats Andersson	Ric Reid
Cindy O'Brien	Frida Bterrani
Tim Eckert	Todd Caldecott
David Wah	Jimmy Tai
Bill Leung	Michael Andaluz
Kirk Huber	Byron Lucas
Doris Huber	Doris Chillcott
Donnie Huber	Tygh Runyan
Theresa Giovanni	Corinne Koslo
Sheena Ellis	Halona Donaghy
Brendan	Forbes March
Sarah McBride	Sarah Sawatsky
Jennifer McBride	Deanna Milligan
Colin McBride	Scott Swanson
Leslie McBride	Linda Darlow
Helen Chen	Natasha Kong
Debbie Williams	Sasha MacLean
Marlene Williams	Gabrielle Rose
Nicole Williams	Maggie O'Hara
Ray Potter	Matt Walker
Lunker	Jorge Vargas
Clarisse	Vanessa Okuma

A sprawling cast of teens in the suburb of Northwood explored love, dating, drug abuse, disability, and other serious issues. The Anderssons were added to placate Swedish investors. The CBC cancelled the series because it claimed the actors were "getting too old." Filmed in North Vancouver.

Nothing Too Good for a Cowboy

CBC
Drama
First Broadcast: Sunday, February 7, 1998, 8:00 p.m.
Final Year Broadcast: 2000
Running Time: 60 min.

Cast:

Richmond P. Hobson	Yannick Bisson
Panhandle Phillips	Ted Atherton
Gloria Hobson (nee MacIntosh)	Sarah Chalke
Tommy	Kristian Ayre
Kit	Kimberley Warnat
Ed	Will Sanderson
Nelson George	Ben Cardinal
Rita George	Carmen Moore
Robert McDaniels	Peter James Bryant
Rupert Mowat	John B. Lowe
Harriet Franklin	Sheelah Megill
Esther	Renae Morriseau
Olivia	Sarah-Jane Redmond

Richard, son of a U.S. congressman; Gloria, his wife; and Panhandle, a career cowboy, try to build the world's largest cattle ranch in northern British Columbia, circa 1940. In their path—lack of cash and manpower (it's WWII, after all), nasty bankers, natural disasters, and scheming British pig farmer Rupert.

Tommy, Ed, and Kit (Ed's sister) were young ranch hands with more enthusiasm than ability. Other characters: kindly ranchers Nelson and Rita; Black Alabama fugitive Robert; and general-store owner Harriet. Esther was Rita's sister and Robert's love interest.

Filmed north of Toronto, and based on a TV movie (with Chad Willett as Hobson), in turn based on the memoirs of Richard P. Hobson, Jr.

Not My Department

CBC
Situation Comedy
First Broadcast: Friday, October 2, 1987, 8:00 p.m.
Final Year Broadcast: 1987
Running Time: 30 min.

Cast:

Gerald Angstrum	Harry Ditson
Margaret Simmons	Shelley Peterson
Mr. Wylie	Barry Stevens

A misfire of epic proportions, which inspired dismal ratings and outright mutiny from CBC's privately owned affiliates, many of whom opted not to run it at all.

Angstrum was the deputy minister of the Department of Regional Incentive Targets, aided by Simmons, and irritated by chief of staff Wylie.

More irritated were audiences, especially fans of the popular British series *Yes, Minister*, which Canadian producers claimed had no influence on their inferior copy.

The fact that Shelley Peterson was the wife of former Ontario Premier David Peterson (he guest-starred as a janitor) whipped audiences into further frenzy.

The series was based on *The Governor General's Bunny Hop*, a novel by journalist Charles Gordon.

The critics jeer: "The series cannot be turned around.... Outright cancellation would seem to be the only solution."
— Jim Bawden, *The Toronto Star*

Nursery School Time

CBC
Children's
First Broadcast: Tuesday, January 21, 1958, 3:45 p.m.
Final Year Broadcast: 1963
Running Time: 15 min.

Montreal Cast:
Maman Fon Fon . . . . Claudine Vallerand (1958)
Miss Madeleine . . . . Madeleine Arbour (1958–63)
Miki the Dog . . . . Himself
Voice of:
Mr. Dick the Beaver . . . . ?

Toronto Cast:
Miss Teddy . . . . Teddy Forman (1958–61, 1962–63)
Miss Toby . . . . Toby Tarnow (1961–62)
Smoky the Kitten . . . . Himself
Voice of:
Hoppy the Bunny . . . . Jack Mather
Puppeteer: Marilyn Booth

Winnipeg Cast:
Miss Shirley . . . . Shirley Knight (1958–59)

The dawn of television as babysitter in Canada, with actors from various cities portraying pre-school teachers, assisted by puppets Mr. Dick and Hoppy, and real-life animals. First seen three days a week, then daily. Vallerand continued in her own extremely popular Quebec series, *Maman Fon Fon*.

O'Keefe Centre Presents

CBC
Variety
First Broadcast: Monday, October 16, 1967, 8:00 p.m.
Final Year Broadcast: 1968
Running Time: 60 min.

Six performances from Toronto's O'Keefe Centre (now The Hummingbird Centre), remembered largely for its premiere episode, "The Rock Scene—Like It Is!" featuring Eric Andersen, Sergio Mendes and Brasil '66, Jefferson Airplane, Dionne Warwick, and the Doors, performing "This is the End." Other programs featured such notables as Harry Belafonte, Al Hirt, Shirley Bassey, Rich Little, George Burns, and Johnny Cash.

Old Testament Tales

CBC
Children's
First Broadcast: Thursday, January 3, 1957, 5:15 p.m.
Final Year Broadcast: 1957
Running Time: 15 min.

Puppeteers: John Keogh, Linda Keogh, John Botterel

A live broadcast presenting stories from the Old Testament, including Daniel in the lion's den, Tobias and the angel, and Jonah and the whale. Performed entirely by marionettes, the programs required twelve hours of rehearsal time.

Ombudsman

CBC
Public Affairs
First Broadcast: Sunday, January 6, 1974, 10:30 p.m.
Final Year Broadcast: 1980
Running Time: 30 min.

Hosts: Robert Cooper (1974–78), Kathleen Ruff (1978–79)

Mild-mannered lawyer Robert Cooper kicked government and corporate asses on behalf of Mr. and Mrs. Average Canadian Citizen.

Digging through layers of bureaucracy, Cooper and his team worked to right thousands of wrongs, only some of which made it to the TV screen. During the series' run, the program received more than sixty thousand complaints and rectified about one-third of them.

Cooper's diminutive stature and high-pitched voice were satirized by Michael Magee in his *Magee and Company* TV show. Cooper left in 1978 to become a film producer, and in 1981 announced plans for a never-made film based on his experiences, tentatively titled *Off the Record* and starring—Robert Redford??!!

On Camera

CBC
Dramatic Anthology
First Broadcast: Saturday, October 16, 1954, 9:00 p.m.
Final Year Broadcast: 1958
Running Time: 30 min.

A showcase earmarked for comedy and drama by Canadian writers, this series of teleplays included offerings by Hugh Garner, Joseph Schull, and Charles Templeton.

Once a Thief

See: *John Woo's Once a Thief*

Once Upon a Hamster

YTV
Children's
First Broadcast: Friday, February 3, 1995, 9:00 a.m.
Final Year Broadcast: 1996
Running Time: 30 min.

Cast:

Story Man . . . . Paul Sutherland
Voices of:

G.P., The Wise Old Frog, Hairbrush Henry, Bernie the Bat,
    Billy-Bob Ferret, Snerdley Snail, Captain Toadie, Timothy
    Tortoise, Lennie the Lizard, Wind, Fog. . . Paul Sutherland
Martha Mouse, Granny Rabbit, Cathy Caterpillar, Lena Lizard,
    Hammy's Cuckoo . . . . Peggy Mahon

A follow-up to *Tales of the Riverbank* and *Hammy Hamster*, featuring live animals, the program restarted the series from the beginning, with Hammy leaving home for the Riverbank. Matthew Mouse became Martha, and a number of new characters appeared, including Hairbrush Henry, a pygmy hedgehog. Inventor G.P. become more prolific, spinning off at least one invention per program. Each episode was introduced by Story Man, although the animals never interacted with humans. Hammy lived inside Story Man's lost boot (the Boothouse) which floated down the river to the Riverbank.

CBC

Four of a kind: (Clockwise, from top left) Allan Manings, Lloyd Bochner, Kathie McNeil, and Rita Greer Allen of CBC game show *One of a Kind*.

100 Huntley Street

Global
Religion
First Broadcast: Friday, June 15, 1977, 10:00 a.m.
Final Year Broadcast: —
Running Time: 60 min. and 90 min.

Host: David Mainse

Mainse is the grand-daddy of Canadian religious broadcasting, with this interview/music program now well into its third decade. A mix of music, interviews, prayer, and preaching. There's also money-raising—the producers purchase air time outright to broadcast the show—but it's a softer sell than other programs of its kind. In the wake of the U.S. *PTL Club* scandal, Mainse guest-hosted for the suddenly absent Jim and Tammy Bakker—but he's kept his own nose clean throughout this show's long run. Toronto's 100 Huntley Street was the studio's real address during its early years. The *Huntley Street* organization also produced *Inside Track*, aimed at teens, and *Circle Square*, aimed at kids.

One of a Kind

CBC
Game Show
First Broadcast: Friday, June 6, 1958, 8:30 p.m.
Final Year Broadcast: 1959
Running Time: 30 min.

Host: Alex Barris
Panelists: Rita Greer Allen, Lloyd Bochner, Betty Kennedy,
    Kathie McNeil, Allan Manings

A popular game show from radio—despised by critics. Panelists identified an object associated with a person, then interviewed related guests. Challengers earned $25 per minute for stumping the panel. Notable guests: Xavier Cugat, Arthur Godfrey, Sir Cedric Hardwicke, Mitch Miller, and Kate Reid, representing such items as Dick Tracy's two-way wristwatch, Stanley Kowalski's torn T-shirt, Ernie Kovacs' cigar, and Perry Como's cockatoo. Some critics charged that the show was rigged. Created by Bernard Slade.

The critics jeer: "One of the phoniest shows the CBC has come up with yet...featuring a regular cast of typical CBC characters, none of whom would stand a chance at a church social amateur hour." — Flash, *The Toronto Star*

"The worst new show of 1958." — Pierre Berton, *CBC Times*

Ooops!

CBC
Children's/Game Show
First Broadcast: Tuesday, September 29, 1970, 5:00 p.m.
Final Year Broadcast: 1971
Running Time: 30 min.

Host: Harry Brown

"What did the doughnut say to the cake?
If I had all that dough, I wouldn't be hanging
around this hole."
— Clarence Gallant, Picadilly, Nfld.

Six contestants worked their way around a game board scoring points with corny jokes sent in by viewers. Players moved ahead if the joke got a laugh (a Gain) or fell behind if it got a groan (a Goof).

The whole program had a duck theme. Brown was known as "The Great Drake" and John O'Leary presented "Ooops! Nooos" bulletins and "Ooops! Weather For Ducks," with lots of ducky puns ("Duck ponds still frozen, but watch out for quacks in the ice.")

Winners chose prizes from six boodle bags containing small items like a camera. One of the bags contained, not surprisingly, a duck. Viewers could purchase a home game from the network.

Open Mike With Mike Bullard

Comedy Network/CTV
Talk Show
First Broadcast: Monday, November 10, 1997, 8:00 p.m.
Final Year Broadcast: —
Running Time: 60 min.

Host: Mike Bullard

Canada finally got the talk show host it deserves: stand-up comic Mike Bullard. Big, gruff Mike spends far too much time needling audience members and laughing at his own jokes, though he features a slate of guests pulled mostly from the Canadian talent pool. The program originated on the Comedy Network, but landed a second simultaneous berth on CTV in January 1998.

The critics jeer: "Bullard, though quick on his feet, isn't what you'd call witty." — John Allemang, *The Globe and Mail*

Rod Coneybeare

A big black eye: for the stars of the disastrous *The Other Eye.* From top: Rod Coneybeare, Jean Templeton, Larry Zolf, and Gary Smith.

The Other Eye

CBC
Satire
First Broadcast: Sunday, July 2, 1967, 10:00 p.m.
Final Year Broadcast: 1967
Running Time: 30 min.

Hosts: Rod Coneybeare, Gary Smith, Jean Templeton, Larry Zolf

A legendary disaster featuring three CBC stalwarts and Gary Smith, a school teacher plucked from obscurity to flounder in prime time. A companion piece to *The Public Eye,* and intended to mount the throne of the cancelled *Nightcap,* the series opener featured an interview with Newfoundland Premier Joey Smallwood. Coneybeare was news anchor, and Zolf conducted street interviews with passers-by.

The critics jeer: "...Smith [is] a grade school Woody Allen...an absolutely appalling half-hour...." — Bob Blackburn, *Toronto Telegram*

"...a catastrophe...a dismal failure." — Jean Templeton, *The Toronto Star*

"Bring back Uncle Chichimus!"—Dennis Braithwaite, *The Globe and Mail*

The Outer Limits

Syndicated: 1995
Science Fiction Anthology
Running Time: 60 min.

Cast:
Control Voice.........................Kevin Conway

A new series bearing the title and trappings of the classic 1960s show. There's still an ominous narrator (the "Control Voice") and a wiggy intro as the producers take control of the viewer's TV set to introduce yet another unusual sci-fi tale.

While some episodes are stand-outs, there's a fairly high pap quotient. The series opener—a two-hour special based on George R.R. Martin's short story "Sandkings"—squandered the promising literary property, transforming it into a hackneyed tale of megalomania. While no single episode has equalled the likes of Harlan Ellison's "Demon With a Glass Hand," from *Outer Limits*' 1960s salad days, some "downer" episodes like "The Deprogrammers," about an alien master race, are admirably pessimistic.

Lots of work for Canadian actors here. Episodes have featured Megan Follows, Matt Frewer, Graham Greene, Scott Hylands, Michael Ironside, Margot Kidder, Nicholas Lea, Nick Mancuso, Howie Mandel, Andrea Martin, Eric McCormack, Catherine O'Hara, Gordon Pinsent, Saul Rubinek, Michael Sarrazin, Peter Stebbings, Alan Thicke, and Amanda Plummer, who won an Emmy on the series.

Entering its sixth year in the 2000–01 season, the new *Outer Limits* has already outlasted its predecessor by four years. Seen originally as a pay-TV presentation on TMN in Canada, and on Showtime in the U.S., repeat broadcasts were seen on Global and other stations.

The Palace

CHCH
Variety
First Broadcast: Friday, September 28, 1979, 10:00 p.m.
Final Year Broadcast: 1980
Running Time: 60 mins.

Host: Jack Jones

Sharp producers convinced Las Vegas-style entertainers to perform in Hamilton, Ontario's, Hamilton Place. Steeltown guests included Pearl Bailey, Diahann Carroll, Charo, Sammy Davis Jr., Lola Falana, Jose Ferrer, Aretha Franklin, Engelbert Humperdinck, Tom Jones, Peggy Lee, Ethel Merman, Melba Moore, Anne Murray, Pat Paulsen, Ginger Rogers, Neil Sedaka, Doc Severinsen, Ben Vereen, and Paul Williams. Canadian support included the Hamilton Philharmonic Orchestra, led by Boris Brott, and the Palace Dancers. The comedy team of Smith and Smith (Steve and Morag) appeared in comedy bits on Canadian cuts, and a Spanish-language segment was filmed for export versions.

Parade

CBC
Musical Variety
First Broadcast: Thursday, July 9, 1959, 8:00 p.m.
Final Year Broadcast: 1964
Running Time: 30 min.

Host: Bill Walker

A showcase for entertainers including Tony Bennett, The Bert Niosi Orchestra, The Billy Van Four, Rosemary Clooney, Sammy Davis Jr., Joan Fairfax, Maynard Ferguson, Oscar Peterson, Pete Seeger, The Smothers Brothers, Denny Vaughan, Jonathan Winters, Johnny Wayne and Frank Shuster. Blasted for headlining U.S. acts over local talent. Seen in Great Britain and, briefly, on NBC.

The Party Game

CHCH
Game Show
First Broadcast: Monday, September 7, 1970, 6:30 p.m.
Final Year Broadcast: 1981
Running Time: 30 min.

Host: Bill Walker
Regular Panelists: Dinah Christie, Jack Duffy, Billy Van

"Sounds like...clock?" This long-running game of charades relied heavily on sexual innuendo from the celebrity panelists. Seen in a supper-time slot and repeated at bedtime (11:30 p.m.), the program became a guilty pleasure for a large, anonymous, late-night audience.

Passport To Adventure

CBC
Film Showcase Serial
First Broadcast: Monday, October 18, 1965, 5:00 p.m.
Final Year Broadcast: 1967
Running Time: 30 min.

Host: Elwy Yost

Classic films, including *King Kong, Lost Horizon,* and even *Abbott and Costello Meet Frankenstein,* were presented in weekday serial format. Films were edited to omit excessive violence and "prolonged clinches" that might bore youngsters. Yost also interviewed actors, including Edward Everett Horton and Douglas Fairbanks, Jr. Reincarnated in the 1970s as TVO's *Magic Shadows.* Also known as *Passport.*

The Patsy Gallant Show

CTV
Variety
First Broadcast: Thursday, September 21, 1978, 7:30 p.m.
Final Year Broadcast: 1979
Running Time: 30 min.

Musical variety featuring Canadian disco-princess Gallant, who was neither a star in New York *or* L.A., despite billing herself as "three-quarters of a superstar." Guest shots included Edwin Starr, and Claudja Barry performing "Boogie Woogie Dancin' Shoes."

The Paul Anka Show

CBC
Musical Variety
First Broadcast: Friday, October 15, 1982, 7:00 p.m.
Final Year Broadcast: 1983
Running Time: 30 min.

Host: Paul Anka

Ottawa's Lonely Boy, singer Paul Anka, tried to revive the glitzy variety show, making a conscientious effort to tuck Canadian stars (Dan Hill, Anne Murray, Wayne Gretzky) into his guest roster (singers Andy Gibb, Helen Reddy, Dionne Warwick, Andy Williams). Don Costa led the house orchestra.

Paul Bernard, Psychiatrist

CBC
Soap Opera
First Broadcast: Monday, September 13, 1971, 4:00 p.m.
Final Year Broadcast: 1972
Running Time: 30 min.

Cast:

Dr. Paul Bernard	Chris Wiggins
Mrs. Patterson	Josephine Barrington
Mrs. Johnson	Anna Cameron
Mrs. Finley	Marcia Diamond
Katie Connor	Nuala Fitzgerald
Mrs. Donaldson	Gale Garnett
Alice Talbot	Dawn Greenhalgh
Mrs. Collins	Kay Hawtrey
Miss Parker	Valerie-Jean Hume
Karen Lampman	Barbara Kyle
Mrs. Brookfield	Carol Lazare
Miss Michaels	Peggy Mahon
Mrs. Connie Walker	Phyllis Marshall
Mrs. Roberts	Paisley Maxwell
Vickie Lombard	Arlene Meadows
Jennifer Barlow	Micki Moore
Mrs. Bradshaw	Diane Polley
Mrs. Wilkins	Vivian Reis
Barbara Courtney	Shelley Sommers
Mrs. Howard	Tudi Wiggins

Regular Performers: Til Hanson, Michele Oricoine

Meet Dr. Paul Bernard, understanding psychiatrist and trusty psychoanalyst to a clientele consisting entirely of rich women. In rigid formula, the good doctor met with his patients, conducted them to the couch, and listened to their dreams, fantasies, and anxieties. Before each commercial, he dropped a minor bombshell: Why do they hate their mothers? When did they stop loving their husbands? Why are they afraid to love?

The stories were based on case histories from the files of the Canadian Mental Health Association. Dr. Bernard's appointments actually made sense in real time. Viewers following Mrs. Talbot's analysis could see her at her next appointment in two weeks. Foreign sales helped finance the program, but a CBC strike halted production long enough for audiences to become disaffected by yet another round of repeats.

A planned second season would have included male patients, the husbands of Dr. Bernard's female clientele. Seen in the U.S., New Zealand, Australia, and Hong Kong.

Pencil Box

CBC
Children's
First Broadcast: Friday, September 17, 1976, 4:30 p.m.
Final Year Broadcast: 1979
Running Time: 30 min.

Voices of:

Bolo Bat, Clara Cactus, Stubby Pencil, Miffy Skunk, Webster (the dictionary)	Noreen Young

Puppeteer: Noreen Young
Regular Performers: Bob Kerner, Holly Larocque, Moira Pyper, Jim Radford

Young actors presented plays written by public-school students, using series creator Noreen Young's puppets, mime, illustrations, and animation. Typical productions included: *The Zombies, The Monsters, Talking Teeth,* and *My Fish and I.*

People in Conflict

CTV
Drama
First Broadcast: Monday, September 10, 1962, various
Final Year Broadcast: 1970
Running Time: 30 min.

Hosts: William McCarthy, Don McGowan

A keyhole-peek at the wretched lives of unfortunates who turned to three TV counsellors—psychologist Gordon Bryenton, social worker Judy Macintosh, and lawyer H.A.D. Oliver—who rescued them, in a mere eight minutes, from their personal quagmires, usually with a stern talking-to. The counsellors were real, the cases were real (based on files from Vancouver Family Counselling Services), but the conflicted were actors, ad libbing to bring a sense of raw angst to their roles. Some portrayals were so convincing that the show received offers of adoption and marriage for distressed characters. Pinch-hitting social workers included Rosemary Brown, Derek Thomas and E.D. McRae. Briefly seen in prime time. In an *SCTV* spoof, panelist Colonel Sanders counselled the distraught to eat more chicken.

The critics jeer: "Any attempt to turn personal problems into mass entertainment is cheap and degrading. Doing so under the guise of family counselling is even worse…." — Joan Irwin, *The Toronto Star*

Pepinot and Capucine

CBC
Children's
First Broadcast: Sunday, January 3, 1954, 5:30 p.m.
Final Year Broadcast: 1955
Running Time: 30 min.

Puppeteers: Charlotte Boisjoli, Jean Boisjoli, Fernand Dore, Marie-Eve Lienard, Robert Rivard

An English adaptation of Montreal's *Pepinot et Capucine* puppet show. Pepinot and Capucine were brother and sister living in Pepinotown, with friends Mr. Pumpion, Mr. Black, inventor Mr. White, and their pet bear Bruin. Bad guy Powpow was reformed in a Christmas show. The characters were adapted from a Montreal comic strip.

The Peppermint Prince

CBC
Children's
First Broadcast: Friday, May 10, 1956, 4:30 p.m.
Final Year Broadcast: 1957
Running Time: 15 min.

Cast:
The Peppermint Prince . . . . John Chappell
Puppeteer: Dave Orcutt

The prince, some puppets, and cartoons.

Performance

CBC
Dramatic Anthology
First Broadcast: Sunday, December 8, 1974, 9:00 p.m.
Final Year Broadcast: 1976
Running Time: 60 min. and 90 min.

A series of teleplays. Notable productions included: Cyril Cusack and Helen Burns in Joe Orton's *The Good and Faithful Servant*; Rick Salutin's *1837*, produced by Toronto's Theatre Passe Muraille; *Baptizing*, adapted from Alice Munro's *Lives of Girls and Women*, starring her daughter, Jenny; *The Last of the Four Letter Words*, with Jayne Eastwood as a woman with cancer; *Ten Lost Years*, with Jackie Burroughs, and *Six War Years*, with Doug McGrath, based on Barry Broadfoot's oral histories of the Depression and WWII; *Mandelstam's Witness*, by Vivian Rakoff with a filmed intro by Arthur Miller; *Red Emma*, by Carol Bolt; and Donald Pleasance in *The Captain of Kopenick*. The series' final productions were dubbed *Camera 76* and featured *The Insurance Man From Ingersoll*, about political corruption, starring Michael Magee and Charlotte Blunt, and Gilles Carle's *A Thousand Moons*, with Carole Laure and Nick Mancuso. Evolved into *For The Record*.

Peter Benchley's Amazon

Syndicated: 1999
Drama
Running Time: 60 min.

Cast:
Andrew Talbott . . . . Rob Stewart
Karen Oldham . . . . Carol Alt
Jimmy Stack . . . . Chris Martin
Pia Claire . . . . Fabiana Udenio
Will Bauer . . . . Tyler Hynes
Dr. Alex Kennedy . . . . C. Thomas Howell
First Elder Cole . . . . John Neville
Falconer John . . . . Gabriel Hogan
Elder Balaam . . . . Joseph Scoren
Korakal . . . . Pedro Salvin
Masteeko . . . . James Gonzalez
Hekka . . . . Deborah Pollitt
Prudence . . . . Katie Emme McIninch
The Shaman . . . . Alejandro Ronceria
Jakuki . . . . Mauricio Rodas
Kinchka . . . . Inga Breede
Amos . . . . Kyle Fairlie

Six survivors of a plane crash in the Amazon jungle must survive snakes, ants, piranhas, and hostile tribes (the Spider Tribe and the Jaguar People, to name but two) to make their way to civilization. Friction-aplenty among: a teacher (Talbott) with six months to live; flight attendant Oldham; unlucky Stack who won the plane trip as a prize; opera singer Claire; teenager Bauer; and egotistical heart surgeon Kennedy. How Canadian are these survivors? Since we don't know their nationalities, some of them *might* be Canadian. Lots of chance meetings with white people where you'd least expect them, including a "lost" tribe, The Chosen, descended from 17th-century explorers. Filmed in Canada and Australia. Based on an idea by author Benchley (and on his thematically similar novel *The Island*).

Pete's Place

Syndicated: 1983
Comedy/Variety
Running Time: 30 min.

Host: Pete Barbutti

Toronto's Brunswick House Tavern stood in for musician/comedian Barbutti's crumbling nightclub, which the principal tried to keep from folding. Pete hosted mostly American guest stars, including actors Morey Amsterdam, Adrienne Barbeau, and Cybill Shepherd, though Canadian guests like John Candy appeared from time to time. Produced by Hamilton's CHCH.

Honest to Pete: Pete Barbutti created and hosted the low-budget variety show, *Pete's Place.*

▼

Pete Barbutti

Pet Peeves

CTV
Magazine
First Broadcast: Wednesday, October 8, 1986, 7:30 p.m.
Final Year Broadcast: 1987
Running Time: 30 min.

Host: Harvey Atkin

Both alleged celebrities and people on the street were asked to tell Harvey what really got their goats. Possibly the decade's worst program idea.

Philip Marlowe: Private Eye

First Choice
Drama
First Broadcast: Thursday May 29, 1986, 8:00 p.m.
Final Year Broadcast: 1987
Running Time: 60 min.

Cast:
Philip Marlowe	Powers Boothe
Annie Riordan	Kathryn Leigh Scott
Lt. Violet Magee	William Kearns

An expensive period piece based on the character created by Raymond Chandler. Sets and costumes were excellent, but audiences failed to click with Boothe's portrayal of Marlowe, previously played by the likes of Humphrey Bogart. Also seen in the U.S. and some European countries.

The Phoenix Team

CBC
Drama
First Broadcast: Tuesday, September 16, 1980, 10:00 p.m.
Final Year Broadcast: 1980
Running Time: 60 min.

Cast:
David Brook	Don Francks
Valerie Koester	Elizabeth Shepherd
The General	Mavor Moore
Graydon	Brian Linehan
Carvallo	Steve Pernie
Moffat	Gerry Crack
Miss Woods	Amelia Hall
Janev	Lee Broker
Theo	Arnie Achtman

The Phoenix Team was Valerie Koester, British secret-service agent, and former lover, David Brook, a top Canadian agent recalled into action from his desk job. The interference of Graydon (yes, *the* Brian Linehan), their overbearing superior, was tempered by the support of The General, head of the Canadian secret service.

Pick a Letter

Syndicated: 1963
Children's
Running Time: 5 min.

Narrator: Peter Mews

George Feyer used his lightning-quick sketching talent to provide visuals for this cartoon feature. Appearing briefly at the start of the program, Feyer worked from behind a special drawing board, making his illustrations appear as if from nowhere. Sketches were related to a single letter, which narrator Mews elaborated on in rhyming couplets. Nice '50s-style studio music included a memorable harmonica and xylophone closing theme. Seen in the U.S., France, England, Australia, Japan, France, Spain, Italy, and the Netherlands.

The critics cheer: "A fresh, inventive TV program for children …it's a little unfortunate that these programs should be rotting in the can while the *Three Stooges* squeal and thump their way through repeat after repeat." — Bob Blackburn, *Toronto Telegram*

Pick the Stars

CBC
Game Show
First Broadcast: Tuesday, September 28, 1954, 9:00 p.m.
Final Year Broadcast: 1957
Running Time: 30 min.

Hosts: Dick MacDougal (1954–56), Lee Stevens (1954–55),
Pat Morgan (1956–57)

A TV version of radio show *Opportunity Knocks*—a talent contest with escalating prizes. Semi-finalists earned $500, while two winners walked away with $1,000 each. Winners were selected by a combination of viewer mail and a judging panel, including Clyde Gilmour. Host Morgan was a previous *Pick the Stars* winner. MacDougal was ordered by sponsor Canada

Packers not to wish contestants "good luck"— the name of a rival brand of margarine.

The critics jeer: "…I have had the impression sometimes that they deliberately lower their sights to pick acrobats and jugglers in an attempt to show that they are just as down to earth as any of us short-hairs in the audience." — Hugh Garner, *Saturday Night*

"Leaves almost everything to be desired." — Robert Fulford, *Toronto Telegram*

Pieces of Eight

CBC
Children's
First Broadcast: Thursday, October 16, 1958, 4:45 p.m.
Final Year Broadcast: 1959
Running Time: 15 min.

Cast:
Ranzo the Pirate . . . . H. Leslie Pigot
Music: Leonard Mayoh and The Chantymen, Jimmy Nas

A-r-r-r, maties! Pirate tales and music from the decks of the *Black Avenger*. From Halifax, naturally, where it was seen months earlier.

The Pierre Berton Show

CTV
Interview
First Broadcast: Monday, September 17, 1962, 11:00 p.m.
Final Year Broadcast: 1972
Running Time: 60 min. and 30 min.

Seen on CTV, followed by CHCH and independents, Berton's was the granddaddy of Canadian interview shows. Conceived by producer Ross McLean and taped in Toronto, London, England, Paris, Washington, New York, and Los Angeles, Berton had a knack for roping in high-profile guests (Lucille Ball, Lenny Bruce, Marguerite Oswald [Lee Harvey's mother], Peter Ustinov, Malcolm X) in part because they were promised that the live-on-tape series wouldn't be edited. Later programs focused more on lower-rung entertainment figures (e.g., Paul Lynde) and historical themes. Berton's moody, whistling theme music was an asset.

The critics cheer: "Berton is more interesting than his guests— watch those beady eyes scurry about like two brown ferrets looking for a hole, nose twitching as he seeks an opportunity." — Heather Robertson, *Maclean's*

Pierre in print: Transcripts of interviews from *The Pierre Berton Show* were sold in book form. ▼

Pifffle & Co.

CBC
Comedy
First Broadcast: Sunday, July 11, 1971, 5:30 p.m.
Final Year Broadcast: 1971
Running Time: 30 min.

Hosts: Terry David Mulligan, Bill Reiter

Sketch comedy focusing on a single topic per program (Canadians, women's lib, etc.). Regular performers included Allan Anderson, Graeme Campbell, Roxanne Erwin, Micki Maunsell, Joseph Golland, Shirley Milliner, and Carol Oczkowska. History may someday reveal to us why the three *f*'s in *Pifffle* were considered funnier than two.

The Pig and Whistle

CTV
Musical Variety
First Broadcast: Monday, September, 1967, 9:30 p.m.
Final Year Broadcast: 1977
Running Time: 30 min.

Host: John Hewer
Regular Performers: Kay Turner, The Carlton Showband, The Roland Dancers

Come on in: Long-running Brit-fest The *Pig and Whistle* spawned numerous record albums.

CTV's answer to *Don Messer's Jubilee*, *The Pig and Whistle* (the program *and* the fictional pub) featured British import John Hewer (in vest and straw boater) as a Cockney innkeeper/master of ceremonies. If listening to maudlin renditions of "Knees Up Mother Brown," "Don't Dilly Dally on the Way," or "Boiled Beef and Carrots" bring a tear to your eye, you were probably one of the million-and-a-half viewers who tuned into this cabbage-scented Britfest each week. Kay Turner played the singing barmaid, serving 150 pub "customers" lemon shandies as the Carlton Showband's miniskirt brigade danced on tables, their cheeky male counterparts slapping the bottoms of dancers and patrons alike. At last call, Hewer handed out beer mugs emblazoned with his porky visage, as cast and audience warbled the closing number, "Time Gentlemen Please." Program guests included singers Vera Lynn and Billy Meek, and Hatti Jacques of numerous *Carry On* films.

The critics jeer: "All those sweaty dancers, all that forced good cheer and those corny jokes represent to me all that is obnoxious about the English." — Heather Robertson, *Maclean's*

Pitfall

Global
Game Show
First Broadcast: Monday, September 14, 1981, 2:30 p.m.
Final Year Broadcast: 1982
Running Time: 30 min.

Host: Alex Trebek

One of the more humiliating game shows in recent memory. Contestants roamed a set that looked like a spaceship from the *Alien* films. Answering questions helped contestants move safely through a technophobe's nightmare—a corridor lined with pipes and odd bits of machinery. Players who blew a question were plummeted into a steamy machine pit, forced to answer another barrage of questions to escape.

Pit Pony

CBC
Drama
First Broadcast: Friday, February 5, 1999, 7:30 p.m.
Final Year Broadcast: 2000
Running Time: 30 min.

Cast:

Willie MacLean	Alex Wrathell
Nellie MacLean	Jennie Raymond
Ned Hall	Shaun Smyth
Charley	Denny Doherty
Molly MacIntyre	Hannah Abenheimer
Angus MacDonald	Brenden Doyle
Spider Davis	Matthew Harris
Jeremiah	Jeremiah Sparks
Stringy Borso	Seamus Morrison
Mr. Everett Frawley	Jeremy Akerman

The tale of a young coal miner, Willie, and his friendship with a mining-pit horse, Gem, in the town of Glace Bay, Cape Breton Island, at the turn of the century. Orphaned Alex is looked after by sister Nellie and her fiancé Ned. Alex's friends are grown-up storyteller Charley and kid pals Molly and Angus. Personnel at the National Coal Company's Ocean Deeps Mine include the boys' brigade manager Spider, pit-pony boss Jeremiah, miner Borso, and manager Frawley. Sable was Willie's pony, foal of pit pony Gem who had died in a mine cave-in. Based on a novel by Joyce Barkhouse and a 1997 TV movie of the same name. Filmed on location in Glace Bay, Cape Breton Island.

Planet Tolex

CBC
Children's
First Broadcast: Tuesday, October 20, 1953, 5:00 p.m.
Final Year Broadcast: 1954
Running Time: 30 min.

Puppeteers: Dora Velleman, Leo Velleman

One of Canada's first science-fiction series, set on puppet-populated Planet Tolex. Blumper the white elephant and Timothy the leprechaun contact their Tolexian counterparts—coil-headed aliens Bricol and Lexo—on their mysterious planet on the other side of the sun.

Playbill

CBC
Dramatic Anthology
First Broadcast: Tuesday, May 19, 1953, 8:30 p.m.
Final Year Broadcast: 1954
Running Time: 30 min.

This series of teleplays included: an adaptation of Oscar Wilde's *Lord Arthur Savile's Crime;* Ted Allan's *Goodbye Hollywood, Hello New York,* with Tobi Robbins, James Doohan, and Lorne Greene; and a science-fiction drama, *The Third Ear,* by Madge Miller and Larry Villani. Also known as *CBC Playbill* and *Ford Theatre Playbill* when sponsored by Ford. A summer replacement series for *CBC Theatre* and *General Motors Theatre.*

Playdate

CBC
Dramatic Anthology
First Broadcast: Wednesday, October 4, 1961, 8:00 p.m.
Final Year Broadcast: 1964
Running Time: 60 min.

Hosts: Robert Goulet, Christopher Plummer (1962–63)

A successor to *GM Presents*, teleplays included *Stop The World I Want To Get Off* by Jacqueline Rosenfeld; *The Prizewinner* by Bernard Slade; Phyllis Lee Peterson's adaptation of *Maria Chapdelaine; The Looking Glass World,* a science-fiction story written by Donald Jack, starring Ted Follows and Austin Willis; Arthur Hailey's *The Troubled Heart;* and The *Cowboy and Mr. Anthony,* by Hugh Kemp, starring Ian Tyson and Sylvia Fricker (later Sylvia Tyson). Also seen in Australia.

The Play's The Thing

CBC
Dramatic Anthology
First Broadcast: Thursday, January 17, 1974, 9:00 p.m.
Final Year Broadcast: 1974
Running Time: 60 min.

Host: Gordon Pinsent

Teleplays by notable Canadian writers, including: *Brothers in the Black Art* by Robertson Davies; *And Then Mr. Jonas* by Morley Callaghan; *The Man From Inner Space* by Eric Nicol; *Roundelay* by Pierre Berton; *Back To Beulah* by W.O. Mitchell; *The Servant Girl* by Margaret Atwood; *The Bells Of Hell* by Mordecai Richler; *How I Met My Husband* by Alice Munro; and *The Executioners,* a self-described "Eskimo drama" by Farley Mowat and Len Peterson.

The Plouffe Family

CBC
Drama
First Broadcast: Wednesday, October 14, 1954, 8:30 p.m.
Final Year Broadcast: 1959
Running Time: 30 min.

Cast:

Théophile Plouffe	Paul Guèvremont
Joséphine Plouffe	Amanda Alarie
Cécile Plouffe	Denise Pelletier
Guillaume Plouffe	Pierre Valcour
Napoleon Plouffe	Emile Genest
Ovide Plouffe	Jean-Louis Roux, Marcel Houben
Uncle Gédéon Plouffe	Doris Lussier
Agathe Plouffe	Clémence Desrochers
Flora Plouffe	Ginette Letondal
Démérise Plouffe	Nana de Varennes
Onésime Ménard	Rolland Bédard
Rita Toulouse	Janin Mignolet, Lise Roy
Blanche Toulouse	Lucie Poitras
Jeanne Labrie	Thérèse Cadorette
Martine Plouffe	Margot Campbell
Aimé Plouffe	Jean Coutu
Flora Plouffe	Ginette Letondal
Rosaire Joyeux	Camille Ducharme
Jacqueline Sévigny	Amulette Garneau
Hélène Giguère	Françoise Graton
Narcisse Vallerand	Daniel Lippe
Alphonse Tremblay	Ernest Guimond
Danielle Delorme	Huguette Oligny
Stan Labrie	Jean Duceppe
Tootsie Duquettte	Denise St. Pierre
Tit-me	Jean Coutu
Father Alaxandre	Guy Provost
Alain Richard	Guy Godin
Juvenal Bolduc	Gratien Glinas

Roger Lemelin's popular 1948 novel, *Les Plouffe*, about life in Quebec, begat a daily French radio series, which begat a French television series, *La Famille Plouffe* (Quebec TV's first drama), which begat (finally) an English-language series. Like Vachon snack cakes, this series bridged the bilingual gap, in this case by providing English-speaking audiences with a French-Canadian family they could care about, in a limited sort of way.

The program caught on in Quebec immediately after its debut in November 1953. A year later English Canada received its first dose of Plouffes, translated (and tidied up to eliminate the occasional "damn"), then performed by the same cast (with a few exceptions).

The gritty, working-class Plouffes lived in Quebec City's Lower Town, in a humble home, about two grades above a hovel. Downstairs was occupied by: henpecked plumber Papa Théophile, moderately incompetent and the symbolic head of his household, buoyed by memories of his cycling-champion days; crusty mama Josephine, the brains of the family; and daughter Cécile, on the verge of permanent spinsterhood. The rest of the brood—Guillaume, Napoleon, and Ovide—bashed each other around upstairs. Guillaume was an all-around jock—hockey a specialty; "little" Napoleon lived his sporting fantasies vicariously through a scrapbook crammed with pictures of famous athletes, and by appointing himself as Guillaume's trainer; Ovide was an opera-loving intellectual who worked in a shoe factory. Cécile was pursued by bus driver Onésime (but wouldn't marry him unless he had a $10,000 bank account), Guillaume loved Danielle, and Ovide fancied Rita, a boogie-woogie fan who dallied with Ovide's rival Stan. Cécile married in 1955, precipitating a change of quarters—a new house with the happy couple on the main floor, and Mama, Papa, and the boys crammed upstairs. Cécile had a baby in 1956, and Napoleon married Jeanne Labrie. Cécile died in 1958 in a motorcycle accident, and Napoleon went into business for himself, selling French fries (no, really) from Onésime's garage. Lorne Greene guested in 1958 as a rival for Rita's affections.

A 1958 script featuring Uncle Gédéon's fantasy about pursuit by a harem of women was deemed too risqué for television, though a dream sequence set in hell squeaked by. Uncle Gédéon earned the wrath of independent Quebec MP, Raoul Poulin, who called the program degrading, immoral, and unrepresentative of the people in his riding of Beauce.

In Quebec, broadcasts effectively shut down the province and forced the rescheduling of hockey playoffs. Ratings outside Quebec told a different story. Omitting one-station towns, the Plouffes were slaughtered in the ratings by routine U.S. fare. Far from a national obsession, perhaps *The Plouffes* can rest comfortably on its success in creating a certain level of celebrity for its French-Canadian cast, and in generating at least some bilingual television appeal.

Followed by: two TV sequels, *The Town Above/En haute de la pente douce* (1959), seen in English and French, and the French-only *Le petit monde du Père Gédéon* (1960); another Lemelin novel, *Le Crime d'Ovide Plouffe*; a feature film *Les Plouffe/The Plouffe Family*; and a miniseries, *Le Crime d'Ovide Plouffe/Death in the Family*. The Plouffes also re-emerged in 1976 (with Lemelin's blessing) as a U.S. sitcom, *Viva Valdez*, about a family of Hispanics who lived in a Los Angeles barrio.

Police Surgeon

CTV
Drama
First Broadcast: Saturday, September 11, 1972, 7:30 p.m.
Final Year Broadcast: 1974
Running Time: 30 min.

Cast:
Dr. Simon Locke . . . . Sam Groom
Lieutenant Detective Dan Palmer . . . . Len Birman
Lieutenant Jack Gordon . . . . Larry Mann
Radio Dispatcher . . . . Nerene Virgin
Tony . . . . Marc Hebet

The offspring of *Dr. Simon Locke*, in which our former country-doctor hero high-tails it to an unidentified city to join the ambiguously titled Emergency Medical Unit of the Metropolitan Police Department as its star "police surgeon." Coincidentally, Dan Palmer left Dr. Locke's same small town to join the MPD as a lieutenant detective. CTV press releases tell it all: "Simon Locke carries a gun in his pocket and a badge in his wallet. He tolerates the badge. And although he hates the weapon, he will use it. But only with the same decisiveness of a surgeon when the tumor is a threat of life!" (I am not making this up.) Tony was Locke's ambulance driver. Guest criminals included Donald Pleasance as a mad bomber, and William Shatner as a vengeful cop. And what the hell is a police surgeon anyway?

Polka Dot Door

TVO
Children's
First Broadcast: Monday, October 4, 1971, 8:00 a.m.
Final Year Broadcast: 1994
Running Time: 30 min.

Hosts: Cindy Cook, Nonnie Griffin, Rex Hagon, Nina Keogh, Alex Laurier, Carrie Loring, Gart Mosbaugh, Gloria Reuben, Gairey Richardson, Denis Simpson, Shelley Sommers, Gordon Thomson, Christopher Trace, Tonya Williams, others

Based on the British series *Playschool*. Four stuffed toys (Humpty, Dumpty, Marigold, Bear) and a spotted kangaroo capable only of speaking its name, Polkaroo, formed the core of this long-running series. Human hosts told kids at home what time it was (*Story Time*, etc.). Polkaroo was played by a succession of male co-hosts who arrived too late, sans costume, to see the mysterious creature.

Spinoffs include *Tell Me a Story* and *Polka Dot Shorts*, which debuted in 1993, replacing *Polka Dot Door* and giving voice (on September 23, 1996) to Polkaroo (Andrew Sabiston) and his companions. Also seen on CBC and around the world, including South Africa and China. The *Polka Dot* series also spawned several live stage shows.

The sounds of silence: The sleeve of this *Polka Dot Door* record album features only characters who, according to the program, were mute.

Police Surgeon— with dice: Board game based on the *Police Surgeon* series, which starred Sam Groom.

Poltergeist: The Legacy

Drama
CTV
First Broadcast: Saturday, September 14, 1996 , 9:00 p.m.
Final Year Broadcast: 1997
Running Time: 60 min.

Cast:
Derek Rayne . . . . Derek de Lint
Alex Moreau. . . . . Robbi Chong
Nick Boyle . . . . Martin Cummins
Patrick Fitzgerald. . . . . Philip Connolly
Dr. Rachel Corrigan . . . . Helen Shaver
Dr. William Sloan. . . . . Daniel J. Travanti
Kat Corrigan. . . . . Alexandra Purvis

No Canadian characters in sight in this Canadian-made series focusing on the supernatural. The Luna Foundation, located on Angel Island near San Francisco, is headed by Dr. Rayne, a "precept" of The Legacy, an ages-old organization dedicated to exploring the supernatural and protecting humankind from its darker side. His team included computer expert Alex, tough guy Nick, fallen priest Patrick, and psychiatrist Rachel. Dr. Sloan was a British precept. When summoned, they fly around the world to battle the forces of evil. Gory and violent (impaling, maggots, gobs of blood), the network received major complaints from offended viewers and a slap on the wrist from the Canadian Broadcast Standards Council, despite heavy editing. CTV showed only one of four seasons.

Power Play

CTV
Drama
First Broadcast: Thursday, October 15, 1998, 8:00 p.m.
Final Year Broadcast: 2000
Running Time: 60 min.

Cast:
Brett Parker . . . . Michael Riley
Colleen Blessed . . . . Kari Matchett
Coach Lloyd Gorman. . . . . Al Waxman
Coach Harry Strand . . . . Neil Crone
Duff McArdle . . . . Gordon Pinsent
Jake Nelson. . . . . Don Cherry
Michele Parker . . . . Caterina Scorsone
Rose Thorton. . . . . Krista Bridges
Renata D'Alessandro . . . . Lori Anne Alter

Al "Shakey" Tremblay. . . . . Normand Bissonnette
Todd "Terminal" Maplethorpe . . . . Jonathan Rannells
Jukka "Braniac" Branny-Acke . . . . Mark Lutz
Mark Simpson. . . . . Dean McDermott
Ray Malone . . . . Sean McCann
Samantha . . . . Jennifer Dale
Hudson James . . . . Jonathan Crombie

Theme Song: "The Good Ol' Hockey Game" performed by Stompin' Tom Connors

Not since CBC's *He Shoots, He Scores* had Canadian television attempted a program about hockey. Big-time New York hockey agent, Parker, was softened up by his junior league coach, Malone, to become general manager of the Hamilton Steelheads. Pinsent was the Steelheads' millionare owner, though he left operations to corporate executive Blessed, who wanted to pack the team off to Houston. Parker and Blessed were involved in a love-hate thing. Thorton was a local sports reporter; Nelson (Cherry's acting debut) was a rival Philly coach. Series highlights: Parker is fired; Blessed resigns; Thorton becomes infatuated with Parker; the Steelheads become wards of the federal government when U.S. interests attempt a takeover; Parker stages a press conference draped in a Canadian flag; and McArdle watches Pinsent's old CBC series *Quentin Durgens, MP*. Steelhead rink scenes were filmed in Hamilton's Copps Coliseum. Popular in Canada, the series' second episode, broadcast on U.S. network UPN, recorded the lowest rating in U.S. broadcast history.

Prisoners Of Gravity

TVO
Interview
First Broadcast: Thursday, October 4, 1990, 7:30 p.m.
Final Year Broadcast: 1994
Running Time: 30 min.

Host: Rick Green

From his spaceship, Earth expatriate Commander Rick conducted interviews on science-fiction-related issues via satellite. Programs were organized thematically (censorship, immortality, sex, stereotypes) and included genre writers (Douglas Adams, Clive Barker, Ray Bradbury, Neil Gaiman, Judith Merril, Harlan Ellison, Frank Miller, Spider Robinson, Robert Sawyer, Peter Straub, Jack Vance, Jack Womack and Roger Zelazny) and comic book artists/writers (Sergio Aragones,

Will Eisner, Gilbert Hernandez, and Bob Kane, creator of Batman.) Also on hand: *Star Trek*'s Nichelle Nichols and Don Harron as Charlie Farquharson. The series' wraparound was a mock documentary, *Second Nature* (hosted by a certain Enrico Gruen), whose broadcast was usurped by Green.

Professor Moffett's Science Workshop

CBC
Children's
First Broadcast: Monday, September 11, 1972, 5:00 p.m.
Final Year Broadcast: 1974
Running Time: 30 min.

Host: Professor Maxwell G. Moffett
Assistants: Claire-Anne Bundy, Stuart Bundy

Irish designer and engineer Moffett, owner of an outrageous beard, demonstrated various scientific principles with two young assistants.

Professor's Hideaway

CFTO
Children's
First Broadcast: Monday, January 2, 1961, 4:00 p.m.
Final Year Broadcast: 1964
Running Time: 60 min. and 90 min.

Cast:
The Professor . . . . Stan Francis
Puppeteers: Hal Marquette, Rene Marquette

Adventures from the Professor's hilltop laboratory, with Sampson the cowardly dog, X and Y, the undercover raccoons, the Raven, and a couple of pixies who dance to Percy Faith's "Swedish Rhapsody." In a typical session the Prof makes plans to visit the moon, catches an episode of the *Three Stooges* or *Tales of the Riverbank*, then tells kids how to grow sprouts from half a sweet potato. Also known as *Hideaway Funtime* and *Professor's Party*.

Profile

CBC
Profile
First Broadcast: Thursday, June 16, 1955, 10:30 p.m.
Final Year Broadcast: 1957
Running Time: 30 min.

Host: Percy Saltzman

Interviews with and biographies of international artists, intellectuals, and newsmakers, usually filmed in their own homes. Subjects included Pablo Casals, Billy Graham, Robert Frost, A.Y. Jackson, Arthur Lismer, Margaret Mead, and Bertrand Russell.

Program X

CBC
Dramatic Anthology
First Broadcast: Thursday, December 17, 1970, 9:00 p.m.
Final Year Broadcast: 1973
Running Time: 30 min.

Host: Charles Oberdorf

Experimental plays made on rock-bottom budgets (they couldn't afford a title, get it?) ranging from gothic horror (*The Ballad of Willie and Rose*) to the Kafkaesque (*The Late Man*). Shot on film and tape, the series showcased some early work by writer/director David Cronenberg.

Psi Factor: Chronicles of the Paranormal

Global
Drama
First Broadcast: Saturday, October 5, 1996, 10:00 p.m.
Final Year Broadcast: 2000
Running Time: 60 min.

Host: Dan Aykroyd
Cast:
Lindsay Donner . . . . Nancy Anne Sakovich
Peter Axon . . . . Barclay Hope
Professor Anton Hendricks . . . . Colin Fox
Dr. Claire Davison . . . . Soo Garay
Matt Praeger . . . . Matt Frewer (1997–2000)
Ray Donahue . . . . Peter MacNeill (1996–99)
Lennox Q. Cooper . . . . Peter Blais (1996–99)
Frank Elsinger . . . . Nigel Bennett (1996–99)
Dr. Curtis Rollins . . . . Maurice Dean Wint (1996–97)
Professor Connor Doyle . . . . Paul Miller (1996–97)
Michael Kelly . . . . Michael Moriarty (1997–98)
Natasha Constantine . . . . Lisa LaCroix (1996–97)
Smithwick . . . . Elizabeth Shepherd (1996–97)
Corliss . . . . Tamara Gorski (1996–97)
Miles . . . . Lindsay Collins (1996–97)
Dr. Mia Stone . . . . Joanne Vannicola (1999–2000)

A docudrama based on the strange cases of the Office of Scientific Investigation and Research (the OSIR actually exists) as they investigate the paranormal. The "docu" part of this drama may have been a more plausible claim during the first season's tamer episodes, mostly consisting of two modest half-hour stories.

The second season came on like gangbusters, ushering in the first of a series of cast changes, a switch to one-hour stories, and a monstrous array of paranormal phenomena, in the form of alien abductions, ghosts, demons, dybbuks, vampires, and zombies.

Fans of the series enjoyed the OSIR team's high-tech approach to investigation, while critics drubbed the show. Host Aykroyd published a book of stories adapted from the series.

The critics jeer: "Help. A ton of gibberish has fallen on me and I can't get up." — Claire Bickley, *The Toronto Sun*

The Public Eye

CBC
Public Affairs
First Broadcast: Tuesday, October 5, 1965, 10:30 p.m.
Final Year Broadcast: 1969
Running Time: 30 min.

Hosts: Philip Deane (1965–67), Warner Troyer (1967–68), Barry Callaghan, Norman DePoe, Peter Jennings, Jeanne Sauvé, Larry Zolf (1968–69)

A successful series that held public policy up to careful scrutiny. Subjects included: Canadian labour unions, a study of the Cuban missile crisis, race relations, riot control, and the bombing of Dresden during WWII.

The program also presented satirical material, including a spoof of *This Hour Has Seven Days*, with host Deane as Patrick Watson. The five hosts of the final season took turns at the show's helm. Guests included David Brinkley and Rich Little. A companion program, *The Other Eye*, was a short-lived disaster.

The critics cheer: "...a hard driving outfit that has produced some excellent shows...." — Leslie Millin, *The Globe and Mail*

Purple Playhouse

CBC
Dramatic Anthology
First Broadcast: Sunday, February 25, 1973, 9:00 p.m.
Final Year Broadcast: 1973
Running Time: 60 min.

Host: Robertson Davies

These taped productions of Victorian melodramas, replete with English accents, had a BBC-ish feel to them. Productions included Barry Morse as *Sweeney Todd, The Demon Barber of Fleet Street;* Norman Welsh as *Dracula;* Leslie Nielsen in a dual role in *The Lyons Mail; The Corsican Brothers;* and *Box and Cox.*

Puttnam's Prairie Emporium

CTV
Children's
First Broadcast: Saturday, September 21, 1988, 11:00 a.m.
Final Year Broadcast: 1991
Running Time: 30 min.

Cast:
Puttnam . . . . George Alexander
Katy . . . . Brandie Mickleborough
Mark . . . . Jeremy Drummond
Ellen . . . . Coral Paul
Ivan . . . . Billy Morton

Ambitious, enjoyable kid's show set in a magical general store located somewhere on the Canadian prairie. A single mom moves her citified kids (Mark, Ellen) to her old homestead above the title store, learning to live with her father (the eccentric proprietor), Ivan (a goofy inventor, creator of the time-travelling closet), poetry-spouting beatnik feline Caldicott C. Catt (a puppet), and a talking moose head mounted on the wall. Typical episodes: Ivan retrieves Sigmund Freud to help Ellen deal with her fear of storms; a failed experiment switches the brains and bodies of Emporium denizens. Sometimes poignant, at other times hip and self-deprecating, the series was filmed in Saskatchewan, where some episodes were broadcast locally as early as 1987.

QED

CTV
Game Show
First Broadcast: Saturday, May 1, 1960, 8:00 p.m.
Final Year Broadcast: 1960
Running Time: 30 min.

Hosts: Joe McCulley, Austin Willis
Panelists: Marcus Long, Rabbi Abraham Feinberg

A cross between *Fighting Words* and *Truth or Consequences,* this early game show featured offbeat discussions, punctuated by brief stunts and limerick contests. The show failed to create any magic among regular panelists Long, left-wing Rabbi Feinberg, and oddly selected guests, including Eva Gabor, Aldous Huxley, and Gypsy Rose Lee. In the show's filmed pilot, McCulley was a panelist and Sir Robert Watson-Watt was the host.

The critics jeer: "Moderator McCulley fails to crack the whip when he should, and chaos always seems just around the corner...suffers from assorted ills." — Bob Blackburn, *The Toronto Star*

Quentin Durgens, MP

CBC
Drama
First Broadcast: Tuesday, December 6, 1966, 9:00 p.m.
Final Year Broadcast: 1969
Running Time: 60 min.

Cast:

Quentin Durgens	Gordon Pinsent
Hannah Durgens	Roxana Bond
Eddie Durgens	Leslie Barringer
Letourneau	Ovila Legare
Jack Sewell	Budd Knapp
Ted Good	Frank Perry
Secretary	Nancy Kerr
'Toinette	Suzanne Levesque
Forget	Jean-Louis Roux
Mrs. Forget	Stevie Wise
Harriot	Bill Needles
Sherwin	Cec Linder

The show started in 1965 as *Mr. Member of Parliament,* a six-part segment of CBC's *The Serial* and a sort of *Mr. Smith Goes to Ottawa.* Idealistic lawyer Quentin Durgens (or Quent), from Moose Falls, Ontario, lived quietly with his wife, his mother Hannah, and his son Eddie. When his politician father died, he became the Honourable Member from Hampton County. As a politician, this boy was green—a scrupulous but naive politician, too honest for national politics, where his rural notions of decency and fair play stuck in the craws of the feds.

In the series, Quent's wife had died. He relied on his Quebécoise secretary,

Mr. Member of Parliament: Promotional flyer for the CBC's first full season of *Quentin Durgens, MP.*

CBC

Episodes set in Moose Falls rather than Ottawa tended toward the silly. In one, Quent tried to get the government to support a local inventor who had developed a fluid that doubled gas mileage. Another, about a liquor plebiscite, was intended as a series spinoff to be known as *The Mayor.* Quent's ally in these episodes was Jack Sewell, editor of the *Moose Falls Times-Examiner.*

Filmed in Ottawa and a recreated parliamentary chamber in a Toronto studio.

The critics cheer: "The tight, bright scripts of George Robertson are gutsily evocative of the Ottawa scene, and Gordon Pinsent's fine-tuned portrayal of a pragmatic politician is variously engrossing, amusing, touching and persuasive."
— John Ruddy, *TV Guide*

Quiz Kids

CBC
Game Show/Children's
First Broadcast: Saturday, April 1, 1978, 11:30 a.m.
Final Year Broadcast: 1982
Running Time: 30 min.

Host: Jim Walsh

A game show for elementary school children, produced in Newfoundland.

'Toinette, and the advice of House Leader Letourneau. As the series progressed, Quent became less impetuous, though he lost as many times as he won: his phone was tapped, his office was ransacked, and he was beaten about the head and neck by hippies. In a rare moment of programming chutzpah, the CBC scheduled a two-part episode about a leadership convention, between Forget and Quent's man Harriot, during an actual Liberal leadership convention.

The Raccoons

CBC
Animated
First Broadcast: Monday, October 7, 1985, 7:30 p.m.
Final Year Broadcast: 1992
Running Time: 30 min.

Narrator: Geoffrey Winter (1985–92)
Voices of:

Bert Raccoon, Mr. Knox, Pig Two, Pig Three . . . . Len Carlson
Melissa Raccoon . . Linda Feige (1985), Susan Roman (1986–92)
Ralph Raccoon, Lady Baden-Baden, Bear . . . . Bob Dermer
Bentley Raccoon . . . . Noam Zylberman (1987–89), Stuart Stone (1990–92)
Broo the puppy, Sophie Tutu . . . . Sharon Lewis
Cyril Sneer, Snag . . . . Michael Magee
Cedric Sneer . . . . Marvin Goldhar
Dan the Forest Ranger . . . . Murray Cruchley
George Raccoon . . . . Dan Hennessey (1990–92)
Julie . . . . Vanessa Lindores
Lisa Raccoon . . . . Lisa Lougheed (1990–92)
Mr. Mammoth, Mr. Willow, Schaeffer . . . . Carl Banas
Nicole Raccoon . . . . Liz Hanna (1990–92)
Pig One . . Nick Nichols (1985–89), Keith Hampshire (1989–92)
Tommy . . . . Noam Zylberman

A long-running animated series about life in the Evergreen Forest where raccoons Bert, Ralph, and Melissa, and dogs Schaeffer and Broo match wits with the evil tycoon aardvark Cyril Sneer and his band of Secret Service Bears. Cedric, Cyril's sensitive son, often aids the raccoons against his nasty dad. The series was introduced as a one-hour special, *Christmas Raccoons* (1980), followed by *Raccoons on Ice* (1981), *The Raccoons and the Lost Star* (1983), and *The Raccoons: Let's Dance* (1984) with some voice actors different from those in the series. Seen around the world, Japanese buyers asked the producers to punctuate the series with a few scenes of violence (they refused). Product spinoffs included books, albums, videos, T-shirts, watches, sleepwear, and running shoes (Sneerkers!).

Radisson

CBC
Adventure
First Broadcast: Saturday, February 9, 1957, 7:00 p.m.
Final Year Broadcast: 1958
Running Time: 30 min.

Cast:

Pierre Esprit Radisson . . . . Jacques Godin
Medard Chouart, Sieur des Groseilliers . . . . Rene Caron
Onenga . . . . Raymond Royer
Theme song: "Radisson" sung by Wally Koster

If Walt Disney could create a Davy Crockett craze with its trumped-up version of life in pioneer America, why couldn't Canada create its own home-grown hero frenzy? And what better subject than the fictionalized adventures of one of Canada's most colourful historical figures, fur trapper Pierre Radisson, hunting for pelts among the Iroquois, with his brother-in-law—a jolly, bearded Des Groseilliers? With a catchy theme song like:

"Radisson, Radisson,
Canada's courageous pioneer!
Radisson, Radisson,
Lord of the Wilderness,
The man who knew no fear..."

how could it fail?

This production, based on Radisson's own journals, and set along the banks of the St. Lawrence and on Ile Perrot, was plagued by rain, mosquitoes, and commercial river traffic, while costs escalated from a mere $7,000 to $25,000 per episode (each was

A couple of cards: Radisson (left) and Des Groseilliers (right) appear on signature cards from Parkhurst's *Radisson* bubble gum trading-card set.

filmed separately in French and English). Four completed scripts disappeared when the series' writer's car was stolen.

Waiting for an eager cavalcade of *Radisson*-crazed juniors, product licencers (and writer John Lucarotti) stocked up on program merchandise, including a recording of the show's theme.

Among the poor-selling TV toys inspired by the program were a Radisson doll, buckskin suit, rifle, belt, music box, T-shirt, and a board game based on Snakes and Ladders, taking Radisson, in a canoe gamepiece, from Three Rivers to Hudson Bay while avoiding obstacles like rapids and Iroquois. A *Radisson* fur hat was crafted from *Davy Crockett* overstock (sold wholesale at a nickel apiece), left behind when the bottom dropped out of Crockett fashion two years earlier. The *Radisson* version was a coonskin cap with a white feather replacing the clipped-off tail. (Unconfirmed rumours suggest that some distraught storekeepers tried to sew raccoon tails *back on* to the hats.)

The opening sequence promised high adventure, but the show was only moderately popular with young audiences, who grew tired of watching our hero paddle through the same short stretch of the St. Lawrence. The series boasted just a few regulars, like Onenga, Radisson's Iroquois blood brother.

The series was also plagued by gaffes. Though designers struggled to be historically accurate (some props were over 300 years old) even junior viewers couldn't forgive a pioneer jet plane zooming across the sky, factory-made canoe paddles, and Iroquois braves in ill-fitting wigs. Canoes tipped constantly; one actor playing an Iroquois told reporters: "If the make-up girl doesn't part my wig dead centre, the whole boat goes over." A Cockney dialogue director taught French-Canadian actors to refer to the Governor of the colonies as "Guv'ner."

In one episode Radisson prepared to blow up an Iroquois fort by lighting the fuse on a powder keg. The next scene? Our hero engaged in a leisurely duck-hunt.

Neither slick nor action-packed enough to face its U.S. competition, the show was killed after two feeble seasons. Twenty-six episodes were retitled *Tomahawk* and sold to the U.S., performing reasonably well in some local markets, including New York City.

The critics cheer: "When a seven-year-old knows and can pronounce des Groseilliers that's proof enough that the series has 'taken.'" — J.E. Belliveau, *The Toronto Star*

The critics jeer: "Pierre lays an egg…. The Canadian taxpayer is a long-suffering individual…. MPs…are already eagerly awaiting an opportunity to bring Pierre Radisson before Parliament…. It shows some highly improbable Indians, plus some highly improbable white people, going through a series of disconnected scenes." — Peter Dempson, *Toronto Telegram*

"He wasn't a cardboard hero, he simply didn't resemble a hero of any kind." — E.H. Hausmann, *Starweek*

The Raes

CBC
Musical Variety
First Broadcast: Friday, June 30, 1978, 9:00 p.m.
Final Year Broadcast: 1980
Running Time: 60 min. and 30 min.

Hosts: Robbie Rae, Cherill Rae
Orchestra Leader: Tommy Banks

This flash-in-the-pan disco duo rose to prominence on their shake-your-booty rendition of Doris Day's "Que Sera, Sera." While they never produced a big follow-up hit, they did provide renditions of then-current hits like "In the Navy" and "Rah Rah Rasputin." Comedy was provided by Jackson Davies and Lally Cadeau. Choreographed numbers were by the James Hibbard Dancers.

An eclectic guest roster included Morey Amsterdam, Patsy Gallant, Susan Jacks, Shari Lewis and Lambchop, Patti Page, Rex Smith, Ian Tyson, Peter Pringle, and Tammy Wynette.

From Vancouver, this was originally a summer series that served as a platform for

Got 'em, need 'em: In politically incorrect trading cards, Radisson's former allies, the "cowardly Hurons," attempt to kill the trapper and steal his furs. Abject defeat results.

the Lucky Seven Loto Canada ticket draw.

Network promotional material claimed the program was "gwell"—a Welsh word meaning "truly superior." But all was not gwell with The Raes, who broke up the act—and their marriage—a few years later. The press subsequently reported that Cherill branded the series a big mistake— all Robbie's idea, and a bad one.

Randy Dandy

CHCH
Children's
First Broadcast: Monday, August 13, 1962, 3:00 p.m.
Final Year Broadcast: 1966
Running Time: 90 min.

Theme Song: "Hey Lah-dee, Lah-dee, Lah-dee"

Cast:
Randy Dandy . . . . Rafael Markowitz

A popular local program featuring Markowitz, who later produced *The Hilarious House of Frightenstein*. As guitar-playing Randy, he introduced *Popeye* cartoons and interacted with the Silly Willy Clown, puppets Ethel and Egbert ("those happy eels from town"), Whopper J. Fibley ("A fib's a fib…") whose inflatable balloon nose exploded after reaching a critical mass of lies. Randy also played Captain Randy Dandy.

The Ray Bradbury Theater

Syndicated: 1985
Dramatic Anthology
Running Time: 30 min. and 90 min.

Host: Ray Bradbury

Author Bradbury adapted his own short stories for television in this interesting anthology series. Some episodes were filmed in Canada, while others were filmed in England, New Zealand (Xena herself, Lucy Lawless, starred in an episode) and France (stories set originally in the U.S. are transposed to Paris). The first six episodes were packaged as *The Ray Bradbury Trilogy 1* in 1985 and *The Ray Bradbury Trilogy 2* in 1986 and seen on HBO in the U.S. and First Choice in Canada. The next five seasons were seen on the USA network and rebroadcast on Global in Canada.

Some notable actors in the series included Denholm Elliott, Elliott Gould, Peter O'Toole,

Que Sera: Disco team Robbie and Cherill Rae spun a B.C. lottery ticket program into their own CBC variety series.

CBC

and James Whitmore. Canadians included Paul Gross, Barry Morse, Leslie Nielsen, Gordon Pinsent, Donald Pleasance, Michael Sarrazin, William Shatner, and John Vernon. While the production on some of the episodes is spotty, Bradbury's superior material carries the series.

Best episodes: "The Crowd," about a man (Nick Mancuso) who sees the same group of people at every accident; "The Town Where No One Got Off," with Jeff Goldblum as a man who leaves a train on a dare; "The Dwarf," with Megan Follows as a carnival employee who finds sympathy for a writer; "Usher II," about a Poe-obsessed megalomaniac; and "The Dead Man," with Louise Fletcher as a woman who marries the wrong guy.

Razzle Dazzle

CBC
Children's
First Broadcast: Monday, October 2, 1961, 5:00 p.m.
Final Year Broadcast: 1966
Running Time: 30 min.

Hosts: Alan Hamel (1961–64), Michele Finney (1961–64), Ray Bellew (1964–66), Trudy Young (1964–66), Sandy Pollock (occasional)

Cast:
Percy Q. Kidpester. . . . . Ed McNamara
Mr. Igotit . . . . Joe Murphy
Mr. Sharpy . . . . Paul Kligman
Hiram Korntassel. . . . . Jack Mather
Mother Mayonnaise. . . . . Barbara Hamilton
Sherlock House . . . . Drew Thompson
Mandarin Tee Hee, Bimbo the Clown, Lord Faversham, Sheik
    Ali Ben Roth, El Rotho . . . . Michael Roth
Dancer . . . . Joey Hollingsworth
Voice of:
Howard. . . . . John Keogh
Puppeteers: John Keogh, Linda Keogh
Theme song: "Tiger Rag"

"Hold everything. Here's the show for kids and turtles."

— Show opener, *Razzle Dazzle*

Set in Razzle Dazzle Alley, this was a conglomeration of every successful kids' show device ever: secret decoder rings, comic strips, serialized movies, dozens of rubber chickens, and more characters and segments than any rational person could keep track of.

Though the hosts were human, the star of the show was spiral-eyed puppet Howard the Turtle, stuck permanently on a pedestal and playing dozens of characters, including: Howard Mellotone, presenting the Pick of the Pops on station C.O.W. (M-o-o-o!), with the Hit Parade Dancers; Howard Footnote, reading Batty Bedtime Stories; Howard Handsome and his Dance Party with the Razzle Dazzle Dancers (performing the dance craze, the Razzle Dazzle, no less); Howard I. Threadneedle, poet; Jimmy Fiddle Faddle, Hollywood gossip columnist for the *Razzle Dazzle Daily;* Howard the chef, presenting Howard's Mad Menu; know-it-all Klaxton Q. Hornblower; and Mr. Showbizz, who produced viewer plays as part of the Razzle Dazzle Genius Department contest.

Popular segments included: Nutty News Reels (re-cut silent films); Groaners (jokes sent in by the audience); The Turtleshell Players in productions including *One Cheap Arabian Night* and *Mutiny on the Bouncy;* The Hinkley-Dinkley News Report; Kooky Commercials; and weird inventions—Rube Goldberg devices designed by viewers and built by staff. Serials included: Australia's

CBC

Turtle power: Michele Finney cozies up to kids' show host extraordinaire, Howard the Turtle.

The Terrible Ten (1961–62), *The Magic Boomerang,* and *The Forest Rangers* (1963).

The program burst at the seams with human characters: frequently booed misanthrope Percy Q. Kidpester (who stopped bugging kids for two seconds at Christmas); incompetent con man Mr. Sharpy, on the lookout for "a knuckleful of nickels"; Mr. Igotit, the storekeeper; Hiram Corntassle, a deceptively intelligent rube from Cucumber Corners (Howard's home town); lazy homemaker Mother Mayonnaise; Sherlock House, "the defective detective" who saved the world from flying saucers; Don "Ace" Baker who coached bizarre games for kids; German inventor Herr Doktor Professor Vee Gates; and mailman Johann Sebastian Bagstrap.

Eric Aldwinkle hosted an educational feature called *Out of His Mind,* and guests included Larry and Gary, the comedy team of Larry Solway and Gary Ferrier. Cartoonist George Feyer drew comic strips featuring Kidpester and other characters, including Boomer Foghorn, Terwilleger Topsoil, Mendel Meek, Daniel the Spaniel (from *Junior Roundup*), and Commander J. Tipton Teabag.

Razzle Dazzle featured a live studio audience, but kids at home participated in Telequiz, a telephone segment, and joined the Razzle Dazzle Club (120,000 members in the U.S. and Canada) which paid off with an official ballpoint pen, button, and decoder, which deciphered secret messages.

So popular, the network received up to 1,200 letters per day, spawning the comment, "Things like this aren't supposed to happen at the CBC" from one harried exec.

The program was inexplicably cancelled in 1967, to be replaced by such stellar fare as *Rocket Robin Hood.*

Limited *Razzle Dazzle* series included: *Razzle Dazzle: Howard Presents The Olympics* (October 1964); *Razzle Dazzle Presents Movie Matinee,* a silent movie showcase, (October 1962); *Razzle Dazzle Presents The Magic Boomerang* (September 1964; June and September 1965); and *Razzle Dazzle With The Forest Rangers* (Fall 1963).

The critics cheer: "Razzle Dazzle entertains brilliantly and in endless variety. It also instructs and informs always with subtlety and humor...."— J. Irwin, *The Toronto Star*

RCMP

See: *Royal Canadian Mounted Police*

Reach for the Top

CBC
Game Show
First Broadcast: Monday, October 4, 1965, 6:00 p.m.
Final Year Broadcast: 1983
Running Time: 30 min.

Launching with its kick-ass guitar-and-drum theme song, this quiz show pitted high school against high school in a battle of brains. Questions ranged from general knowledge to art, sports, and music in cleverly titled rounds: Open Questions; Assigned Questions; Scrambles; What Am I?, Who Am I? and the fast and furious Snapper round that could make or break a match. After a local-team elimination round, winning teams headed to the provincial round and, finally, the nationals. Students won lapel pins, book prizes (not for personal use, selfish louts—for the school library!), or scholarships.

Started as a local Vancouver show in 1961, picked up by Toronto in 1965, then carried nationwide in 1966. Alex Trebek was a quizmaster for Toronto shows; Bill Guest was the most frequent quizmaster in the nationals.

The program was cancelled in 1983 because its half-million viewers were largely over 55—not the audience the CBC hoped to reach. Following cancellation, producer Sandy Stewart continued the show on local stations, including community cable outlets.

The critics jeer: "The quiz kids are about as sensitive as meat grinders. They scratch and claw for every point, lips smacking and eyes glittering…. The losers swear into the microphones." — Heather Robertson, *Maclean's*

The Real Magees

CBC
Discussion
First Broadcast: Monday, May 22, 1973, 1:30 p.m.
Final Year Broadcast: 1973
Running Time: 30 min.

Hosts: Michael Magee, Duddie Magee

A husband-and-wife team in an offbeat show featuring unscripted discussions and interviews with "plain folk" like a cabby, an ambulance driver, a bouncer, and a fortune teller.

ReBoot

YTV
Animated
First Broadcast: Saturday, September 17, 1994, 7:30 p.m.
Final Year Broadcast: 1998
Running Time: 30 min.

Voices Of:

Bob . . . . Michael Benyaer (1994–97), Ian James Corlett (1997–98)
Dot Matrix . . . . Kathleen Barr
Enzo Matrix . . . . . . Jesse Moss (1994–95), Matthew Sinclair (1996–97), Christopher Gray (1997–98)
Big Enzo . . . . Paul William Dobson (1997–98)
Megabyte . . . . Tony Jay
Hexadecimal . . . . Shirley Millner
Cecil, Mike the TV, Phong . . . . Michael Donovan
Andraia. . . . . Andrea Libman (1996–98)
Big Andraia . . . . Sharon Alexander (1997–98)
Hack . . . . Gary Chalk
Slash . . . . Philip Maurice Hayes
Slash-2 . . . . Scott McNeil (1997–98)
Mouse . . . . Louise Vallance

The first television program produced entirely using computer graphic imagery (CGI). *ReBoot* was set inside a computer (the city of Mainframe), and populated by the likes of Bob, a Guardian Program downloaded from the Super Computer. Bob was sweet on Dot, owner of Dot's Diner and big sister to Enzo.

When the unseen User decided to play a computer game, a "game cube" descended on Mainframe, forcing residents to compete in

Reaching for the top: Author (bottom row, second from right) on the Lord Dorchester *Reach for the Top* team. Note "fighting turtle" mascot on desk. Game perks included book prizes, and the opportunity to act like a smartass on television. (Moderator: "What are your career goals?" Smartass kid: "To become a 'Yes' man.")

games of skill, "rebooting" themselves into various gaming roles. Bob was a games expert, aided by a wristwatch gadget called the Glitch. Mainframe's enemies were tough guy Megabyte and Hexadecimal, a super-villainess who lived on the floating city of Lost Angles.

ReBoot was a fun kiddie series with enough wit and intelligence to entertain adults, particularly a spot-on spoof of *The X-Files* and some of the deadpan techno-dialogue (birthdays are known as "upgrades.")

Though the show ran four seasons, the third season consisted entirely of repeat episodes. A rumoured fifth season doesn't appear imminent, though the producers hint at a TV movie to tie up loose ends from the final season.

Red Fisher

Syndicated: 1972
Fishing
Running Time: 30 min.

Host: Red Fisher

Legendary broadcaster Red Fisher shared fishing adventures from Scuttlebutt Lodge, tall tale capital of the world (actually a cheesy indoor cabin set.) Red lured guests on fishing expeditions with him, then recorded the adventure on grainy silent film for later broadcast.

Fishing locales included Iceland, Japan, and Australia, but most often Red wound up at a fishing hole in the good ol' Canadian Arctic. Red's guests included NHL hockey types (Ted Williams), minor celebrities (Alan Hale Jr., the Skipper on *Gilligan's Island,* and Slim Pickens, the guy who rides an A-bomb to his doom in *Dr. Strangelove*), or surprises like Apollo 13 astronaut Jim Lovell. At show's end, Red presented his guests with a self-penned book of verse, *Poems of the Great Outdoors,* which included such memorable fare as "The Curse of the Shifting Sands," or a rhyming commentary on the Vietnam War. Even if you didn't really like fishing, watching Red Fisher was—well, dammit—kind of cozy. Red's other series, all identical, were known as *Our Great Outdoor*s, and *Outdoor Adventures* and ran well into the 1980s. If imitation is the sincerest form of flattery, Red's got a few admirers, including Steve Smith, whose *Red Green Show* was clearly inspired by this one, and the *SCTV* crew, who created *The Fishin' Musician* spoof, with Gil Fisher played by John Candy.

The Red Green Show

Comedy
CHCH, Global, CBC
First Broadcast: Wednesday, September 4, 1991, 8:30 p.m.
Final Year Broadcast: —
Running Time: 30 min.

Cast:

Red Green	Steve Smith
Harold Green	Pat McKenna
Bill Smith	Rick Green
Buzz Sherwood	Peter Wildman
Bob Stuyvesant	Bruce Hunter
Ranger Gord	Peter Keleghan
Dalton Humphries	Bob Bainborough
Glen Braxton	Mark Wilson
Ed Frid	Jerry Schaefer
Hap Shaughnessy	Gordon Pinsent
Mike Hamar	Wayne Robson
Dougie Franklin	Ian Thomas
Edgar Montrose	Graham Greene
Winston Rothschild III	Jeff Lumby
Arnie Doogan	Albert Schultz
Kevin Black	Paul Gross
Postman	Will Millar
Jack	Tim Sims
Dwight Cardiff	George Buza
Bryan Jacobs	Derek Edwards
Walter Smith	Joel Harris
Kelly Cook	Stephanie Beard

What's Red all over?: Steve Smith (left) and Pat McKenna of the very, very manly *Red Green Show.*

S&S Productions

The tales of Possum Lodge, where grizzly, duct-tape-touting woodsman Red Green holds loose court over a cast of oddballs.

The show's format is loosely based on 1960s Canadian TV legend, Red Fisher, master of Scuttlebutt Lodge. The modern Red hangs out with the guys at the lodge, invents things, and engages in verbal sparring with colourful local residents.

Stalwarts among the all-male cast (it's a man's world after all) include: Red's geeky technology-obsessed nephew Harold; naturalist Green; bush pilot Buzz; Natural Resources bureaucrat and golf-addict Stuyvesant; abandoned forester Ranger Gord (his employers have forgotten him); chiseller Bainborough, owner of the Everything Store; Braxton, owner of shoddy Braxton's Marina; timid animal-control officer Frid; Hap, ferry-boat pilot and local prevaricator (former King of England, president of the United States, brain surgeon, and astronaut; handyman and ex-criminal (well, ex-*ish*) Hamar; southern-boy expatriate Franklin, owner of the world's largest trucks; explosives enthusiast Montrose; local magnate Rothschild III, owner of Rothschild's Sewage and Septic Sucking Services; budding songwriter (he's written 13,000) and accident-prone roofer Doogan; and Yuppie developer Black.

Unseen characters include Red's wife Bernice, Old Man Sedgwick, Moose Thompson, Stinky Peterson, Junior Singleton, Buster Hadfield, and Flinty McClintock.

Smith had played the Green character for years until headlining him onHamilton's CHCH in 1991. When CHCH pulled the plug on Red, Smith actually bought a half-hour on Global to continue the program as *The New Red Green Show* (the program's name in seasons four though seven), which moved to the CBC in 1997.

A bona fide cult phenomenon, seen in such diverse countries as Turkey and Denmark, fans travel thousands of miles to attend program tapings. Program merchandise includes cookbooks, episode guide books, T-shirts, boxer shorts, suspenders, bumper stickers, crests, and zipper pulls.

S&S productions, the company behind *Green*, announced plans for a feature film, tentatively titled *Duct Tape Forever*—starring Smith, McKenna, Keleghan, Greene, and Pinsent—in which the Possum Lodge crew embark on a mission to save the lodge from becoming town property.

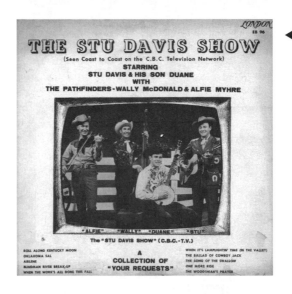

Red River Jamboree

CBC
Musical Variety
First Broadcast: Friday, July 8, 1960, 8:00 p.m..
Final Year Broadcast: 1960
Running Time: 30 min.

Host: Stu Davis

Canada's cowboy troubador provided country music from Winnipeg in this summer replacement for Country Hoedown.

Re: Fraynes

CBC
Sports
First Broadcast: Saturday, October 16, 1954, 10:45 p.m.
Final Year Broadcast: 1955
Running Time: 15 min.

Hosts: June (Callwood) Frayne, Trent Frayne

Interviews of celebrity sports figures conducted by the married couple, both writers, in a rec room set.

The Relic Hunter

Syndicated: 1999
Adventure
Running Time: 60 min.

Cast:
Sydney Fox . . . . Tia Carrere
Nigel Bailey . . . . Christien Anholt
Claudia . . . . Lindy Booth
Stewie Harper . . . . Tony Rosato

The adventures of archaeology professor Sydney Fox, explorer/martial arts expert hired to recover lost or stolen relics (the crown jewels of France, Al Capone's gun, Elvis' guitar, Casanova's *Book of Love*). Bailey is Fox's unadventurous British assistant, Claudia her ditzy secretary, and Harper an underhanded rival (it's a competitive field.) Episodes are formulaic: stranger asks Fox to recover (insert relic here), Fox and Bailey travel to relic's exotic locale, find it, lose it to villains, then kick villains' asses to recover relic. One variation: viewers never know when Fox will find a lame excuse to reveal a G-rated amount of cleavage. A Canada/France co-production.

René Simard

CBC
Musical Variety
First Broadcast: Tuesday, September 27, 1977, 8:30 p.m.
Final Year Broadcast: 1979
Running Time: 30 min.

Host: René Simard
Regular Performers: The Renettes (including Joani Taylor), James Angels Dancers

Quebec singing sensation Simard wooed English Canada with this variety series produced in Vancouver. Already Canada's most popular recording artist, Simard was wowing them in Vegas and Japan. Guests included Salome Bey, Liona Boyd, Chicago, José Feliciano, Anne Murray, Jim Stafford, Peter Ustinov, Andy Williams, Paul Williams, and sports figures, including Toller Cranston, Greg Joy, and The Hockey Rockers (Rogie Vachon, Marcel Dionne, and Boom-Boom Geoffrion). Features included interviews with guest acts, comedy skits, and a "Disco René" feature.

Don't walk away René: Quebec singing sensation René Simard oozed his way into the affections of an English-speaking audience.

The Rez

CBC
Comedy/Drama
First Broadcast: Friday, February 23, 1996, 8:00 p.m.
Final Year Broadcast: 1998
Running Time: 30 min.

Cast:

Silas Crow	Ryan Black
Sadie Maracle	Jennifer Podemski
Frank Fencepost	Darell Dennis
Illiana	Lisa LaCroix
McVey	Kevin Hicks
Eleanor Nanibush	Patricia Collins
Mother Crow	Shirley Cheechoo
Lucy	Tamara Podemski
Etta	Elaine Mills
Tanya	Kari Matchett
Charlie	Adam Beach
Chief Tom	Gary Farmer

A series of stories (some comedic, some dramatic) about life on "The Rez" (the fictitious Kidiabanasee Reserve in Northern Ontario) based on characters created by W.P. Kinsella in the book *Dance Me Outside* and a successful feature film of the same name.

Stories centred around the lives of three young Native Canadians on the periphery of adulthood: Silas (who wanted to be a writer); Sadie (an activist and Silas' girlfriend); and Silas' pal Frank (Frank was always confused). Lucy was Sadie's best friend. Eleanor (who was white) ran the local marina.

Some audience members were challenged by the show's depictions of racism (Sadie supported an avowed anti-white candidate for chief, then backed out when her candidate secretly admitted he actually thought that whites were probably OK) and the not-altogether-sympathetic male leads who cussed, drank beer, smoked cigarettes, and engaged in some questionable behaviour. Beach played Frank in the feature film.

Rita and Friends

CBC
Musical Variety
First Broadcast: Friday, October 28, 1994, 8:00 p.m.
Final Year Broadcast: 1996
Running Time: 60 min.

Host: Rita MacNeil

After committing the unpardonable crime of dumping *Don Messer's Jubilee* more than 20 years earlier, the CBC found salvation with *Rita and Friends*—almost every bit as down-home, folksy, and amateurish a program as modern production methods would allow.

Doomed to repeat their heinous act, CBC execs toyed with the highest-rated series launch in Canadian history (1.7 million viewers), vexing Rita and her fans by banishing her program to Wednesday night and then returning her to Fridays. Confused viewers chased Rita around the schedule until an abrupt (and poorly justified) cancellation.

Compare Rita's treatment to the network's rabid support for the disastrously rated *Friday Night with Ralph Benmergui*. Rita deserved better.

The critics jeer: "She was obese, shy, incapable of reading her lines with any conviction, wooden in her gestures, uneasy when she wasn't singing…the worse she was, the more sincere she became in the eyes of her fans." — John Allemang, *The Globe and Mail*

Ritter's Cove

CBC
Drama
First Broadcast: Sunday, September 19, 1980, 8:00 p.m.
Final Year Broadcast: 1982
Running Time: 30 min.

Cast:
Karl Ritter . . . . Hans Caninenberg
Kate . . . . Susan Hogan
Robert . . . . Dale Walters
Arnie . . . . Craig Kelly

Karl and his grandsons Robert and Arnie lived in a cabin on the British Columbia coast where they operated an aquaplane flying service. When Karl procrastinated with a medical exam he lost his pilot's licence, forcing him to hire female pilot Kate.

These low-key family adventures (air rescues, shipping deadlines, medical emergencies, shady visitors) were set to a backdrop of sexism (women weren't meant to fly, donchaknow) and a gradually emerging mutual respect among the adult characters. A German/British/Canadian co-production.

Riverdale

CBC
Soap Opera
First Broadcast: Monday, September 22, 1997, 7:00 p.m.
Final Year Broadcast: 2000
Running Time: 60 min.

Cast:
Wally Wowczuk . . . . Chris Benson
Jimmy Snow . . . . Christian Potenza
Maurice Long . . . . Dave Nichols
Ben MacKenzie . . . . . Christopher Shyer (1997–98), Hamish McEwan (1998–2000)
Jerome "Tiny" Sheffield . . . . Martin Roach
Costas Stavros . . . . Paul Soles
Chrisa Stavros . . . . Maria Ricossa
Patrick MacKenzie . . . . Alex Campbell
Charles MacKenzie . . . . Stewart Arnott
Alice Sweeney . . . . Lynne Griffin
George Pattillo . . . . Hugo Dann
Gordo Johnson . . . . Merwin Mondesir
Stan Wilkes . . . . Ken James
Gloria Wilkes . . . . Jayne Eastwood
Jenni Hernandez . . . . Yanna McIntosh
Mike Hayes . . . . Tyrone Benskin
Robin Hayes . . . . Ashley Brown
Cassie Coulter . . . . Melissa Thomson
Stephanie Long . . . . Diana Reis
Irene Stavros . . . . Melissa DiMarco
Caroline Walker . . . . Nicole Hughes
Terry Walker . . . . Matt Cooke
Michelle Martin . . . . Jennifer Podemski
Katie MacKenzie . . . . Jessica Greco
Shawn Ritchie . . . . Kristen J. Holdenried
Jake Rose, P.I. . . . . Tom Melissis
Gilmour the dog . . . . Gilmore

Mistakenly (or falsely) billed as Canada's first home-grown soap opera (*Strange Paradise, Paul Bernard: Psychiatrist, Scarlett Hill,* and *Moment of Truth* come immediately to mind), this sudser was Canada's answer to the British series *Coronation Street*. The stories focused on the ordinary lives, loves, and occasional illegal activities of the hard-working folks in Toronto's Riverdale district (actually an expensive set). Hard-core supporters mounted a massive "Save *Riverdale*" campaign on just a rumour of cancellation. They had plenty to worry about, though, since low ratings and few episodes (the 1998–99 season boasted just 11 hours of new material) failed to generate widespread audiences. Like *Coronation Street*, the series was eventually broadcast Sunday mornings (though each episode premiered on Thursday), then rebroadcast in half-hour chunks through the week. The first few episodes were directed by *Coronation* director Eugene Ferguson.

Road to Avonlea

CBC
Drama
First Broadcast: Sunday, January 7, 1989, 7:00 p.m.
Final Year Broadcast: 1996
Running Time: 60 min.

Cast:

Sara Stanley . . . . Sarah Polley
Alec King . . . . Cedric Smith
Janet King . . . . Lally Cadeau
Hetty King . . . . Jackie Burroughs
Olivia King-Dale . . . . Mag Ruffman
Jasper Dale . . . . R.H. Thomson
Felicity King-Pike . . . . Gema Zamprogna
Gus Pike . . . . Michael Mahonen
Felix King . . . . Zachary Bennett
Izzy Pettibone . . . . Heather Brown
Cecily King . . . . Harmony Cramp
Marilla Cuthbert . . . . Colleen Dewhurst
Rachel Lynde . . . . Patricia Hamilton
Eulalie Bugle . . . . Barbara Hamilton
Miss Stacey . . . . Marilyn Lightstone
Clive Pettibone . . . . David Fox
Simon Tremayne . . . . Ian Clark
Pierre Lapierre . . . . Albert Millaire
Nanny Louisa . . . . Frances Hyland

Dare we say *the* Canadian television program of the 1990s? Based on four novels by Lucy Maud Montgomery (*Chronicles of Avonlea, Further Chronicles of Avonlea, The Story Girl,* and *The Golden Road*), the series is set in Prince Edward Island circa 1900 (but was filmed north of Toronto). It focused on Sara Stanley, daughter of a Montreal businessmen who sent her to P.E.I. to spare her the shame of a business scandal. Sara boarded in the Rose Cottage with schoolteacher Hetty King, and her youngest sister Olivia. On the other side of the property lived older brother Alec, wife Janet, and their three kids: Felix, Cecily, and snotty Felicity. Held over from the *Anne of Green Gables* specials that preceded this series were Anne's adoptive mother Marilla, and town gossip Rachel. Dewhurst died in 1992, and Polley left the show in 1995.

The series boasted enough recognizable guest stars to sink the entire island, largely to placate its co-producer The Disney Channel (hence Stockard Channing, Faye Dunaway, Madeline Kahn, Christopher Lloyd, Kate Nelligan, Christopher Reeve, and Michael York.) The series was known simply as *Avonlea* in the U.S. A TV movie, *Happy Christmas, Mrs. King,* followed in 1998.

The critics cheer: "A fine period soap opera, as proudly Canadian as anything our industry has ever produced." — Jim Slotek, *The Toronto Sun*

The critics jeer: "Sticky with sentimentality, loaded with sugary moments and acting that ranges from wooden to irritatingly mannered...." — John Haslett Cuff, *The Globe and Mail*

Robocop—The Series

CTV
Drama
First Broadcast: Saturday, March 12, 1994, 7:00 p.m.
Final Year Broadcast: 1995
Running Time: 60 min.

Cast:

Alex Murphy/Robocop . . . . Richard Eden
Detective Lisa Madigan . . . . Yvette Nipar
Sergeant Stanley Parks . . . . Blu Mankuma
Diana Powers . . . . Andrea Roth
OCP Chair . . . . David Gardner
Gadget (Gertrude Modesto) . . . . Sarah Campbell
Charlie Lipincott . . . . Ed Sahely
Bo Harlan . . . . Dan Duran
Rocky Crenshaw . . . . Erica Ehm
Nancy Murphy . . . . Jennifer Griffin
Jimmy Murphy . . . . Peter Costigan/Jordan Hughes
Pudface Morgan . . . . James Kidnie

In search of more imitation American programming, Canadians turned to the *Robocop* film series, which had recently run out of steam, to produce these adventures set in 21st-century Old Detroit. Robocop was part machine, part Alex Murphy, a deceased police patrolman, maintaining law and order for the omnipresent Omni Consumer Products, which controlled everything from the government to the police force. Madigan knew Robo's secret; Diana, killed in the series opener, survived in electronic form. Gadget was a techno-whiz orphan who helped out at the South Precinct; Lipincott was a tech who maintained Robo's exterior. Robocop only occasionally remembered life with his family, the Murphys. At the start of each episode, Bo and Rocky presented *Media Break,* which capped the daily news. Rumoured to be Canada's most expensive series ever—$36.5 million for its first and only season—it automatically qualifies as Canada's biggest television bomb as well. A new series of darker, more violent Canadian TV movies under the banner *RoboCop: Prime Directives* was announced in 2000.

Rocket Robin Hood

CBC
Animated
First Broadcast: Monday, October 9, 1967, 4:30 p.m.
Final Year Broadcast: 1968
Running Time: 30 min.

Narrator: . . . . Bernard Cowan
Voices of:
Rocket Robin Hood . . . . Len Birman/Don Harron
Friar Tuck . . . . Paul Kligman
Other Voices: Carl Banas, Gillie Fenwick, Ed McNamara, Chris Wiggins, Doug Master, John Scott

Canada's first major colour animated series, this embarrassing effort was a $1,500,000 deal, featuring the adventures of Robin Hood's direct descendant, Rocket Robin Hood, in "the astonishing year 3000." New Sherwood Forest sits atop Sherwood Asteroid, which in turn floats around N.O.T.T. —National Outerspace Terrestrial Territories. Lucky Gordon Pinsent failed to capture the title role. Stretching its slim animation to the point of insult, each episode featured a lo-o-o-n-g theme song ("Band of brothers, marching together…"), while short, serial episodes were sandwiched between interminable previews and recaps, painfully protracted introductions to each of Robin's merry men, and marathon closing credits. One infamous episode re-used the entire background animation from a *Spiderman* cartoon.

Episodes generally followed Robin's encounters with the wicked Prince John and the Sheriff of N.O.T.T. and such outlandish weapons as an atomic-powered vacuum cleaner and the Space Sphinx, a jet-powered Egyptian spacecraft, equipped with chomping jaws. Robin's futuristic arsenal included a bow-and-arrow set that fired lassos, the electro-quarter-staff, and rocket-powered hobby horses. The CBC prohibited cleavage and "crotch lines." Little George, a space hillbilly, was almost introduced to capitalize on the success of *The Beverly Hillbillies*. In the program's favour: cool, jazzy background music. Seen in the U.S., South America, Australia, and Britain, the cartoon was dubbed into French, Italian, Portuguese, and Spanish. Rocker Carol Pope was an animator on the series.

Space travellers surround me: An original production drawing from the wacked-out animated science-fiction series *Rocket Robin Hood*.

Rollin' on the River

CTV
Musical Variety
First Broadcast: Saturday, September 18, 1971, 7:30 p.m.
Final Year Broadcast: 1972
Running Time: 30 min.

Regular performers: Renee Cherrier, Peggy Mahon, Billy Van

Set on a big, phony riverboat set, this feeble excuse for Canadian content featured American Kenny Rogers (pre-"Lucille" days) and his band, the First Edition. Guests included The Beach Boys, The Carpenters, Dr. Music, Ian and Sylvia, Lighthouse, Monty Hall, Murray McLauchlan, and Pat Paulsen. Van provided comedy.

Romper Room

Syndicated: 1959
Children's
Running Time: 30 min.

"Mr. Music, please…"

A private franchise owned by the husband-and-wife team of Bert and Nancy Claster. Local TV stations bought the rights to use the show's trademarks—a smiling jack-in-the-box, a magic mirror, and a Mr. Doo-bee insect costume, the image of a grinning drone. Stations provided their own female host, who went to adult Romper Room School, run by Romper Room Inc. in Baltimore to learn the finer points of interaction with children and six-foot bees.

Romper, stomper, tell me today: Record album sales formed a large segment of the *Romper Room* marketing program.

Standard elements included lessons in manners, overseen by Mr. Doo-bee ("Do be a Doo-bee; Don't be a Don't-bee"), a musical march around the room while kids balanced plastic baskets on their heads ("See me walk so straight and tall, I won't let my basket fall") and a farewell look in the Magic Mirror ("Magic Mirror, tell me today; Did my friends have fun at play?") which became transparent as the local host peered into tuned-in living rooms, listing names at random to the delight of lucky children who happened to be named (and heartbreaking consternation of those who weren't).

A line of Romper Room books and toys was gently pushed as well. Creative licence allowed local stations to use their own books and lessons, making for a distinctly Canadian flavour. Canadian production was consolidated in 1972 under CTV's CKCO affiliate in Kitchener, Ontario. Network hosts included Diane Ippersiel, Cathy Somerville, Betty Thompson, Sarah Thomson, and Fran Pappert. Individual station hosts included CKLW Windsor's Miss Flora Paulin, CKVR Barrie's Miss Lois Welsman, and CHCH Hamilton's Mrs. Lois Jamieson. The program ceased production in 1991.

Also known as *Romper Room School* and *Romper Room and Friends*.

The critics cheer: "*Romper Room* actually holds their attention for one half hour a day. For this relief, much thanks."
— Jocelyn Dingman, *Maclean's*

Ronnie Prophet
See: *Grand Old Country*

Royal Canadian Air Farce

CBC
Comedy
First Broadcast: Friday, October 8, 1993, 8:00 p.m.
Final Year Broadcast: —
Running Time: 30 min.

Cast: Roger Abbott, Don Ferguson, Luba Goy, John Morgan

Cheerful, toothless satire (does anyone really fear being lampooned on *Air Farce*?) poking fun at noteworthy news stories. The cast boasts a string of audience-favourite impersonations and characters including:
• Abbott's Jean Chretien, Peter Mansbridge,

Leonard Cohen, Dave Hodge, and TV critic Gilbert Smythe Bite-Me.
• Ferguson's Lucien Bouchard, Preston Manning, Bill Clinton, Brian Mulroney, Pierre Trudeau, Joe Clark, and Colonel Stacy (of the Chicken Cannon brigade—see below).
• Goy's Sheila Copps, Hana Gartner, Valerie Pringle, Queen Elizabeth, Pamela Wallin, Bingo Lady, and a duck.
• Morgan's Herb Gray, Boris Yeltsin, Jock McBile, and Mike from Canmore.

A popular feature is the show's Chicken Cannon segment, in which bizarre ammo is fired at worthy targets: (e.g., Lucien Bouchard is nailed by B.C. salmon, P.E.I. Superfries, East Coast Fiddleheads, Newfie Screech, Ontario Pennies, and Quebec Maple Syrup). A successor to the CBC radio program of the same name, which hit the airwaves in 1973, and to several CBC television specials.

Royal Canadian Mounted Police

CBC
Drama
First Broadcast: Wednesday, October 28, 1959, 8:00 p.m.
Final Year Broadcast: 1960
Running Time: 30 min.

Cast:

Corporal Jacques Gagnier	Gilles Pelletier
Constable Frank Scott	John Perkins
Constable Bill Mitchell	Don Francks
Mayor Cartwright	Barney McManus
Wilson Tong	William Lee
Mrs. Bell	Helene Winston
Chief the Dog	Apache Golden Chief

Accompanied by rousing theme music vaguely reminiscent of the national anthem, the *R.C.M.P.* opener primed viewers for a visit with Sgt. Preston of the Yukon and a six-pack of loyal huskies. Forget the hoary opening. Part *Dragnet*, part *Highway Patrol*, part *Naked City*, *R.C.M.P.* is a strictly cool slice of TV noir north.

Set in the town of Shamattawa (Manitoba? Saskatchewan?) the program concentrated on the activities of a local RCMP corporal and his two assistants as they investigated the dark underbelly of small-town Canadian life: rape, murder, theft, adultery, and suicide.

The RCMP detachment was headed up by cool, tough, competent Corporal Jacques Gagnier, a French Canadian who wasn't entirely comfortable with his transfer to a predominantly English-speaking town. Gagnier

Getting his man: Corporal Jacques Gagnier collars a crook in *Royal Canadian Mounted Police*.

CBC

was the consummate professional, employing modern crime-fighting and detection methods ('50s-style) to complement the RCMP's noble tradition. He was more comfortable racing down desolate country roads in his 1957 fin-tailed Ford patrol car than riding a horse.

Filmed in stark black-and-white in Ontario, Quebec, and Saskatchewan, this CBC/BBC co-production rarely relied on stage sets for backdrops, using actual locations to depict small-town Canada: '50s diners, gritty log cabin barrooms, and rustic mining camps, surrounded by impenetrable forests. In winter, filthy heaps of exhaust-stained snow lined the town's streets. Was life in rural Canada of the 1950s really like this? Who cares?

Episode titles would comfortably grace the covers of Jim Thompson novels: "Mop-Up," "Killer Instinct," "Crash on 21," and "Day of Reckoning" all reflect the terse style of these compact dramas.

Narrated introductions, delivered in a languid monotone, also stood out against the flag-waving opening sequence. The dialogue was also grimmer than in most programs of its time, dropping the occasional "damn" into the script. And while the Mounties always did seem to get their man, the show rarely settled for pat endings. Example: in a cruel twist, Gagnier talks a teenager out of leaping from the town's water tower, just before the boy slips on an icy rung, critically injuring himself.

Supporting actors included Chris Wiggins, Bruno Gerussi, Douglas Rain (the voice of the HAL 2000 in the movie *2001: A Space Odyssey*), and Wayne and Shuster's stand-in bruiser, Lou Pitoscia, as "Crusher" Murphy.

The show's score was particularly good. While some episodes use canned studio music, others raced along to great '50s jukebox rock or simmered to a cool jazz backdrop. A great forgotten Canadian program, *R.C.M.P.* should be required viewing for fans of good police drama, grim storylines, cool

'R.C.M.P.'

CBC Television

CBC

music, and retro scenery. Also seen in Australia, Cuba, Denmark, Finland, Germany, Japan, Mexico, Norway, Puerto Rico, and as a movie matinee extra in France.

The critics cheer: "Every character, minor and major, is believable…some of the nicest lensing shown in Canadian tv…attention has been paid to suspense and high drama in every show." — Gorm., *Variety*

The critics jeer: "There hasn't been a good gun-battle or even a fist-fight since the series began…they have reduced "RCMP" to something that might be found in a grade three reader." — Dennis Braithwaite, *The Toronto Star*

Rudolph The Red Nosed Reindeer

CBS
Animated
First Broadcast: 1964
Running Time: 60 min.

Voices of:

Rudolph . . . . Billie Mae Richards
Santa/King of Misfit Island . . . . Stan Francis
Dennis . . . . Paul Soles
Yukon Cornelius . . . . Alfie Scopp
Coach . . . . Paul Kligman
Sam the Snowman. . . . . Burl Ives
Other Voices: Larry Mann, Janis Orenstein, Carl Banas, Corinne Conley, Peg Dixon

www.rankinbass.com

Perennial favourite Christmas special featuring a mostly Canadian cast. Rudolph leaves home to find adventure with fellow misfit, Dennis the elf, who has aspirations to dentistry.

The abominable snowman is downright scary, the Land of Misfit Toys is memorable ("Who ever heard of a Charlie-in-the-box?"), and Burl Ives is a pleasant snowman. The reindeer in this version are particularly cruel (Coach: "From now on, we won't let Rudolph play any reindeer games, right team?") and Santa comes off as a grumpy moral pragmatist.

Lots of memorable songs written for the special by Johnny Marks, who wrote the original Rudolph song.

Rupert

Syndicated: 1991
Animated
Running Time: 30 min.

Voices of:

Rupert Bear . . . . Ben Sanford
Bill Badger . . . . Torquil Campbell
Pong Ping . . . . Oscar Hsu
Podgy Pig . . . . Hadley Kay
Tiger Lily. . . . . Stephanie Morgenstern
Mr. Bear. . . . . Guy Bannerman
Mrs. Bear . . . . Lally Cadeau

A beloved British comic staple in England's *Daily Express* for more than 80 years, not just any animator could be chosen to produce cartoons based on the adventures of Rupert the bear.

Enter Toronto's Nelvana studios, licensed to create this series with just the proper British flavour.

The studio produced six seasons' worth of episodes, seen largely on YTV in Canada, and in many other countries around the world.

Saturday Date With Billy O'Connor

CBC
Musical Variety
First Broadcast: Saturday, October 4, 1958, 7:30 p.m.
Final Year Broadcast: 1959
Running Time: 30 min.

Host: Don Parrish
Regular Performers: Billy O'Connor, Allan Blye, Vanda King

A musical warm-up to *Hockey Night in Canada,* and O'Connor's new spot after being bumped from the post-game line-up by former co-star Juliette.

Savoir Faire

HGTV
Lifestyles
First Broadcast: 1996
Final Year Broadcast: —
Running Time: 30 min.

Host: Nik Manojlovich

Meet Nik Manojlovich, perfectionist, and Canada's answer to Martha Stewart. Nik instructs viewers on how to entertain with the sincerity and thoroughness of a boy scout earning a merit badge. While he could be accused of overkill—you'd need a forklift to move all of the inventory in his weekend guest basket to the spare bedroom—he'll never show you a bad time. So overwhelmed is Nik by the niceties of life that he frequently breaks into a broad grin ("Yes!" he exclaims, leaping into the air, when a guest reveals she's preparing a chocolate cake, Nik's favourite). Catering a party for a group of ten-year-old girls, Nik joins them in an enthusiastic affirmation of "girl power." The coy credit sequences, featuring a tuxedoed Nik frolicking in a shower of descending rose petals, should receive some sort of award.

Scarlett Hill

CBC
Soap Opera
First Broadcast: Monday, October 17, 1962, 4:00 p.m.
Final Year Broadcast: 1964
Running Time: 30 min.

Cast:

Amos Currey	John Drainie
Luke Currey	Ron Cohoon
Kate Russell	Beth Lockerbie
Ginny Russell	Lucy Warner
Harry Russell	Ed McNamara
Janice Turner	Suzanne Bryant
David Black	Gordon Pinsent
Tom Harvey	Marty Stetrop
Sidney Quill	Alan Pearce
Pearl Tolliver	Cosette Lee
Sandy	Norman Ettlinger
Dr. Spangle	Tony Kramriether
Walter Pendleton	Ivor Barry

Canada's first soap opera was based on a series of U.S. radio plays written by the late Robert Lindsay and adapted for television by his wife Kathleen. The series started with five-episode story arcs, but later adopted traditional running story lines under the subtitle *Room to Let.* This variation featured the characters who lived in a Scarlett Hill boarding house owned by Kate Russell. A critical failure and modest ratings success, the program was lambasted by critics for lines like: "Admiral Byrd might have been in love with the North Pole, but he didn't take it to bed with him." Seen in Australia, England, and, when syndicated in 1965, in New York as a short-term ratings grabber. A *Scarlett Hill* sound track was recorded in England by Peter Knight.

The critics jeer: "Faced with a heap of scripts of incurable dramatic slackness, the actors have become virtuosos of the pregnant pause, the portentous faraway look...." — Antony Ferry, *Maclean's*

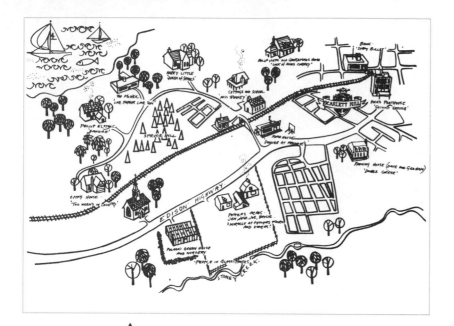

"...brand X detergent drama that forms a half-hour clog in the network schedule...an artesian well of dramatic drivel...contains some of the worst acting I've ever seen or even heard of on television...unsurpassed on television for the predictability of its story lines and for unswerving devotion to tedium." — John Ruddy, *Toronto Telegram*

Schnitzel House

CHCH
Children's
First Broadcast: Friday, September 25, 1964, 10:00 a.m.
Final Year Broadcast: 1968
Running Time: 30 min.

Cast:
Grandpa Schnitzel . . . . Cliff McKay

"Inky dinky, inky dinky, inky dinky, Schnitzel House."
    —From the *Schnitzel House* theme song

Ever wonder what happened to Cliff McKay after *Holiday Ranch* closed its doors? He bought a Schnitzel House franchise, complete with lederhosen, alpine cap, and seedy Swiss-chalet set.

Grandpa's companions were a trio of talking clocks (grandfather, canine, and the Kit Kat variety—a black-and-white feline with eyes that shifted to the beat of its pendulum tail) who played "tricks" on him (flipping the TV image upside-down, for example). Child guests played musical chairs for prizes, and the eliminated were escorted to a table full of mugs of steaming hot chocolate.

SCTV

CBC
Comedy
First Broadcast: Friday, September 19, 1980, 11:45 p.m.
Final Year Broadcast: 1981
Running Time: 30 min.

Regular Performers: Robin Duke, Joe Flaherty, Eugene Levy, Andrea Martin, Rick Moranis, Tony Rosato, Dave Thomas

The *Second City* folks had stopped producing their self-titled program for Global in 1978, but rose, phoenix-like, from the ashes. This sketch comedy series, produced in Edmonton, continued the saga of fictional Melonville TV station SCTV, home of the world's cheesiest staff and programming. Temporarily absent were John Candy, heading the disastrous (and suspiciously titled) *Big City Comedy,* and Catherine O'Hara. Many of the *Second City* characters were reprised, though more sharply focused, and an infusion of cash gave the programs a smarter look.

Back were:

• Flaherty as: station manager Guy Caballero, replete with white suit and hat and a wheelchair he used when he needed "some respect"; Floyd Robertson, alcoholic co-anchor of SCTV news; Sammy Maudlin, unctuous, thigh-slapping, cigarette-puffing talk-show host and dreadful singer ("Take a Load Off, Sammy"); and Count Floyd, a.k.a. Floyd Robertson, vampiric host of *Monster Chiller Horror Theatre,* a showcase for universally unscary fare (*Four for Texas, The Odd Couple*) and the popular catch phrase, "Ooooh, scary eh kids?"

• Levy as: Bobby Bittman, unfunny, helmet-haired, gold-chained stand-up comic—a frequent guest on Maudlin's show; Earl Cannonbear, Floyd's loud-suited, jealous co-anchor (he once told audiences that Floyd lived with someone "who isn't even his wife"); and Rockin' Mel Slirrup, host of dance program *Mel's Rock Pile.*

• Martin as: Mrs. Edith Prickley, sleazy, oversexed station manager in leopard skin suit and cat-eye glasses, and Edna Boil, co-owner of Tex and Edna Boil's Organ Emporium (Tex was played by Thomas).

• Thomas as: acerbic entertainment critic Bill Needles; Scottish cheapskate and cooking-show host Angus Crock; Walter Cronkite; and Bob Hope.

- Moranis as: slick, bearded video DJ Jerry Todd; Rabbi Karloff; Woody Allen; and David Brinkley.

New characters introduced by Rosato and Duke were Italian Chef Marcello and Molly Earl, host of *Crazy Crafts*.

Moranis and Thomas also developed the Bob and Doug McKenzie *Great White North* segment ("Kooo-roo-koo-koo-koo-roo-koo-koooooo") as Canadian content filler designed to round out Canadian broadcasts, which were slightly longer than the U.S. syndicated version.

SCTV Network

First Choice
Comedy
First Broadcast: 1983, various
Final Year Broadcast: 1984
Running Time: 45 min.

Regular Performers: Joe Flaherty, John Hemphill, Eugene Levy, Andrea Martin, Martin Short, Mary Charlotte Wilcox

A sad end for the *SCTV* programs. This version of the series was created for U.S. pay network Cinemax, with the skeleton cast occasionally joined by guests Dave Thomas and John Candy.

New characters were John Hemphill's poignant Happy Marsden, an alcoholic who hosts *Happy Hour,* a kiddie show filmed in a local tavern, and Mary Charlotte Wilcox as pasty-faced matron Idela Voudry.

The final programs are sometimes difficult to watch.

A black-and-white spoof of *Oliver Twist* (*Oliver Grimley*) is technically competent, but not very funny. *Das Boobs,* a witless spoof of the film *Das Boot,* is arguably the program's nadir.

Still, there are a few good bits: *Half Wits,* an obnoxiously cruel game show for stupid people; Jackie Rogers Jr.'s botched run for the presidency; and Sammy Maudlin's nasty spoof of *Thicke of the Night*.

After cancellation, the *SCTV* crew went on to successful solo film and television careers, though they were occasionally reunited (a "best-of" show featuring Caballero and Prickley, a *Second City* television reunion special; Flaherty, Hemphill and Wilcox—and sometimes Levy—in *Maniac Mansion;* and the continuation of the Bob and Doug Mackenzie saga in film and television commercials.

SCTV Network 90

NBC, CBC
Comedy
First Broadcast: Friday, May 15, 1981, 12:30 p.m.
Final Year Broadcast: 1983
Running Time: 60 min. and 90 min.

Regular Performers: John Candy, Joe Flaherty, Eugene Levy, Andrea Martin, Rick Moranis (1981–82), Catherine O'Hara, Martin Short (1982–83), Dave Thomas (1981–82)

In 1982, NBC bought the *SCTV* package, expanding the program to 90 minutes and changing its name to *SCTV Network 90* (some of the old material was recycled for the new show). The CBC ran a roughly edited, 60-minute version under the *SCTV Network* title. The new program represented more money, a bigger writing staff, and complex storylines involving the central characters, punctuated by programs, commercial parodies, and program promos. It also marked the return of John Candy and Catherine O'Hara and the departure of Robin Duke and Tony Rosato (both of whom joined *Saturday Night Live*). In addition to the regular characters created for *SCTV Network* and *SCTV*, new segments included:
- John Candy's Gil Fisher, the Fishin' Musician, who entertained real musical guests (The Plasmatics, The Tubes, Carl Perkins) at his fishing lodge, in a parody of Canada's Red Fisher.
- *The Days of the Week,* a regular soap opera with continuing (and occasionally abandoned) storylines.
- *Mrs. Falbo's Tiny Town,* an appallingly unstructured kids' show with Andrea Martin as the confused Falbo, and John Candy as the neurotic Mr. Messenger.
- The Five Neat Guys, a nostalgic '50s act who cheerfully harmonized through off-colour songs.
- *The Happy Wanderers,* with Candy and Levy as Josh and Stan Schmenge, a pair of homely Leutonian polka musicians who make every song sound the same.

The 90-minute shows provided a perfect format for elaborate episodes—show-long spoofs of films including *Dr. Strangelove, Failsafe, The Godfather,* and *Poltergeist,* for example.

It also allowed the freedom to produce some more eclectic material that might have been excised in a shorter program (the absurd *Adventures of Shake and Bake* in which William Shakespeare and Francis Bacon tussle over word choices while crossing swords with pirate invaders).

Bob and Doug McKenzie's *Great White North* segment caught on with U.S. audiences as well, and popularized several catch phrases ("Hoser," "Beauty," and "Take off, eh?" to name a few), and spawned a best-selling comedy album, a hit single, and a moderately successful feature film, *Strange Brew*.

In the spring of 1982, Moranis, Thomas, and O'Hara left the program, appearing in only a few segments thereafter, while Martin Short joined the cast. Short's arrival seemed to energize the remaining actors to produce some of the program's best work. With him, Short brought new characters: smarmy albino nightclub singer, Jackie Rogers Jr.; pointy-haired misfit Ed Grimley; aging songwriter Irving Cohen; and dead-on impersonations of Jerry Lewis and Pierre Trudeau.

The two years of *SCTV Network 90* represent a highlight of not only Canadian comedy but television comedy itself.

Not only was the program funny, but the Melonvile characters occasionally transcended themselves as mere comic creations: the scene in which Bob and Doug affectionately swap carefully wrapped "smokes" as Christmas presents; the Schmenges actually generating a sense of seasonal goodwill as they share their bizarre Leutonian Christmas with viewers; Johnny LaRue's epiphany as Santa Claus lifts him from drunken degradation with the gift of a massive camera crane.

Alas, after dozens of successful broadcasts, NBC threatened to move the program to a Sunday evening time slot, and the show abruptly ceased production until one last, and not very successful, revival known as *SCTV Network*.

While all of the programs were cut into syndicated half-hour chunks, the 90-minute episodes suffered the worst editing, with the rhythm shattered and the shows jarringly condensed or cut to ribbons. Some of the material has simply disappeared; for example, an entire program about a ratings fluke—in which every SCTV program is replaced by spinoffs of *The Gates of Hell*—is missing. And that awful new theme music…

The critics cheer: "Coolest cathode comedy yet…." — Gene Sculatti, *The Catalog of Cool*

Seaway

CBC
Drama
First Broadcast: Thursday, September 16, 1965, 8:00 p.m.
Final Year Broadcast: 1966
Running Time: 60 min.

Cast:
Admiral Henry Victor Leslie Fox . . . . Austin Willis
Nick King . . . . Stephen Young

Fox, alias "Foxy," a WWII veteran who worked for the Department of Transport, hired ex-U.S. fighter pilot Nick "Nicky" King to keep freight movin' on the St. Lawrence Seaway for the Associated Owners and Shippers. Their legal powers were never clearly explained, but their investigations included insurance fraud, Native land rights, and a shipment of poisoned wheat. A two-part episode about a Communist defector was released as a film, *Don't Forget to Wipe the Blood Off*. Barely Canadian, the producers imported a stream of U.S. actors, guest stars, and directors. The most costly series produced in Canada at the time: $3,000,000 for the first—and only—season. Though ratings were respectable, critics torpedoed the series, which floundered because a lucrative U.S. sale never appeared—not surprising, since U.S. networks were buying colour programs and *Seaway* was filmed in black-and-white. Programs were shot in Toronto, Montreal, Quebec, and Halifax, and seen in local U.S. markets, England, and Finland.

The critics jeer: "The *Seaway* is now on the air and sinking fast…." — Roy Shields, *The Toronto Star*

Second City

Global
Comedy
First Broadcast: Tuesday, September 22, 1976, 7:30 p.m.
Final Year Broadcast: 1978
Running Time: 30 min.

Regular Performers: John Candy, Joe Flaherty, Eugene Levy, Andrea Martin, Catherine O'Hara, Harold Ramis, Dave Thomas

Second City's first shoestring stab at satirizing television, set in the fictional town of Melonville in general and the SCTV television station in particular. This program introduced a host of long-lived characters: Candy as egotistical lech Johnny La Rue; Flaherty as station manager Guy Cabellero (who rides a wheelchair to get sympathy), news anchor Floyd Robertson (and his alter ego, horror-movie host Count Floyd) and obsequious talk-show host Sammy Maudlin; Levy as obnoxious borscht-belt comic Bobby Bittman and broadcaster Earl Cannonbear; Martin as leopardskinned program director Edith Prickley and perpetual ESL student Perrini Sclerozo; O'Hara as obnoxious singer Lola Heatherton; and Thomas as acerbic drama critic Bill Needles, Asian actor Lin Ye Tang, and a painfully accurate Bob Hope. Ramis, who left the series after the first season, played the original station manager and conniving game show host Moe Green, who was kidnapped by the Leutonian Liberation Organization and appeared only in ransom photographs in subsequent episodes. Cheap, cheap, productions on cardboard sets, but funny, especially parodies of *Ben Hur* and TV show *Fantasy Island*. One bizarre skit featured the real Sir Ralph Richardson and Sir John Gielgud, in a pointless (but funny) Pinteresque play. Cheerfully elitist, the program never condescended to explain its humour or cultural references. Followed by CBC's *SCTV* in 1980.

See For Yourself

CBC
Children's
First Broadcast: Thursday, October 15, 1960, 4:30 p.m.
Final Year Broadcast: 1960
Running Time: 30 min.

Host: Ross Snetsinger

Snetsinger and Foster (a dog puppet) presented arts, crafts, and education.

Seeing Things

CBC
Comedy Drama
First Broadcast: Tuesday, September 15, 1981, 8:00 p.m.
Final Year Broadcast: 1987
Running Time: 60 min.

"Dreams are for the night time
Days I'm wide awake
Visions are for crazy men
Not me for goodness sakes
But I'm Seeing Things"
— From the *Seeing Things* theme song

CBC

▲
Seeing Things: Louis Del Grande as Louie Ciccone, a nebbish newspaper reporter beset by unwanted psychic visions.

Cast:

Louie Ciccone	Louis Del Grande
Marge	Martha Gibson
Jason Ciccone	Ivan Beaulieu
Al Ciccone	Al Bernardo
Anna Ciccone	Lynne Gordon
Heather Redfern	Janet-Laine Green
Heather's Husband	Booth Savage
Detective Sergeant Brown	Frank Adamson
Max Perkins	Murray Westgate
Marlon Bede	Louis Negin
Robert Spenser	Cec Linder
Kenny Volker	Ratch Wallace
Falstaff	John Fox
U.S. Federal Marshal Randall Jackson	Maury Chaykin

After several pilot programs, this show about a crime-solving clairvoyant reporter became a popular regular series. When balding Louie goes into a trance, he witnesses details of a recent murder that he's then obliged to solve.

In more unusual episodes, Louie picks up murder vibes from a 3,000-year-old Egyptian mask, and from a stray canine, the murder's only witness.

Louie was a reporter for Toronto tabloid *The Gazette* (he had a brief career in television news). Louie and his wife Marge (the actors were married in real life) were separated, though he desperately wanted to return to hearth, home, and son Jason. Louie lived with parents, Al and Anna, in a storeroom at the family bakery. Real estate agent Marge assisted on investigations, as chauffeur to the non-driving Louie. Louie moved back in with Marge in the fourth season—Marge was jealous of

Assistant Crown Attorney Heather Redfern, who helped Louie on many investigations. Also helpful was Detective Sergeant Brown. Kenny was Marge's hockey-goon boyfriend; Spenser was her boss. Max was Louie's editor; Marlon was the newspaper's food critic.

The show was warmly received around the world, although the CBC's idea of a full season (eight episodes) prevented it from being widely syndicated until it reached 40-plus episodes—just in time for cancellation.

Sesame Park

See: *Sesame Street*

Sesame Street

CBC
Children's
First Broadcast: Monday, September 28, 1970, 11:00 a.m.
Final Year Broadcast: —
Running Time: 60 min. and 30 min.

Canadians watched a direct-import version of *Sesame Street*—PBS's groundbreaking educational series aimed at pre-schoolers—until January 1973, when the CBC began to insert homespun segments.

The first slate of segments illustrated the lives of children from different regions: Peter John Halcrow, a Cree from Manitoba, Daniel Ruest from Quebec, Raymond Doucet from New Brunswick, and Bobbi Edge from Alberta.

Canadian versions of Jim Henson's Muppets included: Dodi, an elderly bush pilot, Basil the bear, and Louis the bilingual otter (1987); Fern, Dr. Bouzouki, Robert, and Katie, a Muppet in a wheelchair (1988); Garth, Barbara Plum, and Hana Gardner (1993); Peter Londonbridge (of *Rhyme Time News*); and Margaret Redwood (1994). A proposed Muppet, Gordon Brightfoot, failed to cut it with test audiences.

Canadian guest personalities included children's entertainers Raffi, Eric Nagler, Fred Penner, and cartoon tour guide Beau Beaver.

By 1974, one-quarter of the program was Canadian-produced; by 1991, it was one-half, becoming the half-hour *Sesame Park* in September 1996, reflecting a less urban setting than the U.S. series did. Canadian segments have been used in other versions of *Sesame Street* around the world. A technical glitch in 1987 treated innocent kiddies to a five-minute porn film segment transmitted over the CBC feed.

701

See: *Tabloid*

Shining Time Station

Syndicated: 1990
Children's
Running Time: 30 min.

Cast:
Mr. Conductor . . . . . . Ringo Starr (1990–91), George Carlin (1991–94)
Stacy Jones. . . . . Didi Conn
Billy Twofeathers. . . . . Tom Jackson (1991–94)
Matt. . . . . Jason Woliner (1990–91)
Tanya. . . . . Nicole Leach (1990–91)
Becky. . . . . Danielle Marcot (1991–94)
Dan Jones. . . . . Ari Magder (1991–94)
Kara. . . . . Erica Luttrell (1991–94)
Harry . . . . Leonard Jackson (1990–91)
Schemer. . . . . Brian O'Connor
Barton Winslow. . . . . Gerard Parkes (1991–94)
J.B. King . . . . Mart Hulswit
Midge Smoot . . . . Bobo Lewis
Schemee . . . . Jonathan Shapiro (1991–94)
Mayor. . . . . Jerome Dempsey
Felix . . . . Aurelio Padron (1991–94)
Ginny . . . . Barbara Hamilton (1991–94)

"Reach for the steam,
reach for the whistle
Go where the railway runs."
— From the *Shining Time Station* theme song

A pleasant kiddie show set in a rustic railroad station in Indian Valley, somewhere on a North American prairie. The station master was Stacy; Harry and Billy were engineers. Schemer (and nephew Schemee) ran an arcade and generally annoyed the cast with harebrained, crooked schemes. Musical numbers were provided by The Jukebox Band, a puppet combo with Tito on piano, Grace on bass, Didi on drums, and Tex & Rex on guitar. The program introduced North American audiences to popular British import *Thomas the Tank Engine*, whose adventures were narrated by the miniature Mr. Conductor, who lived in a picture frame on the wall (Carlin's character was supposed to be a cousin of the original Mr. Conductor.) A Canada/U.S. co-production seen for the most part on YTV in Canada.

Showtime

See: *The CGE Show*

Side Effects

CBC
Drama
First Broadcast: Friday, October 14, 1994 p.m.
Final Year Broadcast: 1996
Running Time: 30 min.

Cast:

Dr. Noah Knelman	Albert Schultz
Dr. Jim Barkin	Joseph Ziegler
Dr. Diane Camilleri	Nadia Capone
Judy Owens	Elizabeth Shepherd
Wanda Gibbs	Barbara Eve Harris
Gail Polidis	Anna Pappas
Donald Chen	Jovanni Sy
Liz Anderson	Jennifer Dale
Michelle Dupont	Janne Mortil
Tom Stockton	Lawrence Dane

The producers of *Street Legal* switched their attentions to the medical profession in this familiar mixture of steamy emotions and issue-oriented drama set in the Kingsview Family Clinic. Dr. Knelman was a skirt-chasing reprobate, more interested in entering the high-flying world of cosmetic surgery than looking after his motley patients; Dr. Barkin was the idealistic doc who believed there was a point to treating heroin addicts (he was also sweet on clinic director Dr. Camilleri). Owens was a nurse.

Sidestreet

CBC
Drama
First Broadcast: Sunday, September 14, 1975, 9:00 p.m.
Final Year Broadcast: 1978
Running Time: 30 min.

Cast:

Inspector Alec Woodward	Sean McCann (1975–76)
Sergeant Johnny Dias	Stephen Markle (1975–76)
Nick Raitt	Donnelly Rhodes (1976–78)
Glenn Olsen	Jonathan Welsh (1976–78)
Inspector Ted Bowman	John Swindells

Another effort to make police programs socially relevant, with cops tackling issues instead of mere criminals. Markle and McCann were fired after the first season to be replaced by more "likeable" leads. The series had a code of non-violence (fires and implied threats were used as substitutes for

CBC

on-screen rough-housing and gunplay). An "international" episode featured the cast heading for the bright lights of Buffalo, New York, to track down a drug shipment. Guest stars included John Colicos, Barry Morse, and Leslie Nielsen. The character of Inspector Bowman was imported from Britain's popular *Z Cars* program, apparently to boost foreign sales.

The critics jeer: "*Sidestreet*...descends on us like a great soggy bowl of Canadian porridge." — Dennis Braithwaite, *The Toronto Star*

Fake-out stake-out: Sean McCann (left) and Steven Markle pretend to patrol a residential neighbourhood in *Sidestreet.*

Singalong Jubilee

CBC
Musical Variety
First Broadcast: Monday, July 3, 1961, 7:30 p.m.
Final Year Broadcast: 1973
Running Time: 30 min.

Hosts: Bill Langstroth, Jim Bennet, Tom Kelly, Patricia Anne McKinnon

Conceived as *Folk Song Jubilee*, starring Pete Seeger, this summer replacement for *Don Messer's Jubilee* became a full series in 1969. Billed as "a friendly meeting-place where people can just sing along together," this Halifax songfest focused on folk and country music, but gradually moved to country-pop-rock. Langstroth played banjo; Bennet and Kelly sang. More visible members of the Jubilee Chorus included: Catherine McKinnon, Anne

TV Singalong: Originally a summer replacement for *Don Messer's Jubilee*, *Singalong Jubilee* outlived its parent by three years.

Murray (she married Langstroth), Ken Tobias, Patricia Anne McKinnon (Catherine's sister), Beverly Welles, Shirley Eikhard, and John Allan Cameron. Other popular members included singer Gene MacLellan (who wrote Murray's mega-hit, "Snowbird"), with familiar eyepatch, and blind Fred McKenna, singing guitar player and graduate of *Don Messer's Jubilee*. Guest acts included the Jubilee Four, the Townsmen Trio, the Don Burke Four, the Dropouts, and Ryan's Fancy.

—*With notes from Blaine Allan*

The critics cheer: "…folk songs very well performed by a relaxed and personable group of people…a thoroughly delightful half-hour." — Joan Irwin, *The Toronto Star*

The critics cheer (and jeer): "…I have always, and will have always, a great love for bad television." — Bob Blackburn, *The Toronto Star*

Sir Arthur Conan Doyle's Lost World

Syndicated: 1999
Drama
Running Time: 60 min.

Cast:

Professor Edward Challenger	Peter McCauley
Marguerite Krux	Rachel Blakely
Lord John Roxton	Will Snow
Ned Malone	David Orth
Dr. Summerlee	Michael Sinelnikoff
Veronica	Jennifer O'Dell

Perhaps someone else's Lost World. Film and television have never been particularly kind to Conan Doyle's 1914 novel, but this incarnation probably has Sir Arthur turning over in his grave. Trapped in a cheesy jungle enclave of rather unconvincing computer-generated dinos are scientist Challenger, heiress Krux, hunter Roxton, journalist Malone and biologist Summerlee. Also on hand is Veronica, the adult child of two now-deceased explorers. The exploring party takes refuge in a giant treehouse and searches the labyrinthian caves below the jungle floor in hopes of finding a convenient exit.

Additional story fodder includes a friendly tribe (the Zanga warriors), numerous visitors, ape men, giant bees, witch doctors, alien invaders, and the not-infrequent deaths and resuscitations of lead characters. William DeVry played journalist John Malone in the series' pilot.

Size Small

Syndicated: 1984
Children's
Running Time: 30 min.

Regular Performers: Helen Lumby, Jeff Lumby, John Lumby Jr., Lisa Lumby Richards

Meet the Lumbys, the hardest working family in Saskatchewan showbiz—this entire program was written and acted by an army of Lumby relatives (John Sr. produced). Gently paced, and soft-spoken, the program has an almost hypnotic effect on adult viewers—but don't become complacent! Out of nowhere comes the nightmarish Friend Record, a giant LP with legs, clinking out an unrecognizable tune on his musical spoons. Puppet pals included Webster, Didi, Tug, Hatchet the beaver, Cooter coyote, Renfrew the dog, Giffer gopher, Gasper skunk, Milkshake the cow, Bijou the poodle, Casablanca the camel, Wallabe salrus, and Of Course the horse. Helen played Miss Helen, Lisa played Great Grandma Gussie, John Jr. played Oliver Sudden, and Jeff played Stampede the cowboy who sang the immortal lines "You've got that horse, so ride him, cause that's what that whopping fellow's for." (Jeff wound up playing Winston Rothschild III on *The Red Green Show*). Spinoff series with special themes and settings included *Size Small Country* and *Size Small Island*. Seen primarily on Global in Canada, on PBS stations in the U.S., and also in Singapore, Malaysia, and Saudi Arabia.

Skipper & Co.

CBC
Children's
First Broadcast: Wednesday, April 3, 1974, 5:00 p.m.
Final Year Broadcast: 1989
Running Time: 30 min.

Cast:
Skipper . . . . Ray Bellew
Corky. . . . . Mack Barfoot

A retired sea captain invites children to visit his lighthouse in this Maritime production with a Newfie spin. Visitors included the postman; magical Vincent Vagabond; loud-mouthed cook, Charlie Lee; and ol' pal Corky. Guests included former Newfoundland Premier Joey Smallwood. Seen only regionally until 1988.

Small Fry Frolics

CBC
Children's
First Broadcast: Sunday December 21, 1952, 6:30 p.m.
Final Year Broadcast: 1955
Running Time: 30 min.

Hosts: Frank Heron (1952–55), Dorothy Heron (1954–55)

A kids' variety show with quizzes and lessons on life skills. Typical segments: opening a bank account; a puppy-naming contest. In the quiz segment, three-day winners were presented with the grand prize—a briefcase! Originally a radio show with host Byng Whittaker, then back to radio for another decade after its television run. Also known as *Children's Corner*.

Snow Job

CTV
Situation Comedy
First Broadcast: Monday, February 21, 1983, 8:00 p.m.
Final Year Broadcast: 1984
Running Time: 30 min.

Cast:
Melvin Courtney. . . . . Jack Creley
Renee Bouvier . . . . Joanne Cote
Jean Paul La Fond . . . . Roger Garand
Hilda Schultz. . . . . Pauline Rathbone
Bernard Graff. . . . . Rummy Bishop
Harold Field . . . . Gabe Cohen
Gigi . . . . Liliane Clune
Bobby Martinson. . . . . Nicholas Kilbertus

Few laughs, as a cantankerous manager tries to run a tight ship at Laurentian ski resort Chateau Royale, while sex-obsessed staff members clown around.

Some Of My Best Friends Are Men

CBC
Public Affairs
First Broadcast: Thursday, September 11, 1973, 10:30 p.m.
Final Year Broadcast: 1975
Running Time: 30 min.

Host: Maxine Samuels
Contributors: Dave Broadfoot, Agota Gabor, Carol Gault, Florynce Kennedy, Sylvia Spring

A feminist discussion program with satirical overtones. Kennedy, self-billed as "radicalism's rudest mouth" provided weekly commentaries, Broadfoot got a pie in the face for conspicuous displays of chauvinism, and the program handed out Shiny Golden Porker awards for particularly notable sexist behaviour. Samuels was producer of *The Forest Rangers* and *Seaway*.

Space Command

CBC
Science Fiction/Children's
First Broadcast: Friday, March 13, 1953, 7:00 p.m.
Final Year Broadcast: 1954
Running Time: 30 min.

Cast: Andrew Anthony, Joe Austin, Bob Barclay, James Doohan, Aileen Taylor, Austin Willis

"Challenging the stars themselves, spaceships pierce the vast blackness of interstellar space, carrying with them the infinitesimal lives of men dedicated to the planet Earth and to her perilous Space Command."
— Opening narration, *Space Command*

Star Trek's James Doohan's first foray into outer space, as part of the crew of Spaceship XSW1, searching outer space for intelligent races on behalf of worldwide organization Space Command. Frank Anderson was the space cadet who was assigned to different functions of Space Command, including the transport division, satellite division, investigation (scientific) division, and exploration division, among others. Designed to compete with U.S. programs like *Rocky Jones, Space Ranger*, the Canadian version tried to emphasize scientific principles. To the consternation of action-hungry audiences, CBC promotional literature promised no "space monsters, moon maidens, space-pirates and space-spies" but did deliver a lot of talk and cheap-looking special effects.

Spider-man

ABC
Animated
First Broadcast: Saturday, September 9, 1967, 10:00 a.m.
Final Year Broadcast: 1970
Running Time: 30 min.

Voices of:

Spider-man/Peter Parker . . . . . Bernard Cowan (1967–68),
    Paul Soles (1968–69)
Betty Brandt . . . . Peg Dixon
J. Jonah Jameson . . . . Paul Kligman
Captain Stacy . . . . Len Carlson

Produced in Canada for ABC using Canadian vocal talent (but only animated here for the first season). Based on Marvel Comics' web-slinging superhero and boasting a catchy theme song ("Spider-man, Spider-man, does whatever a spider can…") and some moody, impressionistic cityscapes courtesy of director/executive producer Ralph Bakshi. Betty Brandt was a reporter at the New York *Daily Bugle* and photographer Peter Parker's sorta girlfriend. Jameson was the *Bugle*'s irritable editor ("I don't care what you do, just get me a picture of Spidah-man!") Popular enemies included: Electro, Doctor Octopus, the Vulture (also Soles), The Green Goblin, and the Rhino (who could *always* be found hiding in the city zoo's rhinoceros caves).

Stargate SG-1

Syndicated: 1999
Science Fiction
Running Time: 60 min.

Cast:

Colonel Jonathan "Jack" O'Neill . . . . Richard Dean Anderson
Major Samantha Carter . . . . Amanda Tapping
Doctor Daniel Jackson . . . . Michael Shanks
Teal'c . . . . Christopher Judge
General George Hammond . . . . Don S. Davis
Doctor Janet Fraiser . . . . Teryl Rothery

The 1994 theatrical film *Stargate* served as the basis of this series: scientists and military types investigate an interdimensional portals that leads to a new planet named Abydos. The series returns the characters of team leader O'Neill, and archaeologist Jackson (played by Kurt Russell and James Spader in the film) and introduces: astrophysicist Carter, alien Teal'c (a Jaffa), commanding officer Davis, and medical officer Fraiser. Using multiple stargates, the team explores new worlds, though many of the planets they visit are vexed by the Gou'ald, a race of powerful, snake-like, alien parasites prone to masquerading as gods. Filmed in British Columbia, episodes premiere on the U.S. Showtime network before appearing in worldwide syndication.

The Starlost

CTV
Science Fiction
First Broadcast: Friday, September 14, 1973, 7:00 p.m.
Final Year Broadcast: 1974
Running Time: 60 min.

Cast:

Devon . . . . Keir Dullea
Rachel . . . . Gay Rowan
Garth . . . . Robin Ward
Mulander 165 . . . . William Osler

Heavily promoted as Canada's Great Hope for international television success. And why not? The series had a considerable number of aces: a respected science-fiction writer Harlan Ellison as story editor; a cast including *2001: A Space Odyssey*'s veteran Keir Dullea; scientific consultation by science-fiction writer Ben Bova, then-editor of *Analog* magazine; state-of-the-art Magicam special effects provided by executive producer Douglas Trumbull, part of the Oscar-winning effects team for *2001*; and a great time slot carved out by key NBC stations.

The program's premise: It's the year 2790 A.D. and the Earthship, *Ark*, drifts helplessly in space. Its crew, charged with moving the population of a dying Earth to a new planet, was killed 500 years earlier. The massive ship houses 500,000 people in a series of gargantuan pods, each a distinct community, separated to prevent homogenization of culture. One problem: most of the inhabitants no longer realize they're on a spaceship.

Devon, a citizen of Amish-inspired Cypress Corners, suspects his pod is part of a larger community. Town Elders banish him, but he's followed by girlfriend Rachel, who's engaged to Garth, the town blacksmith. Garth, in turn, follows Rachel, planning to kill Devon and reclaim his betrothed. Once out of the pod, they form an uneasy alliance to find out just where the hell this massive spacecraft is going and how to turn it around. Ellison imagined a long run for the program, and a blockbuster conclusion: something to do with a black hole. Unfortunately, pre-production disasters eclipsed anything that might have happened to the *Ark*'s navigation centre:

• CTV executives fouled the waters with their meddling; Ellison departed in a huff, leaving a mocking pseudonym, Cordwainer Bird, to mark his place.

• Ellison's departure invalidated writing contracts with some of science fiction's finest names: Philip K. Dick, Thomas M. Disch, Frank Herbert, and A.E. Van Vogt among them. (A solitary script, inspired by Ursula K. LeGuin, made it to production.)

• The *Ark*'s touted special effects were knocked out of orbit by Trumbull's departure. Instead, audiences were treated to cheesy chroma-keys and rear-screen projections.

Episodes involved unconvincing giant bees, stodgy robots, and a dome called New Eden Leisure Village. In hopes of capturing a little *Star Trek* magic, guest stars included John Colicos, who once played a Klingon, and Walter Koenig, *Trek*'s Ensign Chekov, as the alien Oro.

The helpless actors wandered aimlessly around the tiny sets, which had all the atmosphere of a television newsroom. Scripts were silly and illogical, and the trio never seemed to get anywhere. A continuing sub-plot featured hard-up Garth's efforts to win back Rachel—or any other female. Dullea turned in a decent performance, while Rowan's was adequate. Ward turned in his finest work since his 1971 horror flop *Dr. Frankenstein on Campus*. (One bright spot was William Osler as computer Mulander 165, appearing on screens all over the ark as the bushy-eyebrowed image of a stern librarian, repeating, ever more crossly,

"May I help you," once the Library Channel was activated.)

The unadulterated script for the pilot episode won the most outstanding teleplay of the year award from the Writers Guild. Ellison co-wrote a book (with Edward Bryant) based on the program's pilot script: *Phoenix Without Ashes*. A second volume contained both the novel and the script: *Phoenix Without Ashes: The Original Teleplay & Novel for the TV Series the Starlost*. Bova also wrote his own novel, *The Starcrossed*, a spoof of the series and its cursed production, published in 1975. Ten programs were later incongruously jammed into five two-hour TV movies: *The Alien Oro, The Beginning, Deception, The Invasion*, and *The Return*.

The series' worst moments:

• Beset by hallucinations, Garth believes he's under attack by "monster" Devon—actor Dullea daubed with white glue and sporting rustling, construction-paper curls.

• Alien Oro tries to convince the *Ark*'s inhabitants to immigrate to the planet Xar by projecting scratchy 16-mm travelogues as propaganda films. Devon discovers that Xar really looks more like a Tunisian desert than British Columbia and tries to abort the plan. In a slam-bang conclusion, Oro and Devon hold a "debate to the death," scored by a computer. Devon wins. Yawn!

The critics cheer: "…a world ahead of *Star Trek*…the best science fiction series ever to come to television…." — Jack Miller, *The Toronto Star*

The critics jeer: "…its exposition was dull, its pace funereal and its writing poor…. [Ward's] performance is thick-sliced ham…." — Blaik Kirby, *The Globe and Mail*

"…inept, amateurish and silly, and I don't want my name on it." — Harlan Ellison, series creator

Stars on Ice

CTV
Variety
First Broadcast: Thursday, September 21, 1976, 7:30 p.m.
Final Year Braodcast: 1981
Running Time: 30 min.

Host: Alex Trebek (1976–80), Doug Crosley (1980–81)

Skating acts from around the world made this an improbable success, wowing them in places like Saudi Arabia, where ice itself is something of a novelty. Toller Cranston became a semi-regular in 1980.

Ben Bova on *The Starlost*

"What really surprised me is that there was a great deal of national chauvinism on the set. I was a "Yankee." For the first time in life I heard phrases like 'The flea knows how to live with the elephant.' Every piece of advice I gave was completely ignored. As the series progressed, it wasn't just despair I felt, but numb acceptance that this was as good as it was going to get. When I saw the first screening I wanted to run away and hide."

The Stationary Ark

CBC
Science
First Broadcast: Tuesday, September 16, 1975, 5:00 p.m.
Final Year Broadcast: 1975
Running Time: 30 min.

Host: Gerald Durrell

A show about animals, filmed at Durrell's zoo, the Jersey Wildlife Preservation Trust. A U.S./Canada co-production. Followed by *Ark on the Move*.

Stevie-O

CBC
Children's
First Broadcast: Tuesday, July 1, 1958, 3:00 p.m.
Final Year Broadcast: 1958
Running Time: 30 min.

Host: Steve Woodman

Hip, multi-voiced, Montreal DJ Woodman presented cartoons and puppets, man.

Stompin' Tom's Canada

CBC
Musical Variety
First Broadcast: Thursday, September 26, 1974, 9:00 p.m.
Final Year Broadcast: 1975
Running Time: 30 min.

Host: Stompin' Tom Connors
Musicians: Gary Empey, Bill Lewis

Singer/songwriter Stompin' Tom from New Brunswick shared star billing with his continent-wide co-star, featuring studio sessions, live performances, and filmed travelogues.

Story Book
See: *Hidden Pages*

Story Theatre

CTV
Children's
First Broadcast: Sunday, September 12, 1971, 7:00 p.m.
Final Year Broadcast: 1972
Running Time: 30 min.

Regular Performers: Maja Ardal, Peter Bonerz, Jeff Bronstein, Hamilton Camp, Severn Darden, Melinda Dillon, Bob Dishy, Judy Graubart, Mina Kolb, Mickey LaGare, Richard Libertini, Paul Sand, Dick Schaal, Ann Sweeney, Eugene Troobnick

Pretty cool adaptation of a broadway hit based on Grimms' unsanitized fairytales and Aesop's fables, among other source material.

The actors portrayed a travelling troupe riding on horse-drawn wagons, and performed on minimalist studio sets, with actors providing their own narration. Guest stints included Alan Alda as a match-wielding Satan and Avery Schreiber masquerading as a baby who bites off the fingers of his nemesis.

Strange But True

Global
Supernatural
First Broadcast: Sunday, September 11, 1983, 9:30 p.m.
Final Year Broadcast: 1984
Running Time: 30 min.

Host: Barry Morse

An awful Canadian/British co-production (half the shows were filmed in England) featuring supposedly true, weird stories. Poor Barry Morse sat in a library and tried to look ponderous as he thumbed through ancient tomes, searching for "strange" fodder.

Some episodes weren't very strange at all: a man leaves his car with a bank as loan collateral, then reveals his dark secret—he only did it to save on parking charges while vacationing.

Some episodes belonged in the so-bad-it's-good category. Personal favourites: a starfish beckons rescuers to find a man in mortal danger; a ghost bugs his old pals to help him find his leg, which was lost in a train accident (they find it on someone's roof).

Strange Paradise

CBC
Soap Opera
First Broadcast: Monday, October 20, 1969, 2:00 p.m.
Final Year Broadcast: 1970
Running Time: 30 minutes

Cast:

Jean Paul Desmond/Jacques Eloi Des Mondes . . . . Colin Fox
Erica Desmond/Helene Des Mondes . . . . Tudi Wiggins
Holly Marshall . . . . Sylvia Feigel
Dr. Alison Carr . . . . Dawn Greenhalgh
Raxl . . . . Cosette Lee
Quito . . . . Kurt Schiegl
Elizabeth Marshall . . . . Paisley Maxwell
Vangie Abbott . . . . Angela Roland
Reverend Matthew Dawson . . . . Dan McDonald
Tim Stanton . . . . Bruce Gray
Dan Forrest. . . . . John Granik
Susan O'Clair . . . . Trudy Young
Emily Blair . . . . Lucy Warner
Huaco . . . . Patricia Collins
Ada. . . . . Peg Dixon
Irene . . . . Pat Moffat
Laslo . . . . Jack Creley
Cort . . . . David Wells
Philippe Desmond . . . . Neil Dainard

Weird, synthesized flute harmonies and pounding jungle drums accompany a kaleidoscope of swirling colour. A drug-induced hallucination? A futuristic test pattern? No—it's the opening credits for this weekday soap about voodoo, cryogenics, reincarnation, and family curses.

Dubbed *Pagan Place* by critics, the program was a Canada/U.S. co-production—the first daily soap produced for syndication. Also seen in Mexico, it was inspired by *Dark Shadows* (ABC 1968–73), the wildly successful U.S. soap starring Canadian Jonathan Frid as tortured vampire heartthrob, Barnabas Collins.

The series was set on the forbidding Caribbean island of Maljardin (but filmed in Ottawa), where all plant and animal life are poisonous.

After his wife Erica dies, wealthy Jean Paul Desmond retreats to an island mansion to perform cryogenic experiments to return her to life, assisted by servant and part-time sorceress, Raxl, and her mute, bald aide, Quito. Summoning the powers of darkness, Jean Paul invokes the spirit of Jacques Eloi Des Monde (who hides in a 300-year-old painting), a 17th-century lookalike ancestor damned to eternal torment by a pact with the Devil. Jacques (sometimes referred to as Jacques *du Brevert* Des Mondes) possesses Jean Paul and revives Erica as a demon, intent on murdering the island's few inhabitants.

The new Jean Paul uses video surveillance and hidden microphones to spy on a litany of guests: Vangie, a medium; biochemist Alison Carr (Erica's sister); Dan Forest, business manager; artist Tim Stanton; Holly Marshall, a too-cool teenage heiress in bell bottom pants; Elizabeth, Holly's "uptight" mother; and the Reverend Matthew Dawson.

When U.S. stations cancelled the show, producers imported Robert Costello, who had produced *Dark Shadows*. In short order, the island's hapless inhabitants are murdered—except for Holly, who is rescued by Jean Paul in a rare lucid moment. He escapes with Raxl and Quito to the mainland, after torching the portrait of his ancestor who provides, in retrospect, the rationale for the program's title: "Whether you live or die, Jean Paul Desmond, wherever you choose to run, your curse will follow you, and life will be for you always a Strange Paradise."

In the revamped show, Jean Paul returns to his mainland mansion in Desmondton, where he's beset by a family curse that turns him into (what else?) an insane murderer. The transformation is preceded by a pulsating red star and the appearance of the Devil's Mark—a crudely rendered magic-markered figure—on Jean Paul's palm. Other complications: Jacques is back; Trudy Young arrives as a reincarnated witch; Holly falls in love with a spirit; Erica's double moves in; Raxl engages in Snake God worship; Jean Paul falls in love with a woman targeted for extermination by a witch coven; brother Philippe returns from a sabbatical with a mystic Native tribe; and missing father Julian returns (he may be dead). In the

Strange literature: *Strange Paradise* spawned three creepy pocketbooks by Dorothy Daniels, the same author who penned dozens of *Dark Shadows* novels.

series' illogical blockbuster, Raxl is killed by the capricious Snake God after Jean Paul discovers she is responsible for the family curse. With the image of Jacques destroyed, Jean Paul is freed of curses, disloyal servants, and Desmondton.

Colin Fox (who holds the record for most television portrayals of Sir John A. MacDonald) chews the scenery suitably, providing the most pervasive sound bite; the drawn-out, mocking laughter of ancestor Jacques: Jean Paul: Why will you not free me of this curse? Jacques: Haaaaaa-ha-ha-ha-ha-haaaaaaa!—an inexpensive substitute for dialogue. A special nod goes to Kurt Schiegl, for bringing some sensitivity to the thankless role of Quito.

Dialogue is generally uninspired and often amusing ("It is all becoming clear—this is a contract with the Devil!"), and spooky background music, repeated endlessly, will be familiar to the few fans of *The Starlost*.

Unfortunately, comparison to *Dark Shadows* doomed *Strange Paradise* to television oblivion. Those who recall the program often confuse it with its vampiric counterpart ("...and the vampire had this mute servant, see..."). *Strange Paradise* deserves a little more recognition than that, simply for blazing a trail of weirdness across

the bland Canadian television landscape of 1969. Despite its shortcomings, the series provides occasional rewards, given a chance to weave its peculiar spell.

Filmed in Ottawa and Old Chelsea, Quebec; stills of Toronto's Casa Loma stood in for the mansion.

The critics jeer: "... kookiness gone amuk [sic]...after a couple of samplings a viewer comes away only with a new appreciation of the confusion of metaphysical gobbledygook and unlimited sympathy for an entrapped cast." — *New York Times*

"On first sight alone [it's] the funniest show on the air." — Patrick Scott, *The Toronto Star*

Strategy

CBC
Game Show
First Broadcast: Monday, April 1, 1969, 2:00 p.m.
Final Year Broadcast: 1969
Running Time: 30 min.

Host: Alex Trebek
Announcer: Jay Nelson
Assistant: Dee Miles

CBC's entry into the big-prize (major appliances) game-show sweepstakes. Program promotion says: "What makes *Strategy* different from other television game shows is the circle. It is painted in different colors to denote four separate zones. It is a maze, much like the snakes and ladders game of years ago." Contestants headed to the centre of the board as they answered questions and avoided booby-traps set by the opposition. Winners left the show after one victory. Miles presided over a map marking contestants' progress and some of the booby traps.

The critics jeer: "...none of the four players yesterday stepped on [a booby trap]. We were all waiting for that.... Poor host Alex Trebek, what's he ever done to inherit the TV roles he gets?" — Roy Shields, *The Toronto Star*

Street Legal

CBC
Drama
First Broadcast: January 6, 1987, 9:00 p.m.
Final Year Broadcast: 1994
Running Time: 60 minutes

Colin Fox on *Strange Paradise*:

"Filming was terrible. We began shooting in August in a cinder block building with no air conditioning. The aptly named Crawley Studio was infested with cluster flies. Millions of them were released by the heat, to the point that it looks like video break-up on the screen. On the threat of a staff walk-out, they were forced to put in air conditioning.

"Most of the time we were trying to stop ourselves from laughing out loud, as we delivered faux period dialogue. We lasted three or four months with the first set of writers until they realized they had to get us off Maljardin and the repetition based on an island setting—there was no one left to knock off.

"The show had a fan club and a large following. There's still a large group of now-middle-aged viewers who were horrified by the strange goings-on in *Strange Paradise*. I'm still often recognized from the program. It just doesn't seem to die."

Cast:

Charles "Chuck" Tchobanian	C. David Johnson
Leon Robinovitch	Eric Peterson
Carrington "Carrie" Barr	Sonja Smits (1987–92)
Olivia Novak	Cynthia Dale (1988–94)
Dillon Beck	Anthony Sherwood (1989–94)
Alana Newman Robinovitch	Julie Khaner (1989–94)
Rob Diamond	Albert Schultz (1991–94)
Laura Crosby	Maria del Mar
Brian Malony	Ron Lea
Mercedes	Alison Sealy-Smith
Nick Del Gado	David James Elliott (1987–89)
Lisa	Maria Ricossa
Gloria Beachum	Diane Polley
Steve Winton	Mark Saunders
Legal Secretary	Pamela Sinha
Student	Venus Terzo
R.J. Williams	Donnelly Rhodes
Ted Barr	Gordon Thomson
Harold Vickers	Gordon Pinsent
Judge Appleby	Lawrence Dane
Tom	Nicholas Campbell
Businessman	Gary Reineke
Jill	Tanja Jacobs

The continuing saga of Toronto legal firm Barr, Robinovitch, Tchobanian and Associates. Somewhat at odds with each other were Leon Robinovitch and Carrie Barr, left-of-centre nice guys, vs. Chuck Tchobanian and wannabe partner, entertainment lawyer Olivia Novak on the right.

Based on a gritty 1986 TV movie, *Shell Game,* featuring some of the show's characters (Barr, Tchobanian, and Rabinovitch were played by Brenda Robin, Tony Rosato and Nicholas Rice, respectively), the new series took on a soap opera sheen—and a huge cast of characters to keep the series' many plots and sub-plots rolling.

Chief secondary characters were Crown attorney Beck, litigation lawyer Newman (she became a judge), slick corporate lawyer Diamond, and no-goodnik lawyer Malony.

Whenever audience numbers waned, the show's producers had a simple answer—claim that the new season would be hotter!, steamier!!, sexier!!! than the season before. The first strategy was the introduction of the ambitious, manipulative, and tarty Olivia Novak in the second season. Further campaigns included "the HEAT is on the STREET" and a series of Toronto Transit Commission bus and streetcar ads featuring horizontal characters under the banner "each week they embrace the law." (One

reviewer suggested that the new photos made the actors look like they had "ingested toxic shellfish.")

Series highlights: Olivia comes on to (insert name of any character here), jockeys for full partnership, and becomes pregnant with Chuck's baby; Leon marries Newman, runs for mayor, has an affair, and defends himself against sexual harassment charges; Chuck is wrongly convicted of murder, fights a custody battle with ex-wife Lisa over their son, and obsesses over Olivia; Carrie has a relationship with undercover cop Del Gado, marries Dillon, adopts a daughter, and is run over and killed by an alcoholic judge (her 1992 swan song); and the near-bankruptcy of the law firm, targeted for takeover by an American firm headed by R.J. Williams.

A follow-up TV movie, *Last Rights,* was telecast in November 1994, and featured Olivia's murder trial for assisting in the suicide death of a terminal AIDS patient, and Chuck's efforts to defend her in court.

Life imitated art when series co-creator William Deverell fought in court with the CBC over the rights to use the series name in a further novel. After a long legal battle the book was published in 1995 as *Street Legal: The Betrayal,* though it featured only characters created by Deverell.

Guidelines for the series warned writers that Canadian judges do not use gavels, though they might slap the bench with their hand. Seen in 30 countries, including Germany, Australia, Switzerland, Norway, and Turkey. The City of Toronto (featured heavily in outdoor scenes) celebrated December 13, 1992, as "*Street Legal* Day."

The critics cheer: "Dependability is what made *Street Legal* a hit with viewers—dependable characters, dependable plots, dependable renewals, year after year." — Tony Atherton, *Ottawa Citizen*

The critics jeer: "There is already a surfeit of over-sexed and simple-minded drama on television and most of it features far more compelling and attractive actors and actresses." — John Haslett Cuff, *The Globe and Mail*

Stump The Experts

CBC
Game Show
First Broadcast: Thursday, September 11, 1952, 7:30 p.m.
Final Year Broadcast: 1952
Running Time: 30 min.

Host: Stephen Brott
Panel: Maxwell Cohen, Hugh MacLennan, Dr. D.L. Thompson.

Viewers submitted tough questions to a panel, then won cheap handicraft prizes for stumping the experts.

Sunshine Sketches

CBC
Comedy/Drama
First Broadcast: Tuesday, September 9, 1952, 7:30 p.m.
Final Year Broadcast: 1953
Running Time: 30 min.

Narrator: John Drainie
Cast:

Peter Pupkin	Timothy Findley
Judge Pepperleigh	Alex McKee
Zena Pepperleigh	Peggi Loder
Reverend Dean Drone	John Bethune/Eric House
Lillian Drone	Peg Dixon
Theodora Drone	Barbara Hamilton
Henry Mullins	Bill Needles
Jefferson Thorpe	?
Mallory Tompkins	Frank Perry
Josh Smith	Paul Kligman
Golgotha Gingham	Robert Christie

Stephen Leacock's *Sunshine Sketches of a Little Town* formed the apt subject matter for English Canada's first television drama. Episodes featured daydreaming bank teller Pupkin, his paramour Zena, innkeeper Smith, Gingham the undertaker, and Thorpe the barber.

Since Leacock penned only a dozen *Sunshine Sketches,* writers (including Don Harron) elaborated on the original material by expanding single paragraphs into full episodes.

Filmed in Beaverton, Ontario. Also known as *Addison Spotlight Theatre,* after its car dealership sponsor.

The critics cheer: ""Best show on TV." — Peter Francis, *Mayfair Magazine*

Super Dave

Global
Comedy Variety
First Broadcast: Wednesday, October 12, 1988, 10:30 p.m.
Final Year Broadcast: 1992
Running Time: 30 min.

Cast:

Super Dave Osborne	Bob Einstein
Fuji Hakayito	Art Irizawa
Donald Glanz	Don Lake
Mike Walden	Himself

Einstein created stuntman Super Dave for the short-lived variety show *Van Dyke and Company* (1976), then continued to develop the character on CTV's *Bizarre* (he was the show's producer)before launching his own headliner.

The program's structure was simple: introduce a guest star (The Smothers Brothers, Ray Charles, Joe Cocker) then lope off to "the compound" where Dave would announce his next great stunt. Thanks to the incompetence of engineer Fuji and assistant Donald, each stunt would lead to the Super One's near-demise. Real-life L.A. sportscaster Mike Walden provided heartless play-by-play, often abandoning Super with (apparent) grievous mortal injuries.

While the slapstick stunt (a beheading, a fall, a monstrous crushing) capped each program, the show succeeded because of Einstein's careful characterization, highlighting Super Dave's barely concealed contempt for his audience, his ever-renewed faith in Fuji, his increasingly shaky bravado as he attempts a new stunt, and, finally, his utter devastation after being left to perish, alone, from his injuries. The show spawned a Saturday morning cartoon, cable sitcom, and full-length film.

The Superior Sex

CBC
Game Show
First Broadcast: Wednesday, July 5, 1961, 10:00 p.m.
Final Year Broadcast: 1961
Running Time: 30 min.

Host: Elwy Yost
Panelists: Corinne Conley, Susan Fletcher, Paul Kligman, Royce Frith

Teams of four men and four women (half of them guests) battled each other in tests of skill (e.g., darts, miniature golf, croquet, ballet) and intelligence. Criticized as impatient, excitable, and dictatorial, host Yost called the disastrous program "fantastic" despite savage reviews. Electrical malfunctions allowed sneaky players to block other contestants. Female scorekeepers, sans surnames, were June and Gail.

The critics jeer: "Not since the very early days of CBC-TV...has there been anything on the screen so comprehensively clumsy and coy and cluttered." — Nathan Cohen, *The Toronto Star*

"Moderator Elwy Yost...had to keep shouting: 'Somebody is treading on the light button.'" — John Ruddy, *Toronto Telegram*

Swingaround

CBC
Children's/Game Show
First Broadcast: Tuesday, September 10, 1967, 4:30 p.m.
Final Year Broadcast: 1970
Running Time: 10 min. and 30 min.

Host: Lloyd Robertson (1968–69), Trevor Evans (1969), Bill Paul (1969–70)

A quiz show for Toronto-area Grade Seven students, used, until 1968, to pad episodes of *Barney Boomer* and *Upside Town* (on which Evans also appeared). Each show pitted two new teams of four students against each other in a stand-alone competition, with cash prizes going to the winners. A National Telephone Quiz segment had the host phone two lucky students from across Canada, who helped an on-screen team answer four questions.

Other segments were: Singaround Matches, games of fun and skill; Isolation Booth, in which team members tried to guess a secret object placed with an opposition team member; and Who Am I?, a guessing game.

The Swiss Family Robinson

CTV
Adventure
First Broadcast: Friday, September 13, 1974, 7:00 p.m.
Final Year Broadcast: 1975
Running Time: 30 min.

Cast:
Johann Robinson . . . . Chris Wiggins
Elizabeth Robinson . . . . Diana Leblanc
Marie Robinson . . . . Heather Graham
Franz Robinson . . . . Micky O'Neill
Ernest Robinson . . . . Michael Duhig

This fairly faithful adaptation of the Johann Wyss literary classic scored big ratings points in 17 countries, particularly Germany and England, where it spawned a children's book based on the series. Jungle footage was shot in Jamaica, with tree-house sets located in Toronto.

Prematurely cancelled, thanks to a deal arranged by the program's producers, selling the series to ABC television and selling an option to CBS—at the same time! While CBS retained script control, ABC waited impatiently for its episodes, until it created its own version: a big-budget disaster produced by Irwin Allen, featuring a tour de force of unconvincing special effects, including hurricanes and exploding volcanoes. By the time Allen's show premiered on ABC, CBS had dropped its Canadian option. Without U.S. funding, and with other countries fearing slaughter from the big-budget competition, the Canadian Robinsons faded from the picture. The U.S. competitor folded 26 episodes later.

Tabloid

CBC
News Magazine
First Broadcast: Monday, March 9, 1953, 7:01 p.m.
Final Year Broadcast: 1963
Running Time: 30 min.

Hosts: Dick MacDougal (1953–58), Percy Saltzman (1953–63), Max Ferguson (1958–61), Elaine Grand (1953–56), Joyce Davidson (1956–61), Betty Jean Talbot (1961–62), Alan Millar (1961–62)

Newscasters: Gil Christy (1953–54), John O'Leary (1954–62), Rex Loring (1962–63)

Free-form weather: Percy Saltzman's *Tabloid* forecasts sometimes took up two-thirds of the show.

▼

CBC

Contributors: Allan Anderson, Gregory Clark, Earl Cox, Blair Fraser, Trent Frayne, Robert Fulford, Sydney Katz, Paisley Maxwell, Robert McKeown, Dave Price, Wilfred Sanders, John Saywell, Lister Sinclair, Jean Templeton, Bruce West

"A program with an interest in anything that happens anywhere, bringing you the news at seven."

—Opening narration, *Tabloid*

Producer Ross McLean's melange of news, newsreels, entertainment, and viewer mail was billed as "Facts with Fun."

Hosted by TV's "Mr. Relaxation," MacDougal, and bespectacled weatherman Saltzman, who was so popular with viewers that his weather reports were open-ended, occasionally taking up half the show. (Saltzman's glasses were props used to make him more likable.) The program started out delivering headline news, but dropped that in 1953 when a news program preceded it. After a disgruntled viewer mailed in a damning review of MacDougal's "mugging" performance, the host invited viewers to write or phone the unhappy critic, who sued successfully for $3,000 after receiving a barrage of calls and mail and an endless procession of cab drivers sent to his home. MacDougal, self-described as a "tripe-and-onions, fish-and-chips chap," died in 1958, to be replaced by popular radio figure Max Ferguson.

When popular Elaine Grand left the show, she was replaced by the controversial Joyce Davidson, who offended viewers by expressing indifference to a Royal Visit. Viewer outrage forced her resignation after telling Pierre Berton, on television, that any woman still a virgin at age 30 was "unlucky." Talbot replaced Davidson after a casting call of more than 500 applicants.

On Monday, October 1, 1960, after 2,250 broadcasts, "the nightly habit of nearly everyone" changed its name to *701*—the program's official starting time—to satisfy a drug company who had registered the trade name "Tabloid."

The program moved to Montreal for the summer of 1962 and was hosted by Norman Kihl and popular French-Canadian "weather girl," Marthe Choquette. After a major revamping, only holdover Saltzman joined the new on-air staff in the show's final year.

The series' best moments: Gregory Peck tossing Joyce Davidson's research notes on the floor; a pantomime interview with

Harpo Marx; Saltzman's record 20-minute weather segment; and the day cameras caught a sleeping stagehand sawing logs behind the scenery.

A filmed 1955 episode of *Tabloid* rests in a time capsule inside a cornerstone of the Imperial Oil Building in Toronto.

The critics cheer: "It has a style and a mood all its own...a comfortableness that no other Canadian show has ever been able to achieve." — Dennis Braithwaite, *The Toronto Star*

"Night in and night out you won't find a better television program." — Trent Frayne, *The Globe and Mail*

The critics jeer: "...has to be done away with out of kindness to the show itself and the viewers." — Pierre Maple, *TV Guide*

"...a poor man's *Jack Paar* show." — Arthur Treacher, *Tabloid* guest, in an appearance on *The Jack Paar Show*

Take 30/Take Thirty

CBC
Discussion
First Broadcast: Monday, September 17, 1962, 3:30 p.m.
Final Year Broadcast: 1984
Running Time: 30 min.

Hosts: Anna Cameron (1962–65), Paul Soles (1962–78), Adrienne Poy (Clarkson) (1965–75), Moses Znaimer (1967–68), Ed Reid (1971–75), Mary Lou Finlay (1975–77), Hana Gartner (1977–1982), Harry Brown (1978–84), Nadine Berger (1982–84)

This weekday staple started as *Open House* with Fred Davis and Anna Cameron, but was relaunched, minus Davis. The show was aimed at "housewives" and produced an impressive array of documentaries and interviews during its 30-year run. Topics covered included the sexual revolution, contentious religious issues, Vietnam, reports from Moscow and Japan, and a dramatization from Richard Rohmer's novel *Exoneration* (with Percy Saltzman as the U.S. president).

Notable guests included Dr. Benjamin Spock, Phyllis Diller, Charlton Heston, and Peter Ustinov. Contributors included culinary favorite Jehane Benoit, consumer reporter Ruth Fremes, and financial adviser Brian Costello. Eventual co-host Adrienne Poy (later Clarkson), the program's book reviewer, was billed as the "first performer

Mid-afternoon stretch: Paul Soles (left) and Adrienne Clarkson were the longest-running hosts of *Take 30*.

of Oriental origin to have a daily program...in the western world." (Actress Michael Learned of *The Waltons* fame, applied for the job.)

During several summers, the program changed to *Take 30 From...* (fill in the blank) featuring broadcasts from various Canadian cities.

During the 1970s, the program occasionally became *Take 30 Access* during summers, giving TV exposure to various organizations. An hour-long version, *Take 60*, appeared briefly in prime time.

The critics cheer: "Anna Cameron...is the personification of everybody's sister and Paul Soles is everybody's brother. *Take Thirty* should do well." — Roy Shields, *The Toronto Star*

"A program of consistently high standards and wide-ranging interests." — Pat Pearce, *Montreal Star*

The critics jeer: "Shows like *Take 30* have become disaster freaks, reeling with furrowed brow and wringing hands [on issues] from overpopulation to crippled kids to pollution to divorce in a necrophiliac orgy of doom.... It's a guilt-ridden old show which is sloppily produced and suicidally depressing; it should be taken off the air."—Heather Robertson, *Maclean's*

Take Time With Noel Harrison

CBC
Musical Variety
First Broadcast: Saturday, October 19, 1974, 6:30 p.m.
Final Year Broadcast: 1976
Running Time: 30 min.

Host: Noel Harrison

Rex's son welcomed folk and country music guests including John Allan Cameron, Shirley Eikhard, Tom Gallant, Tommy Makem, The Stringband, and Brent Titcombe.

Taking the Falls

CTV
Crime Drama
First Broadcast: Saturday, September 23, 1995, 10:00 p.m.
Final Year Broadcast: 1995
Running Time: 60 min.

Cast:
Terry Lane . . . . Cynthia Dale
Katherine McVicar . . . . Sandra Nelson
Bernie McVicar . . . . Ken James
Dominic DiFranco . . . . Alex Carter
Stanley Prendergast . . . . Michael Copeman
Kenny Malloy . . . . Richard McMillan
Tessa . . . . Michele Muzzi

Dale was a struggling private eye who drove a junk heap, and Nelson was the lawyer in this crime series set in Niagara Falls (the Canadian side). Bernie was Katherine's dad, DiFranco and Prendergast were cops, Tessa was a coroner, and Kenny was an informant who ran a local spook house.

An action-comedy, critics charged the show failed on both counts. It's apparently easier to take the Falls than to hold onto them—the series pooched in just a few weeks.

The critics jeer: "One of the worst Canadian-made shows I've ever seen." — Greg Quill, *The Toronto Star*

Talent Caravan

CBC
Variety
First Broadcast: Friday, February 6, 1959, 8:00 p.m.
Final Year Broadcast: 1960
Running Time: 30 min.

Host: George Murray
Orchestra Leader: Ricky Hyslop

A travelling talent show highlighting young performers. Producers tallied viewer mail to select the brightest performers.

Tales of Adventure

CBC
Children's
First Broadcast: Saturday, September 13, 1952, 7:30 p.m.
Final Year Broadcast: 1953
Running Time: 30 min.

Ambitious drama for kids, with serialized adaptations of novels, including: Jules Verne's *20,000 Leagues Under the Sea* (pre-Disney); Thomas Raddall's *Roger Sudden;* and Wilkie Collins' *The Moonstone.* Performers in the dramas included Eric Clavering, Colin Eaton, Earle Grey, William Holland, Murray Kash, Ed McNamara, Alan Pearce, and Warren Wilson.

Tales of the Riverbank

CBC
Children's
First Broadcast: Saturday, October 5, 1963, 12:00 p.m.
Final Year Broadcast: 1964
Running Time: 30 min.

Voices of:
Hammy Hamster, Roderick Rat, Guinea Pig, Sir Reginald Raccoon, Blossom Skunk, Chippie Chipmunk, Wise Old Frog, Turtle, Mrs. Duck, Old Mother Hen, Mr. Weasel, Mr. Squirrel . . . . Paul Sutherland

Paul Sutherland

What's his motivation?: Dave Ellison (bottom left) and Paul Sutherland (bottom right) direct Guinea Pig in a taxing aerial stunt in *Tales of the Riverbank.*

Producers Dave Ellison and Paul Sutherland created this live-action series featuring real animals with human voices. Conceived as an adaptation of the children's book *The Wind in the Willows,* a dearth of moles in the Toronto area caused delays. When a reward was offered, one enterprising Toronto student located a nest of moles, then killed them all before presenting them to the producers.

The program's revised premise: Hammy Hamster emigrates to the Riverbank, where he meets Roddy, a white rat who introduces him to Riverbank denizens, including inventor Guinea Pig, a W.C. Fields sounda-like who fashions bizarre machinery, lives in an old mill and drives a car (Hammy prefers a small motorboat).

These non-violent programs, filmed around Toronto, featured a memorable guitar-music score.

Animals on the program were non-professionals (up to a dozen Hammys and three Rodericks), and no animal was allowed to work for more than ten minutes at a stretch. They were encouraged to act by liberal smearings of cheese and peanut butter on set props.

Sold to the BBC (and 34 other countries), British narrator Johnny Morse dubbed new character voices for the British market. Sequels include *Hammy Hamster* and *Once Upon a Hamster.*

Tales of the Wizard of Oz

Syndicated: 1961
Animated
Running Time: 30 min.

Voices of:
Dorothy, The Munchkins . . . . Susan Morse
The Wizard, Dandy Lion. . . . . Carl Banas
Socrates. . . . . Alfie Scopp
Rusty . . . . Larry Mann
The Wicked Witch of the West . . . . Peggi Loder

"We're three sad souls, oh me, oh my
No brain, no heart, I'm much too shy…"
— From the *Tales of the Wizard of Oz*
theme song

A pretty dreadful adaptation of L. Frank Baum's classic, seen originally in a half-hour format and relentlessly recycled as five-minute cartoons. The cartoons featured *very* limited animation, but memorable voice char-

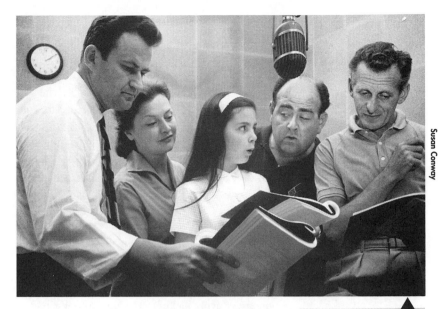

acterizations: the Wiz was a crusty misanthrope who sounded like W.C. Fields, and Rusty the Tin Man emoted like a 20-locomotive train wreck. Dandy Lion's signature line was an elongated "maaaa-maaaaa," and the teardrop-shaped Munchkins sounded like long-play records spun at 78. Though the Wicked Witch of the West is credited as Peggi Loder, she sounds a lot more like Larry Mann in drag. *Star Trek*'s James Doohan was listed as a voice actor in original press releases. Occasional guest characters included Robby the Rubberman, a stuttering spare tire. The series had only one truly funny gag: scarecrow Socrates nailed a diploma to his head to advertise his smarts. Also notable was the raucous, free-form incidental music.

Followed by a one-hour 1964 NBC special, *Return to Oz,* with *The Forest Rangers'* Susan Conway filling in as Dorothy.

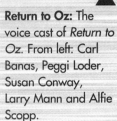

Return to Oz: The voice cast of *Return to Oz.* From left: Carl Banas, Peggi Loder, Susan Conway, Larry Mann and Alfie Scopp.

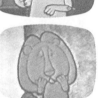

Cartoon counterparts: At left (from top to bottom) are cartoon characters Rusty, Dandy Lion, Socrates, Dorothy and Toto, and The Wizard.

T and T

Global
Drama
First Broadcast: Saturday, September 10, 1988, 7:30 p.m.
Final Year Broadcast: 1991
Running Time: 30 min.

Cast:

T.S. Turner . . . . Mr. T
Amanda Taler . . . . Alex Amini
Terri Taler. . . . . Kristina Nicoll
Danforth Decker . . . . David Nerman
Martha Robinson . . . . Jackie Richardson
Detective Dick Hargrove . . . . David Hemblen
Detective Jones . . . . Ken James
Renee. . . . . Rachael Crawford
Sophie . . . . Catherine Disher
Joe Casper . . . . Sean Roberge

Pitying the fools who missed him after the implosion of *The A-Team,* Mr. T gave in to Canadian producers who sought him for this tongue-in-cheek series. Playing a detective and former boxer, he assisted lawyer Amanda Taler by impulsively kicking criminal butt (he had a very short fuse) at least once per episode. Never one for subtlety, he literally hauled suspects to court for legal disposal. In 1990, Amanda was replaced by another "T"—her younger sister Terri. Necessarily fast-paced (episodes were only a half-hour long), the programs were filmed around Toronto. Seen one year earlier on the U.S. Family Channel. Pilot film: *Straight Line.*

Target The Impossible

See: *Here Come The Seventies*

Telepoll

CTV
Public Opinion
First Broadcast: Sunday, December 3, 1961, 7:00 p.m.
Final Year Broadcast: 1965
Running Time: 30 min.

Hosts: Royce Frith, Arnold Edinborough

Well-known intellectuals debated the issues while everyday Canadians were polled on their opinions regarding important questions

Broadcaster Magazine

of the day. Pipe-smoking Frith was host.

Opinions on questions of the day? More than 76% of respondents felt interracial marriage between White and Black individuals was a bad idea, though almost 90% favoured non-discrimination (October 1962); more than 63% said divorce should be made easier (January 1962); and more than 57% felt Russia was a threat to the West (December 1962).

Guest debaters included Pierre Berton, Kildare Dobbs, Frank Drea, Trent Frayne, Lloyd Percival, Leslie Roberts, Gordon Sinclair, and Jack Webster. Sponsors were Telex (a Telex machine figured heavily in the proceedings) and *Saturday Night* magazine (Edinborough was editor). A New York City version of the show was hosted by Ron Cochran.

Telescope

CBC
News Magazine
First Broadcast: Sunday, June 30, 1963, 9:00 p.m.
Final Year Broadcast: 1973
Running Time: 30 min.

Host: Fletcher Markle

A documentary series that concentrated on profiles of Canadians "in depth," among them actors Christopher Plummer (during filming of *The Sound of Music*) and Bruno Gerussi, singers Tommy Hunter and Gordon Lightfoot, pianist Glenn Gould, conductor Guy Lombardo, skier Nancy Greene, and writer Arthur Hailey. Non-Canadian subjects included writer Ray Bradbury, director John Huston, and The Beatles, who were tailed through their hotel rooms during a Toronto appearance. Guest commentators included Buckminster Fuller, John Kenneth Galbraith, and Piet Hein, who had the dubious distinction of inventing a new form of poetry called Grooks. Host Markle directed the Disney film classic, *The Incredible Journey.*

Telestory Time

CBC
Children's
First Broadcast: Thursday, January 1, 1953, 5:00 p.m.
Final Year Broadcast: 1954
Running Time: 15 min.

Host: Pat Patterson

Patterson read a storybook written by Dorothy Robb to musical accompaniment by organist Doris Ord in this series aimed at pre-schoolers. Sketch-a-minute favourite George Feyer illustrated the story as it was being read.

The Ten Thousand Day War

CBC
Documentary
First Broadcast: Wednesday, October 22, 1980, 9:00 p.m.
Final Year Broadcast: 1982
Running Time: 60 min.

Narrator: Richard Basehart

A massive undertaking for newsman Michael Maclear, the first western journalist in North Vietnam, who produced this epic look at the Vietnam conflict, from the French takeover in 1945 to the fall of Saigon in 1975. A mixed critical success: some detractors felt the series lacked focus, biting off more than it could chew in 26 episodes. Also published as a book.

That Maritime Feelin'

CBC
Music
First Broadcast: Friday, April 8, 1977, 7:30 p.m.
Final Year Broadcast: 1977
Running Time: 30 min.

Another apology for cancelling *Don Messer's Jubilee*, this time bringing back Marg Osburne. Guests included singers John Allan Cameron, Wilf Carter, Anne Murray, Stompin' Tom Connors, Patsy Gallant, Shirley Eikhard, Catherine McKinnon, Ken Tobias, and Noel Harrison. Osburne died while the series was still in production.

Theatre Canada

CBC
Dramatic Anthology
First Broadcast: Thursday, September 17, 1970, 9:00 p.m.
Final Year Broadcast: 1970
Running Time: 30 min.

This series of filmed dramas included: Morley Callaghan's *Rigmarole* with Donnelly Rhodes and Margot Kidder; *The Magic Hat* with Gordon Pinsent; *The Mariposa Bank Mystery* by Stephen Leacock; *Postcard* by Alice Munro; and *Roberta and her Robot* by Richard J. Needham. The series was also seen in Great Britain. Also known as *Canadian Short Stories*.

Theodore Tugboat

CBC
Children's
First Broadcast: Tuesday, October 26, 1993, 10:00 a.m.
Final Year Broadcast: —
Running Time: 15 min.

Cast:
The Harbour Master . . . . Denny Doherty

Theodore Tugboat looks an awful lot like Thomas the Tank Engine (face forward, they might be mistaken for each other in a police line-up) but never mind that—they were probably built at the same factory.

The Harbour Master narrates the moralistic tales of thoughtful, hard-working Theodore and his seafaring pals of The Great Ocean Tug and Salvage Company fleet at Big Harbour, then applies the lessons learned to his own life. Other tugs, directed by the Dispatcher, include: conscientious Emily the Vigorous; burly blowhard George the Valiant; safety tug Foduck the Vigilant, a solid-state electronic marvel; and diminutive but enthusiastic Hank Tugboat. Other characters include The Pilot Boats (Pearl and Petra), Benjamin Bridge, Bedford Buoy, and Owan the Oil Rig. A life-sized Theodore was commissioned to visit children in port cities.

They're Playing Our Song

CBC
Music
First Broadcast: Tuesday, August 26, 1975, 9:30 p.m.
Final Year Broadcast: 1975
Running Time: 30 min.

Host: Jim McKenna

What do you get when you offer famous Canadians a chance to request their favourite musical chestnuts? Why, a playlist composed largely of non-Canadian music and performers: José Feliciano performed "California Dreamin'" for Gary Carter; Kathy McAuliffe performed "Amazing Grace" for W.O. Mitchell; and Brook

Benton performed "More" for Gordie Howe. Nancy Greene Raine requested a patriotic favourite—Susan Jacks performing "Which Way You Goin', Billy?" A three-episode series.

A Third Testament

CBC
Documentary
First Broadcast: Wednesday, November 13, 1974, 9:30 p.m.
Final Year Broadcast: 1975
Running Time: 60 min.

Host: Malcolm Muggeridge

Muggeridge looked at faith through the eyes of theologians St. Augustine and Soren Kierkegaard, writers William Blake and Leo Tolstoy, Lutheran pastor Dietrich Bonhoeffer, and scientist/philosopher Blaise Pascal. Their collected works might have comprised a Third Testament of the Bible. Filmed separately in English and French.

This Hour Has Seven Days

CBC
Public Affairs
First Broadcast: Sunday, October 4, 1964, 10:00 p.m.
Final Year Broadcast: 1966
Running Time: 60 min.

Hosts: John Drainie (1964–65), Laurier LaPierre, Patrick Watson (1965–66)
Reporters: Dinah Christie, Robert Emmett Hoyt, Warner Troyer, Larry Zolf

Executive producers Douglas Leiterman and Patrick Watson shared this news program's mission statement with the public: "Using special camera techniques we will probe dis-

CBC

Current affairs cool: From left, Laurier LaPierre, Patrick Watson, and Dinah Christie in CBC's classic public affairs program *This Hour Has Seven Days.*

honesty and hypocrisy. By encouraging leads from our viewers and inviting their alertness, we will provide a kind of TV ombudsman to draw attention to public wrongs and encourage remedial action." Each program was an eclectic mix of filmed reports, interviews, songs, or satiric skits written by Robin Grove-White, of *That Was The Week That Was* fame. A studio audience and a mail segment helped ensure the appearance of two-way communication with viewers.

Drainie, a popular actor, and LaPierre, a professor of Canadian history at McGill University, were the original anchors. Christie became a regular in the second season, singing the week's headlines. Covering contentious issues in an uncompromising fashion, the program earned the well-publicized wrath of CBC management.

First-season fracases included: management nixing a sketch depicting Queen Elizabeth as a housefrau in curlers, and one with program staff, disguised as relatives, sneaking into the Ontario Hospital for the Criminally Insane in Penetanguishene to interview inmate Fred Fawcett.

Things got hotter next season, when Watson replaced Drainie as co-host. LaPierre threatened to resign when management forbade him from conducting interviews with politicians. Management relented, but his interviews were criticized for "emotional involvement." A sketch about Pope Paul V, "infallibly" umping a ball game between the Yankees and the Cardinals, had the CBC apologizing to viewers, while Leiterman held a press conference supporting the sketch. Execs also objected to the sensationalism of inviting Ku Klux Klan members to shake hands with a Black minister in the studio (they refused). Management threatened cancellation unless producers agreed to play ball and stop talking to the press. Naturally, LaPierre complained to *Maclean's*.

Further crises: in covering the trial of Steven Truscott, a 14-year-old charged with murder, LaPierre filled the emotional void left by Truscott's composed mother when he wiped a tear from his eye. Critics charged that LaPierre had became "emotionally involved" with the material.

When LaPierre was criticized for revealing an anti-capital punishment bias during an interview with Quebec Attorney General Claude Wagner, he publicly criticized the CBC and was cited for "Disloyalty to Management."

In April 1966, Watson was told that his and LaPierre's contracts would not be renewed;

Leiterman leaked the story to *The Globe and Mail*, sparking a "Save Seven Days" campaign among the program's three million viewers. Thousands of phone calls, petitions, and letters failed to sway Prime Minister Pearson or Secretary of State Judy LaMarsh. When the Toronto Producers' Association threatened to strike if the host's contracts were dropped, Pearson appointed a mediator.

After six weeks of hearings by the Parliamentary Broadcasting Committee, the program remained dead. The campaign had failed to bring the show back to the air.

The critics cheer: "It is impossible to simply watch it; you become involved in it…it remains, for millions…something to talk about come Monday…to see whether there's another Pope sketch…or to see whether Laurier LaPierre will lose his temper…or Pat Watson his unflappable urbanity." — Alan Edmonds, *Maclean's*

The critics jeer: "The bigger the audience it draws, the more it becomes enslaved by what it believes—erroneously most of the time—the audience wants…. It rationalizes debasement of standards with the demagogic and self-deluding claim that 'nobody likes us but the people.'" — *The Globe and Mail*

This Hour Has 22 Minutes

CBC
Satire
First Broadcast: Monday, October 11, 1993, 10:30 p.m.
Final Year Broadcast: —
Running Time: 30 min.

Regular Performers: Cathy Jones, Rick Mercer (1992-2001), Greg Thomey, Mary Walsh

Twenty-two minutes after commercials, that is. The remnants of *CODCO* re-formed in something of an homage to *This Hour Has Seven Days,* using a loose news program format to satirize current issues, most of them political. A popular segment is Mercer's satirical ranting as he stomps around the city (a volume of Mercer's monologues, *Streeters: Rants and Raves From This Hour Has 22 Minutes,* is available).

Memorable characters include: Jones' Babe Bennett, sexual affairs commentator ("I'm just goofin' around!"); Walsh's Prairie correspondent Connie Bloor, redneck Dakey Dunn, and in-your-face reporter Marg Delahunty (who frequently accosts real politicians); and Thomey's Jerry Boyle, clumsy head of the Newfoundland Separatist Party. Cast members take fre-

This half-hour has high ratings: The cast of *This Hour Has 22 Minutes.* From left, Mary Walsh, Greg Thomey, Cathy Jones, and Rick Mercer.

Salter Street Films

quent breaks to perform in side projects: Mercer's *Made in Canada* and Thomey's *Daily Tips For Modern Living* among them.

This Is the Law

CBC
Game Show
First Broadcast: Monday, June 21, 1971, 8:30 p.m.
Final Year Broadcast: 1976
Running Time: 30 min.

Host: Paul Soles (1971), Austin Willis (1972–76)
Panelists: Julie Amato (1976), Bill Charlton (1971–76), Susan Gay (1971–72) Susan Keller (1972–75), Madeleine Kronby (1971), Dini Petty (1971), Hart Pomerantz (1971–76), Larry Solway (1971–75)
Cast:
The Lawbreaker . . . . Paul Soles
The Cop . . . . Robert Warner
Regular Performers: Paul Bradley, Valri Bromfield, Eric Clavering, Trudy Desmond, Dougal Fraser, Gale Garnett, Robert McHeady, Monica Parker, Patrick Sinclair, Jo Penny, Harry Van Doren, Diane Wainman

Originally a radio program, this popular game show asked panelists to identify obscure laws. In one segment, the panel had to uncover a legal oddity (submitted by viewers for a $25

In Victoria, B.C., this is the law!: Host Austin Willis provided clues to help panelists identify outlandish illegalities in *This Is the Law.*

CBC

"bounty") based on clues supplied by the host. Other infractions were acted out in silent film clips featuring Soles as The Lawbreaker, a sad nebbish pursued by The Cop, who seemed to exist only to throw Soles in prison. (The Cop was rewarded in 1974 with a promotion to sergeant after hauling The Lawbreaker into prison 268 times).

Though comedian Pomerantz (*The Hart and Lorne Terrific Hour*) was also a lawyer, he snagged the most laughs with outrageously convoluted wrong answers, only occasionally stumbling on a correct one. Guest commentators who explained legal details included Roy McMurtry and Dr. Morton Shulman. When Solway and Keller left, substitute panelists included Patricia Bates, Peter Cook, Barbara McLeod, Patricia Murphy, Margaret Pascu, Billy Van, and Ben Wicks. The end credit sequence featured an animated Lawbreaker escaping from prison.

This Living World

CBC
Children's
First Broadcast: Thursday, October 10, 1959, 5:00 p.m.
Final Year Broadcast: 1964
Running Time: 30 min.

Host: Steve Bloomer

Bloomer played host to live animals, presented in artificial habitats recreated in the studio. Regular animal performers included a cheetah and Momba the gorilla, named in a viewer contest. Produced in French (*La vie qui bat* with Guy Provost) beginning in 1955. So popular, it generated up to 23,000 viewer letters *per week*.

Tidewater Tramp

CBC
Children's
First Broadcast: Friday, October 2, 1959, 5:00 p.m.
Final Year Broadcast: 1962
Running Time: 30 min.

Cast:
Captain Martin . . . . Reg McReynolds
Gail Martin . . . . Maureen Cook
Peter. . . . . Robert William Chambers
Regular Performers: Edith Matheson Dean, Brendan Dillon, Ted Greenhalgh, Wally Marsh

A drama for kids based on a radio program. The Flying Kestrel, a tramp steamer, sailed the coast of British Columbia. Captain Martin, a widower, was accompanied by daughter Gail and assisted by coast cadet Peter. Occasionally seen on *Junior Roundup*.

Time For Sunday School

CBC
Religion
First Broadcast: Sunday, October 7, 1962, 11:00 a.m.
Final Year Broadcast: 1966
Running Time: 30 min.

Hosts: Helene Nickerson, Gloria Chetwynd, Ann Graham

"But Davy, I thought we didn't have to go to Sunday School today." Former Montreal "weather girl" Nickerson was the first host of this kids' program designed to provide Sunday School to a home audience through Bible stories, songs, hymns, and the perennially popular Lutheran cartoon, *Davy and Goliath*. A home-grown segment, *Crabapple Island*, featured animal characters Mayor Basil Bullfrog and Myopia Mole in adventures of moral significance.

Tiny Talent Time

CHCH
Children's Variety
First Broadcast: Sunday, September 8, 1957, 4:00 p.m.
Final Year Broadcast: 1992
Running Time: 30 min.

Host: Bill Lawrence

This 35-year marathon of baton twirlers, ballerinas, and small boys with accordions was a spinoff of an earlier program, *Ken Soble's Amateur Hour*. Seems that adult performers were miffed to see prize money handed over to the likes of a tuneless three-year-old with a harmonica. Kindly Uncle Bill kept kid performers at ease, asking them the same familiar questions each week ("If you could make a wish come true, what would you wish for?") A ratings powerhouse, the *Tiny Talent* brigade routinely slaughtered NFL football in the ratings. A new series, broadcast in 2000, featured Sandie Savelli and Mike Gravina as hosts.

The critics jeer: "I swear it's true—CHCH-TV says the Tinies are in its top 10 shows." — Roy Shields, *Toronto Telegram*

Titans

CBC
Interview
First Broadcast: Friday, July 3, 1981, 8:00 p.m.
Final Year Broadcast: 1982
Running Time: 30 min.

Host: Patrick Watson

Watson recreated his old *Witness to Yesterday* series as he interviewed historical figures including: Marilyn Lightstone as Nefertiti; Chris Wiggins as Galileo; Frances Hyland as Queen Elizabeth I; W.O. Mitchell as Stephen Leacock; John Neville as Confucius; John Marley as Albert Einstein; and Watson himself as Alexander Graham Bell. Provocative and entertaining.

Toby

CBC
Situation Comedy
First Broadcast: Friday, October 4, 1968, 4:30 p.m.
Final Year Broadcast: 1969
Running Time: 30 min.

Cast:

Toby Mitchell . . . . Susan Petrie
Mark Mitchell . . . . Peter Young
Leonard Mitchell . . . . Arch McDonnell
Jennifer Mitchell . . . . Micki Moore
Jean-Jacques "Jay-Jay" Roberge . . . . Robert Duparc

Canada's answer to *Gidget*, Toby was described as "a 16-year-old Canadian high-schooler with the I.Q. of Einstein and the imagination of Salvador Dali. Her ambition is to be 'Queen of the Universe' and her destiny is to be a mother of three." (Love those '60s!)

Toby lived in the suburbs with her parents, Leonard and Jennifer, and pudgy brother Mark, who had "ambitions to be a gynecologist or a pilot." Jay-Jay, a Quebec exchange student, provided a nominal love interest.

"There's a lot of laughs north of the border," said a CBC press release, "Your average Parry Sound farmer may seem a funny fellow, but there are plenty of kooks living in the city too."

To help alert teens to the copious humour, producers invested in a special laugh track geared to a younger audience.

Teen comedy: From left, Arch McDonnell, Micki Moore, Peter Young, Robert Duparc, Susan Petrie in *Toby*. Smiling fellow reclining at rear is unidentified.

CBC

Petrie was chosen from a cattle call of 260 prospective Tobys.

The critics jeer: "The...show seemed somewhat light weight and square...(Toby) has Robert Goulet eyes and a fixed endearing cute little grin, like something drawn with your finger on a moist orange juice jug." — Natalie Edwards, *Starweek*

The Tom Green Show

Comedy Network
Comedy
First Broadcast: Friday, February 13, 1998, 11:00 p.m.
Final Year Broadcast: —
Running Time: 30 min.

Host: Tom Green
Co-Host: Glenn Humplik
Hangers-On: Phil Geroux, Derek Harvie

Tom Green's a real card, lying in front of the Eaton Centre sucking on a cow's teat, or dragging a rotten animal carcass onto Mike Bullard's *Open Mike* set.

Green got his start on Ottawa cable television in 1994, taping his parents' reactions to stunts like painting their house plaid or replacing the hood of Dad's car with a new one, replete with pornographic illustration, and dubbing it the Slutmobile.

Other popular features include Green's Scuba Hood, a guy who steals coins from public fountains, and Green's rendition of the "Bum Bum Song."

Exploding fame saw Green's program broadcast on MTV, though segments filmed in New York City stiffed—New Yorkers were just too savvy for this sort of thing. Long-suffering co-host Humplik (he once ate a pickle soaked in urine) continued to appear on the MTV series, though he refused to move to L.A. with Green.

Naturally, dealing in popular obscenities made Tom a corporate darling—he's been offered major sponsorship deals (Pepsi, for example) and you're probably sitting there thinking "This ain't fair—I could have done that." True, but Green ate that pile of feces and you didn't.

Green made the transition to film in such undistinguished fare as *Road Trip* (2000), and *Freddy Got Fingered* (2001) and starred in *The Tom Green Cancer Special*, about his experience with testicular cancer.

The Tommy Ambrose Show

CBC
Musical Variety
First Broadcast: Friday, September 22, 1961, 9:00 p.m.
Final Year Broadcast: 1963
Running Time: 30 min.

Host: Tommy Ambrose
Music: Gordon Kushner Chorus, Lucio Agostini Orchestra

Squeaky clean singer-songwriter Ambrose tried manfully to pilot this lopsided mix of local talent (largely young, unknown Canadian singers getting their "big break") and big-name U.S. imports like Ann-Margret and The Smothers Brothers.

The Best of Tommy Ambrose (summer 1962) featured repeats.

The Tommy Banks Show

CBC
Musical Variety
First Broadcast: Wednesday, December 29, 1971, 10:30 p.m.
Final Year Broadcast: 1974
Running Time: 30 min.

Host: Tommy Banks

The program featured interviews, conducted by brassy nightclub star Banks, sandwiched between musical acts.

An eclectic guest roster included Edgar Bergen and Charlie McCarthy, Sebastian Cabot, Rosemary Clooney, Max Ferguson, Rod McKuen, Murray McLauchlan, Peter C. Newman, Slim Pickens, Joey Smallwood, The Stampeders, Jackie Vernon, and interviews with Mr. Chang, a 700-year-old spirit guide housed in the body of British psychic Douglas Johnson.

The Tommy Hunter Show

CBC
Musical Variety
First Broadcast: Friday, September 17, 1965, 8:30 p.m.
Final Year Broadcast: 1992
Running Time: 30 min. and 60 min.

Canada's Country Gentleman, singer/guitar player Tommy Hunter graduated from *Country Hoedown*, inheriting its time slot and taking some cast members on a near 30-year run. A highly rated series, the program was still pulling audiences of almost a million in its final year.

One reason for the show's success was Hunter's insistence on playing to a wider audience than hard-core country fans. His stipulation to CBC before signing up for the series was "no barns and no bales of hay." Shows were taped mostly in Toronto, with occasional visits to other Canadian cities.

Hunter's supporting performers have been the Rhythm Pals (Mike Ferbey, Mark Wald, and Jack Jensen), fiddler Al Cherney, and the Bert Niosi Orchestra.

Other regular performers included singer Pat Hervey, guitarist Jim Pirie, banjo player Maurice Bolyer, singer Debbie Lori Kaye, the Country Guys and Gals, the Allan Sisters, the Coach 'n' Four, the Travelling Men, guitarist Red Shea, Whiskey Jack, and the OK Chorale. Musical guests included Garth Brooks, Crystal Gayle, The Judds, Kris Kristofferson, Reba McEntire, and Eileen (Shania) Twain.

The show's title changed, for the 1976 season, to *Tommy Hunter Country*. Hunter was awarded the Order of Canada in 1986, and made an Honorary Citizen of the State of Tennessee in 1987. The show was popular on the U.S. country network, TNN, and briefly syndicated in the U.S.

— *With notes from Blaine Allan*

Canada's country gentleman: Tommy Hunter and canine catch some rays between tapings of the long-running *Tommy Hunter Show.*

CBC

The Town Above

CBC
Drama
First Broadcast: Monday, October 12, 1959, 10:30 p.m.
Final Year Broadcast: 1960
Running Time: 30 min.

Cast:

Fred Chevalier	Roland Chenail
Pauline Chevalier	Denise Pelletier
Denis Chevalier	Louis Turenne
Diane Chevalier	Catherine Begin
Pierre Chevalier	Yvon Thiboutot
Uncle Gédéon	Doris Lussier
Onésime Ménard	Rolland Bédard

The flip-side of life with the lower-class Plouffes, as creator Roger Lemelin turned to the upper-middle class Quebec City suburb of Sillery, and a new family, the Chevaliers. The family was stalled on the path of upward mobility, trying to keep up appearances while struggling with a changing society. Pauline was mother to three teenage kids: Denis, who wanted to study medicine, flirtatious Diane, and adolescent tough Pierre. Father Fred was a grim accountant on the verge of nervous breakdown, wringing his hands week after week over family spending habits. Two *Plouffes* holdovers were bus driver Onésime (whose deceased wife Cécile was played by Pelletier) and Uncle Gédéon.

A critical and ratings failure, particularly in English Canada, where the program's second season wasn't even carried. The series was known as *En haut de la pente douce* in Quebec.

The critics jeer: "Wise men head for the nearest exit after they've heard the only good feature of the show. (That's the theme song.) If the exit's locked, hide under the bed." — Ron Poulton, *Toronto Telegram*

"Why must TV stories of family life always be set in Quebec?" — Dennis Braithwaite, *The Toronto Star*

Traders

Global/CBC
Drama
First Broadcast: Thursday, February 1, 1996, 10:00 p.m.
Final Year Broadcast: 2000
Running Time: 60 min.

Cast:

Sally Ross	Sonja Smits
Adam Cunningham	Bruce Gray
Marty Stephens	Pat McKenna
Barb Stephens	Gloria Slade
Jack Larkin	David Cubitt
Cedric Ross	David Gardner
Ayn Krywarik	Kymberley Huffman
Susannah Marks	Janet C.A. Bailey
Monika Barnes	Terri Hawkes
Donald D'Arby	Rick Roberts
Grant Jansky	David Hewlett
Benny Siedleman	Ron Gabriel
Christopher Todson	Chris Leavins
Ian Farnham	Gabriel Hogan
Paul Deeds	Peter Stebbings
Carl Davison	Philip Akin
Ziggy McLeod	Angela Vint
Niko Back	Rachael Crawford
Ben Sullivan	Shaun Johnston
M.J. Sullivan	Lexa Doig
Mike Pinetti	Richard Zeppieri
Cathy Blake	Kristina Nicoll, Sabrina Grdevich
Tommy "Ryke" Rykespoor	Alex Carter

A surprise for timid producers of programs set in Anywhere, North America; international audiences didn't seem to mind watching Toronto Bay Street traders unashamedly buying and selling Canadian stocks and bonds.

Sally headed up the financial firm Gardner, Ross (later Gardner, Ross, Cunningham) after dad Cedric was disgraced in a financial scandal. Other traders included: charismatic, crackerjack trader Larkin; stab-you-in-the-back, second-in-command Cunningham, who'd love to sell the firm to the highest bidder; maniacal head trader Stephens; and Krywarik, a retail broker who specialized in elderly male investors.

The series derived dramatic tension (amid a flurry of financial-babble) from the firm's complex business dealings, as well as the lives, loves, and aspirations of its management and employees. Series highlights: Cedric stages a coup; Sally has a lesbian affair, suffers a cancer scare, and marries Ben; Marty is stabbed; Krywarik and Larkin are murdered. The program was seen on both Global and CBC from its third season on.

The critics cheer: "There is not a single moment of that kind of imitative awkwardness that has characterized Canadian TV shows in the past." — John Haslett Cuff, *The Globe and Mail*

▲

The trouble with Tracy: was hackneyed plots like this one, with brother Paul (Franz Russell) making out as a maid to assist ditzy sis, Tracy (Diane Nyland).

"LIFE...
COM'ON, KIDS. I'LL TREAT YOU
EACH TO A TUNA FISH SANDWICH.
PAUL, COULD YOU MAKE MINE
PASTRAMI?
ANYTHING YOU SAY, PAUL. ♯
[FIN]

▲

The final cue: The last cue card used in the wrap episode of *The Trouble With Tracy.*

The Trouble With Tracy

CTV
Situation Comedy
First Broadcast: Wednesday, September 15, 1971, various
Final Year Broadcast: 1972
Running Time: 30 min.

Cast:

Tracy Young	Diane Nyland
Doug Young	Steve Weston
Tracy's Mother	Sylvia Lennick
Paul Sherwood	Franz Russell
Tony Marshall	Ben Lennick
Sally Anderson	Bonnie Brooks
Jonathan Norris	Arch McDonnell
Margaret Norris	Sandra Scott

Three decades after its premiere, viewers declare *The Trouble With Tracy* the worst Canadian show ever made—even if they've never seen it. There may be ample support for that supposition, right from the opening sequence: the zany (and annoyingly unforgettable) theme music; actress Diane Nyland bowing to the wild applause of a non-existent audience; the stale canned laughter dogging the opening gag as Tracy slams a door into hapless husband Doug's face (perhaps the first show in history to cue a laugh track before the program begins).

A Canada/U.S. production taped in Toronto for daily syndication, it was briefly the most successful Canadian TV export of all time. To help secure U.S. sales, the program feigned a New York setting—using two snapshots of the New York skyline, strategic placement of the Stars and Stripes, and myriad script references to Central Park, Bellevue Hospital, and the American Dream, courtesy of American scriptwriter Goodman Ace, who wrote every episode. Ace was the highest-paid comedy writer of the 1950s, scripting for such stars as Sid Caesar and Perry Como. Tempted to write off the program's campy storylines and stale one-liners to the tastes of a 1970s audience? A misconception: Tracy was uncool even by the standards of the day. Ace wrote the scripts in the '40s and '50s for a radio (and short-lived TV) program called *Easy Aces*. L.A. script doctors made a half-hearted effort to adapt these scripts to 1970s sensibilities. (Ace's 1958 film, *I Married a Woman,* starring George Gobel, also features characters, plot, and dialogue lifted wholesale for *Tracy.*)

Some script gems:
• Doug, referring to his mother-in-law's extended visit: "Mother was set to stay the summer—good old Somerset Mom."
• Doug, on a local politician: "All the polls had picked him to lose—but luckily he wasn't running in a Polish district."
• Doug to secretary using dictaphone: "Miss Anderson, please take that plug out of your ear."
Miss Anderson: "I can't hear you, I've got a plug in my ear."

Creaky plots revolved around dim-witted Tracy's attempts to help her husband get ahead at the advertising agency of Hutton, Dutton, Sutton and Norris. Budget conscious, the program ignored bad takes, blithely rolling tape as actors recovered from missed cues and forgotten lines. The action was largely limited to two cheaply constructed sets: the Youngs' avocado-and-gold living room and the sparsely furnished agency offices. Actors shamelessly filled multiple roles. In one episode, Doug expresses surprise when the Youngs' writer/neighbour appears as a television announcer. "Didn't you know?" asks Tracy, with a budget-stretching explanation, "Tony's been doing that show for years."

Costumes (also heavily recycled), were supplied by Simpson's, featuring unholy marriages of cotton, vinyl, and polyester, with occasional flashes of dangerously sharp, impossibly pointy collars.

Despite its ability to stupefy, *Tracy* retains a certain macabre, though innocent, appeal. Perhaps it's the relentless repetition of signature gags: Tracy consistently answering: "Just fine thanks," to unrelated questions. Or Doug's oft-repeated aside to the audience after a heinous Tracyism: "Isn't that awful?" What about Nyland's ultimately engaging portrayal of sweet, ditzy Tracy or the antics of Tracy's perpetually unemployed "hippie" brother, Paul?

Perhaps *Tracy* is merely a fond and gentle reminder of Canada's own confusing cultural identity: a home-grown program, masquerading as American, relying on 20-year-old imported scripts and German laugh-track machines to reach its intended international audience. Even its profound failure makes it still more Canadian—and a perfect metaphor for early-'70s Canadian culture.

Franz Russell

The critics cheer: "…highly competent and fun…. Day after day, it comes out funny." — Bob Blackburn, *Toronto Telegram*

The critics jeer: The show's biggest weakness is the gross miscasting of Diane Nyland…." — Patrick Scott, *The Toronto Star*

Diane Nyland Proctor on *The Trouble With Tracy*

"It was the most bizarre audition ever. I met with (producer) Sy Burns, who gave me a bit of a script to read. He just said: 'Be at CFTO-TV tonight at seven.' I even had to find my own wardrobe. The first thing we taped was that long opening sequence. Steve and I hardly knew each other's names—we hadn't really been introduced. We begged them to let us change the opening later on, but they wouldn't go for it. We were taping seven shows every five days, which was insanity. We went through three directors in three weeks. My dressing room was a lean-to beside the set. They wouldn't even stop tape when I switched wardrobe.

"For the first 40 episodes we didn't have a hairdresser. We had a skater who was relatively adept as a hairdresser, which is why I wore those sausage curls around my ears. I hated the wardrobe and also the laugh track machine they'd imported from Germany. That laughter sounds so canned. In ten months, we finished taping 130 episodes—most of which I haven't seen.

"I realized it had almost become a cult thing when I took my son to Kindergarten for the first time, five years after the show. Some of the teachers stopped dead in their tracks when I walked in. They admitted they'd skipped school to watch the program. I still get recognized—sometimes my laugh gives me away. But I have never done a television show since, except a single appearance in *Street Legal*, because of *Tracy*."

Tugboat Annie

CBC
Situation Comedy
First Broadcast: Monday, October 7, 1957, 9:00 p.m.
Final Year Broadcast: 1958
Running Time: 30 min.

Cast:

"Tugboat" Annie Brennan	Minerva Urecal
Horatio Bullwinkle	Walter Sande
Murdoch McArdle	Stan Francis

This Canadian/British/American co-production featured crusty skipper Tugboat Annie, the Ma Kettle of the Pacific Northwest sea lanes, with a heart of gold plate. McArdle owned Annie's craft, the *Narcissus*. Bullwinkle was Annie's rival and owner of the *Salamander* (both boats were played by the *J.C. Stewart*). Set in the fictional town of Secoma (but filmed in Toronto) and based on stories by Norman Reilly Raine who modelled the character on real-life tugboat skipper Thea Foss of Tacoma, Washington. Great fun for those who never tired of watching Bullwinkle being dunked in the drink, ad nauseam, at the end of each program. A 1933 film, *Tugboat Annie*, starred Canadian actress Marie Dressler. Also known as *The Adventures of Tugboat Annie*.

The critics jeer: "…notable for its elephantine humor. Sande mugs continuously. Urecal seems more raucous than even this role calls for." — Ron Poulton, *Toronto Telegram*

:20 Minute Workout

Syndicated: 1982
Physical Fitness
Running Time: 30 min.

Workout Team: Sharon Bisset, Michelle Brimacombe, Laurie Briscoe, Holly Butler, Sue Carter, Ella Collins, Sharon Hasfal, Alison Hope, Nerise Houghton, Bess Motta, Nicole Nardini, Annie Schumacher, Leslie Smith, Arlaine Wright

Exercise or sexercise? Taped in Toronto this aerobics show *did* feature tastefully attired female "instructors," though lingering shots of upturned buttocks and pouty rouged lips sucking air to a disco beat were interpreted as a come-on by some male viewers. The most recognizable aerobicizer was Bess Motta (with her sing-song delivery—"I know you're strong, I know you're strong, I know that you can do it now...four more...three more...") who appeared in the first *Terminator* film and played a pair of lips in the syndicated series *The New Monkees*. Producer Ron Harris later released *Totally Nude Aerobics* direct to video.

Twice in a Lifetime

CTV
Drama
First Broadcast: Saturday, September 18, 1999, 7:00 p.m.
Final Year Broadcast: 2001
Running Time: 60 min.

Cast:
Othniel . . . . Al Waxman
Mr. Jones . . . . Gordy Brown
Mr. Smith . . . . Paul Popowich

Imagine the horror of shuffling off life's mortal coil, casting open the Pearly Gates and encountering—Al Waxman!!?? The folks at CTV were obviously *Touched by an Angel* when they dreamed up this series about guest stars who begged for a "life sentence"—a second chance to fix the messes they made of their lives. The catch? Souls could return to Earth only as other people, who had to convince their younger selves to straighten up. Othniel judged the cases, and angels helped the departed to present their arguments. The series was commissioned by PAX-TV, a U.S. family network.

The critics jeer: "...disappointingly transparent with the outcome of the character's journey immediately predictable."— Tyler McLeod, *The Calgary Sun*

Twilight Zone

Syndicated: 1988
Dramatic Anthology
Running Time: 30 min.

Narrator: Robin Ward

Enterprising producers revived the original *Twilight Zone* in 1985 on CBS. The new series had one thing going for it—a nifty opening with creepy theme music by The Grateful Dead and a sly appearance by an ethereal Rod Serling. Unfortunately, the many weak stories were too familiar to even casual viewers of fantasy television. After sputtering along on CBS until 1987, Canadian producers filmed a 1987–88 season of 30 syndicated shows. The new episodes were largely no worse than the CBS efforts, and Robin Ward did a nice turn as narrator, replacing Charles Aidman.

Twitch City

CBC
Situation Comedy
First Broadcast: Monday, January 19, 1998, 9:30 p.m.
Final Year Broadcast: 2000
Running Time: 30 min.

Cast:
Curtis . . . . Don McKellar
Hope. . . . . Molly Parker
Nathan . . . . Daniel MacIvor
Newbie . . . . Callum Keith Rennie
Rex Reilly . . . . Bruce McCulloch/Mark McKinney
Lucky the Cat. . . . . Himself

Meet the new King of Kensington, Curtis, an unemployed dork who never left his apartment, preferring to experience life through TV. When Curtis' roommate, Nathan, was arrested for murder (he symbolically dispatched the original King of Kensington—Al Waxman, playing a vagrant), Curtis took over the apartment and Nathan's girlfriend, Hope. Satirical storylines revolved around a never-ending succession of boarders, Nathan's return from prison, the all-important TV schedule, Nazis, cat invasions, and a shipment of hallucinogenic pineapple-almond cookies left in a room rented by a Vietnamese businessman. Newbie was a fellow couch potato and convenience store clerk. Curtis' favourite program, presented in clips, was the trashy *Rex Reilly Show*. McKinney replaced fellow *Kids in the Hall* alumnus McCulloch as Rex, when the host had a "cranium transplant."

Uncle Bobby

CTV
Children's
First Broadcast: Monday, January 20, 1964, 10:00 a.m.
Final Year Broadcast: 1980?
Running Time: 30 min.

Cast:
Uncle Bobby . . . . Bobby Ash

"Hello, hello, we're glad to have you with us
Hello, hello, we're going to have some fun!"
— Uncle Bobby's *theme song*

Former circus clown, the very British Bobby Ash appeared as a television fixture up to six days a week, for more than 20 years. Eccentric Uncle Bobby sported longish (slightly greasy) hair and a mile-wide tie with a Windsor knot big enough to choke a horse. In its early years, the program was padded with cartoons like *The Mighty Hercules,* but later shifted its emphasis to live guests. Viewers were known as "Bobby-Soxers," and a considerable part of each show was devoted to viewer birthdays, introduced in basso profundo by Bimbo the Birthday Clown, a 6-foot cut-out whose theme song ("Bimbo, Bimbo, he's a happy clown you know") gave way to a rendition of "Happy Birthday to You" by Happy, a giggling puppet monstrosity made of yarn. Frequent guests included magician Ron Leonard ("You know what it is? It's m-a-a-g—ic!") and friendly traffic cops. Uncle Bobby wound up each

show by telling kids to be good: "But not so very, very good that someone comes up to you and asks 'What have you been up to?'" The final incarnation of the show, *Uncle Bobby and Friends,* featured a talent-show segment, and a *Star Wars*-type robot, R-2, as co-host.

The critics cheer: "He is avuncular without being condescending, and the show is on a higher level than most kids' programs in the States." — Richard Gehman, *Maclean's*

Uncle Chichimus/Uncle Chichimus Tells a Story
See: *The Adventures of Chich*

Uncle Ed's Party

CBC
Children's
First Broadcast: Tuesday, December 30, 1952, 5:00 p.m.
Final Year Broadcast: 1954
Running Time: 30 min.

Host: Ed McCurdy
Cast:
Fireman/Postman/Moose Head/The Shadow . . . . Joe Austin

Singer/guitarist McCurdy interspersed stories with folk songs. Set in a weird house that could be entered only through a coal chute and inhabited by a talking moose head and an odd shadowy figure in a rocking chair, who spouted platitudes. Broadcast twice a week in 1953. Also known as *Ed's Place, Uncle Ed's Place,* and *Ed McCurdy.*

Uncle Ed's Place
See: *Uncle Ed's Party*

Under Attack

Syndicated: 1967
Debate
Running Time: 60 min.

Hosts: Pierre Berton (1967–68), Fred Davis (1968–72), Bill Walker (1972–74)

Real-life squares squared off in debates against a bearpit full of frothing students. Guest combatants included Prime Minister Pierre Trudeau, Lawyer Melvin Belli, assorted Marxists, racists, separatists, and cartoonist Al Capp, who explained why he hates youth.

Under Twenty-One

CBC
Discussion
First Broadcast: Tuesday, September 25, 1956, 10:00 p.m.
Final Year Broadcast: 1956
Running Time: 30 min.

Host: Jeanne Sauvé

The future Governor General led discussions with a youth-oriented panel.

The Unforeseen

CBC
Dramatic Anthology
First Broadcast: Thursday, October 2, 1958, 8:30 p.m.
Final Year Broadcast: 1960
Running Time: 30 min.

An anthology of dramas linked by surprise endings.

The show's most infamous production, *Spider in the Night*, was Canada's sole entry into the giant-monster-spawned-by-radiation sweepstakes of the 1950s. Larry Mann played the dad who defends his family from an unconvincing giant spider dummy, blown to bits by the Canadian Army.

Other subjects included a haunted death mask that possessed its possessors, a monstrous mechanical chess player, and a deceased mystery writer searching for his own killer.

The critics jeer: "... the play in question turned out not so much horrifying as just plain awful...hairy arms [were] rather feebly simulated by black-dyed ostrich feathers...the CBC should do some explaining over this one." — Dennis Braithwaite, *The Toronto Star*

CBC

Web site: Larry Mann emotes amid a tangle of tatty yarn in *The Unforeseen*'s infamous giant spider episode.

Up At Ours

CBC
Comedy/Drama
First Broadcast: Thursday, October 2, 1980, 10:30 p.m.
Final Year Broadcast: 1980
Running Time: 30 min.

Cast:
Verna Ball	Mary Walsh
Jack Howse	Ray Guy
Dolph	Kevin Noble
Mrs. O'Mara	Janis Spence

Gordon Pinsent created this show set in a St. John's, Newfoundland, boarding house owned by Verna. Howse was a lodger, Mrs. O'Mara lived next door, and Dolph was a cab driver for Outport Taxi. Pinsent guest-starred in one episode as a priest. Produced in St. John's.

Up Canada

CBC
News Magazine
First Broadcast: Tuesday, October 23, 1973, 10:00 p.m.
Final Year Broadcast: 1975
Running Time: 30 min.

Host: Rob Parker
Reporters/Regular Players: Valri Bromfield, Michael Callaghan, John Allan Cameron, Doug Collins, Maxine Crook, Don Cumming, John Kastner, Patrick MacFadden, John Martin, Rex Murphy, John Zaritsky, Larry Zolf

The CBC tried on "cheeky" in this uneven mix of sloppy reporting and feeble topical sketch comedy (e.g., womanizing MP George Fraser serves in a B.C. riding called Nookie-in-the-Islands).

The critics jeer: "Must we endure a lifetime of adolescent snickering, incompetent documentaries and yet one more unctuous fish-faced host in horn-rims who reads his line off a clipboard?" — Heather Robertson, *Maclean's*

Upside Town

CBC
Children's
First Broadcast: Tuesday, January 9, 1968, 4:30 p.m.
Final Year Broadcast: 1968
Running Time: 20 min.

Cast:

Florence Kozy . . . . Lynn Gorman
Hazel Kozy . . . . Pam Hyatt
Councillor Edgar Q. Russell . . . . Franz Russell
Trudy Young . . . . Trudy Young
Captain Boomer . . . . Rex Sevenoaks
Ma Parkin . . . . Claire Drainie
Mr. Andrews . . . . Claude Rae
Sam Oliver . . . . Gerard Parkes
Susan . . . . Belinda Montgomery
Ernie Power . . . . Jack Duffy
Harvey Fleetwood . . . . Trevor Evans
Brian Scobie . . . . Ted Follows

Barney Boomer, axed from his own show, left residents of Cedarville to their own devices in this sequel to *Barney Boomer*. Major returning characters included: stuffy Councillor Edgar Q. Russell; Barney's uncle Captain Boomer; convenience store owner Florence Kozy; and Trudy Young, inexplicably playing herself. New characters included newspaper publisher Sam Oliver, epicure and newspaper columnist Ernie Power (author of *The Power Line*), and trusty copy boy Harvey Fleetwood, Canada's oldest high school student "and future brain surgeon." Harvey's apprenticeship consisted largely of performing domestic duties for Power. Scobie was the director of local TV station WOW. Only 20 minutes long, the half-hour program was padded out with *Swingaround*, a short game show for kids.

Urban Angel

CBC
Drama
First Broadcast: Friday, February 8, 1991, 8:00 p.m.
Final Year Broadcast: 1992
Running Time: 60 min.

Cast:

Victor Torres . . . . Justin Louis
Dino Moroni . . . . Vittorio Rossi
Francine Primeau . . . . Dorothee Berryman
Bob Vanverdan . . . . Jack Langedijk
Bill Rack . . . . Arthur Grosser
Rachel Kane . . . . Ellen Cohen
Hubie Collison . . . . Michael Rudder
Martine Beaudoin . . . . Jocelyne Zucco
Sylvie Belanger . . . . Sophie Lorain
Nicole . . . . Francois Robertson
Lt. Drabeck . . . . Vlasta Vrana
Alex Noble . . . . Berke Lawrence

Franz Russell

Torres was an ex-con working as an undercover investigative reporter for the *Montreal Tribune;* Moroni was his ex-partner-in-crime, a fence.

Newspaper staff included: editor Primeau; city editor Bob; reporters Bill, Rachel, and Sylvie; copy editor Hubie; and photographer Martine.

The paper's staff hung out at Babes where Nicole was a waitress. Filmed in Montreal and also seen on CBS's late night schedule.

The Urban Peasant

CBC
Cooking
First Broadcast: Monday, September 6, 1993, 3:30 p.m.
Final Year Broadcast: —
Running Time: 30 min.

Host: James Barber

"Oh, James it's true, I get hungry when I think of you."
— From the *Urban Peasant* theme song

Scruffy but kindly host James Barber shows viewers that turning simple ingredients into sterling examples of international cuisine is "dead easy."

Though some of his recipes are deliberately healthy, the Peasant doesn't skimp on butter ("because I like butter") or flavour. Watch out for the dessert recipes, though, which are often slathered with a big dollop of yogurt or honey where it doesn't belong. Filmed in Vancouver. Also seen on the U.S. TLC network.

The critics cheer: "He's the Pied Piper of simple and his main ingredient is always love." — *The Kitchener/Waterloo Record*

Vanderberg

CBC
Drama
First Broadcast: Sunday, October 9, 1983, 8:00 p.m.
Final Year Broadcast: 1983
Running Time: 30 min.

Cast:
Hank Vanderberg	Michael Hogan
Elizabeth Vanderberg	Susan Hogan
Lewis Vanderberg	Jan Rubes
Sandra Evans	Jennifer Dale
Ralph Barrett	Barry Flatman
Pierre Sylvan	Yvan Ponton
Robert Unger	George Touliatos
Calvin Richards	Stephen Markle
Christine Tompson	Deborah Grover
Patrick Vanderberg	Simon Reynolds
Ryan Evans	Allan Royal

Canadian tycoon Hank Vanderberg plans to build a natural gas pipeline across northern Manitoba directly to Europe. Standing in his way: a disloyal wife, an eccentric cowboy landowner and the federal government. Filmed in Toronto, New York, Ottawa, Washington, Paris and Brussels, the six-episode mini-series had delusions of *Dallas*, but failed to graduate to a full-fledged series. Based on an episode of *For the Record*.

The Vic Obeck Show

CBC
Sports
First Broadcast: Monday, February 8, 1954, 8:00 p.m.
Final Year Broadcast: 1955
Running Time: 30 min.

Host: Vic Obeck

Mostly football, hockey, and baseball coverage with a few other sports (dog sled racing, billiards, table tennis) and some instruction thrown in. Among the show's live interview subjects were swimmer Marilyn Bell on water safety and Sir Edmund Hillary on his ascent of Mount Everest. Also known as *Vic Obeck's Parade Of Sports*.

Vic Obeck's Parade Of Sports
See: *The Vic Obeck Show*

Video One

CBC
Children's
First Broadcast: Wednesday, May 5, 1971, 5:00 p.m.
Final Year Broadcast: 1972
Running Time: 30 min.

Hosts: Ian McCutcheon, Reiner Schwartz

A *Drop-In* spinoff, this public-affairs magazine for high schoolers was notorious for tackling tough topics like birth control. Rock group Chilliwack was a guest.

Vision On

CBC
Children's
First Broadcast: Thursday, September 18, 1975, 4:30 p.m.
Final Year Broadcast: 1982
Running Time: 30 min.

Hosts: Ben Benison, Tony Hart, Pat Keysell, Wilf Makepeace Lunn

A program for children with hearing impairments, stressing visuals. A British/Canadian co-production.

War of the Worlds

Syndicated: 1988
Science Fiction
Running Time: 60 min.

Cast:

Dr. Harrison Blackwood. . . . . Jared Martin
Dr. Suzanne McCullough . . . . Lynda Mason Green
Norton Drake . . . . Philip Akin (1988–89)
Lt. Col. Paul Ironhorse . . . . Richard Chaves (1988–89)
Debi McCullough . . . . Rachel Blanchard
Mrs. Pennyworth . . . . Corinne Conley (1988–89)
John Kincaid. . . . . Adrian Paul (1989–90)
Advocate 1 . . . . Richard Comar & David Calderisi (1988–89)
Advocate 2 . . . . Ilse von Glatz (1988–89)
Advocate 3 . . . . Michael Rudder (1988–89)
Malzor . . . . Denis Forest (1989–90)
Mana . . . . Catherine Disher (1989–90)
Ardix. . . . . Julian Richings (1989–90)
Cito. . . . . John Gilbert (1989–90)

A Canadian series that followed the 1953 feature film of the same name (the film constituted the series' premiere). In the series, the invasion that Orson Welles described on radio in 1938 was identified as a trial run for the invaders (who are from Mortax, not Mars).

The aliens have revived, but radiation poisoning forces them to assume the bodies of Earthlings, which quickly deteriorate; dispatched aliens dissipate into pools of green, glowing slime. Astrophysicist Dr. Blackwood and biologist Dr. McCullough join forces with no-nonsense Colonel Drake and computer whiz Norton to sideline the aliens. Debi (well-played by Blanchard) is Suzanne's daughter; Norton's voice-activated wheelchair is named Gertrude. The Advocates are the alien leaders.

In the series' darker second season, *The Second Invasion,* both Drake and Ironhorse are killed and freedom fighter Kincaid joins up, housing the new team in an underground lair. Earth is worse for wear as it plunges into anarchy and invasion by new humanoid Morthrans, from the planet Morthrai, who execute the first invaders (they were the Morthrans' shock troops) and employ clones and bio-weapons against our planet. In the season's finale, the Morthrans ultimately mutiny against murderous leader Malzor and settle into uneasy peace with the Earthlings.

A favourite episode finds the team in Canada, where aliens have taken over the bodies of a prison hockey team (the series had a sense of humour). Forced to bear the beatings of the opposition, an enraged alien defends himself by tearing his opponent limb from limb. An undeservedly ignored effort, with some clever scripts, and nice art direction, sets, and atmosphere, particularly in the series' final season. Canadian guest stars included semi-regular John Vernon as Suzanne's uncle, a general, and John Colicos as a troublemaking alien defector.

The Waterville Gang

CTV
Children's
First Broadcast: Saturday, September 16, 1972, 10:30 a.m.
Final Year Broadcast: 1973
Running Time: 30 min.

Voices of:

Ace Seagull . . . . Len Carlson
Sergeant Perch . . . . Franz Russell
Other Voices: Julia Amato, Sid Brown, Donna Miller

Undersea puppet adventures with the denizens of Waterville, a submerged city playing home to Dodger Dolphin, his bubble-headed girlfriend Angel Fish, rival Sharky Shark, Eloise "Frenchie" the Seahorse, and Sergeant Perch of the Perch Patrol.

Other marine life included aristocratic Pearl Van Oyster, cranky Tucker Turtle, and Ace Seagull.

The Watson Report

CBC
Public Affairs
First Broadcast: Thursday, October 9, 1975, 10:00 p.m.
Final Year Broadcast: 1981
Running Time: 30 min.

Host: Patrick Watson

Watson's public affairs program was the then-current flagship of CBC's current affairs programming, offering interviews, and domestic and foreign reports.

The Wayne and Shuster Show

CBC
Comedy
First Broadcast: Wednesday, October 16, 1957, 10:00 p.m.
Final Year Broadcast: 1990
Running Time: 60 min.

Hosts: Frank Shuster, Johnny Wayne
Announcer: Bernard Cowan
Regular Performers: Joe Austin, Renee Cherrier, Eric Christmas, Don Cullen, John Davies, Jack Duffy, Nuala Fitzgerald, Barbara Franklin, Tom Harvey, Bill Kemp, John Kozak, Ben Lennick, Sylvia Lennick, Peggi Loder, Larry Mann, Robert McEwan, Harvey Patterson, Lou Pitoscia, Carol Robinson, Sheila Rutanen, Paul Soles, Marilyn Stuart, Rudy Webb, Roy Wordsworth

Wayne and Shuster (originally Shuster and Wayne) were already familiar to Canadian audiences when they launched their own television show on CBC in 1957. Widely known through their radio program and a succession

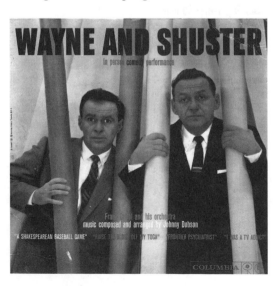

Wayne and Shuster on vinyl: An early comedy album by the duo, featuring popular sketches. ▶

of stage appearances, the duo was a logical choice to fill an hour on Canada's fledgling television network.

The humour was one part collegiate, one part topical satire, and four parts vaudeville with the occasional song thrown in. Shuster was the capable slightly more-than-straight man and Wayne was...well, Johnny Wayne, playing himself under thin disguise (his most common alter ego was pompous Professor Waynegartner). Assisting the team was a rotating cast of stalwart supporting players (including short-lived stints by Jack Albertson, Beatrice Arthur, McLean Stevenson, and Donald Sutherland), occasional musical guests and dance numbers by the likes of Don Gillies.

Comedy features included commercial spoofs, a news feature (News Nose) and satires of films and TV programs: *Cross-Canada Hit Parade*, *The Man from U.N.C.L.E.*, *Star Trek*, and Bruce Lee movies, for example. More literate sketches included take-offs on *Hamlet*, *Cyrano de Bergerac*, and the celebrated "Kiss the Blood Off My Toga," a hard-boiled take on Shakespeare's *Julius Caesar*.

The duo originally appeared once per month, eventually settling on a four-a-year schedule under various titles: *The Wayne and Shuster Hour*, *The Wayne and Shuster Comedy Special*, *The Wayne and Shuster Comedy Hour*, *Super Comedy With Wayne and Shuster*, etc. The programs often appeared under omnibus CBC titles including *Show of the Week*, *Sunday at Nine*, *CBC Super Special*, and *CBC Super Show*.

Side projects for the duo included *Holiday Lodge* (1961), a CBS summer series about social directors at an uppity summer camp, and *Wayne and Shuster Take an Affectionate Look At...* (1966), a CBS summer series highlighting famous comedians. Material repackaged for syndication included *Wayne and Shuster* (1980), eighty 30-minute episodes with new introductions by the team, and *Wayne and Shuster in Black & White* (1996), a compilation of older sketches.

Critics frequently treat us to polarized views of Wayne and Shuster's record: either they're comic geniuses who racked up a record 67 appearances on *The Ed Sullivan Show* (eat your heart out Topo Gigio), or irrelevant purveyors of comedy so ancient that new audiences couldn't possibly appreciate them. What's missing? The incredible good will these guys built up over their 50-year career. Whether you heard them on radio, or saw them on innumerable TV specials, Gulf Oil commercials, or public service announcements urging us to "do good," the boys radiated an accessible charm that made you want to like them—even meet them halfway on gags that weren't quite coming off. Let critics argue over whether "Julie, don't go!," is the pinnacle of Canadian television comedy or whether 50-year-old skits pass muster against *This Hour Has 22 Minutes*, Wayne and Shuster were a couple of good ol' Canadian boys who told old jokes well, and surprised us with some new ones. We liked them, and they genuinely seemed to like us.

W-5

CTV
Documentary
First Broadcast: Sunday, September 11, 1966, 10:00 p.m.
Final Year Broadcast: —
Running Time: 60 min.

Hosts: Isabel Bassett, Ken Cavanagh, Henry Champ, Tom Clark, Tom Gould, Helen Hutchinson, Jack McGaw, Trina McQueen, Craig Oliver, Valerie Pringle, Jim Reed, Peter Reilly, Lloyd Robertson, Gail Scott, Warner Troyer

Who, What, When, Where, Why—are the five Ws of *W-5*, a long-running hour of investigative journalism. Originally resembling CBC's *This Hour Has Seven Days*, early shows placed a greater emphasis on satire, with the likes of Rich Little providing topical comedy. Reporters on the series have included Heinz Avigdor, Wei Chen, Bill Cunningham, Frank Drea, Barry Dunsmore, Ruth Fremes, Peter Kent, Susan Ormiston, Jim Reed, Morley Safer, Jeanne Sauvé, Sylvia Sweeney, Charles Templeton, and Patrick Watson. The program went on sabbatical during the 1977-78 season. When CTV lured *fifth estate*'s Eric Malling to host the show in 1990, its name changed to *W-5 With Eric Malling* until his departure in 1996. The revamped show was daringly redubbed *W-Five*. The program switched formats in 1999, changing to *W-Five Presents*, and featuring longer documentaries instead of short news story segments.

Whatever Turns You On

CTV
Children's
First Broadcast: Monday, September 25, 1979, 7:30 p.m.
Final Year Broadcast: 1980
Running Time: 30 min.

Regular Performers: (Adults) Ruth Buzzi, Les Lye (Kids) Marc Baillon, Jonathan Gebert, Rodney Helal, Christine McGlade, Elizabeth Mitchell, Kevin Schenk, Kevin Sommers

Kung who?: Frank Shuster (right) investigates while Johnny Wayne (left) hams it up as a martial artist.

An evening version of *You Can't Do That on Television*, predating the popular Saturday morning series featuring dozens of teen thespians in irreverent sketch comedy. Lye was the tormentor/victim of the show's young actors; U.S. actress Buzzi, imported to spur foreign sales, played his female counterpart.

What On Earth

CBC
Game Show
First Broadcast: Monday, January 4, 1971, 2:00 p.m.
Final Year Broadcast: 1975
Running Time: 30 min.

Host: Warren Davis
Panelists: Mavis Davis, Peter Hesky, Walter Kenyon, Franz Russell, Peter Swan, Sybill Turnbull, Molly Wilson, William Withrow, T. Cuyler Young

Up to five panelists (most of them experts from art galleries and museums) tried to identify historical objects and artifacts (mummies' ears, quill cutters, etc.) from the museum's collection. Seen up to five days per week. Taped at the Royal Ontario Museum in Toronto. Appeared as a local Toronto production in 1970.

What am I?: Panelists attempt to identify a secret object in *What On Earth*.

What's New?

CBC
Children's
First Broadcast: Thursday, September 14, 1972, 5:00 p.m.
Final Year Broadcast: 1990
Running Time: 30 min.

Hosts: Lon Appleby, Jennifer Gibson, Howard Green, David Kitching, Sandy Lane, Marie-Claude Lavallée, Harry Mannis, Suhana Meharchand, David Schatzky, Wayne Thompson, Sara Wolch

Current affairs show for teens featuring young-ish hosts, with quizzes, viewer feedback, and features ranging from rock-group profiles to more serious subjects, including AIDS and sexual abuse. Also appearing were Noreen Young's political-figure puppets (Pierre Trudeau, Jimmy Carter, Joe Clark, etc.), with voices by Max Ferguson, Judy Sinclair, and David Hughes and a puppet named Captain Canada.

What's The Good Word?

CTV
Game Show
First Broadcast: Monday, January 17, 1972, various
Final Year Broadcast: 1975
Running Time: 30 min.

Host: John Barton

Panelists competed in guessing a mystery word for piddling prizes. Contestants were helped out by word clues (e.g., fair, mark, and end = book) and illustrations. From Vancouver.

Where It's At

CBC
Music
First Broadcast: Monday, September 30, 1968, 5:30 p.m.
Final Year Broadcast: 1969
Running Time: 30 min.

A weekday after-school rockfest for teens, from various cities. Hosts included Fred Latremouille in Vancouver, The Guess Who in Winnipeg, Jay Jackson and Colleen Peterson in Toronto, Robert Demontigny in Montreal, and Frank Cameron in Halifax.

Staple acts included Anne Murray, The Poppy Family, Papa Bear's Medicine Show, The Northwest Company, The Wiggy Symphony, Jason Hoover and the Epics, The Collectors, The Five Sounds, The Lincolns, The Majestics, The OutCrowd, The Yeoman, and The Rajah (with their patented "raga" sound). International guest acts included Lulu. Programs from Halifax and Vancouver were broadcast in black-and-white.

Whistle Town

CBC
Children's
First Broadcast: Tuesday, September 30, 1958, 5:00 p.m.
Final Year Broadcast: 1959
Running Time: 30 min.

Cast:
Mr. Bean	Larry Beattie
Mr. Bean's Assistant	Jack Mather
Danny	Rex Hagon
Mayor Jacques	Jean Cavall
Mr. Haggarty	Hugh Webster
Postman	Claude Rae
Mr. Gentlefella	Doug Romaine

Voice of:
Foster	John Keogh

Music: Ed McCurdy
Puppeteers: John Keogh, Linda Keogh

Sketches, news, music, and cartoons on a small-town set. Shown twice a week, with settings varying from city hall, to a toy shop, to the fire station. Foster was a dog puppet; McCurdy presented filmed folk songs. Hagon graduated to *The Forest Rangers*.

The Whiteoaks Of Jalna

CBC
Drama
First Broadcast: Sunday, January 23, 1972, 9:00 p.m.
Final Year Broadcast: 1972
Running Time: 60 min.

Cast:
Renny Whiteoak	Paul Harding
Adeline Whiteoak (elder and junior)	Kate Reid
Meg	Amelia Hall
Ernest II	Don Scardino
Alayne	Maureen O'Brien
Roma Fitzsturgis	Antoinette Bower

Pheasant Vaughan	Blair Brown
Uncle Ernest	Gillie Fenwick
Piers Whiteoak (man)	John Friesen
Piers Whiteoak (boy)	Douglas Birkenshaw
Victoria	Linda Goranson
Christian	Gary McKeehan
Ruth	Toby Tarnow
Aunt Augusta	Josephine Barrington
Uncle Nicholas	Don McGill
Mip	Jaro Dick
Old Finch	Joseph Shaw
Young Finch	Vincent Dale
Philip I	David Schurman
Philip II and Philip III	Paul Craig
Old Eden	James Hurdle
Young Eden	Tom Lewis
Mary Wakefield	Aileen Taylor Smith
Maurice Vaughan	David Hughes
Amy Stroud	Dawn Greenhalgh
Chris Dayborn	Patricia Collins
Jim Dayborn	Nicholas Simons
Wragge	Roy Wordsworth
Dilly Warkworth	Nonnie Griffin
Wright	Paul Bradley
Maggie	Maja Ardal
Charlesworth	Kenneth Dight
Tony Roberts	J.B. Douglas
Mrs. Potsler	Gertrude Goransson
Mr. Potsler	Michael Ferens
Noah Bins	Eric Clavering
Maitland Fitzsturgis	Sean Mulcahy
Lomax	Charles Palmer

An imitation *Forsyte Saga* based on Mazo de la Roche's novels about the Whiteoak family.

CBC press releases trumpeted a quote from a British publisher who claimed that de la Roche was "...a gold mine to anyone who has ever had anything to do with her." Instead, this $2-million flop made a fool of the unnamed publisher and itself, squandering initial audience goodwill on ridiculously complicated dual storylines, random flashbacks, and the addition of Christian and Victoria, two characters invented for the series to carry the plot to 1971 (the novels ended in the 1950s). The network provided thousands of free family-tree charts, just to help viewers keep track of the characters.

Cancelled after just 12 episodes (a technicians' strike caused major delays), the series was re-edited and rebroadcast in 1974, with the cast reassembled to plug some gaping plot holes and to complete the

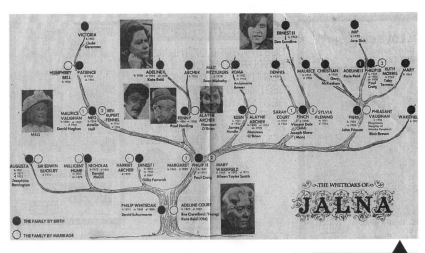

unseen 13th episode. The 1974 broadcast also dropped the 1971 storyline and provided desperately needed narration by Renny Whiteoak.

While viewers were impressed by some performances and the elaborately staged battle sequences, everybody wondered why the Whiteoaks were so attached to their family estate, seen only as a front porch, bedroom, and stairway. The program was blacked out in Windsor where the CBC assumed eager Detroit viewers would destroy the market for a never-realized big U.S. sale.

Chief scriptwriter was Timothy Findley, though imported U.S. writer Claude Harz shared the blame. Seen in England, France, and Norway (where it became a surprise hit). NBC had already taken a stab at the series in the mid-50s and a new series, produced in France, was filmed in 1994.

The critics jeer: "Who *are* these people? And what…is going on?" — Heather Robertson, *Maclean's*

"The whole thing cries for dramatic snap and some semblance of pace instead of this diminishing crawl." — Jack Miller, *The Toronto Star*

Whozit

CBC
Game Show
First Broadcast: Friday, October 16, 1953, 10:00 p.m.
Final Year Broadcast: 1953
Running Time: 30 min.

Host: Michael Cashin

Panelists unmasked a mystery guest with clues provided by caricaturist Bert Grossick's drawings.

Get yer programs: Viewers received Jalna family trees to help keep track of *Whiteoaks'* dozens of characters and fuzzy plot lines.

Ben's world:
Cartoonist Ben Wicks
interviewed off-beat
characters in *Wicks*.

Wicks

CBC
Drama
First Broadcast: Monday, September 10, 1979, 12:30 p.m.
Final Year Broadcast: 1981
Running Time: 30 min.

Host: Ben Wicks

Cartoonist Wicks interviewed unusual guests, including window washers on the Empire State Building and a woman who trained wild beavers.

Willie Wonderful

CBC
Children's
First Broadcast: Tuesday, December 30, 1952, 5:30 p.m.
Final Year Broadcast: 1953
Running Time: 15 min.

Stories performed by marionettes.

Willy and Floyd

Syndicated: 1973
Children's
Running Time: 30 min.

Cast:
Uncle Willy . . . . Bill Luxton
Floyd Swyne/Morley the Mailman . . . . Les Lye

An ambitious local effort from CJOH Ottawa in the days when local programming formed a large part of television schedules. Doddering Uncle Willy and his ambitious nephew Floyd broadcast for more than two decades and several formats, with the pair running a movie theatre, a talent agency, a computer company, and a hotel, the Willy and Floyd Arms. While the original local program starting in 1966 included cartoons, later versions were devoted to a sitcom format. Notable guests included actor Bruno Gerussi, singer Alanis Morissette, cartoonist Jim Unger and Margaret Trudeau. Also known as *Uncle Willy and Floyd*.

Wind At My Back

CBC
Drama
First Broadcast: Sunday, December 1, 1996, 7:00 p.m.
Final Year Broadcast: —
Running Time: 60 min.

Cast:
Grace Bailey . . . . Kathryn Greenwood
Honey Bailey . . . . Cynthia Belliveau (1996–99), Laura Bruneau (2000–)
Hubert "Hub" Bailey . . . . Dylan Provencher
Henry "Fat" Bailey. . . . . Tyrone Savage
May Bailey. . . . . Shirley Douglas
Toppy Bailey . . . . Robin Craig
Max Sutton . . . . James Carroll
Jim Flett. . . . . Robert Bockstael
Pritchard Flett. Bradie Whetham
Jack Bailey. . . . . Booth Savage
Ollie . . . . Neil Crone

Tales of the Bailey family surviving the Great Depression of the 1930s in the mining town of New Bedford, Ontario. When husband Jack dies, Honey Bailey is forced to leave her children, Hub and Fat, with vindictive (but wealthy) mother-in-law May (she blames Honey for her son's death). Grace is May's unmarried daughter who searches for love and a fulfilling career; Jim is a love interest. When Honey returned from a stay at a sanitarium, she was played by a new actress, Bruneau. Athletics coach Max is Honey's new husband. Loosely based on a series of books about the Depression by Max Braithwaite and Barry Broadfoot. Filmed in Toronto and broadcast in 40 countries.

Wojeck

CBC
Drama
First Broadcast: Tuesday, September 13, 1966, 9:00 p.m.
Final Year Broadcast: 1968
Running Time: 60 min.

Cast:

Dr. Steve Wojeck . . . . John Vernon
Marty Wojeck . . . . Patricia Collins
Stevey Wojeck . . . . Jamey Weyman
Judy Wojeck . . . . Tanis Montgomery
Crown Attorney Arnie Bateman . . . . Ted Follows
Detective Sergeant Byron James . . . . Carl Banas

Based on the real-life experiences of Toronto's crusading coroner, Dr. Morton Shulman, *Wojeck* was a bona fide Canadian dramatic hit—a rare critical success that hooked audiences to the tune of three million viewers a week. As Wojeck, (North America's first drama starring a Polish hero—sorry, *Banacek*) Vernon was angry!, angry!, angry!, bringing a grim realism to the role as he locked horns with the establishment on major issues: abortion, drug addiction, unsafe working conditions, police brutality, elder abuse, Native rights, auto safety, and drug abuse. Marty was Mrs. Wojeck and Stevey and Judy were their children. They lived in an unglamorous home, replete with plumbing problems and kitchen clutter. Arnie was Wojeck's legal ally.

The pilot film, *Tell Them the Streets Are Dancing*, seen in 1966, featured the coroner's attack on shoddy working conditions in the construction industry. The first episode of the series, "The Last Man in the World," about the suicide of a lonely aboriginal Canadian, won an award at the Monte Carlo Film Festival. Hand-held cameras helped bring a gritty cinéma vérité to the television screen, particularly in first-season black-and-white episodes.

While Dr. Shulman initially approved of the program, allowing access to his files and offering his office for filming, he disassociated himself when the series ran Chrysler commercials featuring new, faster cars—death machines in the eyes of the coroner.

Ultimately, *Wojeck* was a victim of its own success, gobbling up major issues until the cupboards were bare. The program wasn't quite what U.S. networks were looking for (too controversial, too much saucy language), but they liked Vernon and the show's creator, Phillip Hersch, who headed south for greener pastures after 20 episodes. Vernon had also been frustrated in his attempts to bring a little humour to the unrelenting grimness of the program. The concept was relaunched a few years later as NBC's milder *Quincy, M.E.* Ironically, Vernon guest-starred on the U.S. series as a dying mobster.

An angry coroner: Wojeck (John Vernon, left) and Sergeant James (Carl Banas) crack another socially relevant case in *Wojeck*.

Rarely rerun, the episodes hold up well, though low-rise Toronto is almost unrecognizable except for the looming Royal York Hotel.

Only occasionally does the series betray its age. "After All, Who's Art Morrison?," for example, features Jack Creley as a mincing closet queen, outed by a blackmailer. "I guess you're the man of the family now," says his wife to their teenage son, who confides to his girlfriend (Margot Kidder, no less) that he's worried homosexuality might be hereditary.

Wojeck returned in a 1992 TV movie, *Wojeck: Out of the Fire*. Dumped by his long-suffering wife in 1978, Wojeck returned to Toronto in search of a baby killer and marital reconciliation after a 15-year hiatus in Sudan.

The series was exported to Belgium, England, Finland, Holland, Ireland, Sweden, and Yugoslavia.

Wojeck in print: A rare paperback adaptation of the first *Wojeck* episode.

The critics cheer: "…any sane television viewer can come to only one conclusion, *Wojeck* is the best television series being produced in North America." —Roy Shields, *The Toronto Star*

Wok With Yan

CBC
Cooking
First Broadcast: Monday, May 26, 1980, 12:30 p.m.
Final Year Broadcast: 1992
Running Time: 30 min.

Host: Stephen Yan

Appalling punster Stephen Yan demonstrated Chinese cuisine, employing the ancient and honourable wok in this combination of cooking and stand-up comedy.

CBC

The Wolfman Jack Show

CBC
Musical Variety
First Broadcast: Tuesday, October 5, 1976, 7:30 p.m.
Final Year Broadcast: 1977
Running Time: 30 min.

Host: Wolfman Jack (Bob Smith)
Regular Performers: Peter Cullen, Sally Sales, Danny Wells

Another disgraceful excuse by Canada's national network to make big foreign sales, this time courtesy of famous U.S. disc jockey Wolfman "I'll do anything for a buck" Jack. Presented mainly foreign acts (Bay City Rollers, Fifth Dimension, Helen Reddy, Glen Campbell, Tony Orlando) but allowed local talent (Gloria Kaye, the Stampeders, Bachman-Turner Overdrive) to provide the occasional number.

The Famous People Players, a troupe of physically and mentally challenged performers who manipulated life-sized puppets, were regulars. Sketch comedy was provided by three regulars and the Wolfman himself, matching wits with a talking horse in his dressing room. *The Gong Show*'s Unknown Comic, Murray Langston, was a writer.

Wonderful World of Professor Kitzel

Syndicated: 1972
Animated
Running Time: 5 min.

Narrator: Paul Soles
Voice of:
Professor Kitzel . . . . Paul Soles

Professor Kitzel used a time machine to visit sketchily animated scenes from world history, including the ascent of Mt. Everest, and the stories of Thomas Paine, Samuel De Champlain and Thomas Edison among them. Kitzel was accompanied by his doddering grandpa who never said a word. Memorable theme music would stop aficionados of retro canned library music dead in their tracks. A companion piece to *Max, the 2,000-Year-Old Mouse*.

W.O.W.

CBC
Children's
First Broadcast: Saturday, September 15, 1979, 12:00 p.m.
Final Year Broadcast: 1980
Running Time: 30 min.

The "Wonderful One-of-a-Kind Weekend" featured children's films and special guest hosts, including Sharon, Lois and Bram, and David Suzuki accompanied by Ami the robot (Luba Goy).

Yes You Can

CBC
Children's/Fitness
First Broadcast: Friday, September 19, 1980, 7:30 p.m.
Final Year Broadcast: 1982
Running Time: 30 min.

Host: Kevin Gillis
Co-Hosts: Tammy Bourne, Trevor Bruneau
Cast:
Coach Cuddles Ford . . . . Patrick Ford
Voices of:
Harry Hogg/Body Man . . . . Michael Magee

Designed to promote fitness, this program featured songs, exercise, sporting tips, and interviews with amateur and professional athletes.

Animated Harry Hogg promoted laziness and massive food consumption. Coach Cuddles demonstrated injury prevention by winding up in hospital, where a doctor explained the injury and Michael Magee gave voice to the Coach's injured organ (in tones more suitable to an obscene phone call—"I'm, uh, the spleen, and when I was injured, I bled a lot.")

Composer-singer Gillis sang original non-sporty songs, including the show's theme song: *You can do it, yes you can!*

Guests included: Toller Cranston, Gordie Howe, Karen Kain, and a raft of young athletes.

Yoga

CTV
First Broadcast: Monday, September 13, 1971, 9:00 a.m.
Final Year Broadcast: 1975
Running Time: 30 min.

Host: Kareen Zebroff

New Age, psychedelic yoga lessons, with something that sounded like a cover version of the Beatles' "Hey Jude" as theme music. Zebroff's long-running program inspired a how-to book.

Also known as *Kareen's Yoga.*

You Can't Do That on Television

Syndicated
Children's
First Broadcast: 1979
Running Time: 30 min.

Regular Performers: Kevin Akyeampong, Jordan Arron, Marc Baillon, Stephanie Bauder, Nick Belcourt, Aneal Bhartia, Chris Bickford, Wyatt Boyd, Jennifer Brackenbury, Carlos Braithwaite, Todd Brewer, Charlie Brien, Andrew Burke, Jami Burning, Andrea Byrne, Mike Cameron, Justin Cammy, Stephanie Chow, Angie Coddett, Eugene Contreras, Roddy Contreras, Matt Cook, Todd Corrigon, Tim Douglas, Kai Engstad, Robert Enns, Vicki Essex, Iain Fingler, Corey Fraser, Jonothan Gebert, Alasdair Gillis, Amyas Godfrey, Matthew Godfrey, Naida Gosselin, Karen Grant, Abby Hagyard, Brad Hampson, Ramona Helal, Rodney Helal, David Halpin, Mike Hora, Adam Kalbfleisch, Sarah Keelan, Cindy Kennedy, Martin Kerr, Pauline Kerr, Tanya King, Kevin Kubusheskie, Tony Lefebvre, Vanessa Lindores, Libby Livingston, Darryl Lucas, Simone Lumsden, Mike Lyon, Mike Maguire, M.J. Malcolm, Robin Marpack, Jamie Martin, Korbett Matthews, Kyle Matthews, Christine (Moose) McGlade, Luke McKeehan, Deidre McIsaac, Patrick Mills, Elizabeth Mitchell, Eugene Miyagawa, Forest Wolf Mohawk, Alanis Morissette, Jody Morris, Jeff Mousseau, Chris Nolan, Brodie Osome, Mike Patton, William Pohoresky, Doug Ptolemy, Natalie Radmore, Adam Reid, Elizabeth Richardson, Lisa Ruddy, Sidharth Sahay, Vikram Sahay Natalie Salat, Scott Sandeman, Kevin Schenk, Ben Schreiner, Klea Scott, Rekha Shah, Sariya Sharp, Marjorie Silcoff, Gordon Smith, Kevin Somers, Amy Stanley, Jill Stanley, Jim Stechyson, Michelle Taylor, Christian Tessier, Chantal Tremblay, James Tung, Claude Valiquette, Kevin Ward, Sarah West, Ruth Westdal, Jennifer White, Steve Wilson, Ted Wilson, Bradfield Wiltse

Barth the chef, Blip, Peter Cockroach, Ross Ewich, Mr. Lance
      Prevert, Mr. Shidler, Snake Eyes, et al . . . . Les Lye
Valerie, et al . . . . Abby Hagyard

Anarchic children's show with a rotating cast of a hundred or so. Sassy kids took on lazy, dishevelled parents, slovenly chefs, and nasty teachers (most of them played by Lye), while dropping great buckets full of slime on each other (the words "I don't know" triggered the green torrent). Occasionally, the program actually *did* provide moments you might not expect to see on television (e.g., a Native boy tells a white boy that his people gave white men tobacco so they would "die of lung cancer"). A show about adoption was run once and pulled from syndication. Adults hated the show, but U.S. pay network Nickelodeon loved it, footing the bill for the series, which it credited for keeping the network alive. Though actors took turns hosting, the most prominent hosts were Christine McGlade, Alasdair Gillis ,and Chris Bickford. Alanis Morissette appeared briefly in the cast. Originally seen live on CJOH in Ottawa, early episodes weren't taped. Seen mostly on CTV stations, then YTV, new programs were produced until 1990. Exported to Australia, England, Finland, and Spain.

The Young Chefs

CBC
Children's
First Broadcast: Wednesday, October 6, 1976, 5:00 p.m.
Final Year Broadcast: 1976
Running Time: 30 min.
Host: Mme Jehane Benoit
The Young Chefs: Karim Kovacevich, Lisa Schwartz

Mme Benoit taught cooking skills to two youngsters at her farm in Quebec. "Cuddle your bread! Play with it!"

Youth Takes a Stand

CBC
Discussion
First Broadcast: Monday, October 18, 1954, 4:30 p.m.
Final Year Broadcast: 1955
Running Time: 30 min.

Hosts: Gordon Blackford, Vernon Trott

Discussions between the adult hosts and a panel of respectful Toronto teens, 1950s-style. Typical topic: juvenile delinquency. Filmed in Toronto.

Cooking for kids: Mme Jehane Benoit (centre) instructs Karim Kovacebich (left) and Lisa Schwartz (right) in the culinary arts on *The Young Chefs*.

CBC

Zut!

CBC
Comedy
First Broadcast: Saturday, October 17, 1970, 7:00 p.m.
Final Year Broadcast: 1971
Running Time: 30 min.

Regular Performers: Al Boliska, Barrie Baldaro, Dave Broadfoot, Peter Cullen, David Harriman, Donald Lautrec, Wally Martin, Joan Stuart

Yet another failed attempt to create a successful English comedy produced in Montreal—this time a thinly revised *Comedy Crackers*, loosely built around French-English relations and current events. Lautrec sang, Broadfoot left.

Zoboomafoo

Syndicated: 1999
Children
Running Time: 30 min.

Hosts: Chris Kratt, Martin Kratt
Cast:
Jackie . . . . Samantha Tolkacz
Voice of:
Zoboomafoo. Gordon Robertson

Canadian co-produced nature series for kids. From their headquarters (Animal Junction) the Kratt brothers teach simple lessons about the animal kingdom with the assistance of a talking lemur named Zoboomafoo. A little girl, Jackie, provides a feature on domestic animals. A claymation segment, set in imaginary Zoboland, features additional creatures Bugly, Noggendrill, Slimantha, Gooble and Wiggy Waxwing. A cleverly crafted, fast-moving series, the Kratt brothers expend enough energy in 30 minutes to power a small city.

GEMINI AWARD WINNERS

Initiated in 1986, the Geminis honour all aspects of English-language television production in Canada. Gemini winners are chosen by members of the Academy of Canadian Cinema & Television, a national, non-profit, professional association created in 1979 to serve the Canadian film and television industry. This partial listing of Gemini award winners covers programming most closely represented by *TV North*. The Gemini sculpture was created by designer Scott Thornley.

15th Gemini Awards (2000)

Best TV Movie or Dramatic Mini-Series
Dr. Lucille: The Lucille Teasdale Story — Francine Allaire, Claude Bonin, Rob Forsyth

Best Dramatic Series
Da Vinci's Inquest — Laszlo Barna, Lynn Barr, Tom Braidwood, Chris Haddock

Best Comedy Program or Series
This Hour Has 22 Minutes — Geoff D'Eon, Michael Donovan, Ginny Jones-Duzak, Mark Farrell, Jack Kellum

Best News Information Series
the fifth estate — David Studer, Susan Teskey

Best Talk/General Information Series
Skylight — Rita Shelton Deverell

Best Lifestyle Series
Foodessence — Charles Bishop

Best Music, Variety Program or Series
East Coast Music Awards 2000 — Michael Lewis, Jac Gautreau, Geoff D'Eon

Best Documentary Series
The View From Here — Rudy Buttignol

Best Performing Arts Program or Series or Arts Documentary Program or Series
Tall Tales From The Long Corner — Gordon Henderson

Best Animated Program or Series or Short Animated Program
Angela Anaconda — Neil Court, Steven DeNure, Sue Rose, John Mariella, Joanna Ferrone, Beth Stevenson

Best Children's or Youth Program or Series
Incredible Story Studio — Kevin DeWalt, Virginia Thompson, Robert de Lint, Rob King

Best Pre-School Program or Series
Polka Dot Shorts — Jed MacKay

Best Performance by an Actor in a Leading Role in a Dramatic Program or Mini-Series
Jonathan Scarfe — *The Sheldon Kennedy Story*

Best Performance by an Actress in a Leading Role in a Dramatic Program or Mini-Series
Colleen Rennison — *A Feeling Called Glory*

Best Performance by an Actor in a Continuing Leading Dramatic Role
Michael Riley — *Power Play*

Best Performance by an Actress in a Continuing Leading Dramatic Role
Torri Higginson — *The City*

Best Performance in a Children's or Youth Program or Series
Matt Frewer — *Mentors*

Best Performance in a Pre-School Program or Series
Sheila McCarthy — *Sesame Park*

Best Performance in a Comedy Program or Series
Cathy Jones, Rick Mercer, Greg Thomey, Mary Walsh — *This Hour Has 22 Minutes*

Best Performance or Host in a Variety Program or Series
Brigitte Gall — *Brigitte Gall: Joan of Montreal*

Best Performance in a Performing Arts Program or Series
Juan Chioran — *Dracula*

Best Performance by an Actor in a Featured Supporting Role in a Dramatic Program or Mini-Series
Robert Wisden — *The Sheldon Kennedy Story*

Best Performance by an Actress in a Featured Supporting Role in a Dramatic Program or Mini-Series
Shirley Douglas — *Shadow Lake*

Best Performance by an Actor in a Featured Supporting Role in a Dramatic Series
Pedro Salvin — *Peter Benchley's Amazon*

Best Performance by an Actress in a Featured Supporting Role in a Dramatic Series
Shannon Lawson — *The City*

Best Performance by an Actor in a Guest Role, Dramatic Series
Geordie Johnson — *The City*

Best Performance by an Actress in a Guest Role, Dramatic Series
Alisen Down — *Cold Squad*

Best Host or Interviewer in a News or Talk/General Information Program or Series
Robert Mason Lee — *Mason Lee: On The Edge*

Best News Anchor
Diana Swain — *Manitoba Votes 1999*

Best Host in a Lifestyle or Performing Arts Program or Series
Peter Jordan — *It's a Living with Peter Jordan*

14th Gemini Awards (1999)

Best TV Movie or Dramatic Mini-Series
Milgaard — Vibika Bianchi, Laszlo Barna, Ritchard Findlay, Martin Harbury, Laura Lightbown

Best Dramatic Series
Da Vinci's Inquest — Chris Haddock, Laszlo Barna

Best Comedy Program or Series
Made in Canada — Gerald Lunz, Michael Donovan, Linda Nelson, Marilyn Richardson

Best News Information Series
the fifth estate — David Studer, Susan Teskey

Best Talk/General Information Series
Open Mike With Mike Bullard — John Brunton, Barbara Bowlby, Al Magee

Best Lifestyle Series
Weird Homes — Mike Collier

Best Music, Variety Program or Series
This Hour Has 22 Minutes — Michael Donovan, Paul Bellini, Geoff D'Eon, Jack Kellum, Andrew McInnes

Best Documentary Series
The View From Here — Rudy Buttignol

Best Performing Arts Program or Series or Arts Documentary Program or Series
The Genius of Lenny Breau — Jim Hanley, Phyllis Laing, Paul McConvey

Best Animated Program or Series or Short Animated Program
Rolie Polie Olie — Michael Hirsh, Fabrice Giger, William Joyce, Patrick Loubert, Clive Smith

Best Children's or Youth Program or Series
The Inventors' Specials: Edison: The Wizard of Light — David Devine, Richard Mozer

Best Pre-School Program or Series
Sesame Park — Duncan Lamb, Susan Sheehan, Wendy Smith

Best Performance by an Actor in a Leading Role in a Dramatic Program or Mini-Series
Ian Tracey — *Milgaard*

Best Performance by an Actress in a Leading Role in a Dramatic Program or Mini-Series
Wendy Crewson — *At the End of the Day: The Sue Rodriguez Story*

Best Performance by an Actor in a Continuing Leading Dramatic Role
Michael Riley — *Power Play*

Best Performance by an Actress in a Continuing Leading Dramatic Role
Arsinée Khanjian — *Foolish Heart*

Best Performance in a Children's or Youth Program or Series
Meredith Henderson — *The Adventures of Shirley Holmes*

Best Performance in a Pre-School Program or Series
Jayne Eastwood — *Noddy*

Best Performance in a Comedy Program or Series
Cathy Jones, Rick Mercer, Greg Thomey, Mary Walsh — *This Hour Has 22 Minutes*

Best Performance or Host in a Variety Program or Series
Jesse Cook, Natalie McMaster — *Juno Awards 1999*

Best Performance in a Performing Arts Program or Series
Joni Mitchell — *Joni Mitchell: Painting With Words and Music*

Best Performance by an Actor in a Featured Supporting Role in a Dramatic Program or Mini-Series
Hrothgar Matthews — *Milgaard*

Best Performance by an Actress in a Featured Supporting Role in a Dramatic Program or Mini-Series
Sabrina Grdevitch — *Milgaard*

Best Performance by an Actor in a Featured Supporting Role in a Dramatic Series
Gordon Pinsent — *Power Play*

Best Performance by an Actress in a Featured Supporting Role in a Dramatic Series
Marion Gilsenan — *Riverdale*

Best Performance by an Actor in a Guest Role, Dramatic Series
Sean McCann — *Power Play*

Best Performance by an Actress in a Guest Role, Dramatic Series
Martha Henry — *Emily of New Moon*

Best Host or Interviewer in a News or Talk/General Information Program or Series
Wendy Mesley — *Undercurrents*

Best News Anchor
Peter Mansbridge — *The National*

Best Host in a Lifestyle or Performing Arts Program or Series
Brian Linehan — *Linehan*

13th Gemini Awards (November 1998)

(Two sets of awards were offered in 1998 to shift the Geminis into a fall presentation schedule.)

Best Dramatic Series
Traders — Alyson Feltes, Hart Hanson, Sandie Pereira

Best Comedy Series
This Hour Has 22 Minutes — Michael Donovan, Geoff D'Eon, Jack Kellum, Gerald Lunz, Andrew McInnes

Best Information Series
Undercurrents — F. M. Morrison, Pam Bertrand

Best Lifestyle Information Series
Moving On — Shafik Obrai

Best Music, Variety Program or Series
Yo-Yo Ma Inspired By Bach: Six Gestures — Niv Fichman, Rudy Buttignol

Best Documentary Series
The Nature of Things with David Suzuki — Michael Allder, Michael Bennett

Best Performing Arts Program or Series or Arts Documentary Program
Yo-Yo Ma Inspired By Bach: Falling Down Stairs
— Niv Fichman, Rudy Buttignol

Best Animated Program or Series
Sam & Max — Patrick Loubert, Gwenn Saunders Eckel, Michael Hirsh, Stephen Hodgins, Robert Ross, Clive A. Smith, J. D. Smith

Best Children's or Youth Program or Series
Ready or Not — John Brunton, Barbara Bowlby, Moira Holmes

Best Pre-School Program or Series
Theodore Tugboat — Andrew Cochran

Best Sports Program or Series
Sports Journal — Ken Dodd, Jay Mowat, Terry Walker

Best Performance by an Actor in a Leading Role in a Dramatic Program or Mini-Series
Nicholas Campbell — *Major Crime*

Best Performance by an Actress in a Leading Role in a Dramatic Program or Mini-Series
Liisa Repo-Martell — *Nights Below Station Street*

Best Performance by an Actor in a Continuing Leading Dramatic Role
Patrick McKenna — *Traders*

Best Performance by an Actress in a Continuing Leading Dramatic Role
Sheila McCarthy — *Emily of New Moon*

Best Performance in a Children's or Youth Program or Series
Sarah Polley — *Straight Up*

Best Performance in A Pre-School Program or Series
Rick Mercer — *The Adventures of Dudley the Dragon*

Best Performance in a Comedy Program or Series
Steve Smith, Patrick McKenna — *The New Red Green Show*

Best Performance or Host in a Variety Program or Series
Brent Carver — *Young At Heart*

Best Performance in a Performing Arts Program or Series
Yo-Yo Ma — *Yo-Yo Ma Inspired By Bach: Falling Down Stairs*

Best Performance by an Actor in a Featured Supporting Role in a Dramatic Series
Kris Lemche — *Emily of New Moon*

Best Performance by an Actress in a Featured Supporting Role in a Dramatic Series
Kim Huffman — *Traders*

Best Performance by an Actor in a Supporting Role in a Dramatic Program or Mini-Series
Diego Matamoros — *The Sleep Room*

Best Performance by an Actress in a Supporting Role in a Dramatic Program or Mini-Series
Nicky Guadagni — *Major Crime*

Best Performance by an Actor in a Guest Role, Dramatic Series
Brent Carver — *Due South*

Best Performance by an Actress in a Guest Role, Dramatic Series
Wendy Crewson — *Due South*

Best Host, Anchor, or Interviewer in a News or Information Program or Series
Linden MacIntyre — *the fifth estate*

Best Host in a Lifestyle Information, Variety, or Performing Arts Program or Series
Peter Jordan — *It's A Living*

Academy Achievement Award
Jim Burt

John Drainie Award
Bernie Lucht

Earle Grey Award
Al Waxman

Canada Award
The Rez — Brian Dennis

Chrysler's Canada's Choice Award
Nikita — Jamie Paul Rock, Jay Firestone

12th Gemini Awards (March 1998)

(Two sets of awards were offered in 1998 to shift the Geminis into a fall presentation schedule.)

Best Dramatic Series
Traders — Alyson Feltes, Hart Hanson, Mary Kahn, Seaton McLean

Best Comedy Program or Series
This Hour Has 22 Minutes — Michael Donovan, Geoff D'Eon, Jack Kellum, Gerald Lunz, Marilyn Richardson

Best Information Series
the fifth estate — David Studer, Susan Teskey

Best Lifestyle Information Series
Future World — Andrew Johnson, Alice Hopton, Maria Mironowicz

Best Music, Variety Program or Series
The 1997 Juno Awards — John Brunton, Sue Brophey, Martha Kehoe, Lee Silversides

Best Documentary Series
Man Alive — Robin Christmas, Joy Crysdale, Sydney Suissa

Best Animated Program or Series
Stickin' Around — Michael Hirsh, Patrick Loubert

Best Pre-School Program or Series
Little Bear — Michael Hirsh, Patrick Loubert, Clive A. Smith

Best Children's or Youth Program or Series
Street Cents — John Nowlan, Jonathan Finkelstein, Barbara Kennedy

11th Gemini Awards (1997)

Best Dramatic Series
Due South — Jeff King, Bob Wertheimer, George Bloomfield, Kathy Slevin

Best Comedy Series
This Hour Has 22 Minutes — Michael Donovan, Jack Kellum, Marilyn Richardson, Gerald Lunz, Geoff D'Eon

Best Information Series
the fifth estate — David Studer, Susan Teskey

Best Lifestyle Information Series
Gilmour on the Arts — Maria Mironowicz, Donna Lee Aprile

Best Music, Variety Program or Series
September Songs: The Music of Kurt Weill — Niv Fichman, Larry Weinstein

Best Documentary Series
Witness — Mark Starowicz, Hilary Armstrong

Best Performing Arts Program or Series or Arts Documentary Program
Dido and Aeneas — Daniel Iron, Niv Fichman

Best Animated Program or Series
Reboot — Christopher Brough, Ian Richard Pearson, Stephane Reichel

Best Children's Program or Series
The Adventures of Dudley the Dragon — Ira Levy, Peter Williamson, Paula Smith

Best Youth Program or Series
The Composer's Specials: Handel's Last Chance — David Devine, Richard Mozer, Jan Oparty

Best Sports Program or Series
Athens to Atlanta: The Olympic Spirit — Doug Sellars, Terry Ludwick, Carl Karp

Best Performance by an Actor in a Leading Role in a Dramatic Program or Mini-Series
Aidan Devine — *Net Worth*

Best Performance by an Actress in a Leading Role in a Dramatic Program or Mini-Series
Barbara Williams — *Diana Kilmury: Teamster*

Best Performance by an Actor in a Continuing Leading Dramatic Role
David Cubitt — *Traders*

Best Performance by an Actress in a Continuing Leading Dramatic Role
Tina Keeper — *North of 60*

Best Performance in a Children's or Youth Program or Series
Callum Keith Rennie — *My Life as a Dog*

Best Performance in a Comedy Program or Series (Individual or Ensemble)
Cathy Jones, Rick Mercer, Greg Thomey, Mary Walsh — *This Hour Has 22 Minutes*

Best Performance in a Variety Program or Series
Buffy Sainte-Marie — *Buffy Sainte-Marie: Up Where We Belong*

Best Performance in a Performing Arts Program or Series
Ashley MacIsaac, Laura Smith — *Governor General's Performing Arts Awards*

Best Performance by an Actor in a Supporting Role in a Dramatic Program or Mini-Series
Al Waxman — *Net Worth*

Best Performance by an Actress in a Supporting Role in a Dramatic Program or Mini-Series
Teresa Stratas — *Under the Piano*

Best Performance by an Actor in a Supporting Role in a Dramatic Series
Lubomir Mykytiuk — *North of 60*

Best Performance by an Actress in a Supporting Role in a Dramatic Series
Kay Tremblay — *Road To Avonlea*

Best Performance by an Actor in a Guest Role, Dramatic Series
David Gardner — *Traders*

Best Performance by an Actress in a Guest Role, Dramatic Series
Frances Bay — *Road To Avonlea*

Best Host, Anchor, or Interviewer in a News or Information Program or Series
Lloyd Robertson — *Quebec Referendum '95: A Nation in Question*

Best Host in a Lifestyle Information, Variety, or Performing Arts Program or Series
David Suzuki — *The Nature of Things*

10th Gemini Awards (1996)

Best Dramatic Series
Due South — Paul Higgis, Jeff King, Kathy Slevin, George Bloomfield

Best Comedy Series
This Hour Has 22 Minutes — Michael Donovan, Jack Kellum, Gerald Lunz, Jenipher Ritchie, Geoff D'Eon

Best Information Series
Venture — Joe Crysdale, Linda Sims

Best Lifestyle Information Series
On the Road Again — Paul Harrington

Best Music, Variety Program or Series
Brian Orser: Blame It on the Blues — Morgan Earl, Peter Mann

Best Documentary Series
Man Alive — Louise Lore

Best Performing Arts Program or Series or Arts Documentary Program
The Planets — Niv Fichman

Best Animated Program or Series
Reboot — Christopher Brough, Ian Pearson, Stephane Reichel, Steve Barron

Best Children's Program or Series
Are You Afraid of the Dark? — Ronald A. Weinberg, Micheline Charest, D.J. MacHale

Best Youth Program or Series
Ready or Not — John Brunton, Alyse Rosenberg

Best Sports Program or Series
For the Love of the Game — Aiken Scherberger

Best Performance by an Actor in a Leading Role in a Dramatic Program or Mini-Series
Michael Riley — *Adrienne Clarkson Presents: The Facts Behind the Helsinki Roccamatios*

Best Performance by an Actress in a Leading Role in a Dramatic Program or Mini-Series
Jessica Steen — *Small Gifts*

Best Performance by an Actor in a Continuing Leading Dramatic Role
Paul Gross — *Due South*

Best Performance by an Actress in a Continuing Leading Dramatic Role
Joely Collins — *Madison*

Best Performance in a Children's or Youth Program or Series
Ernie Coombs — *Mr. Dressup*

Best Performance in a Comedy Program or Series (Individual or Ensemble)
Mary Walsh, Cathy Jones, Rick Mercer, Greg Thomey — *This Hour Has 22 Minutes*

Best Performance by an Actress in a Guest Role, Dramatic Series
Tantoo Cardinal — *North of 60*

Best Performance by an Actor in a Guest Role, Dramatic Series
Gordon Pinsent — *Due South*

Best Performance in a Variety Program or Series
Rita MacNeil — *Rita & Friends*

Best Performance in a Performing Arts Program or Series
Joni Mitchell — *Joni Mitchell: Intimate and Interactive*

Best Performance by an Actor in a Supporting Role in a Dramatic Program or Mini-Series
Brent Carver — *Street Legal Finale: The Last Rights*

Best Performance by an Actress in a Supporting Role in a Dramatic Program or Mini-Series
Catherine Finch — *Butterbox Babies*

Best Performance by an Actor in a Supporting Role in a Dramatic Series
Nigel Bennett — *Forever Knight*

Best Performance by an Actress in a Supporting Role in a Dramatic Series
Patricia Hamilton — *Road To Avonlea*

Best Host, Anchor, or Interviewer in a News or Information Program or Series
Hana Gartner — *the fifth estate*

Best Host in a Lifestyle Information, Variety, or Performing Arts Program or Series
Rex Murphy — *Proud and Free*

Academy Achievement Award
W. K. Donovan

John Drainie Award
Dodi Robb

Earle Grey Award
Bruno Gerussi

Canada Award
Nuhoniyeh: Our Story — Allen Code, Mary Code

Chrysler's Canada's Choice Award
Due South

9th Gemini Awards (1995)

Best Dramatic Mini-Series
Dieppe — Bernard Zukerman

Best Dramatic Series
Due South — Paul Higgis, Kathy Slevin, Jeff King

Best Comedy Series
This Hour Has 22 Minutes — Michael Donovan, Jack Kellum, Gerald Lunz, Jenipher Ritchie, Geoff D'Eon

Best Information Series
the fifth estate — Kelly Crichton, David Studer

Best Lifestyle Information Series
On the Road Again — Paul Harrington

Best Music, Variety Program or Series
Kurt Browning: You Must Remember This — John Brunton, Joan Tosoni, Sandra Bexic

Best Documentary Series
Witness — Mark Starowicz

Best Animated Program or Series
Reboot — Christopher Brough, Ian Pearson

Best Children's Program or Series
The Big Comfy Couch — Cheryl Wagner, Robert Mills

Best Youth Program or Series
Street Cents — John Nowlan, Jonathan Finkelstein, Barbara Kennedy

Best Sports Program or Series
Elvis: Airborne — Morgan Earl, Catherine McCartney, Edward Futerman

Best Performance by an Actor in a Leading Role in a Dramatic Program or Mini-Series
Stephen McHattie — *Life With Billy*

Best Performance by an Actress in a Leading Role in a Dramatic Program or Mini-Series
Nancy Beattie — *Life With Billy*

Best Performance by an Actor in a Continuing Leading Dramatic Role
Paul Gross — *Due South*

Best Performance by an Actress in a Continuing Leading Dramatic Role
Lally Cadeau — *Road To Avonlea*

Best Performance in a Children's or Youth Program or Series
Laura Bertram — *Ready or Not*

Best Performance in a Comedy Program or Series (Individual or Ensemble)
Cathy Jones, Rick Mercer, Greg Thomey, Mary Walsh — *This Hour Has 22 Minutes*

Best Guest Performance in a Series by an Actor
Bruce Greenwood — *Road To Avonlea*

Best Guest Performance in a Series by an Actress
Sarah Strange — *Neon Rider*

Best Performance in a Variety Program or Series
Sarah McLachlan — *Sarah McLachlan: Fumbling Towards Ecstasy*

Best Performance in a Performing Arts Program or Series
Holly Cole — *Intimate and Interactive with The Holly Cole Trio*

Best Performance by an Actor in a Supporting Role
Bernard Behrens — *Coming of Age*

Best Performance by an Actress in a Supporting Role
Jennifer Phipps — *Coming of Age*

Best Anchor or Interviewer
Linden MacIntyre — *the fifth estate*

Best Host in a Lifestyle Information, Variety, or Performing Arts Program or Series
Albert Schultz — *1994 Gemini Awards*

John Drainie Award
Knowlton Nash

Earle Grey Award
John Candy, Joe Flaherty, Eugene Levy, Andrea Martin, Rick Moranis, Catherine O'Hara, Harold Ramis, Martin Short, Dave Thomas
(SCTV Comedy Troupe)

Canada Award
For Angela — Joe MacDonald, Nancy Trites Botkin

Chrysler's Canada's Choice Award
1994 Molson Hockey Night in Canada on CBC, The Stanley Cup Final — Ron G. Harrison, Larry Isaac

8th Gemini Awards (1994)

Best Dramatic Mini-Series
The Boys of St. Vincent — Claudio Luca, Sam Grana

Best Dramatic Series
E.N.G. — Robert Lantos, Jennifer Black, Greg Copeland

Best Comedy Series
The Kids in the Hall — Lorne Michaels, John Blanchard, Jeffery Berman, Cindy Park, Joe Forristal

Best Information Series
Marketplace — Sig Gerber, Paul Moore

Best Variety Program or Series
The Trial of Red Riding Hood — Bernard Rothman

Best Documentary Series
Acts of War — Michael Maclear, David Kirk

Best Animated Program or Series
Jim Henson's Dog City — Michael Hirsh, Patrick Loubert, Clive A. Smith

Best Children's Program or Series
Lamb Chop's Play-along — Jon Slan, Richard Borchiver, Bernard Rithman

Best Youth Program or Series
Street Cents — Jonathan Finkelstein, Barbara Kennedy, John Nowlan

Best Sports Program or Series
The Spirit of the Game — Andy Blicq, Noah Erenberg

Best Performance by an Actor in a Leading Role in a Dramatic Program or Mini-Series
Henry Czerny — *The Boys of St. Vincent*

Best Performance by an Actress in a Leading Role in a Dramatic Program or Mini-Series
Kelly Rowan — *Adrift*

Best Performance by an Actor in a Continuing Leading Dramatic Role
James Purcell — *Counterstrike*

Best Performance by an Actress in a Continuing Leading Dramatic Role
Jackie Burroughs — *Road To Avonlea*

Best Performance in a Comedy Program or Series (Individual or Ensemble)
Cathy Jones, Greg Malone, Tommy Sexton, Mary Walsh — *CODCO*

Best Guest Performance in a Series by an Actor or Actress
Philip Granger — *Neon Rider*

Best Performance in a Variety Program or Series
Jinny Jacinto, Laurence Racine Choiniere, Nadine Louis-Binette, Isabelle Chasse — *1993 YTV Achievement Awards*

Best Performance in a Performing Arts Program or Series
Holly Cole — *The Holly Cole Trio: My Foolish Heart*

Best Performance by an Actor in a Supporting Role
Wayne Robson — *The Diviners*

Best Performance by an Actress in a Supporting Role
Lise Roy — *The Boys of St. Vincent*

Best Anchor or Interviewer
Lloyd Robertson — *CTV National News*

Best Host in a Lifestyle Information, Variety, or Performing Arts Program or Series
Rob Buckman — *Magic or Medicine?*

John Drainie Award
Max Ferguson

Earle Grey Award
Ernie Coombs

Canada Award
Speak It! From the Heart of Black Nova Scotia
— Marilyn A. Belec, Mike Mahoney, D. Sylvia
Hamilton

7th Gemini Awards (1993)

Best Dramatic Mini-Series
Conspiracy of Silence — Bernard Zukerman

Best Dramatic Series
E.N.G. — Robert Lantos, Jeff King, R. B. Carney,
Jennifer Black

Best Comedy Series
The Kids in the Hall — Lorne Michaels, Joe Forristal,
Jeffery Berman, Cindy Park

Best Variety Series
*The Best of Just For Laughs, Montreal International
Comedy Festival* — Andy Nulman, Gilbert Rozon

Best Information Series
the fifth estate — Kelly Crichton, David Nayman

Best Light Information Series
Life: The Program — Duncan McEwan

Best Documentary Series
The Valour and the Horror — Arnie Gelbart, Andre
Lamy, Adam Symansky

Best Performing Arts Program
Cirque du Soleil: Nouvelle Experience — Helene
Dufresne

Best Animated Program or Series
The Adventures of Tintin — Michael Hirsh, Patrick
Loubert, Clive A. Smith

Best Children's Program or Series
Shining Time Station — Britt Allcroft, Rick
Siggelkow, Nancy Chapelle

Best Youth Program or Series
The Jellybean Odyssey — Michael Chechik

Best Sports Program or Series
Sports Weekend — Doug Sellars, Joan Mead

**Best Performance by an Actor in a Leading Role in a Dramatic
Program or Mini-Series**
Michael Mahonen — *Conspiracy of Silence*

**Best Performance by an Actress in a Leading Role in a Dramatic
Program or Mini-Series**
Kate Nelligan — *Diamond Fleece*

**Best Performance by an Actor in a Continuing Leading
Dramatic Role**
Cedric Smith — *Road To Avonlea*

**Best Performance by an Actress in a Continuing Leading
Dramatic Role**
Sara Botsford — *E.N.G.*

**Best Performance in a Comedy Program or Series
(Individual or Ensemble)**
Dave Foley, Bruce McCulloch, Kevin McDonald,
Mark McKinney, Scott Thompson — *The Kids in
the Hall*

Best Guest Performance in a Series by an Actor or Actress
Kate Nelligan — *Road To Avonlea*

Best Performance in a Variety Program or Series
Anne Murray, k. d. lang — *Country Gold*

Best Performance in a Performing Arts Program or Series
Barenaked Ladies — *Ear to The Ground: Barenaked
Ladies*

Best Performance by an Actor in a Supporting Role
Jonathan Welsh — *E.N.G.*

Best Performance by an Actress in a Supporting Role
Brooke Johnson — *Conspiracy of Silence*

Best Anchor or Interviewer
Peter Mansbridge — *CBC News National Town Hall*

**Best Host in a Light Information, Variety, or Performing Arts
Program or Series**
Adrienne Clarkson — *Adrienne Clarkson Presents*

John Drainie Award
Barbara Frum (posthumous)

Earle Grey Award
Barbara Hamilton

Canada Award
It's About Time — Rita Shelton Deverell, Peter
Flemington

John Labatt Entertainment Award For Most Popular Program
Road To Avonlea

6th Gemini Awards (1992)

Best Dramatic Mini-Series
Young Catherine — W. Paterson Ferns, Michael
Deeley, Stephen Smallwood

Best Dramatic Series
E.N.G. — Robert Lantos, Jeff King, R. B. Carney,
Jennifer Black

Best Comedy Series
CODCO — Michael Donovan, Stephen Reynolds,
J. William Ritchie, Jack Kellum

Best Variety Series
The Tommy Hunter Show — Lynn Harvey

Best Information Series
The Journal — Mark Starowicz

Best Light Information Series
The New Music — Moses Znaimer, Denise Donlon

Best Documentary Series
The Nature of Things — James Murray

Best Animated Program or Series
Babar — Michael Hirsh, Patrick Loubert, Clive A. Smith

Best Children's Program or Series
The Garden — Stephen Onda

Best Youth Program or Series
Lost in the Barrens — Seaton McLean, Derek Mazur, Joan Scott MacMillan, Mike Scott

Best Performance by an Actor in a Leading Role in a Dramatic Program or Mini-Series
Bernard Behrens — *Saying Good-Bye*

Best Performance by an Actress in a Leading Role in a Dramatic Program or Mini-Series
Brenda Bazinet — *Saying Good-Bye*

Best Performance by an Actor in a Continuing Leading Dramatic Role
Eric Peterson — *Street Legal*

Best Performance by an Actress in a Continuing Leading Dramatic Role
Jackie Burroughs — *Road To Avonlea*

Best Performance in a Comedy Program or Series (Individual or Ensemble)
Sandra Shamas — *Adrienne Clarkson Presents: Sandra Shamas — Spitting Nickels*

Best Guest Performance in a Series by an Actor or Actress
Michelle St. John — *E.N.G.*

Best Performance in a Variety Program or Series
k. d. lang with Tommy Banks, conductor of the Edmonton Symphony Orchestra — *The 1990 Canadian Country Music Awards*

Best Performance in a Performing Arts Program or Series
Diana Leblanc — *Legacy: La Maison Suspendue*

Best Performance by an Actor in a Supporting Role
Kenneth Welsh — *Journey Into Darkness: The Bruce Curtis Story*

Best Performance by an Actress in a Supporting Role
Sarah Polley — *Lantern Hill*

Best Anchor or Interviewer
Lloyd Robertson — *CTV National News*

Best Host in a Light Information, Variety, or Performing Arts Program or Series
David Suzuki — *The Nature Connection*

Best Performance by a Host, Interviewer, or Anchor
Norm Perry — *Canada AM*

John Drainie Award
Gordon Pinsent

Earle Grey Award
Colleen Dewhurst

Canada Award
Drums! — Andy Blicq, Pnina Bloch, Jennifer Campbell

John Labatt Entertainment Award for Most Popular Program
Road To Avonlea

5th Gemini Awards (1990)

Best Dramatic Mini-Series
Love and Hate — Bernard Zukerman

Best Dramatic Series
E.N.G. — Robert Lantos, Jeff King, R. B. Carney, Jennifer Black

Best Comedy Series
Material World — Katie Ford, Joe Partington

Best Variety Series
CODCO — Michael Donovan, J. William Ritchie, Stephen Reynolds, Jack Kellum

Best Information Series
The Journal — Mark Starowicz

Best Light Information Series
On the Road Again — Karl Nerenberg

Best Documentary Series
The Nature of Things — James Murray

Best Animated Program or Series
Babar — Michael Hirsh, Patrick Loubert, Clive A. Smith

Best Children's Program or Series
Raffi in Concert With the Rise and Shine Band — Richard Mozer, David Devine, Raffi

Best Youth Program or Series
Talkin' About AIDS — Daphne Ballon, Rachel Low, Seaton McLean

Best Performance by an Actor in a Leading Role in a Dramatic Program or Mini-Series
Kenneth Welsh — *Love and Hate*

Best Performance by an Actress in a Leading Role in a Dramatic Program or Mini-Series
Michelle St. John — *Where the Spirit Lives*

Best Performance by an Actor in a Continuing Leading Dramatic Role
Art Hindle — *E.N.G.*

Best Performance by an Actress in a Continuing Leading Dramatic Role
Jackie Burroughs — *Road To Avonlea*

Best Guest Performance in a Series by an Actor or Actress
Victoria Snow — *Street Legal*

Best Performance by an Actor in a Supporting Role
Joe Flaherty — *Looking For Miracles*

Best Performance by an Actress in a Supporting Role
Ann-Marie MacDonald — *Where the Spirit Lives*

John Drainie Award
Allan S. McFee

Earle Grey Award
Jan Rubes

Canada Award
Batiya Bak! — Werner Volkmer

John Labatt Entertainment Award For Most Popular Program
Road To Avonlea

Special Gemini Award For Outstanding Contribution to Canadian Television
Johnny Wayne (posthumous), Frank Shuster

4th Gemini Awards (1989)

Best Dramatic Mini-Series
Glory Enough for All — Gordon Hinch, Joseph Green, W. Paterson Ferns, David Elstein

Best Dramatic Series
Degrassi Junior High — Linda Schuyler, Kit Hood

Best Comedy Series
CODCO — Michael Donovan, J. William Ritchie

Best Variety Program
The Kids in the Hall — Joe Forristal, Lorne Michaels

Best Variety Series
Smith & Smith Comedy Mill — Steve Smith, Morag Smith

Best Information Series
The Journal — Mark Starowicz

Best Light Information Series
On the Road Again — Susan Stranks

Best Documentary Series
The Struggle For Democracy — Ted Remerowski, Nancy Button, Michael Levine

Best Animated Program or Series
Babar — Michael Hirsh, Patrick Loubert, Clive A. Smith

Best Children's Program or Series
Mr. Dressup — Shirley Greenfield

Best Youth Program or Series
Wonderstruck — Liz Fox

Best Performance by an Actor in a Leading Role in a Dramatic Program or Mini-Series
R. H. Thomson — *Glory Enough For All*

Best Performance by an Actress in a Leading Role in a Dramatic Program or Mini-Series
Martha Henry — *Glory Enough For All*

Best Performance by an Actor in a Continuing Leading Dramatic Role
Eric Peterson — *Street Legal*

Best Performance by an Actress in a Continuing Leading Dramatic Role
Stacie Mistysyn — *Degrassi Junior High*

Best Guest Performance in a Series by an Actor or Actress
Gordon Pinsent — *Street Legal*

Best Performance in a Variety or Performing Arts Program or Series
Dave Foley, Bruce McCullough, Kevin McDonald, Mark McKinney, Scott Thompson — *The Kids in the Hall*

Best Performance by an Actor in a Supporting Role
Jan Rubes — *Two Men*

Best Performance by an Actress in a Supporting Role
Martha Gibson — *Two Men*

Best Performance by a Host, Interviewer, or Anchor
Peter Mansbridge — *China in Crisis*

John Drainie Award
Peter Gzowski

Earle Grey Award
Sean McCann

Canada Award
Inside Stories

***TV Guide* Most Popular Program Award**
The Journal

3rd Gemini Awards (1988)

Best Dramatic Mini-Series
Anne of Green Gables: The Sequel — Kevin Sullivan

Best Dramatic Series
Degrassi Junior High — Kit Hood, Linda Schuyler

Best Comedy Series
N/A

Best Variety Series
It's Only Rock 'n Roll — Joe Bodolai, John Brunton, Judith Dryland

Best Information Series
Venture — Duncan McEwan

Best Light Information Series
Live it Up — Alan Edmonds, Jack McGaw

Best Documentary Series
The Nature of Things — James Murray

Best Animated Program or Series
The Raccoons — Kevin Gillis, Sheldon Wiseman

Best Children's Series
Ramona — Kim Todd

Best Performance by an Actor in a Leading Role in a Dramatic Program or Mini-Series
Kenneth Welsh — *And Then You Die*

Best Performance by an Actress in a Leading Role in a Dramatic Program or Mini-Series
Megan Follows — *Anne of Green Gables: The Sequel*

Best Performance by an Actor in a Continuing Leading Dramatic Role
Pat Mastroianni — *Degrassi Junior High*

Best Performance by an Actress in a Continuing Leading Dramatic Role
Sonja Smits — *Street Legal*

Best Guest Performance in a Series by an Actor or Actress
Martha Henry — *Mount Royal*

Best Performance in a Variety or Performing Arts Program or Series
k. d. lang — *The 1987 Canadian Country Music Awards*

Best Performance by an Actor in a Supporting Role
Wayne Robson — *And Then You Die*

Best Performance by an Actress in a Supporting Role
Colleen Dewhurst — *Anne of Green Gables: The Sequel*

Best Performance by a Host, Interviewer, or Anchor
Peter Mansbridge — *Sunday Report*

John Drainie Award
Davidson Dunton

Earle Grey Award
Kate Reid

Canada Award
Degrassi Junior High

***TV Guide* Most Popular Program Award**
Night Heat

2nd Gemini Awards (1987)

Best Dramatic Mini-Series
Ford: The Man and the Machine — David J. Patterson

Best Dramatic Series
Night Heat — Sonny Grosso, Andras Hamori, Larry Jacobson, Stephen J. Roth

Best Comedy Series
Seeing Things — David Barlow, Louis Del Grande, Martin Wiener

Best Variety Series
S&M Comic Book — Cynthia Grech

Best Information Series
The Journal — Mark Starowicz

Best Light Information Series
N/A

Best Documentary Series
The Nature of Things — James Murray

Best Animated Program or Series
Babar and Father Christmas — Alison Clayton, Merilyn Read

Best Children's Series
Degrassi Junior High — Kit Hood, Linda Schuyler

Best Pay TV Dramatic Program or Series
Daughters of the Country — Norma Bailey, Michael Scott, Ches Yetman

Best Performance by an Actor in a Leading Role in a Dramatic Program or Mini-Series
Booth Savage — *The Last Season*

Best Performance by an Actress in a Leading Role in a Dramatic Program or Mini-Series
Victoria Snow — *Daughter of the Country*

Best Performance by an Actor in a Continuing Leading Dramatic Role
Eric Peterson — *Street Legal*
Winston Rekert — *Adderly*

Best Performance by an Actress in a Continuing Leading Dramatic Role
Dixie Seatle — *Adderly*

Best Performance by a Lead Actor in a Continuing Role in a Comedy Series
Louis Del Grande — *Seeing Things*

Best Performance by a Lead Actor in a Comedy Program or Series
Dinah Christie — *Check It Out!*

Best Guest Performance in a Series by an Actor or Actress
Ed McNamara — *Seeing Things* (posthumous)

Best Performance in a Variety or Performing Arts Program or Series
Tommy Sexton, Greg Malone — *S&M Comic Book*

Best Performance by an Actor in a Supporting Role
Eugene Clark — *Night Heat*

Best Performance by an Actress in a Supporting Role
Vivian Reis — *The Marriage Bed*

Best Performance by a Host, Interviewer, or Anchor
Hana Gartner — *the fifth estate*

John Drainie Award
Ross McLean

Earle Grey Award
Lorne Greene

***TV Guide* Most Popular Program Award**
Night Heat

1st Gemini Awards (1986)

Best Dramatic Mini-Series
Anne of Green Gables — Kevin Sullivan, Ian McDougall

Best Continuing Drama Series
Night Heat — Andras Hamori

Best Comedy Series
Seeing Things — David Barlow, Louis Del Grande, Martin Wiener

Best Variety Series
N/A

Best Information Program or Series
the fifth estate — Robin Taylor, Ron Haggart

Best Light Information Series
N/A

Best Documentary Single Program or Series
Glenn Gould: A Portrait, Parts 1 & 2 — Eric Till, Vincent Tovell

Best Animated Program, Single Program, or Series
The Bestest Present — W. H. Stevens Jr.

Best Children's Series
Fraggle Rock — Larry Mirkin

Best Pay TV Dramatic Program or Series
Bradbury Trilogy — Seaton McLean

Best Performance by a Lead Actor in a Single Dramatic Program or Mini-Series
August Schellenberg — *The Prodigal*

Best Performance by a Lead Actress in a Single Dramatic Program or Mini-Series
Megan Follows — *Anne of Green Gables*

Best Performance by an Actor in a Continuing Leading Dramatic Role
Robert Clothier — *The Beachcombers*

Best Performance by an Actress in a Continuing Leading Dramatic Role
Marnie McPhail — *The Edison Twins*

Best Performance by a Lead Actress in a Comedy Program or Series
Martha Gibson — *Seeing Things*

Best Performance by a Lead Actor in a Comedy Program or Series
Louis Del Grande — *Seeing Things*

Best Performance in a Variety, Entertainment, Performing Arts Program or Series
Heath Lamberts — *One for the Pot*

Best Performance by an Actor in a Supporting Role
Richard Farnsworth — *Anne of Green Gables*

Best Performance by an Actress in a Supporting Role
Colleen Dewhurst — *Anne of Green Gables*

Best Performance by a Host or Interviewer
David Suzuki — *The Nature of Things*

John Drainie Award
Pat Patterson

Earle Grey Award
Ed McNamara

***TV Guide* Most Popular Program Award**
Anne of Green Gables

INDEX of
Television Actors and Personalities

B

E

F

G

N

T

X

Y

Z

About the Authors

Peter Kenter is a writer, editor and award-winning design consultant. His work appears in a wide range of publications, from articles in *Toronto Life*, *Canadian Business*, *Marketing*, and *Report on Business* to *Cottage Life*. He writes book reviews (for the *Financial Times of Canada*), celebrity interviews and trivia quizzes, and articles on film, popular culture, computer technology, environmental issues and economics.

Peter Kenter is not only an observer of Canadian television, but a participant. At an early age he appeared on CBC's *Reach For the Top*, and later on such television game shows as *Guess What?* and *Definition* (on which he almost won a car). In addition, he co-hosted an avant garde cable-access program, the *10-Night Show*, on Rogers Cable. He maintains a large collection of books and items related to popular culture, including Canadian television soundtrack albums, books based on Canadian programs and a video collection containing some rare Canadian programs, including the infamous *The Trouble With Tracy*.

Martin Levin is Books Editor for the *Globe and Mail*. Prior to this, his Fifth Column appeared regularly in the Facts and Arguments page of the newspaper. He is sports editor of the *Canadian Global Almanac* published annually by MacMillan of Canada as well as editor of its Canadian Hall of Fame section. He is a former columnist and book editor for the *Financial Times of Canada*, a contributor to *Toronto Life*, the *Financial Post* and other publications. He has been a book reviewer and baseball writer for the *Toronto Star*. He was founding editor of *Innings*, a baseball periodical, and of *Seniors Today*, Canada's first weekly for adults over 55 years. He was a reviewer for the *Thunder Bay Chronicle-Journal* and has won several international awards for editorial writing.

Martin Levin has also been an active participant in Canadian television, first appearing on Manitoba's *Touchdown Quiz*—his school won the province—and later on *Canada A.M.*, among other programs.